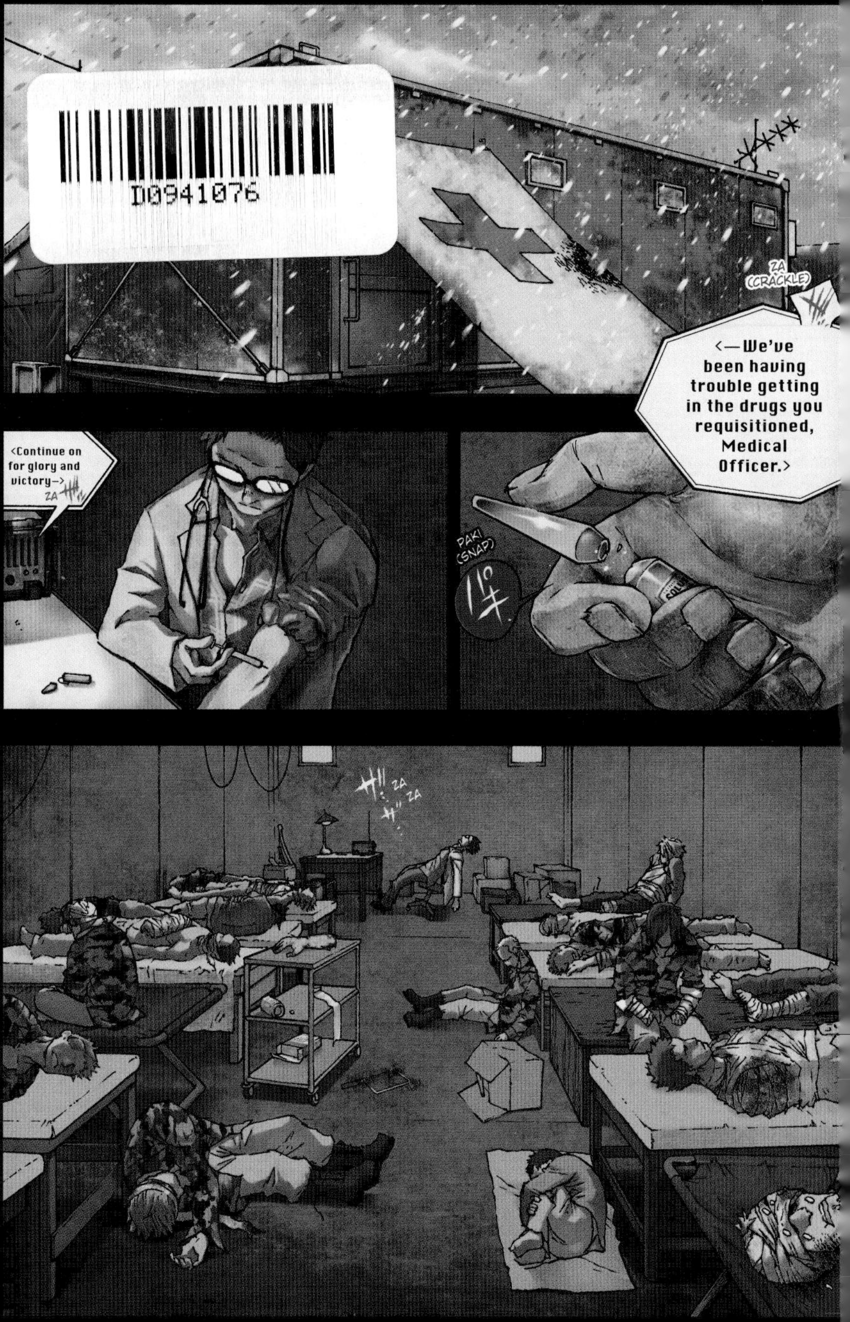
ZA (CRACKLE)
<—We've been having trouble getting in the drugs you requisitioned, Medical Officer.>
PAKI (SNAP)
パキ
<Continue on for glory and victory—>
ZA
ZA ZA

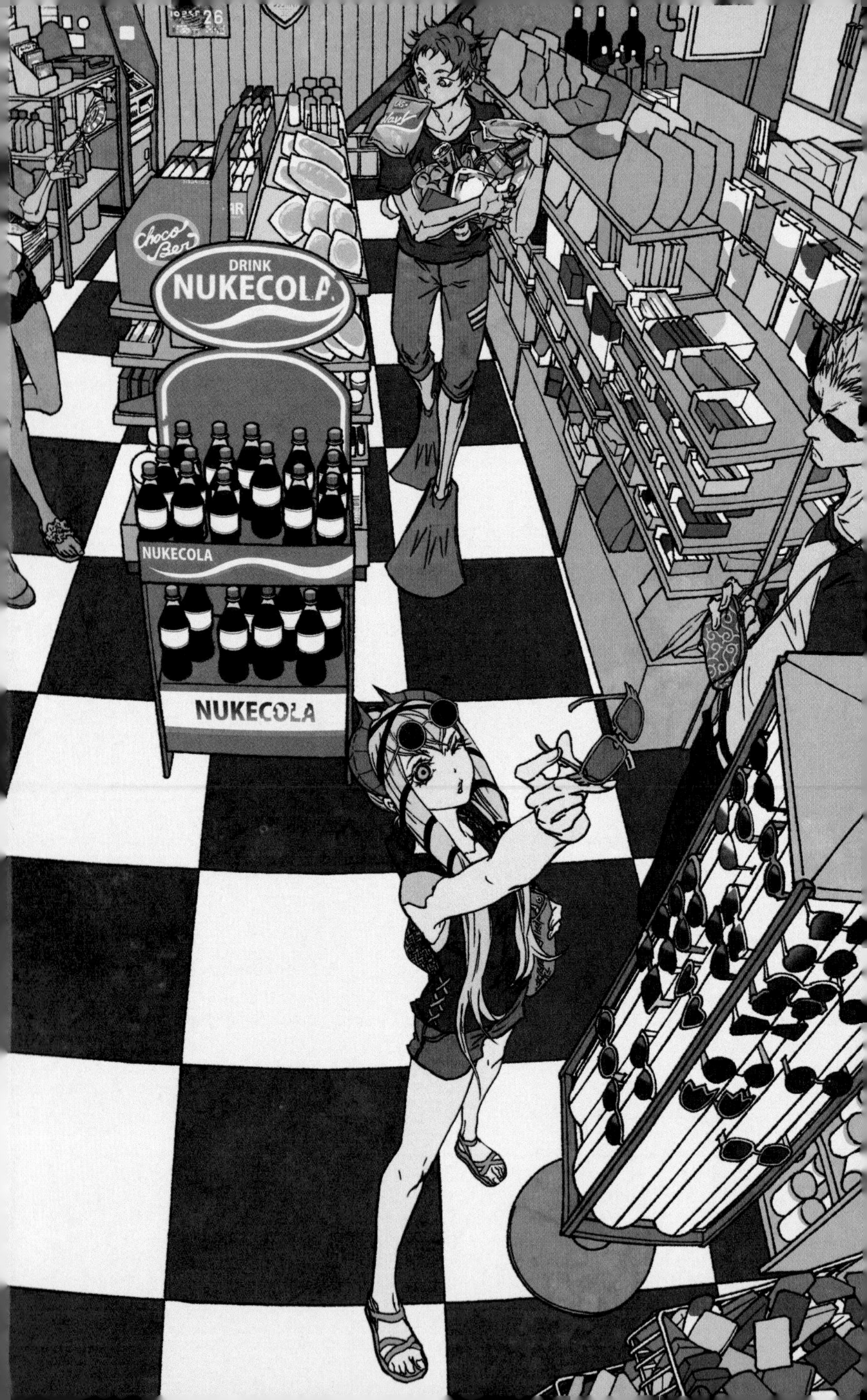

DRINK
NUKECOLA
NUKECOLA
NUKECOLA

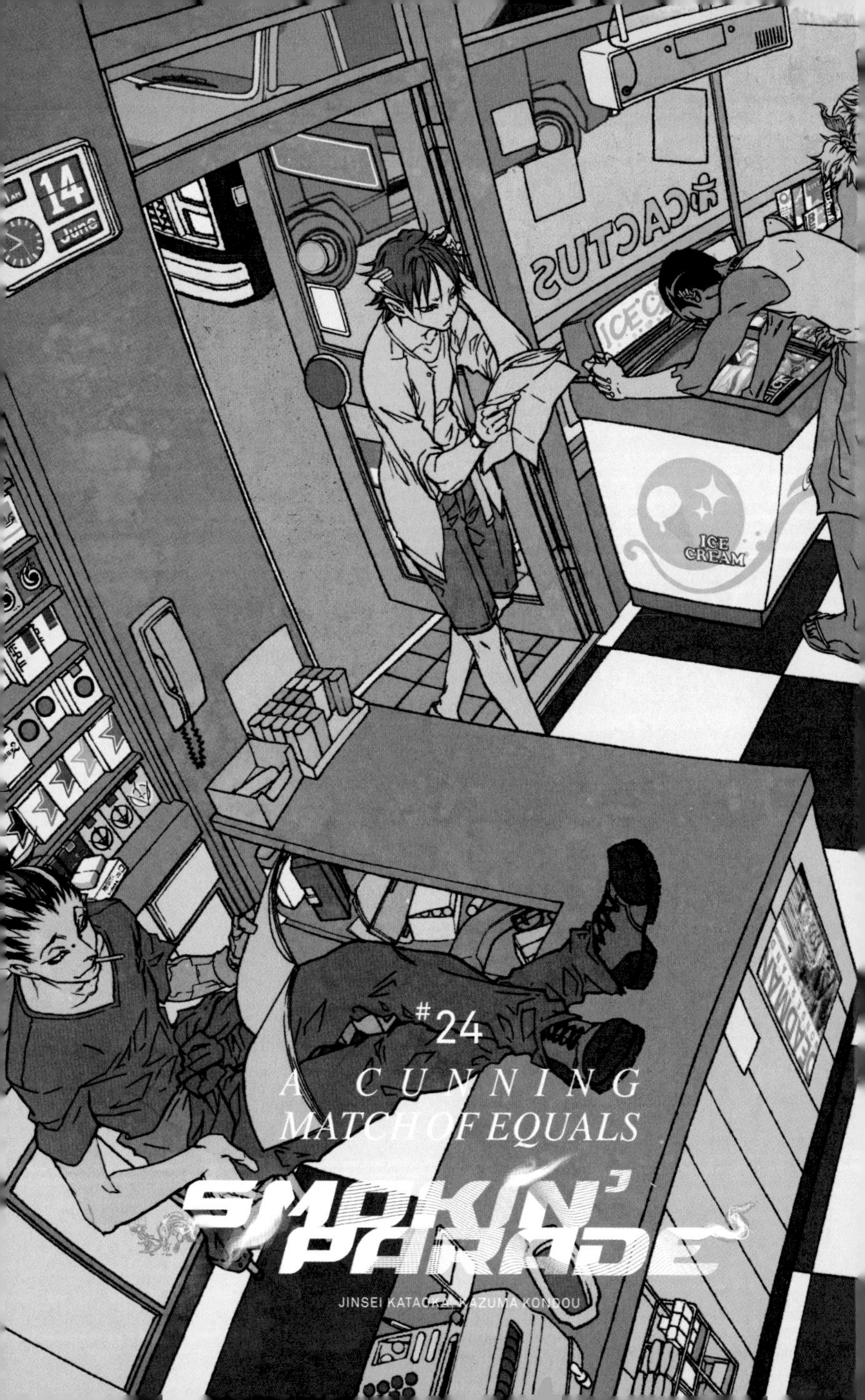

14
June
CACTUS
ICE CREAM
#24
A CUNNING MATCH OF EQUALS
SMOKIN' PARADE
JINSEI KATAOKA KAZUMA KONDOU

SMOKIN' PARADE

JINSEI KATAOKA, KAZUMA KONDOU

CONTENTS

SMOKIN' PARADE 3

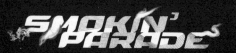

C H A R A C T E R S

AKUTA

A Jackalope who has taken a liking to Youkou because he sees himself in the kid. A heavy smoker with a sweet tooth.

YOUKOU KAKUJOU

A boy who lost both arms and his right leg when his younger sister turned into a Spider. He has replaced one missing arm with a Gear and joined the Jackalopes.

KOTOHARU

A member of the Jackalopes. He has an incredible amount of respect for Akuta and keeps a collection of items related to him.

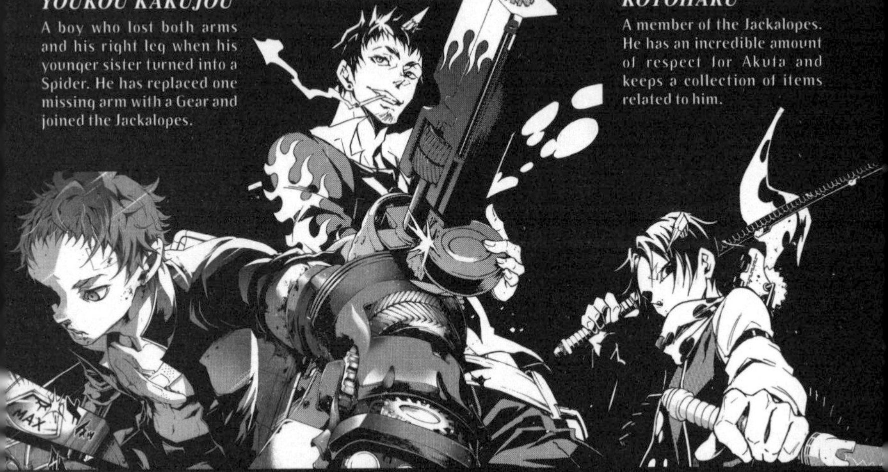

MAX

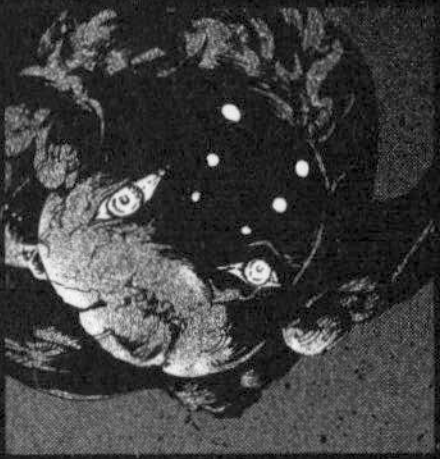

THE LORD

Believed to be the largest and fiercest Spider currently in existence. It is terrorizing the northern region.

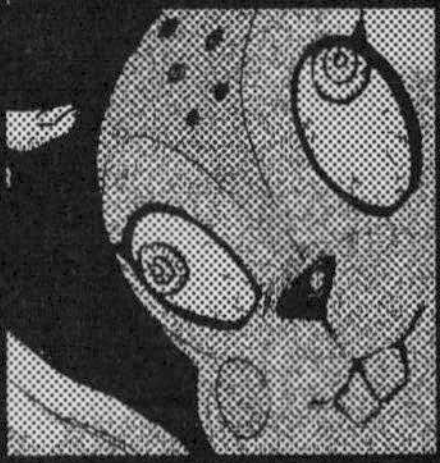

SPIDERS

Monsters with heightened physical abilities who rage out of control according to their base instincts.

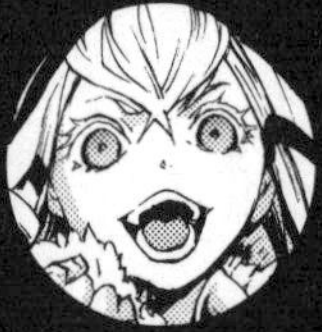

KUKURI

The captain of the Jackalopes' northern base.

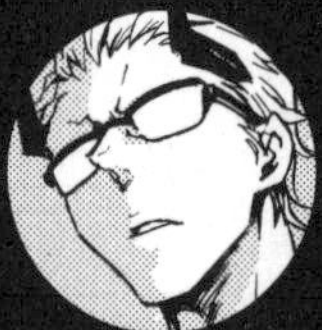

UDOU

The deputy director of the Jackalopes' northern base.

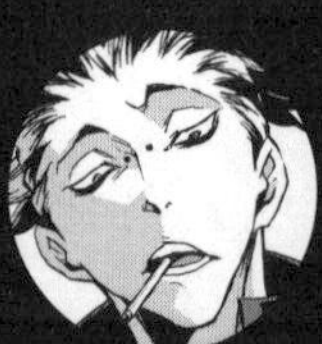

JIMO

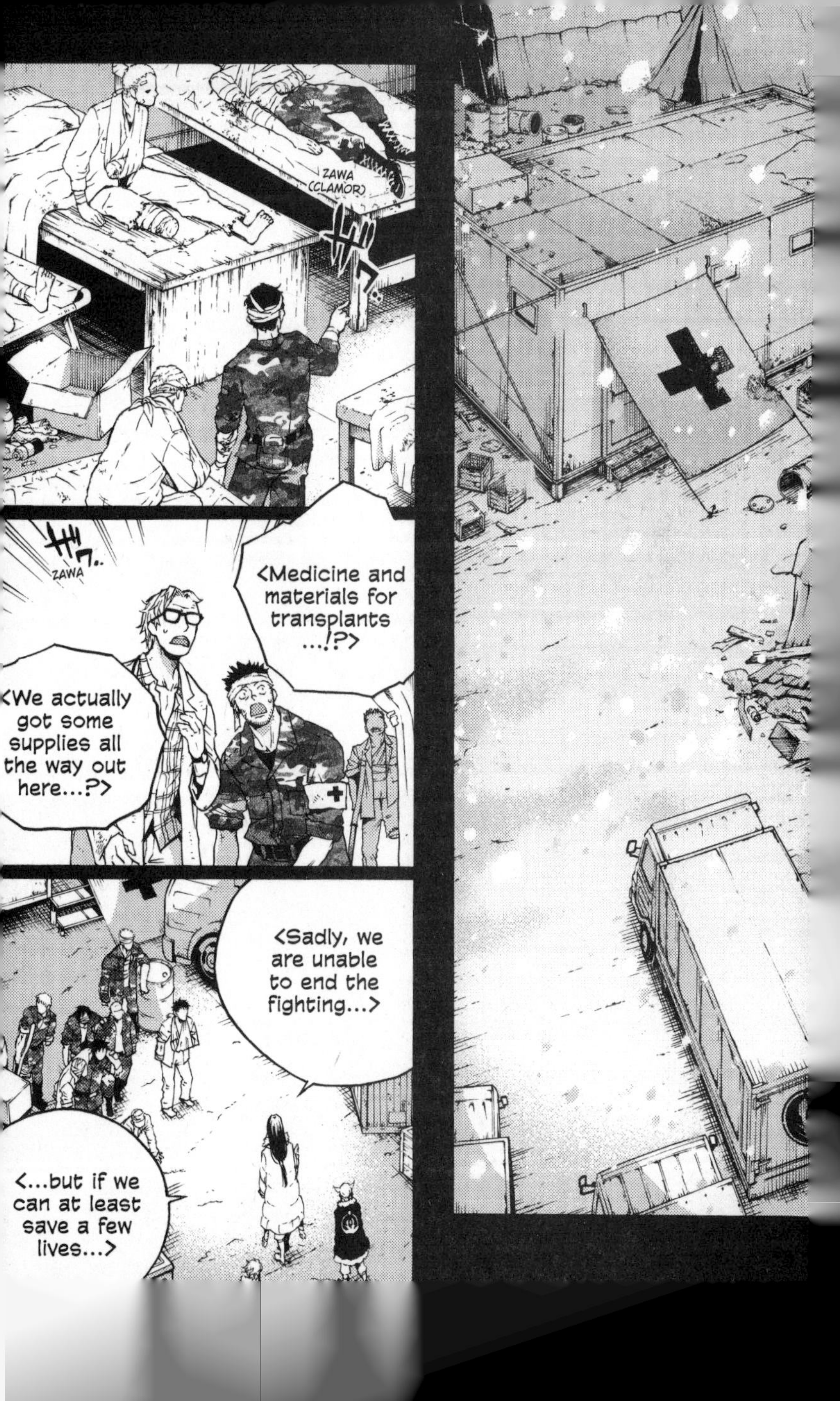
ZAWA (CLAMOR)
ZAWA
<Medicine and materials for transplants ...!?>
<We actually got some supplies all the way out here...?>
<Sadly, we are unable to end the fighting...>
<...but if we can at least save a few lives...>

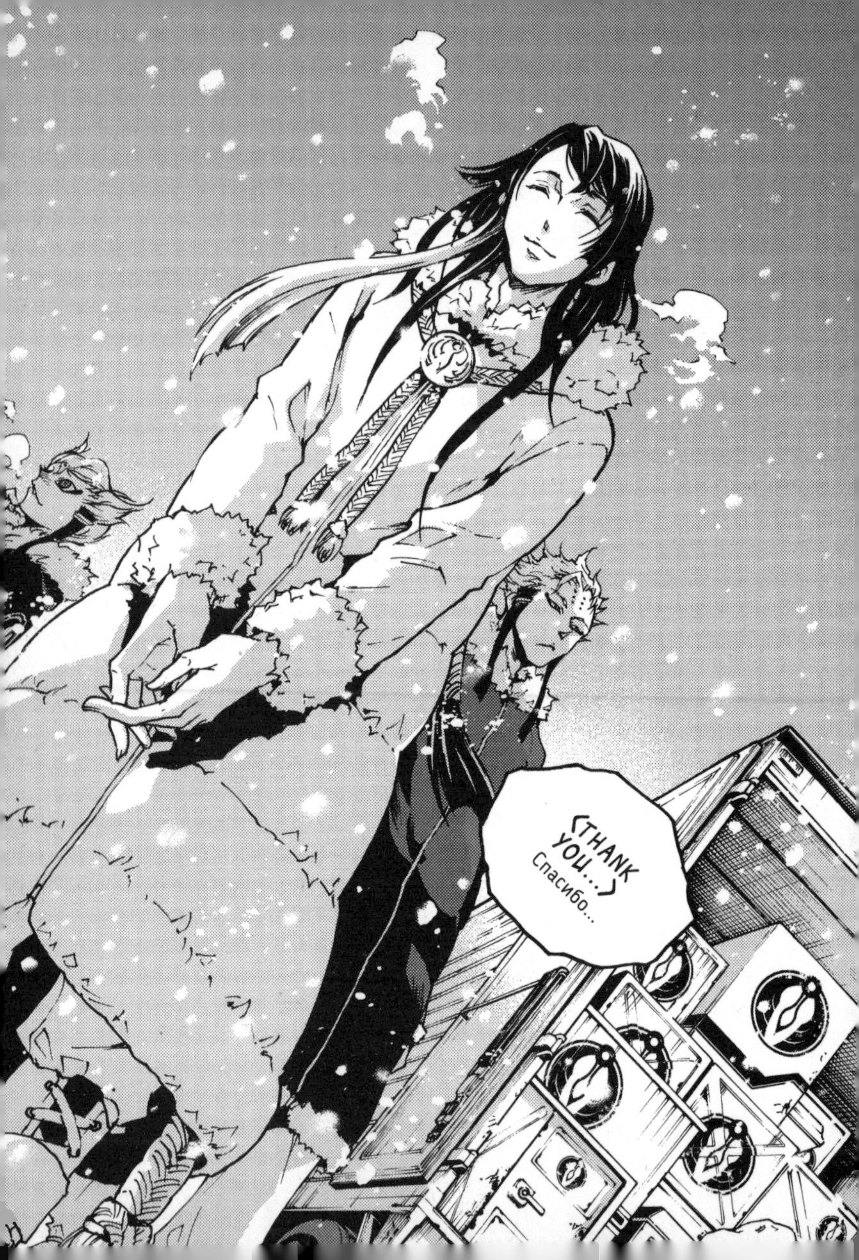
<THANK YOU...> Спасибо...

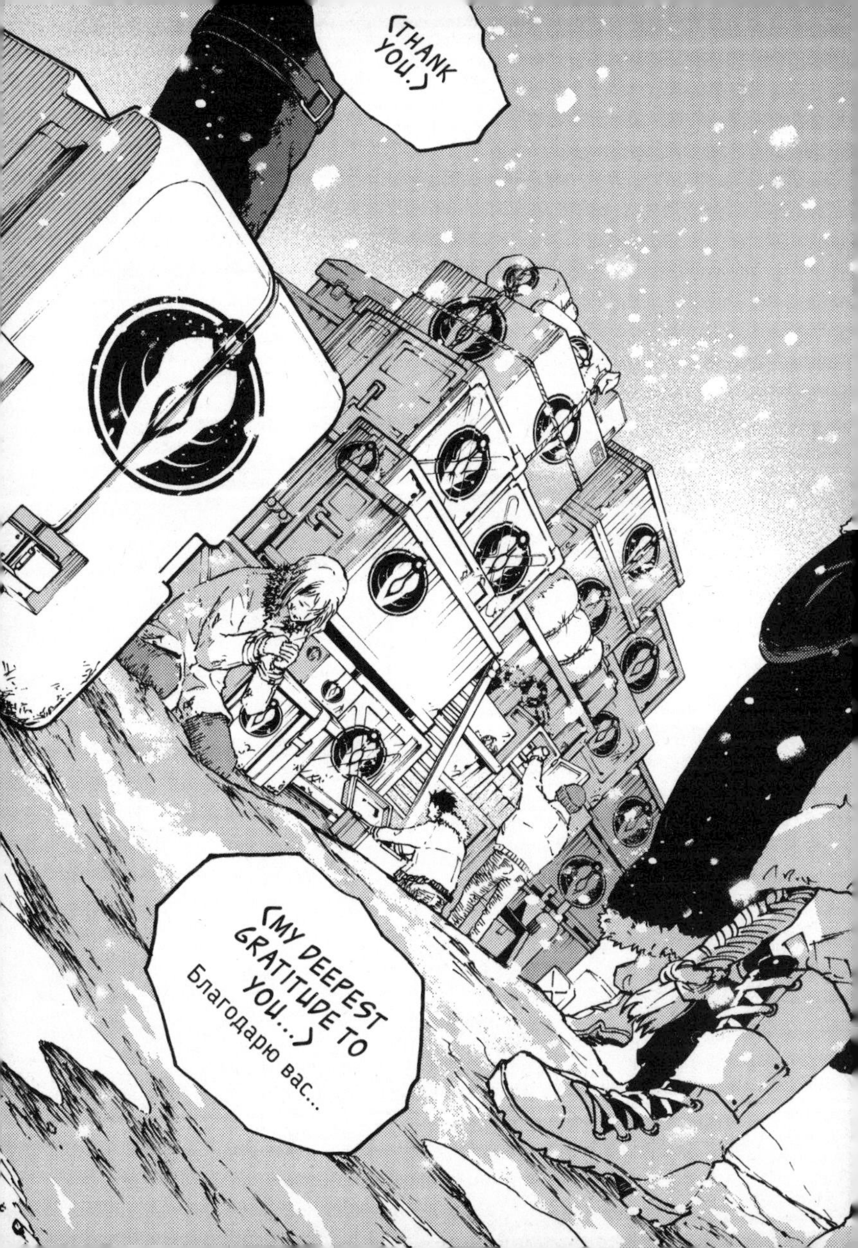
<THANK YOU.>
<MY DEEPEST GRATITUDE TO YOU...> Благодарю вас...

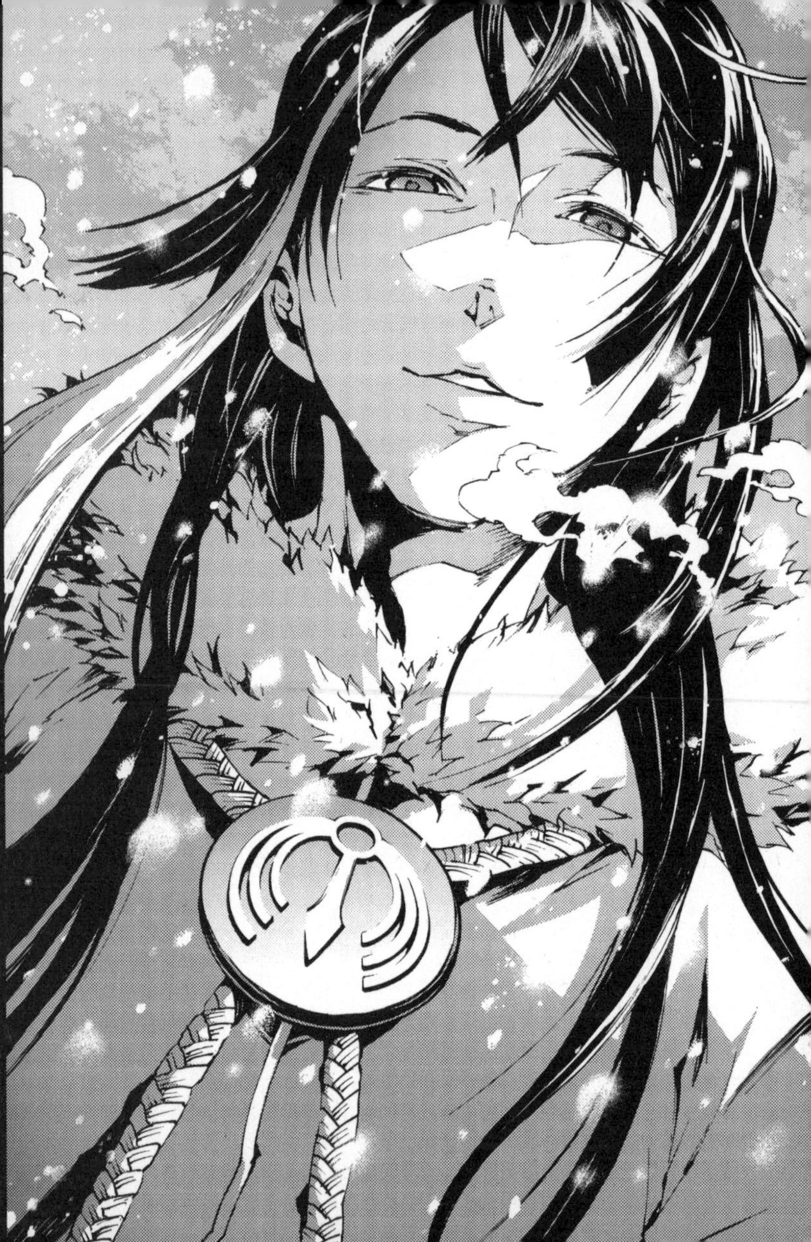

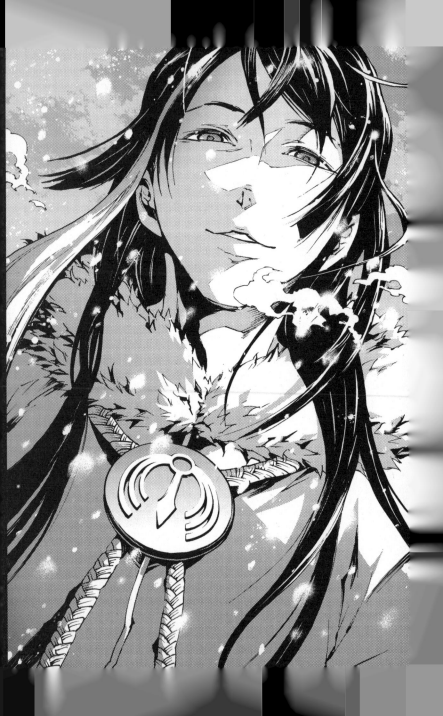

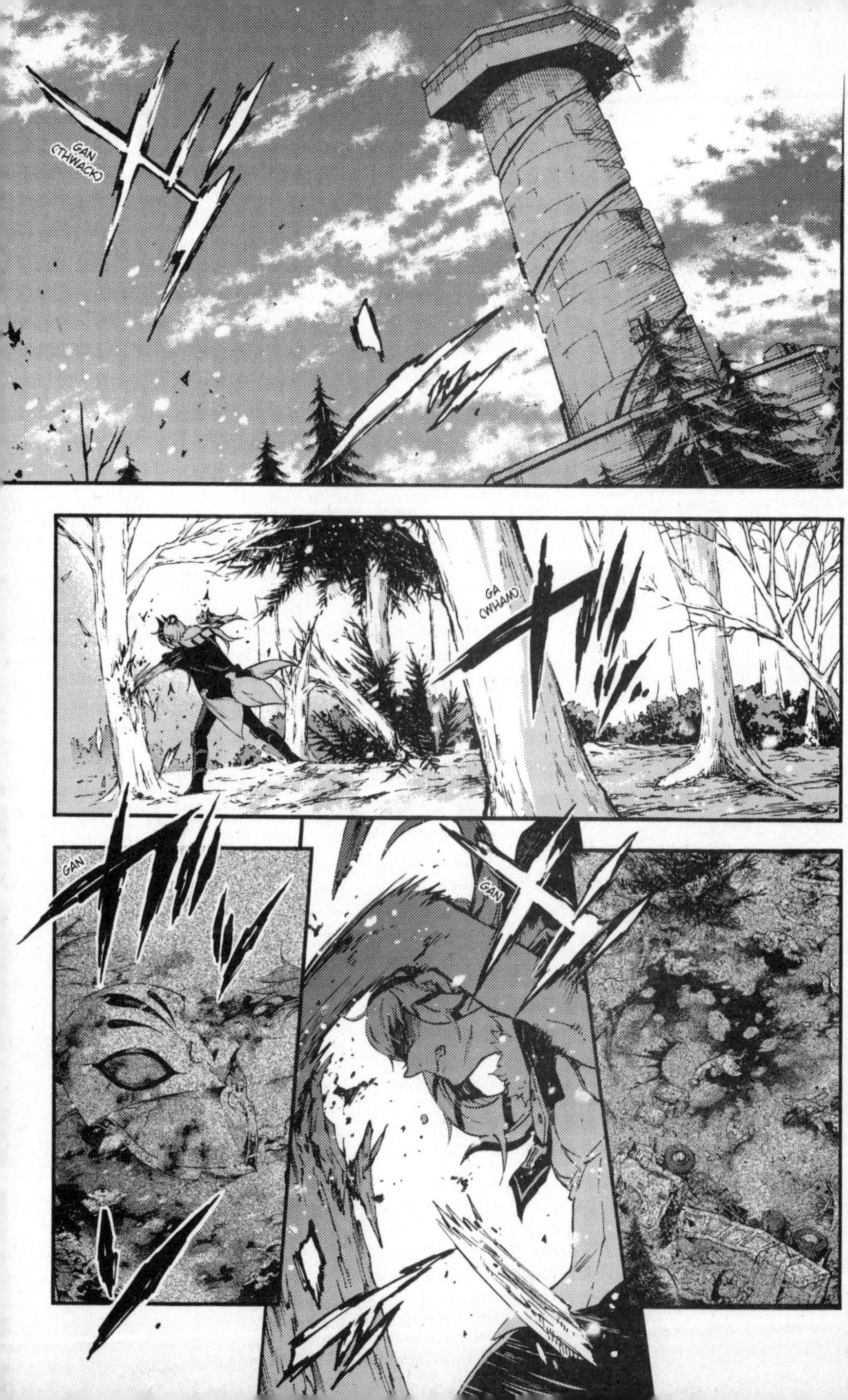
GAN (THWACK)
GA (WHAM)
GAN
GAN

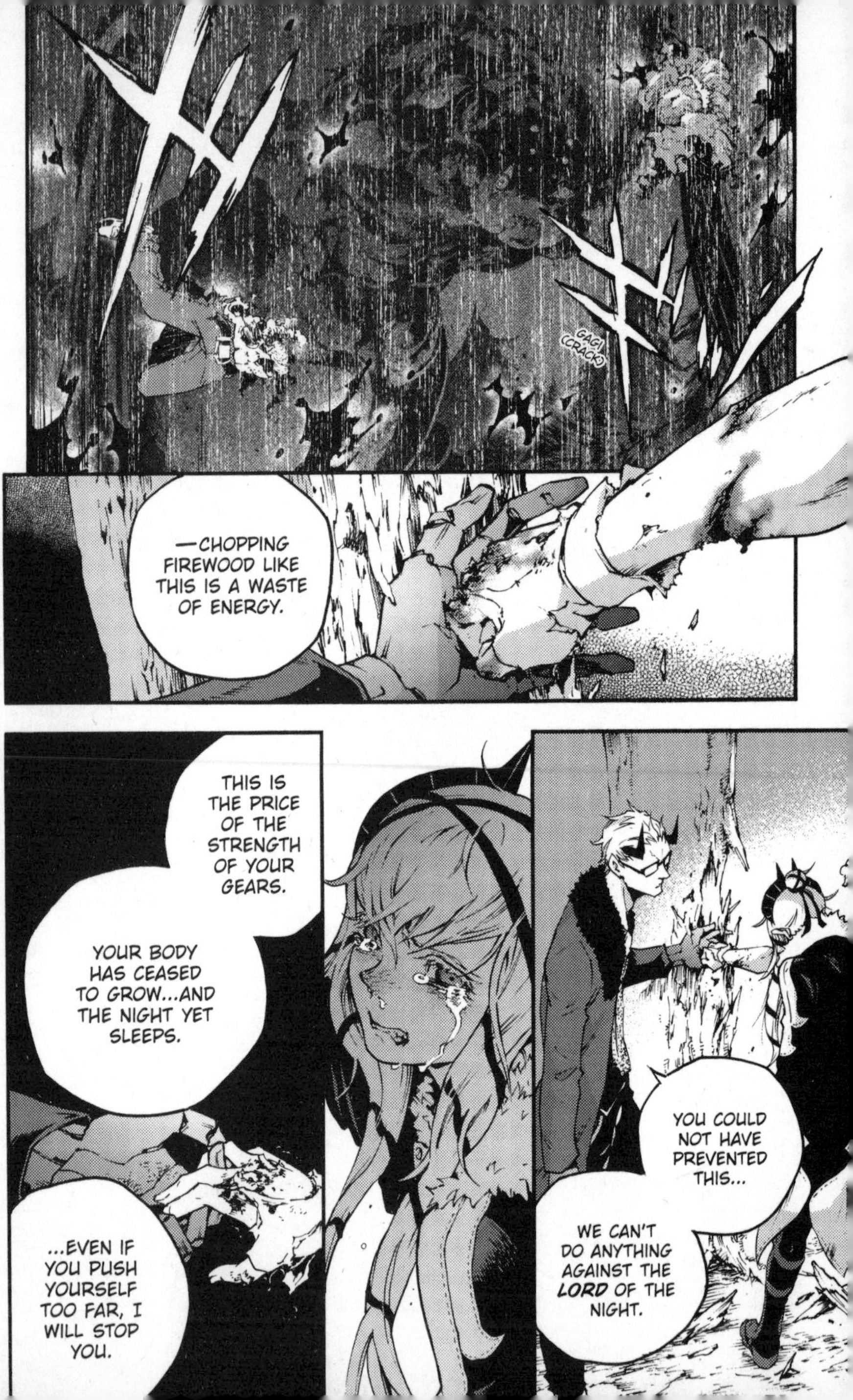
GAGI (CRACK)
—CHOPPING FIREWOOD LIKE THIS IS A WASTE OF ENERGY.
YOU COULD NOT HAVE PREVENTED THIS...
WE CAN'T DO ANYTHING AGAINST THE **LORD** OF THE NIGHT.
THIS IS THE PRICE OF THE STRENGTH OF YOUR GEARS.
YOUR BODY HAS CEASED TO GROW...AND THE NIGHT YET SLEEPS.
...EVEN IF YOU PUSH YOURSELF TOO FAR, I WILL STOP YOU.

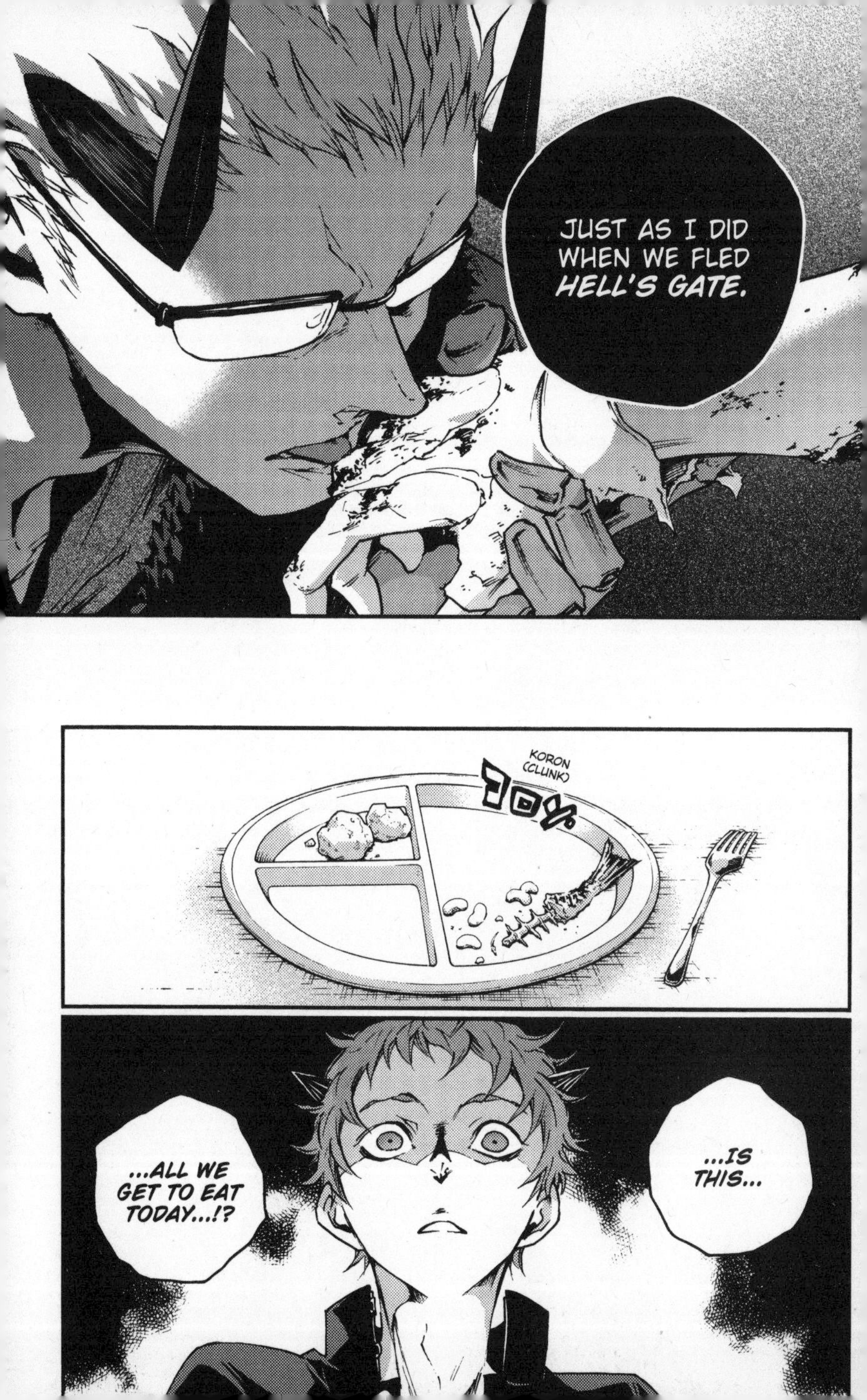
JUST AS I DID WHEN WE FLED HELL'S GATE.
KORON (CLINK)
...IS THIS...
...ALL WE GET TO EAT TODAY...!?

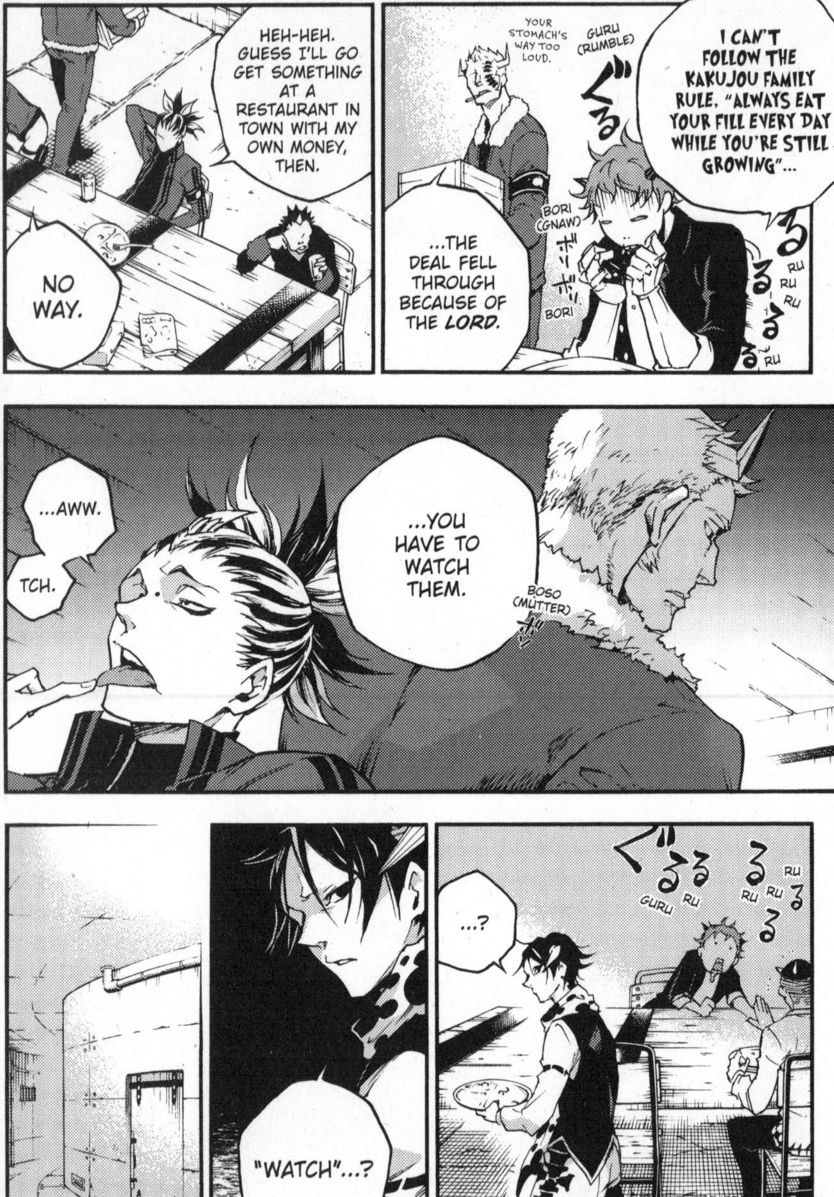
I CAN'T FOLLOW THE KAKUJOU FAMILY RULE, "ALWAYS EAT YOUR FILL EVERY DAY WHILE YOU'RE STILL GROWING"...
GURU (RUMBLE)
YOUR STOMACH'S WAY TOO LOUD.
RU RU RU RU
BORI (GNAW)
BORI
...THE DEAL FELL THROUGH BECAUSE OF THE *LORD*.
HEH-HEH. GUESS I'LL GO GET SOMETHING AT A RESTAURANT IN TOWN WITH MY OWN MONEY, THEN.
NO WAY.
BOSO (MUTTER)
...YOU HAVE TO WATCH THEM.
...AWW.
TCH.
RU RU RU RU
GURU RU
...?
"WATCH"...?

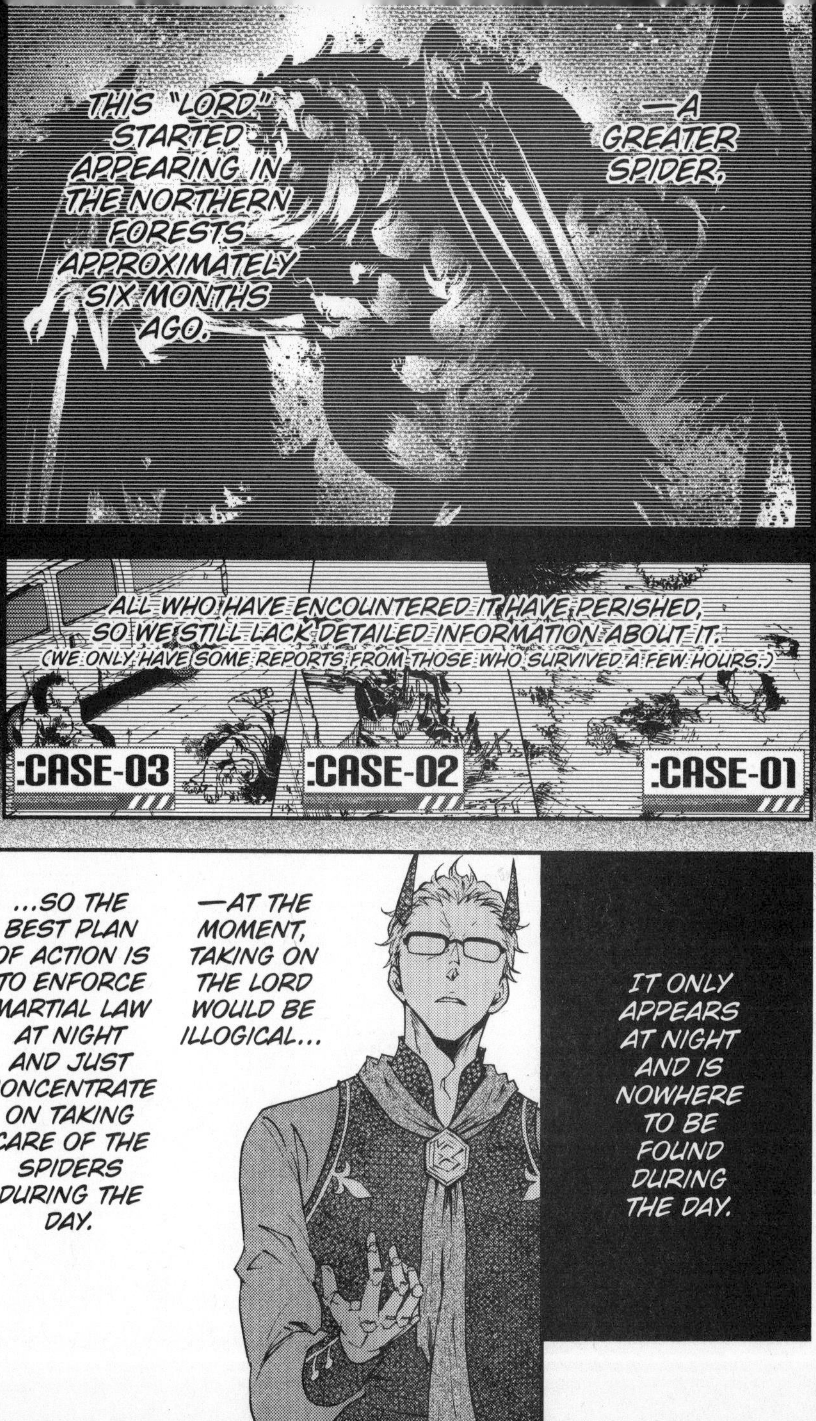
—A GREATER SPIDER.
THIS "LORD" STARTED APPEARING IN THE NORTHERN FORESTS APPROXIMATELY SIX MONTHS AGO.
ALL WHO HAVE ENCOUNTERED IT HAVE PERISHED, SO WE STILL LACK DETAILED INFORMATION ABOUT IT.
(WE ONLY HAVE SOME REPORTS FROM THOSE WHO SURVIVED A FEW HOURS.)
:CASE-01
:CASE-02
:CASE-03
IT ONLY APPEARS AT NIGHT AND IS NOWHERE TO BE FOUND DURING THE DAY.
—AT THE MOMENT, TAKING ON THE LORD WOULD BE ILLOGICAL...
...SO THE BEST PLAN OF ACTION IS TO ENFORCE MARTIAL LAW AT NIGHT AND JUST CONCENTRATE ON TAKING CARE OF THE SPIDERS DURING THE DAY.

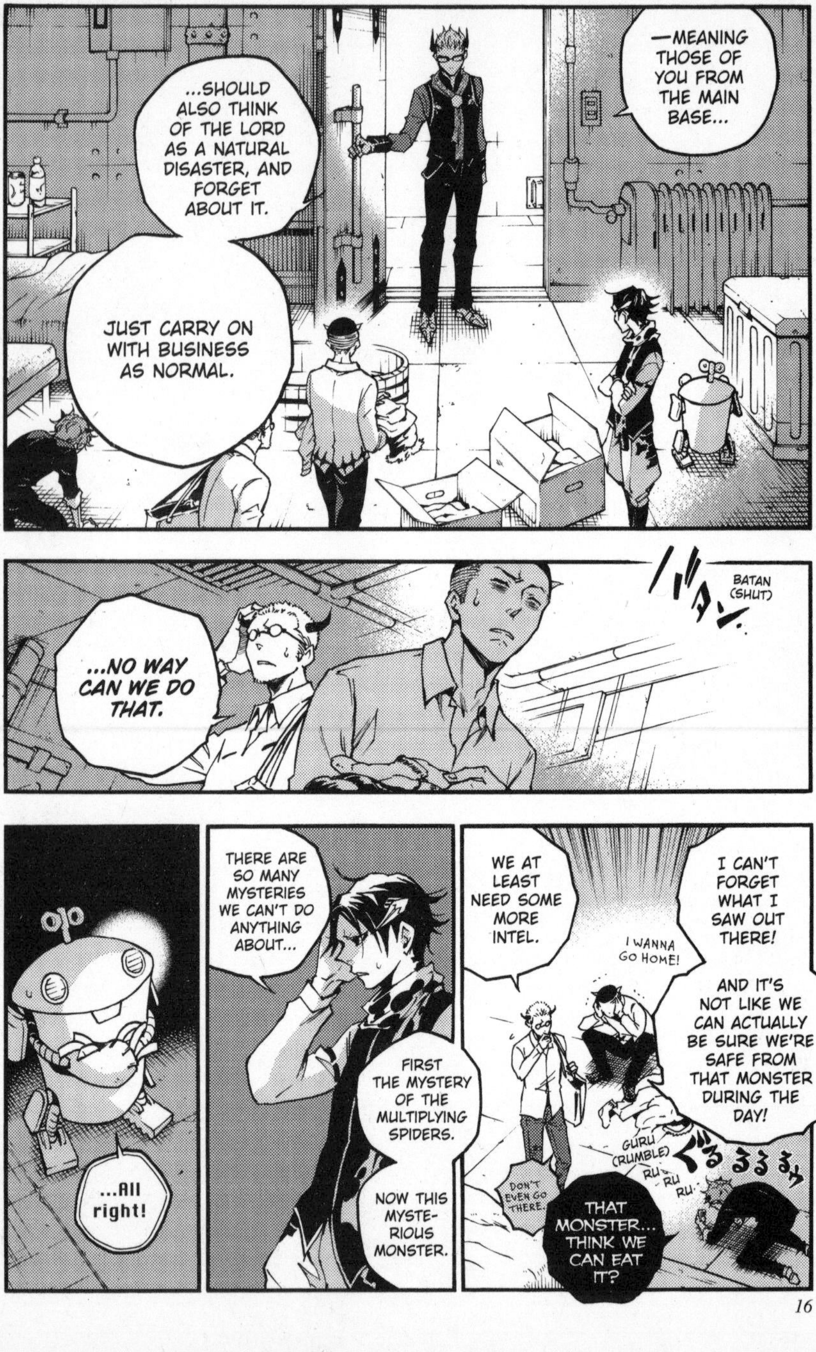
—MEANING THOSE OF YOU FROM THE MAIN BASE...
...SHOULD ALSO THINK OF THE LORD AS A NATURAL DISASTER, AND FORGET ABOUT IT.
JUST CARRY ON WITH BUSINESS AS NORMAL.
BATAN (SHUT)
...NO WAY CAN WE DO THAT.
I CAN'T FORGET WHAT I SAW OUT THERE!
WE AT LEAST NEED SOME MORE INTEL.
I WANNA GO HOME!
AND IT'S NOT LIKE WE CAN ACTUALLY BE SURE WE'RE SAFE FROM THAT MONSTER DURING THE DAY!
GURU (RUMBLE) RU RU RU
THAT MONSTER... THINK WE CAN EAT IT?
DON'T EVEN GO THERE.
THERE ARE SO MANY MYSTERIES WE CAN'T DO ANYTHING ABOUT...
FIRST THE MYSTERY OF THE MULTIPLYING SPIDERS.
NOW THIS MYSTE-RIOUS MONSTER.
...All right!

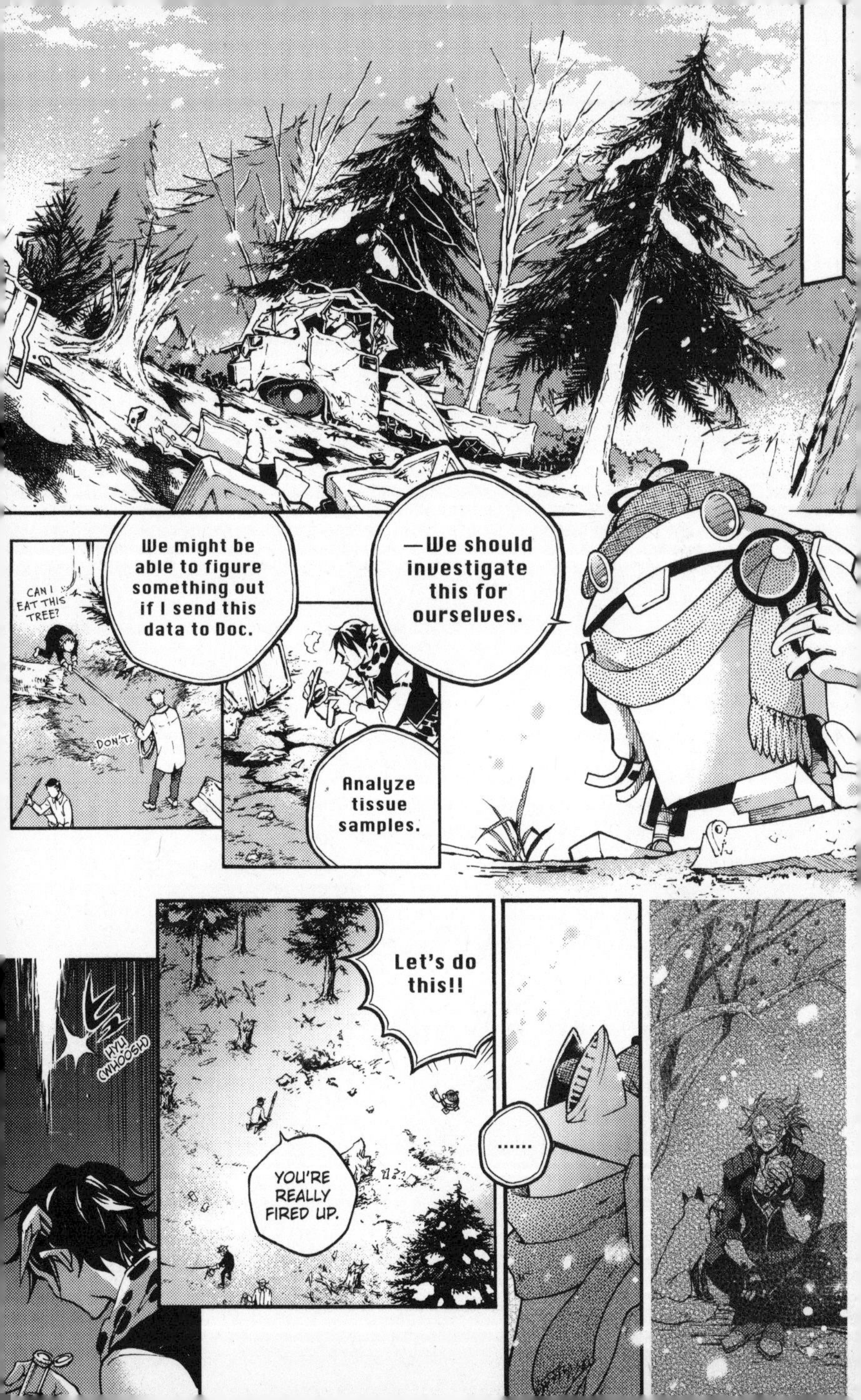
—We should investigate this for ourselves.
We might be able to figure something out if I send this data to Doc.
Analyze tissue samples.
CAN I EAT THIS TREE?
DON'T.
......
Let's do this!!
YOU'RE REALLY FIRED UP.
HYU (WHOOSH)

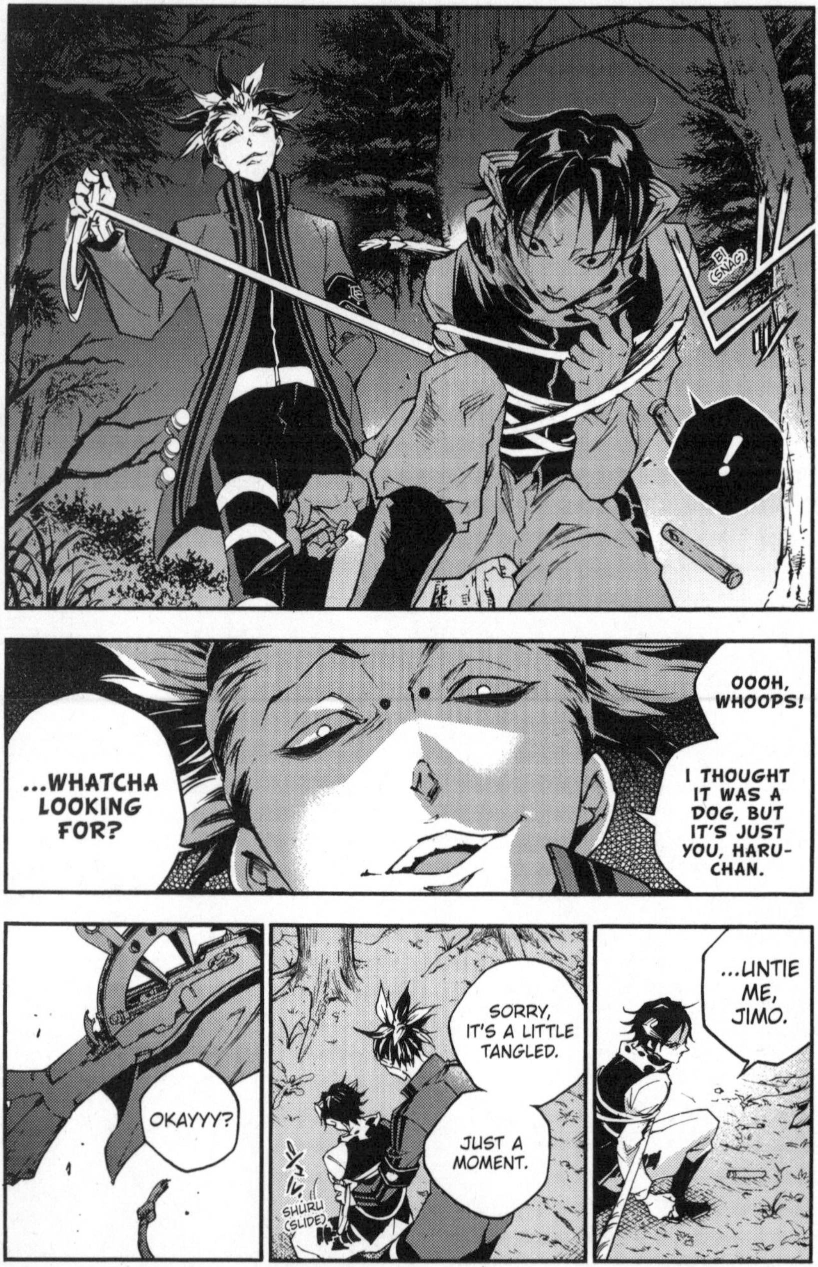
BI (SNAG)
!
OOOH, WHOOPS!
I THOUGHT IT WAS A DOG, BUT IT'S JUST YOU, HARU-CHAN.
...WHATCHA LOOKING FOR?
...UNTIE ME, JIMO.
SORRY, IT'S A LITTLE TANGLED.
JUST A MOMENT.
SHURU (SLIDE)
OKAYYY?

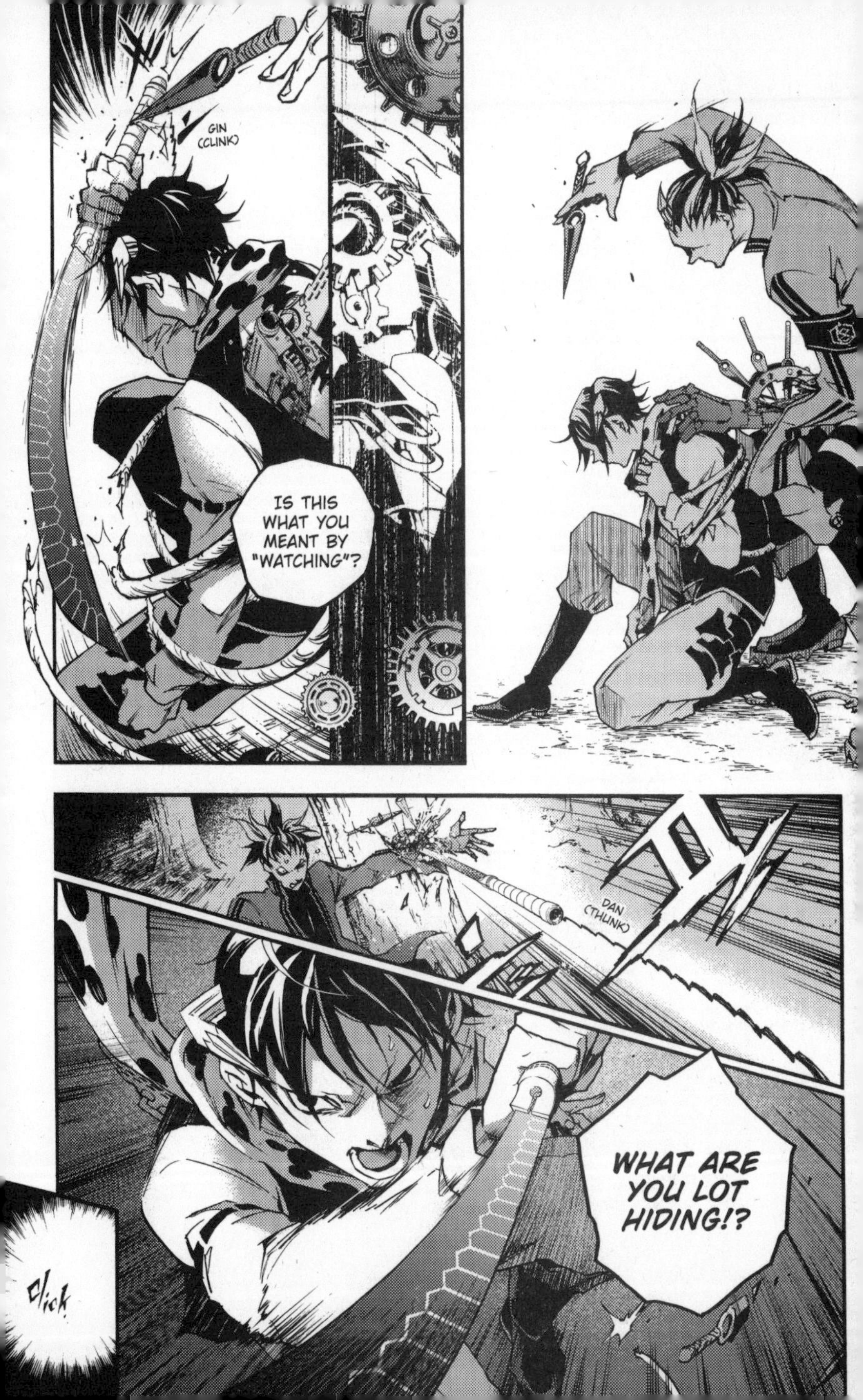
GIN (CLINK)
IS THIS WHAT YOU MEANT BY "WATCHING"?
DAN (THUNK)
WHAT ARE YOU LOT HIDING!?
Click

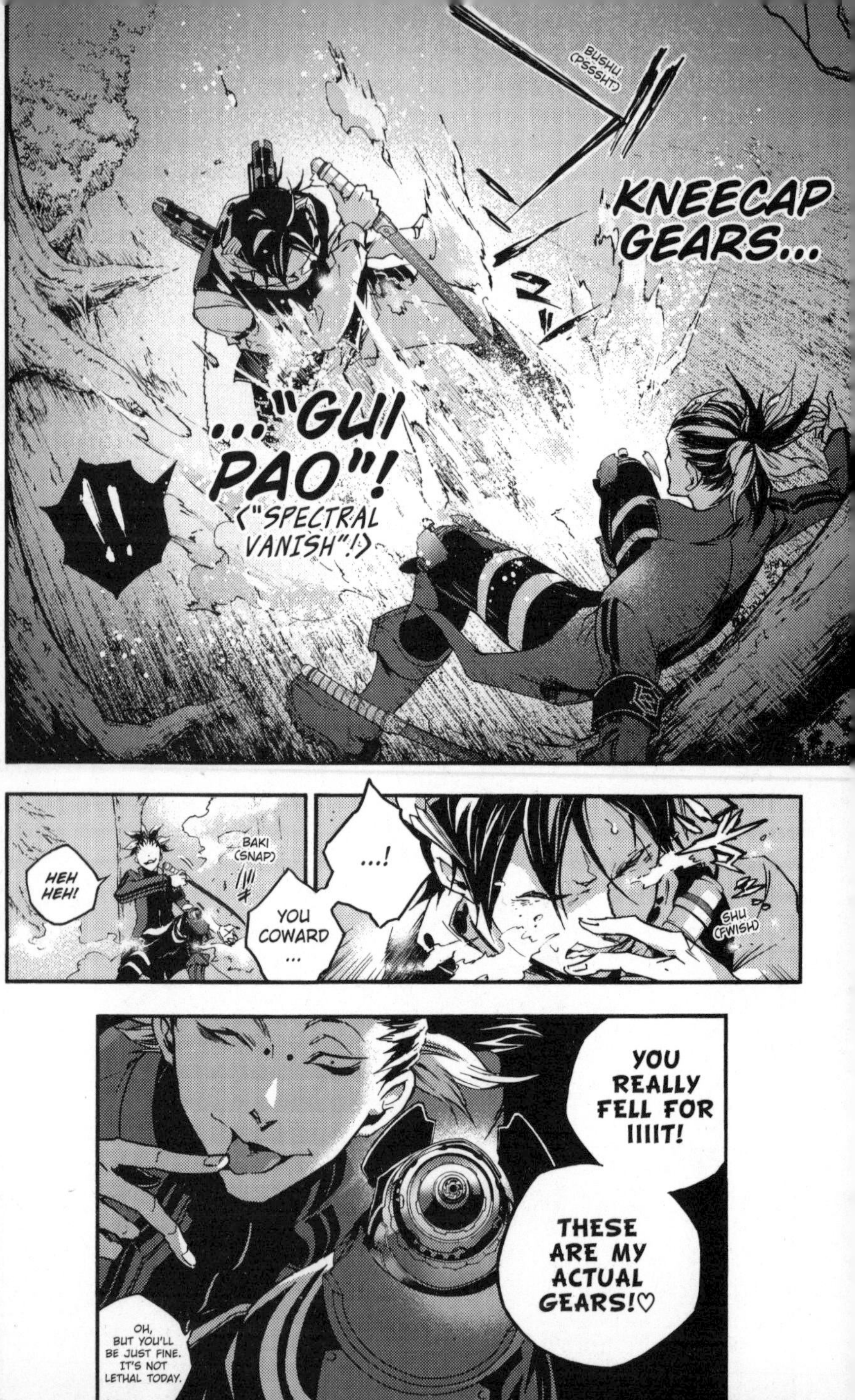
BUSHU (PSSSHT)
KNEECAP GEARS...
..."GUI PAO"!
〈"SPECTRAL VANISH"!〉
!!
...!
YOU COWARD ...
SHU (FWISH)
BAKI (SNAP)
HEH HEH!
YOU REALLY FELL FOR IIIIT!
THESE ARE MY ACTUAL GEARS!♡
OH, BUT YOU'LL BE JUST FINE. IT'S NOT LETHAL TODAY.

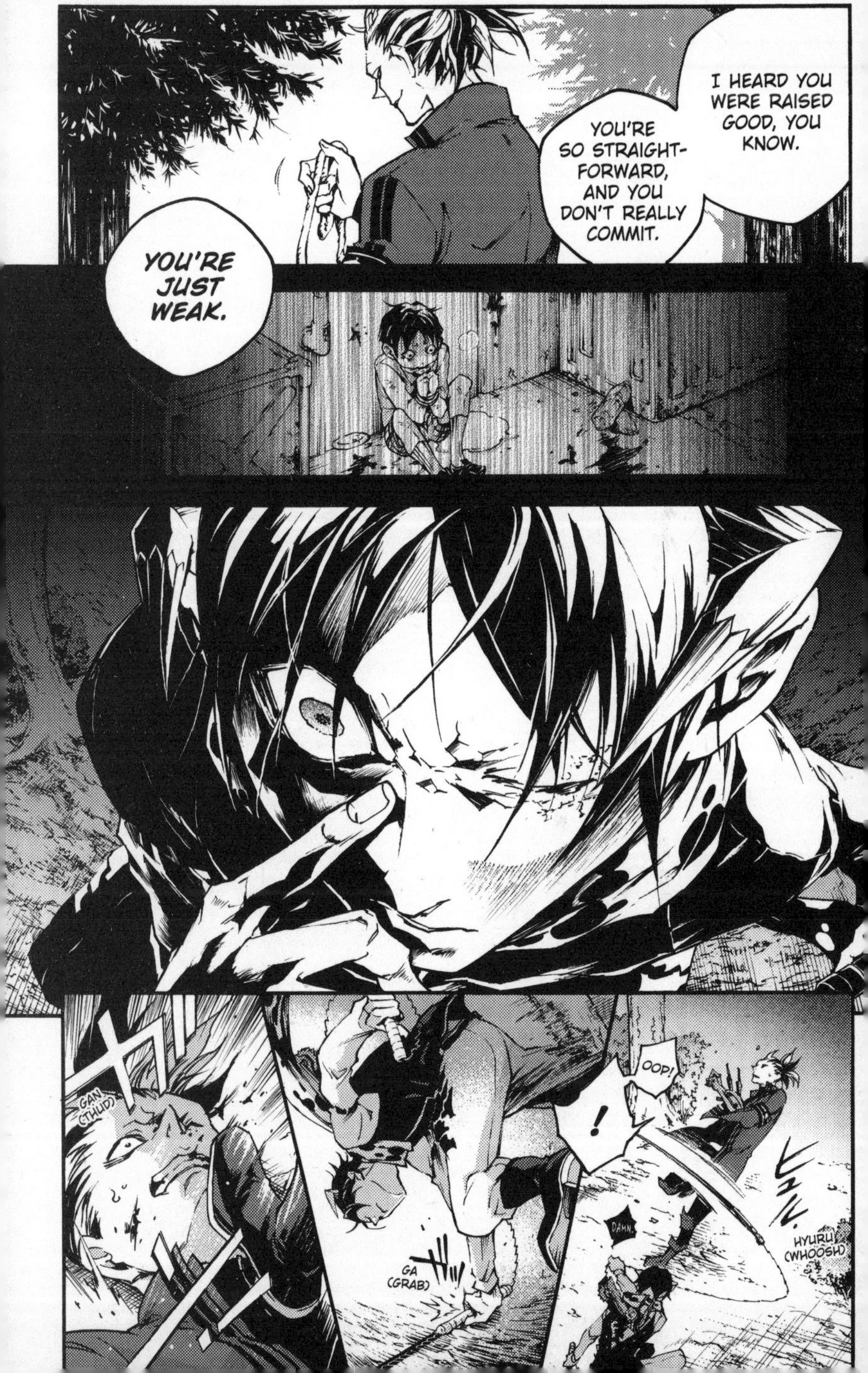
I HEARD YOU WERE RAISED GOOD, YOU KNOW.
YOU'RE SO STRAIGHT-FORWARD, AND YOU DON'T REALLY COMMIT.
YOU'RE JUST WEAK.
OOP!
!
HYURU (WHOOSH)
DAMN.
GA (GRAB)
GAN (THUD)

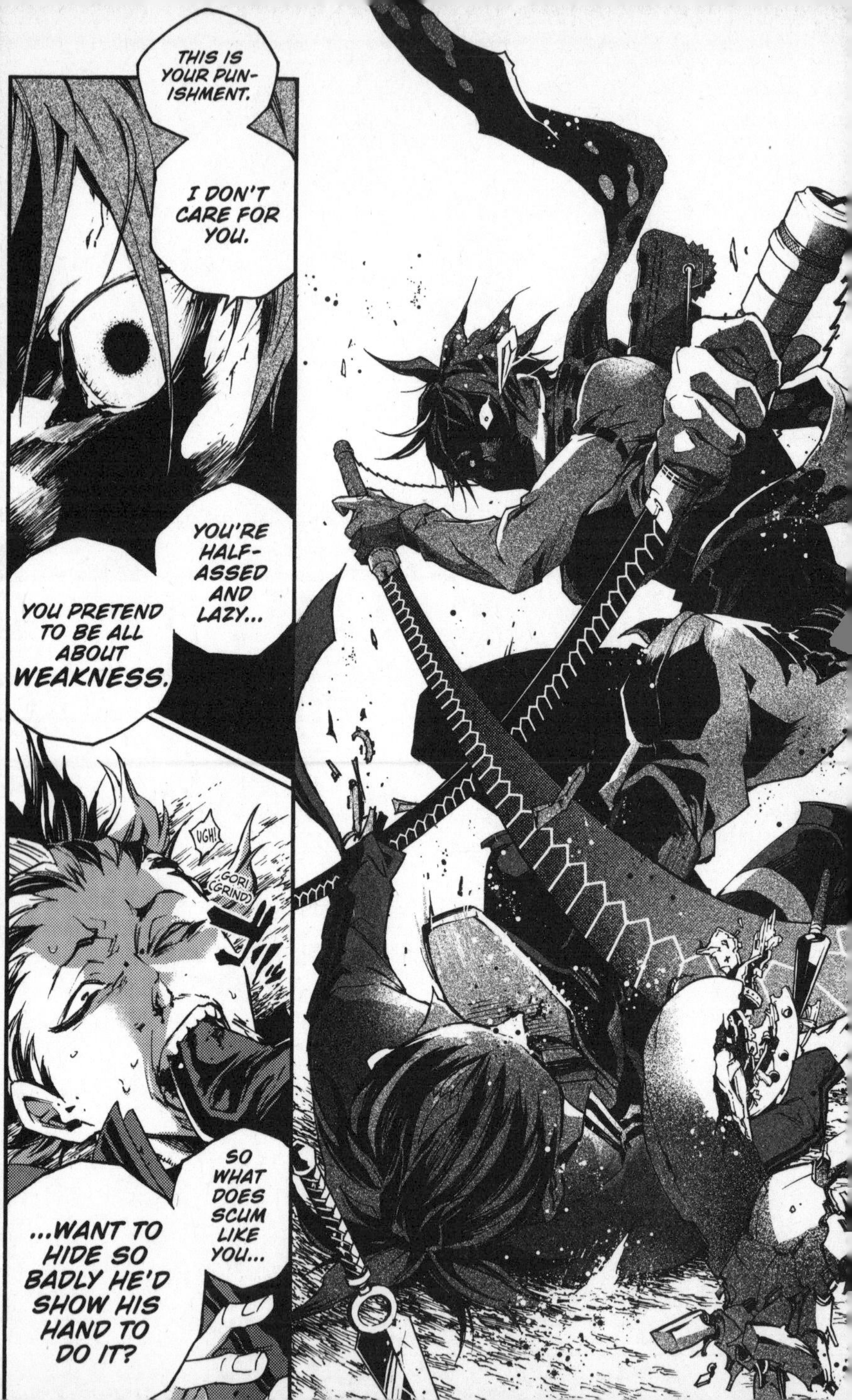
THIS IS YOUR PUN-ISHMENT.
I DON'T CARE FOR YOU.
YOU'RE HALF-ASSED AND LAZY...
YOU PRETEND TO BE ALL ABOUT WEAKNESS.
UGH!
GORI (GRIND)
SO WHAT DOES SCUM LIKE YOU...
...WANT TO HIDE SO BADLY HE'D SHOW HIS HAND TO DO IT?

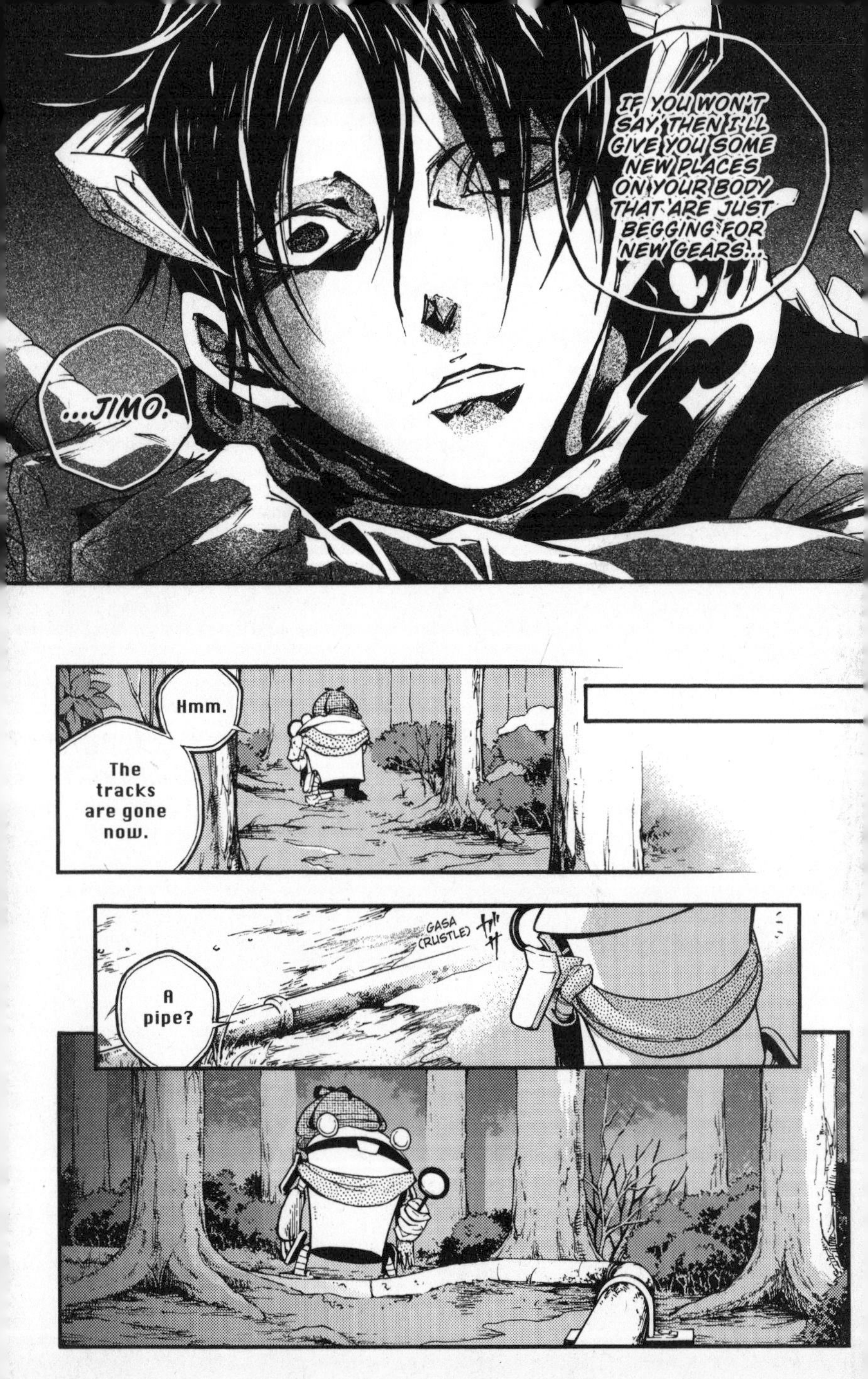
IF YOU WON'T SAY, THEN I'LL GIVE YOU SOME NEW PLACES ON YOUR BODY THAT ARE JUST BEGGING FOR NEW GEARS...
...JIMO.
Hmm.
The tracks are gone now.
GASA (RUSTLE)
A pipe?

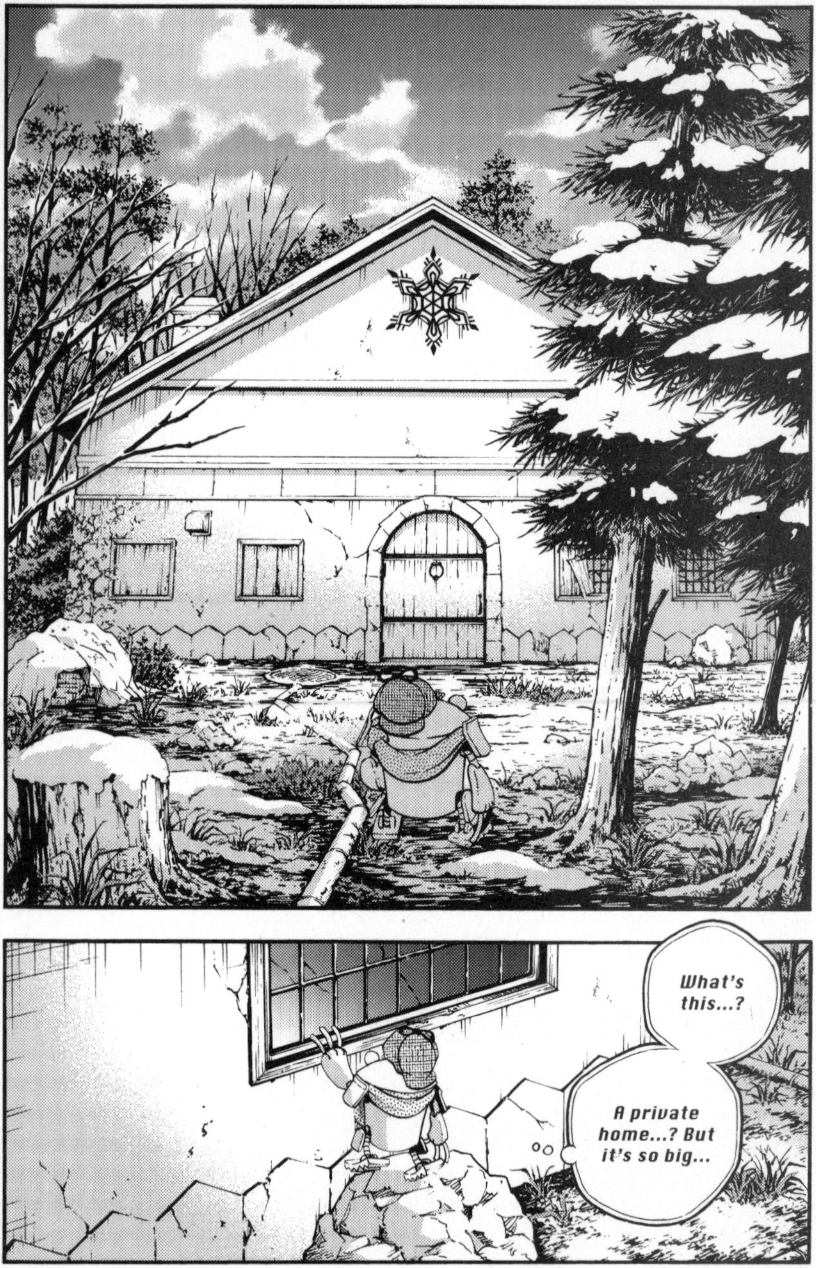
What's this...?
A private home...? But it's so big...

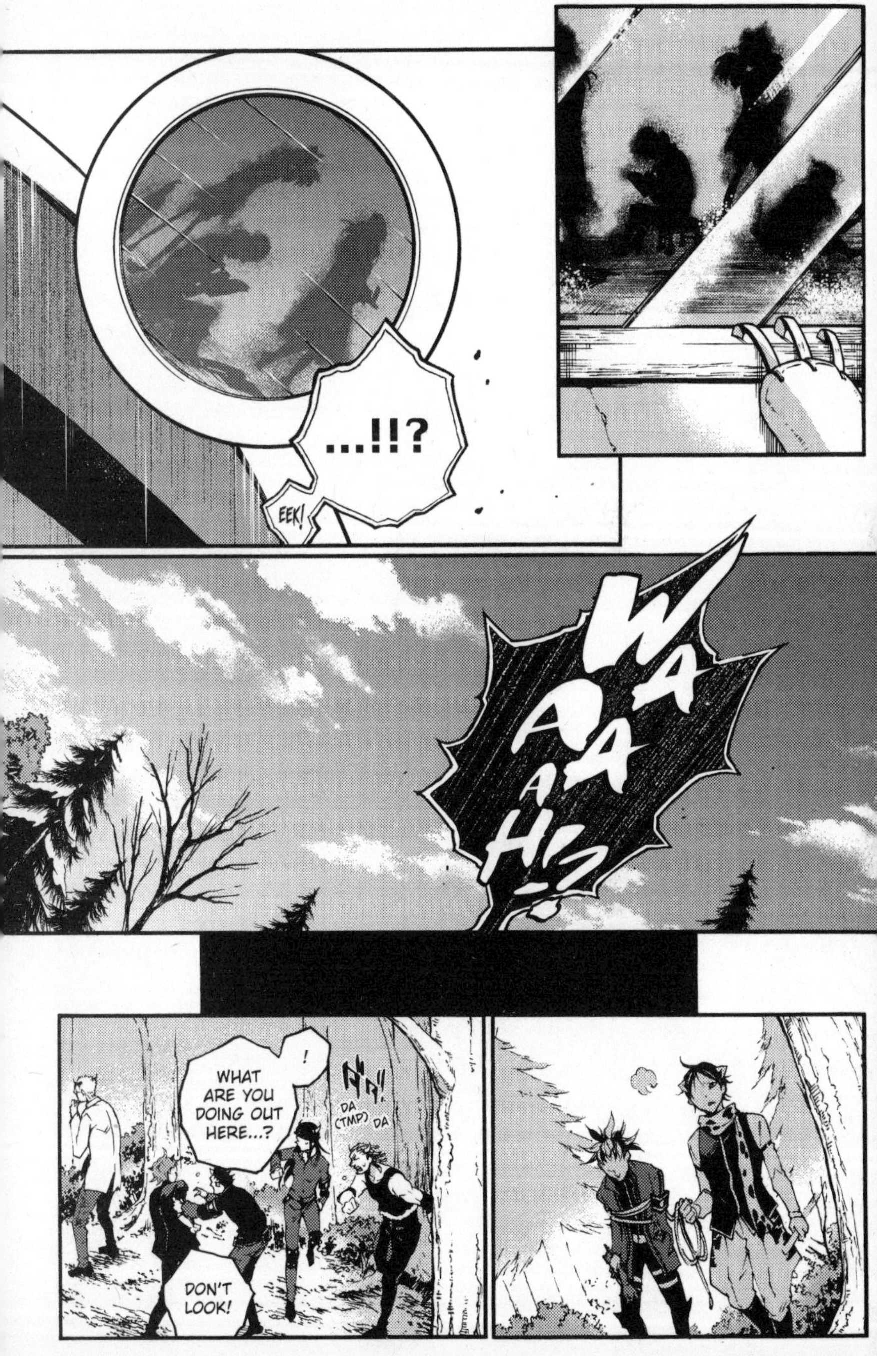
...!!?
EEK!
WAAAAH!?
!
WHAT ARE YOU DOING OUT HERE...?
DA (TMP) DA
DON'T LOOK!

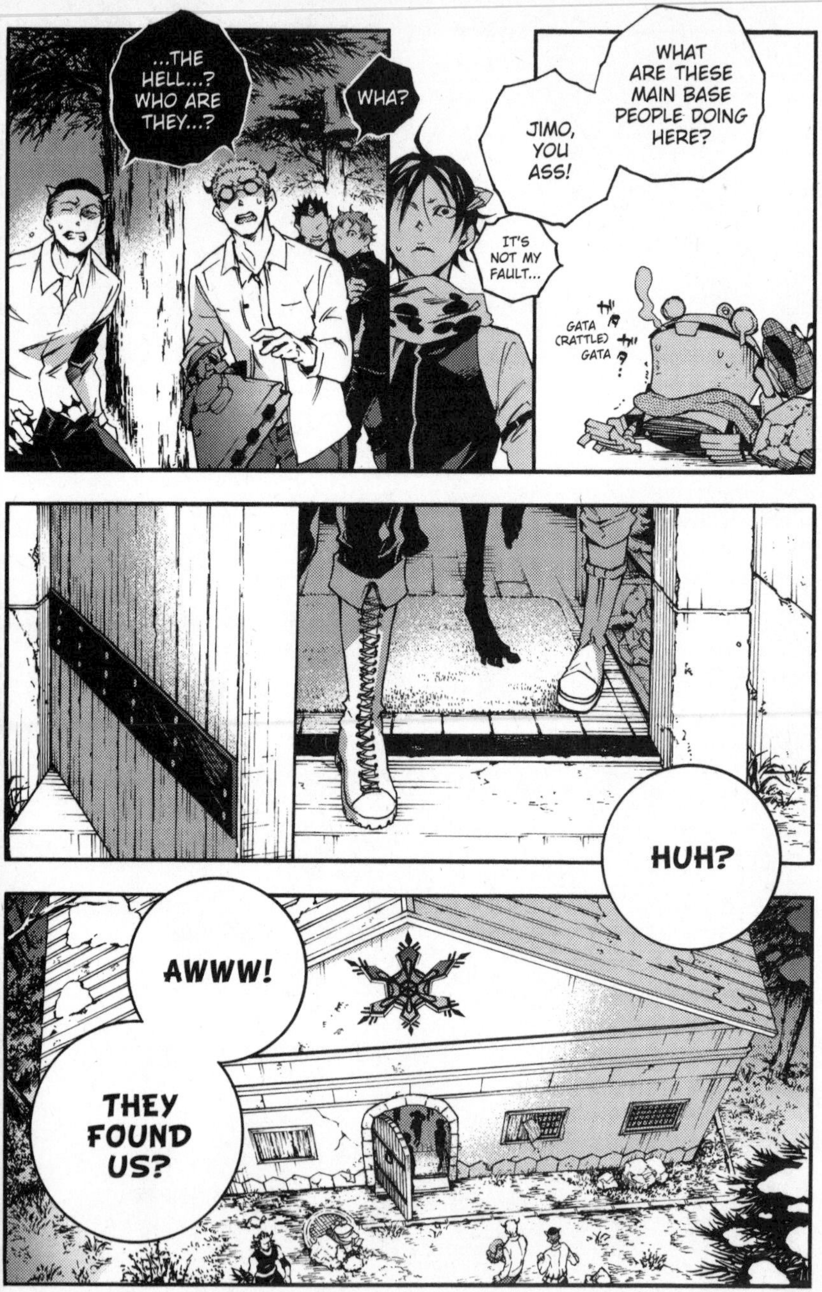
WHAT ARE THESE MAIN BASE PEOPLE DOING HERE?
JIMO, YOU ASS!
IT'S NOT MY FAULT...
GATA (RATTLE) GATA
WHA?
...THE HELL...? WHO ARE THEY...?
HUH?
AWWW!
THEY FOUND US?

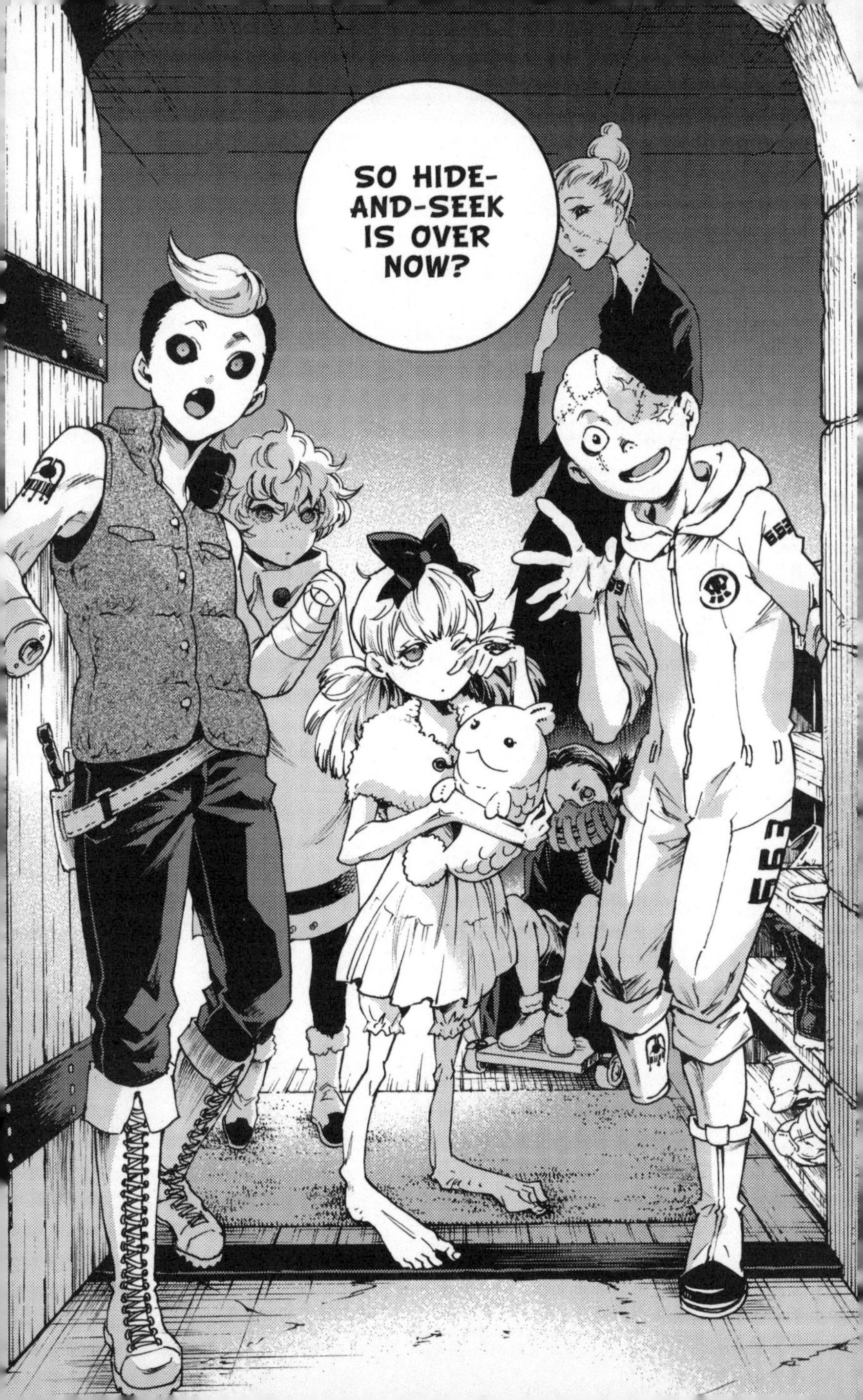
SO HIDE-AND-SEEK IS OVER NOW?

SMOKIN' PARADE

THE WORLD IS DEAD, THE PARADE WILL START.

JINSEI KATAOKA, KAZUMA KONDOU

SMOKIN' PARADE

THE WORLD IS DEAD, THE PARADE WILL START.

JINSEI KATAOKA, KAZUMA KONDOU

SMOKIN' PARADE

THE WORLD IS DEAD, THE PARADE WILL START.

JINSEI KATAOKA, KAZUMA KONDOU

SMOKIN' PARADE

THE WORLD IS DEAD, THE PARADE WILL START.

JINSEI KATAOKA, KAZUMA KONDOU

SMOKIN' PARADE

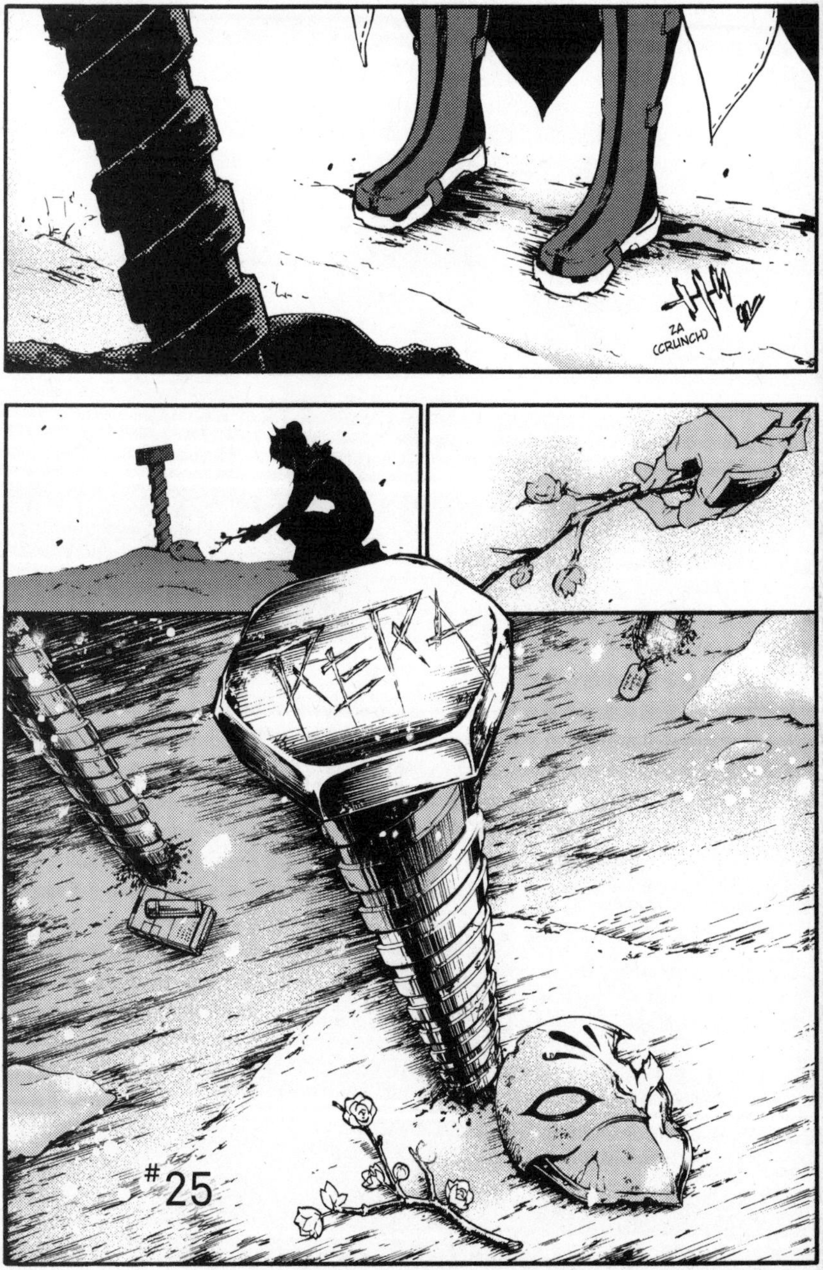
ZA
(CRUNCH)
#25

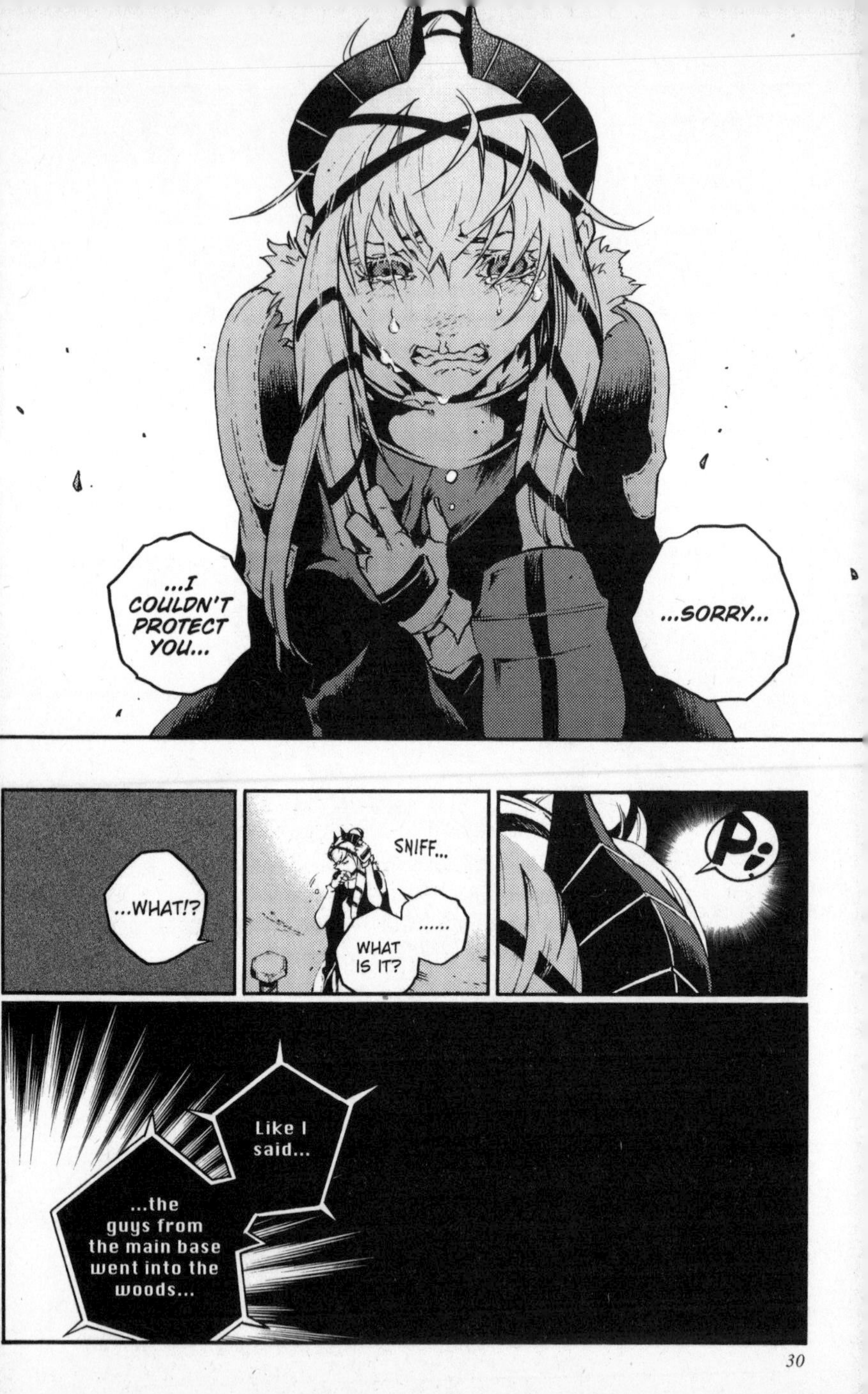
...SORRY...
...I COULDN'T PROTECT YOU...
SNIFF...
......
WHAT IS IT?
...WHAT!?
Like I said...
...the guys from the main base went into the woods...

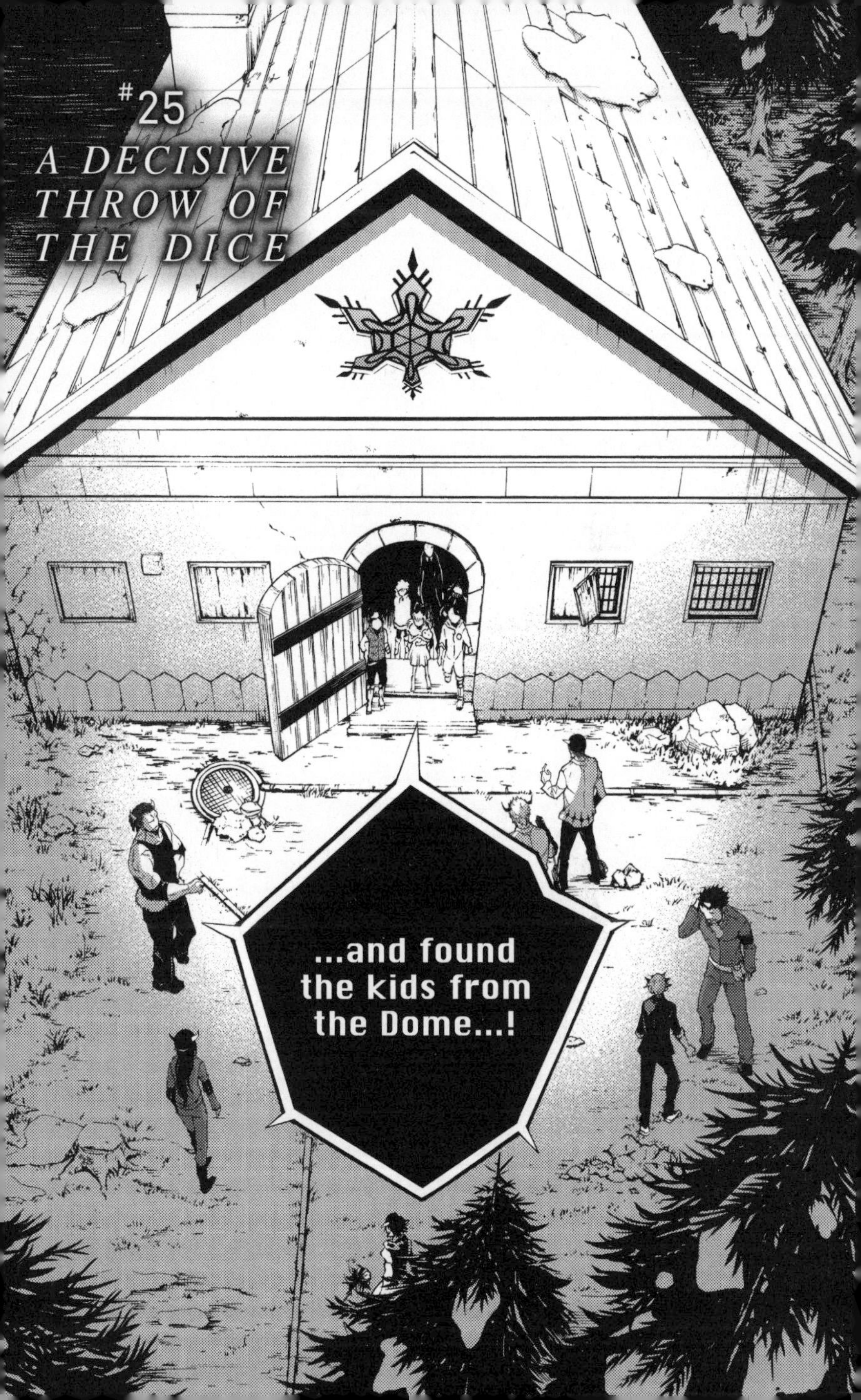
#25
A DECISIVE THROW OF THE DICE
...and found the kids from the Dome...!

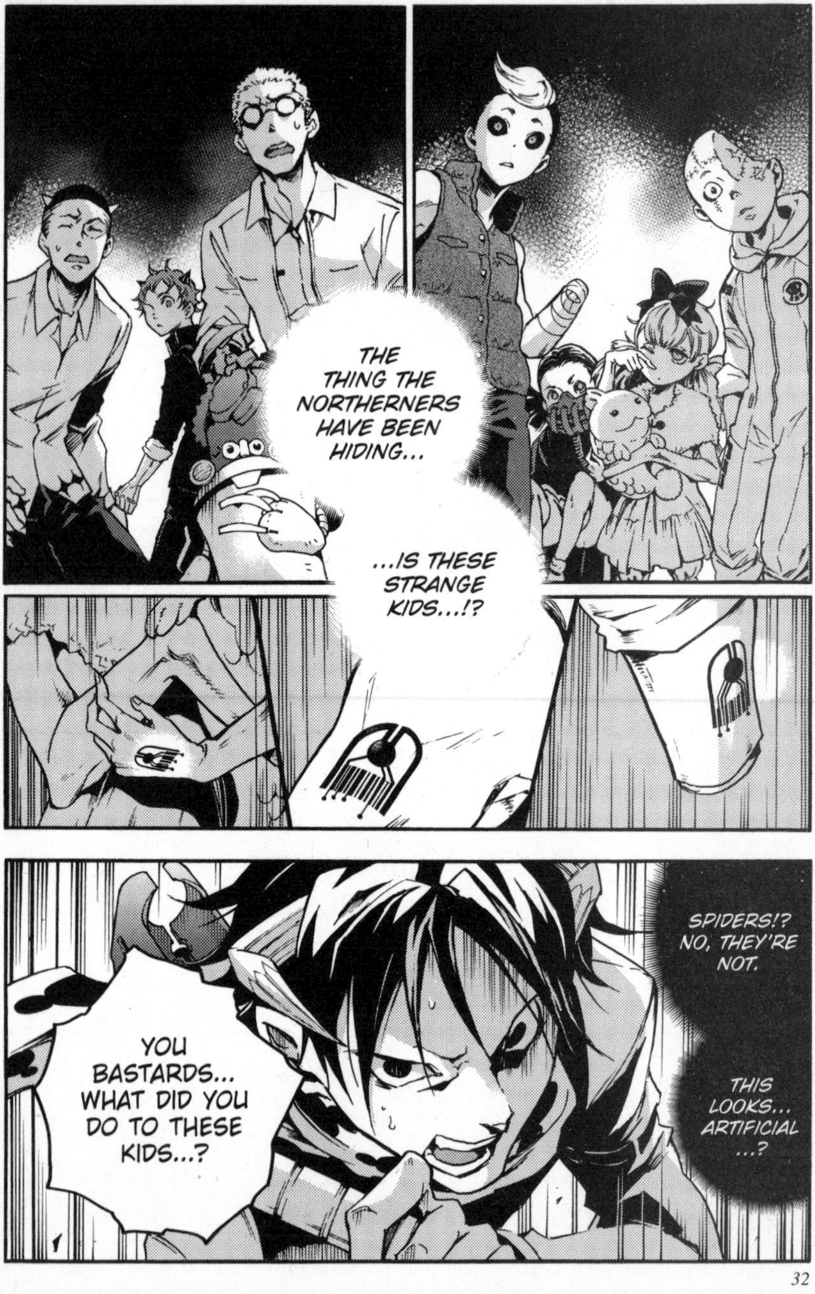
THE THING THE NORTHERNERS HAVE BEEN HIDING...
...IS THESE STRANGE KIDS...!?
SPIDERS!? NO, THEY'RE NOT.
THIS LOOKS... ARTIFICIAL ...?
YOU BASTARDS... WHAT DID YOU DO TO THESE KIDS...?

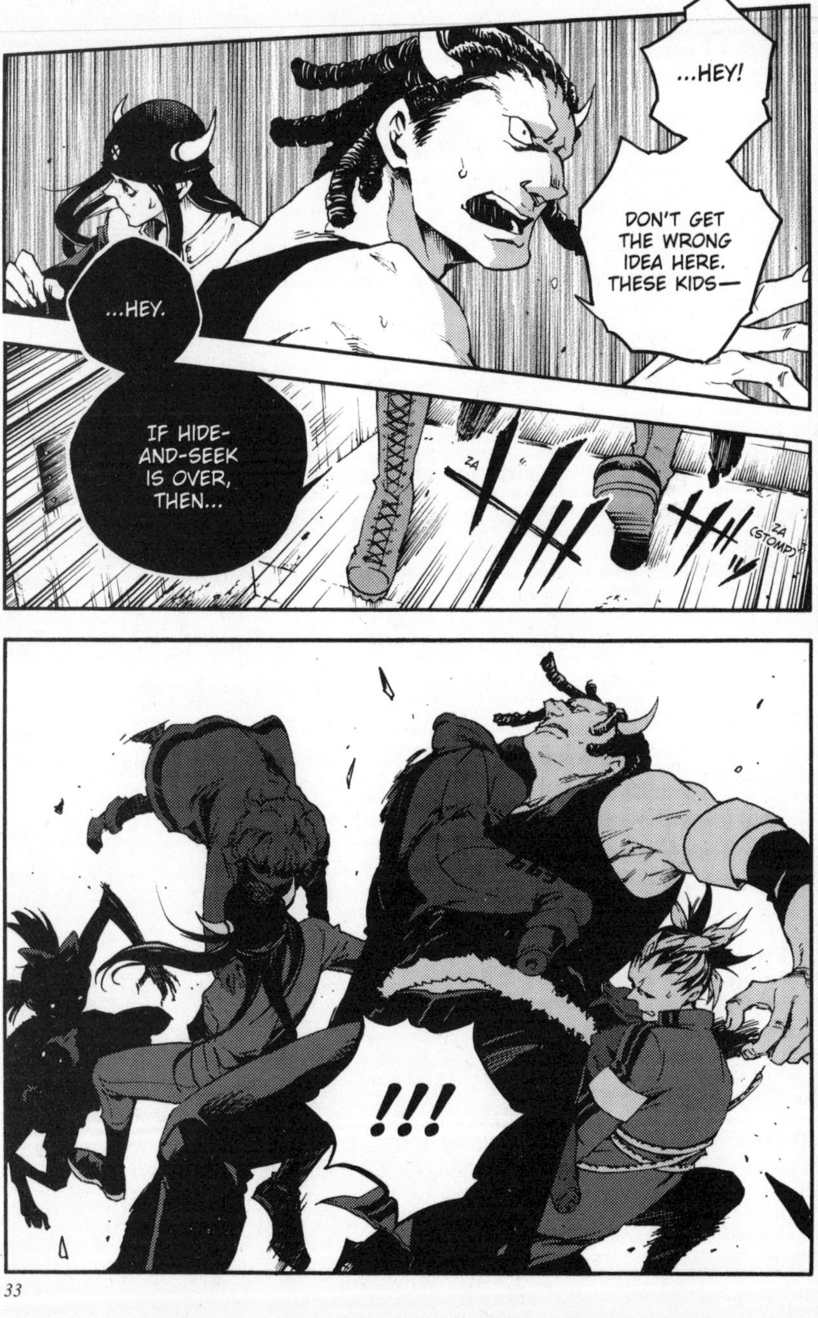
...HEY!
DON'T GET THE WRONG IDEA HERE. THESE KIDS—
...HEY.
IF HIDE-AND-SEEK IS OVER, THEN...
ZA
ZA (STOMP)
!!!

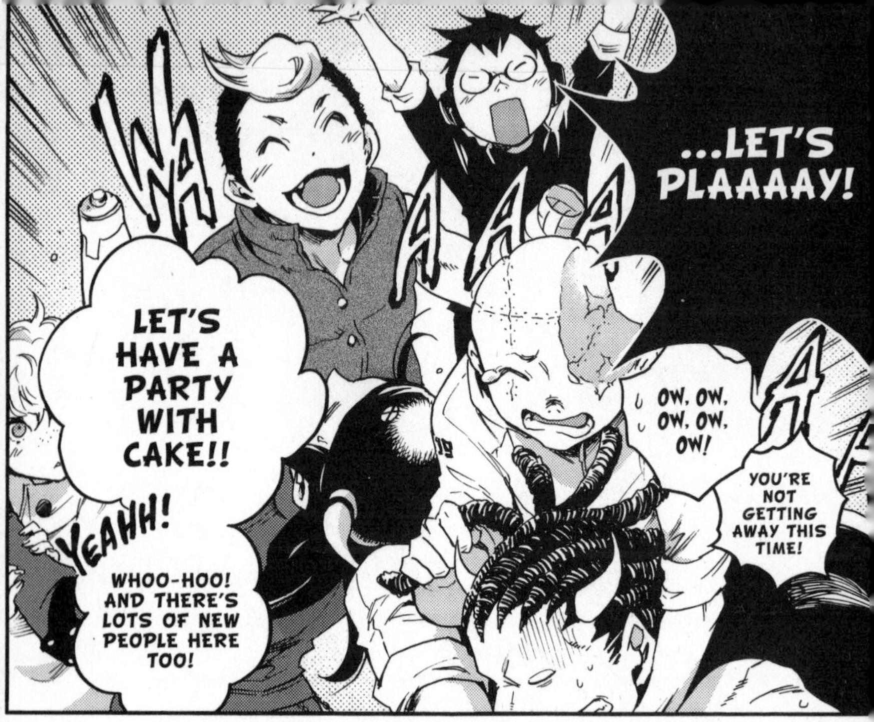
...LET'S PLAAAAY!
WAAAAAA
OW, OW, OW, OW, OW!
YOU'RE NOT GETTING AWAY THIS TIME!
LET'S HAVE A PARTY WITH CAKE!!
YEAHH!
WHOO-HOO! AND THERE'S LOTS OF NEW PEOPLE HERE TOO!
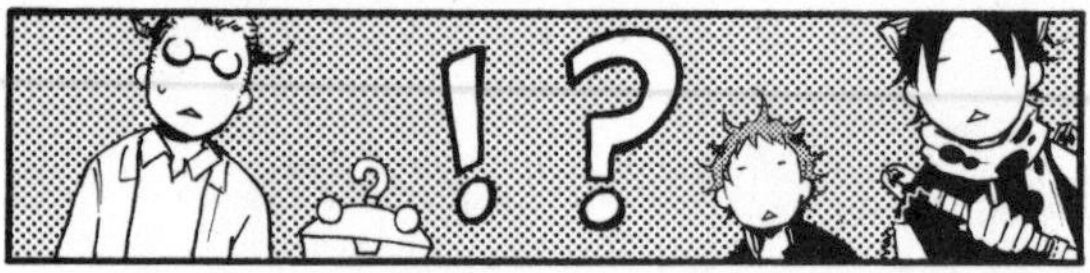
!?
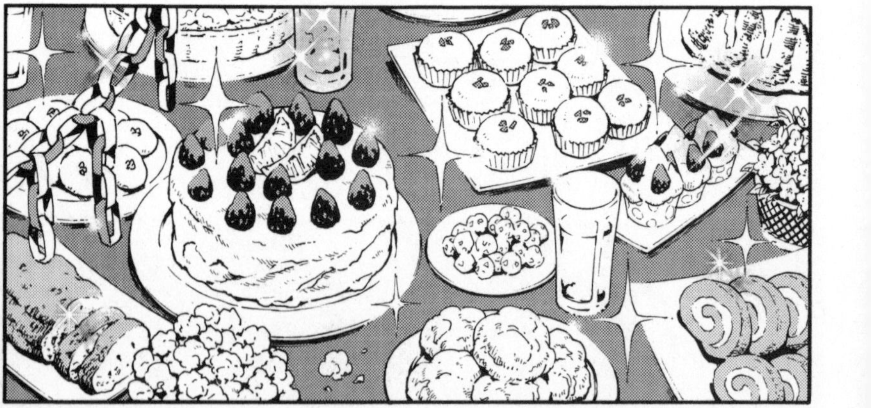

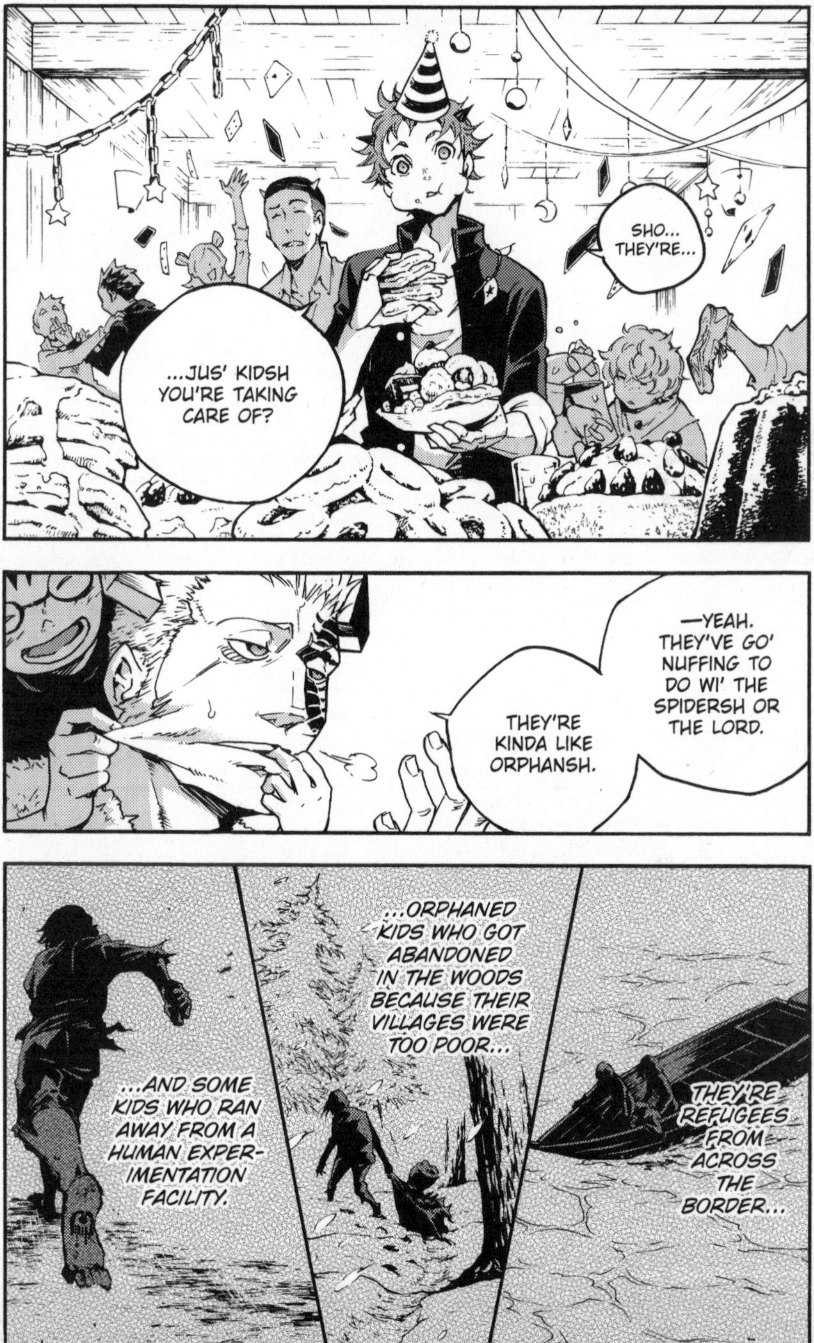
SHO... THEY'RE...
...JUS' KIDSH YOU'RE TAKING CARE OF?
—YEAH. THEY'VE GO' NUFFING TO DO WI' THE SPIDERSH OR THE LORD.
THEY'RE KINDA LIKE ORPHANSH.
THEY'RE REFUGEES FROM ACROSS THE BORDER...
...ORPHANED KIDS WHO GOT ABANDONED IN THE WOODS BECAUSE THEIR VILLAGES WERE TOO POOR...
...AND SOME KIDS WHO RAN AWAY FROM A HUMAN EXPERIMENTATION FACILITY.

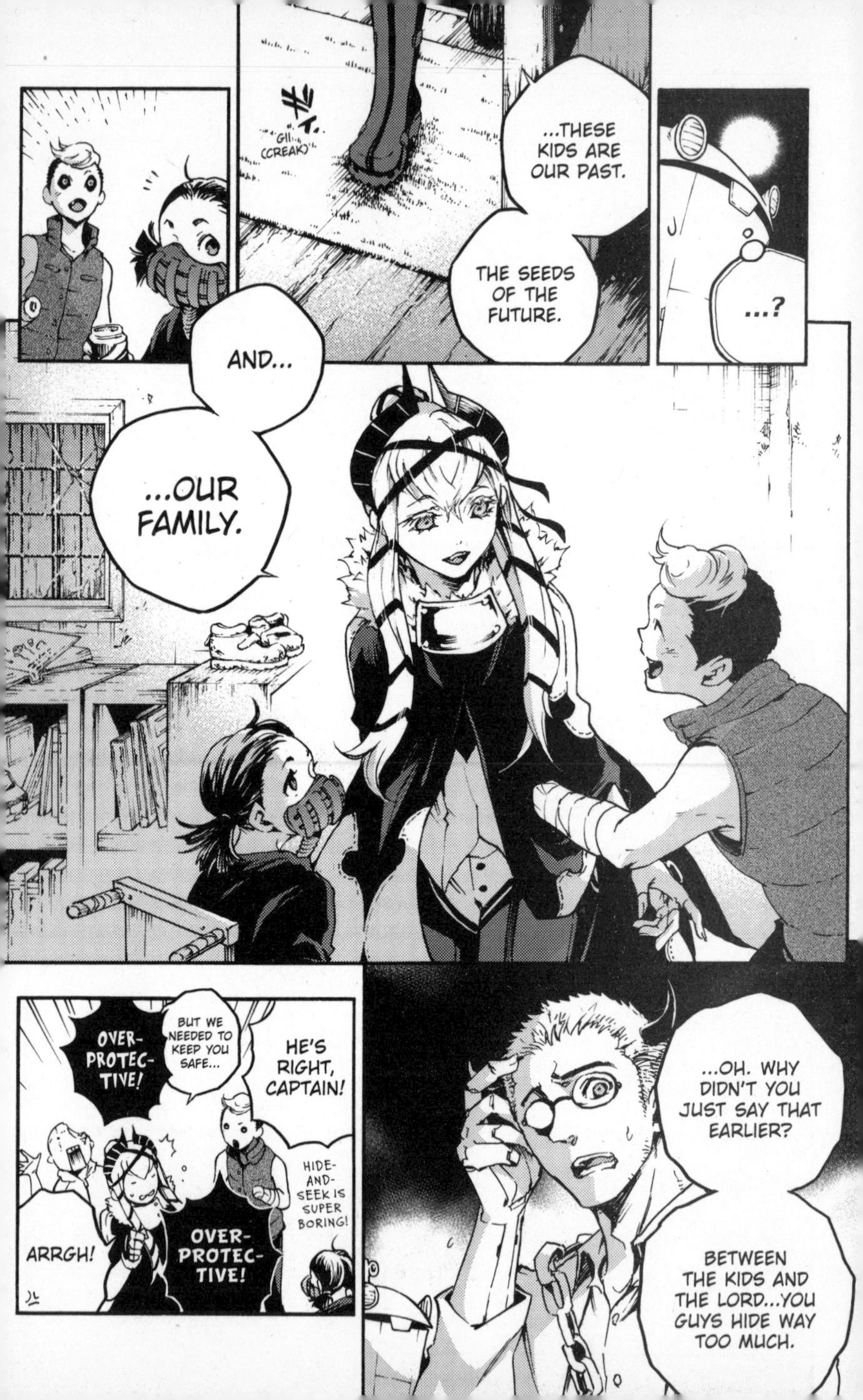
...?
...THESE KIDS ARE OUR PAST.
THE SEEDS OF THE FUTURE.
GII (CREAK)
AND...
...OUR FAMILY.
...OH. WHY DIDN'T YOU JUST SAY THAT EARLIER?
BETWEEN THE KIDS AND THE LORD...YOU GUYS HIDE WAY TOO MUCH.
HE'S RIGHT, CAPTAIN!
BUT WE NEEDED TO KEEP YOU SAFE...
OVER-PROTECTIVE!
HIDE-AND-SEEK IS SUPER BORING!
OVER-PROTECTIVE!
ARRGH!

—THINGS HAVE ONLY GOTTEN MORE COMPLICATED BECAUSE YOU WENT AGAINST MY ADVICE AND BROUGHT THE PEOPLE FROM THE MAIN BASE HERE.

URGH...

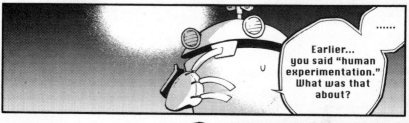

......

Earlier... you said "human experimentation." What was that about?

......SEE? COMPLICATED.

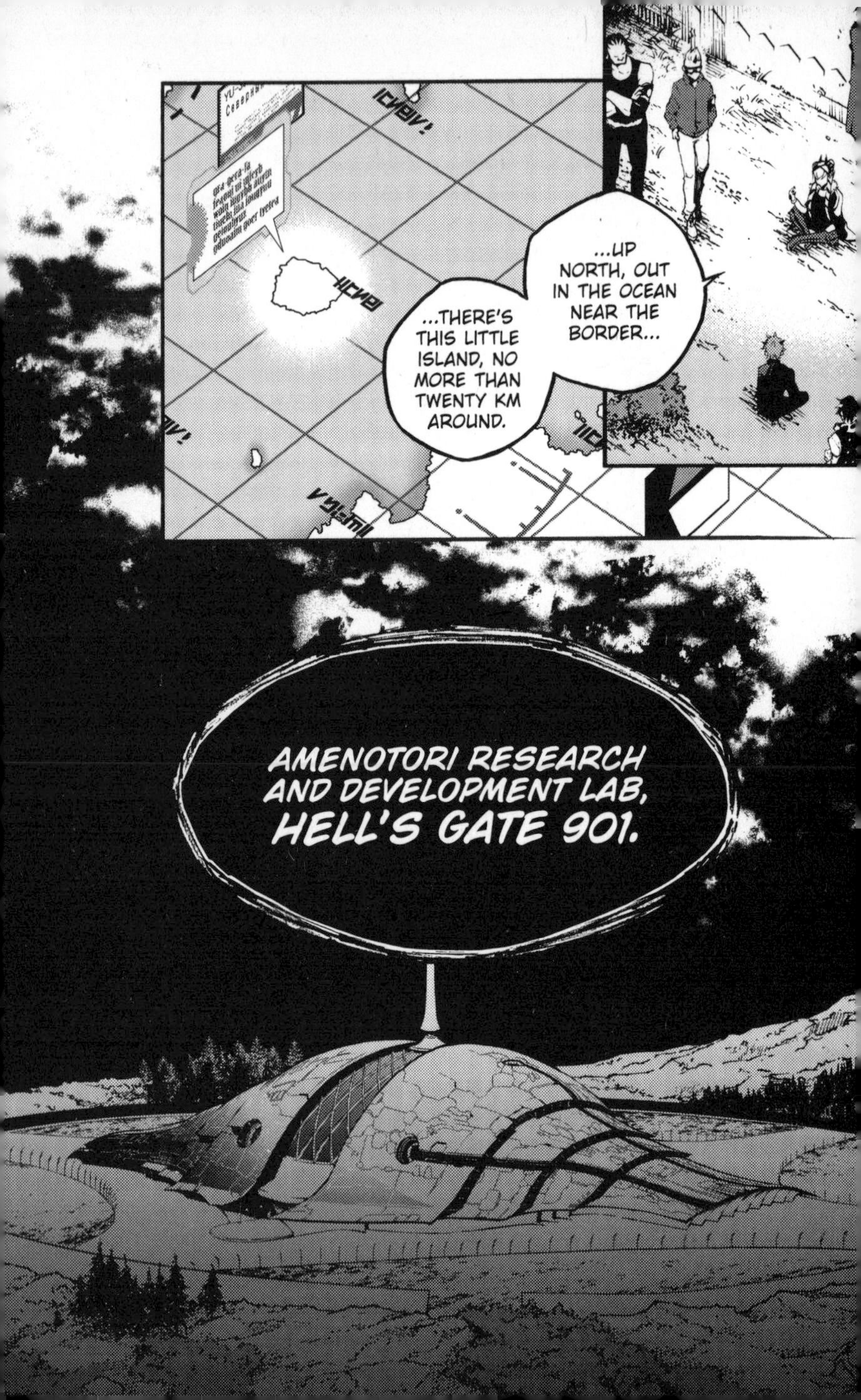
...UP NORTH, OUT IN THE OCEAN NEAR THE BORDER...
...THERE'S THIS LITTLE ISLAND, NO MORE THAN TWENTY KM AROUND.
AMENOTORI RESEARCH AND DEVELOPMENT LAB, HELL'S GATE 901.

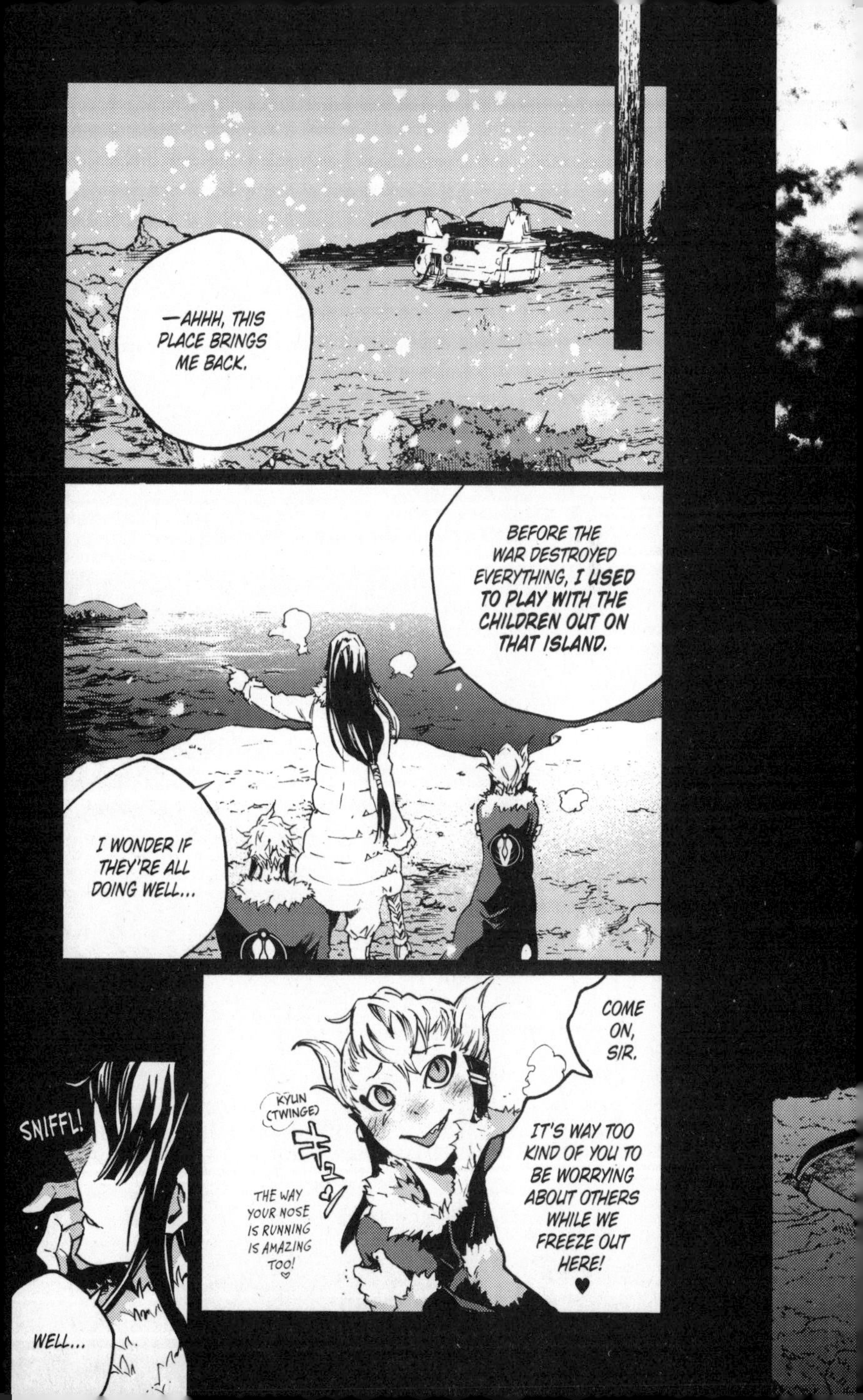
—AHHH, THIS PLACE BRINGS ME BACK.
BEFORE THE WAR DESTROYED EVERYTHING, I USED TO PLAY WITH THE CHILDREN OUT ON THAT ISLAND.
I WONDER IF THEY'RE ALL DOING WELL...
COME ON, SIR.
IT'S WAY TOO KIND OF YOU TO BE WORRYING ABOUT OTHERS WHILE WE FREEZE OUT HERE! ♥
KYUN (TWINGE)
THE WAY YOUR NOSE IS RUNNING IS AMAZING TOO! ♡
SNIFFL!
WELL...

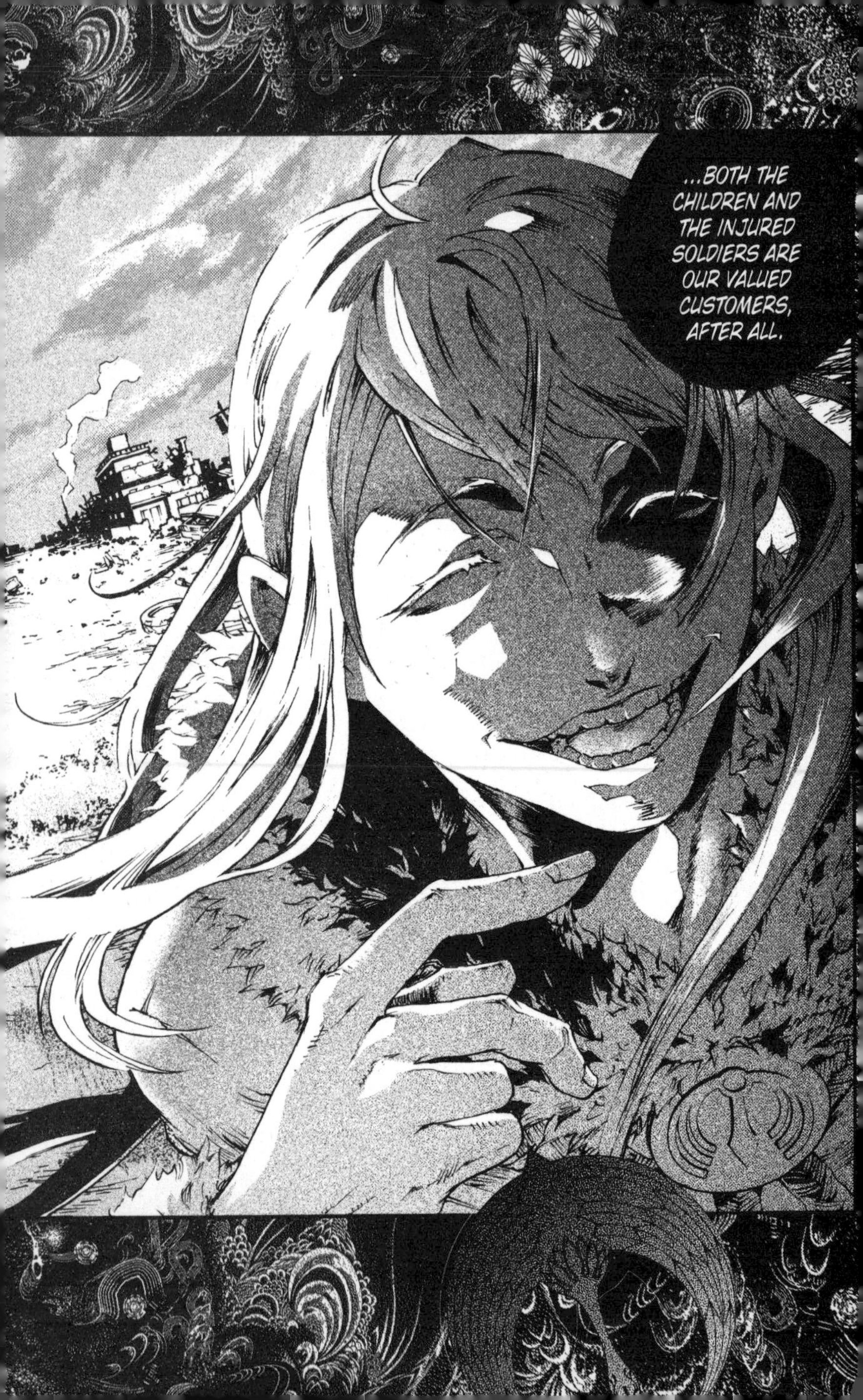
...BOTH THE CHILDREN AND THE INJURED SOLDIERS ARE OUR VALUED CUSTOMERS, AFTER ALL.

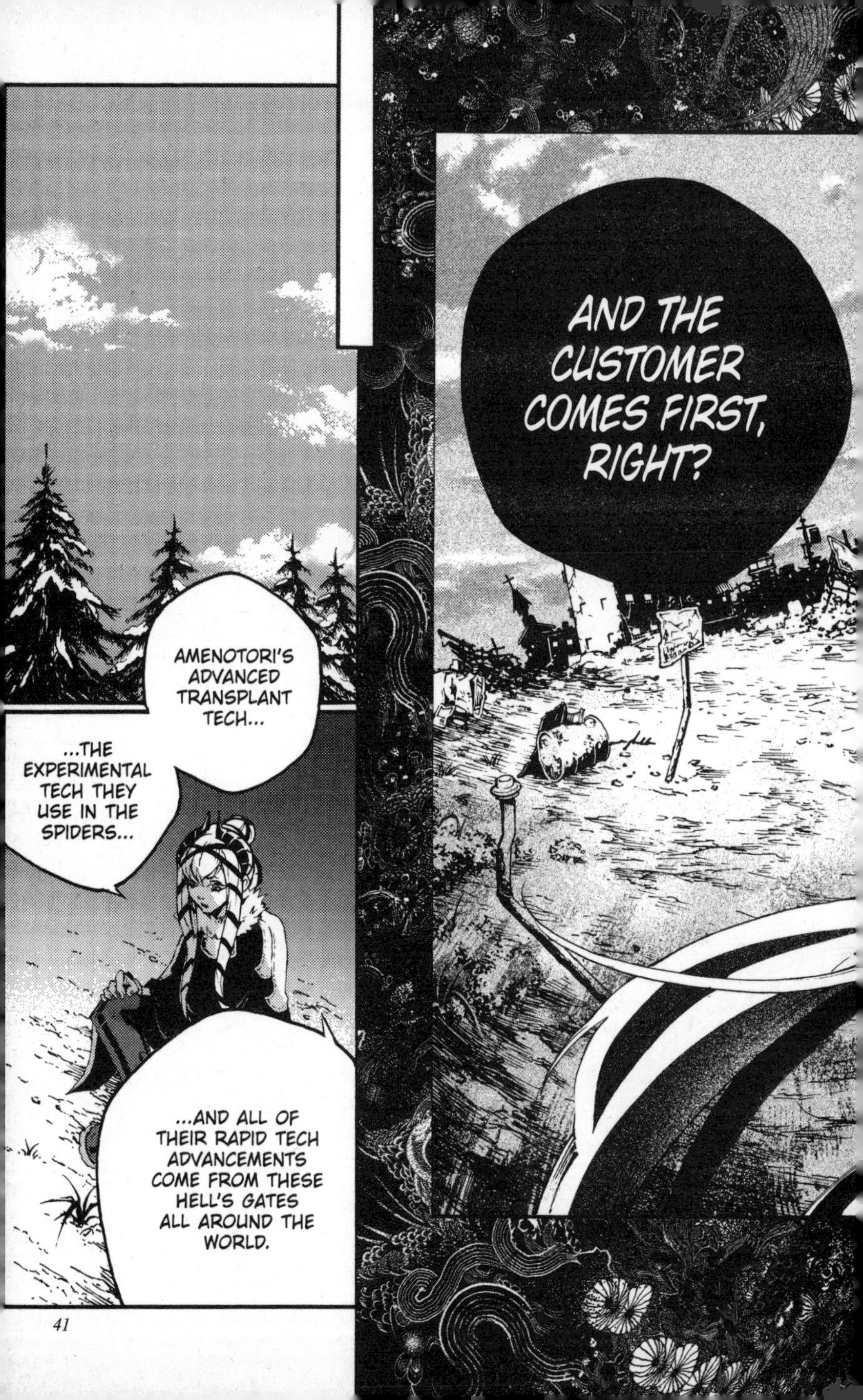
AMENOTORI'S ADVANCED TRANSPLANT TECH...
...THE EXPERIMENTAL TECH THEY USE IN THE SPIDERS...
...AND ALL OF THEIR RAPID TECH ADVANCEMENTS COME FROM THESE HELL'S GATES ALL AROUND THE WORLD.
AND THE CUSTOMER COMES FIRST, RIGHT?

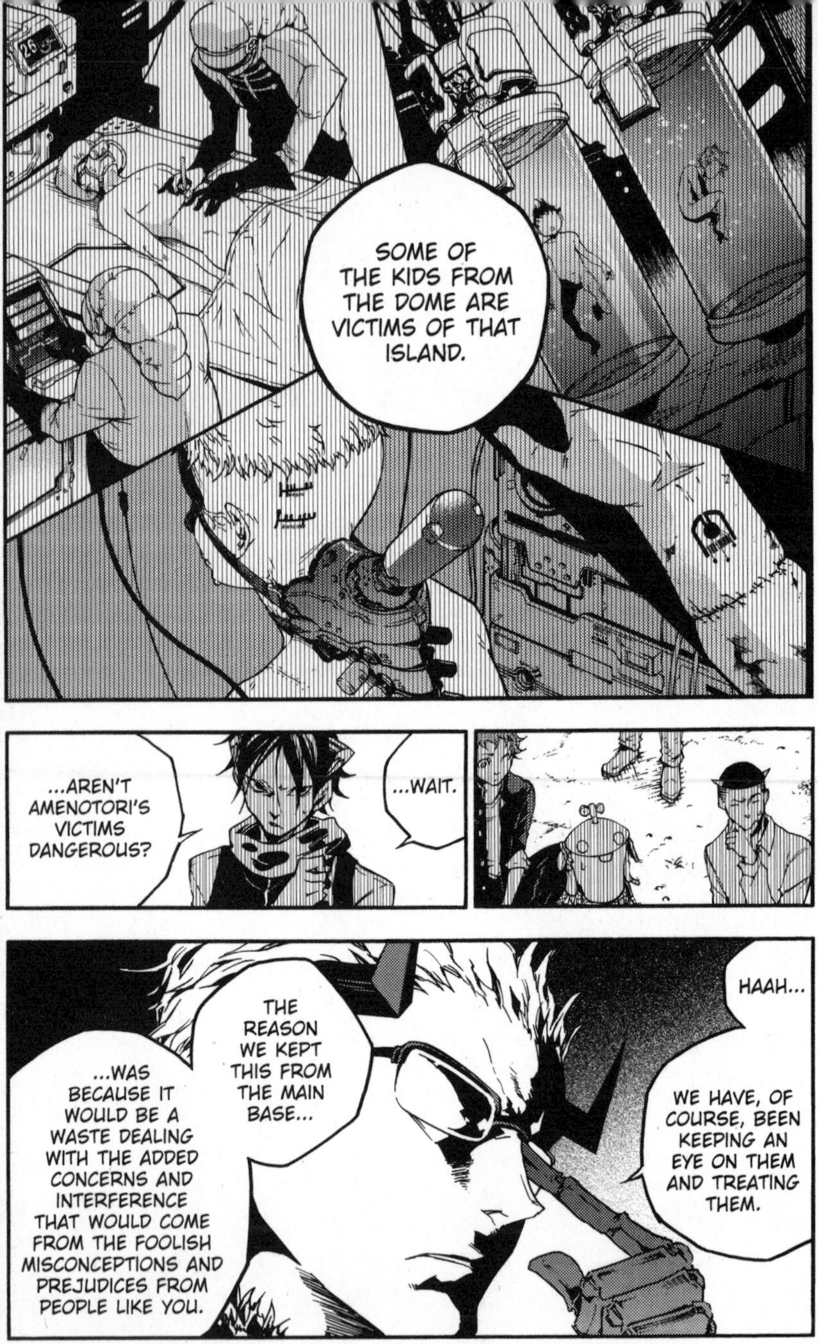
SOME OF THE KIDS FROM THE DOME ARE VICTIMS OF THAT ISLAND.
...WAIT.
...AREN'T AMENOTORI'S VICTIMS DANGEROUS?
HAAH...
WE HAVE, OF COURSE, BEEN KEEPING AN EYE ON THEM AND TREATING THEM.
THE REASON WE KEPT THIS FROM THE MAIN BASE...
...WAS BECAUSE IT WOULD BE A WASTE DEALING WITH THE ADDED CONCERNS AND INTERFERENCE THAT WOULD COME FROM THE FOOLISH MISCONCEPTIONS AND PREJUDICES FROM PEOPLE LIKE YOU.

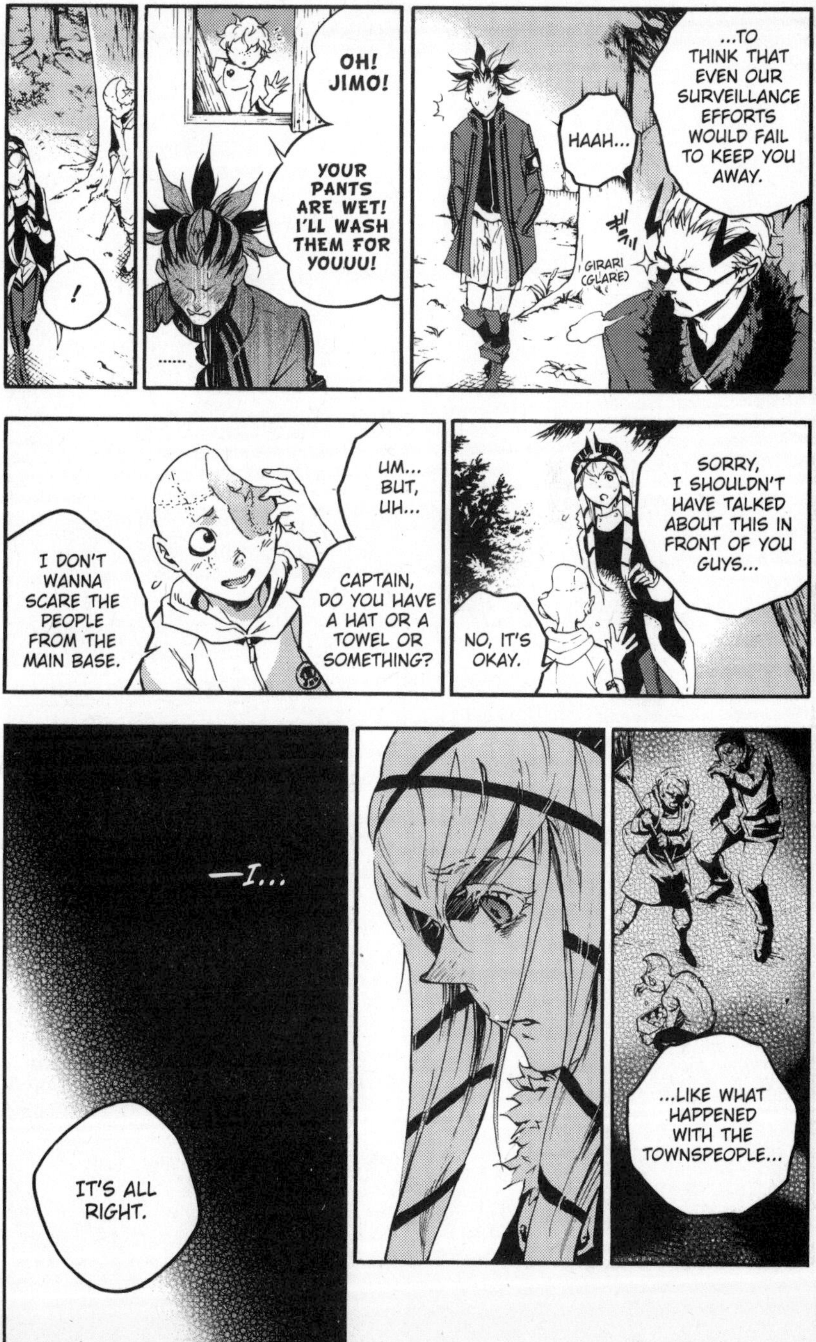
...TO THINK THAT EVEN OUR SURVEILLANCE EFFORTS WOULD FAIL TO KEEP YOU AWAY.
HAAH...
GIRARI (GLARE)
OH! JIMO!
YOUR PANTS ARE WET! I'LL WASH THEM FOR YOUUU!
......
!
SORRY, I SHOULDN'T HAVE TALKED ABOUT THIS IN FRONT OF YOU GUYS...
NO, IT'S OKAY.
UM... BUT, UH...
CAPTAIN, DO YOU HAVE A HAT OR A TOWEL OR SOMETHING?
I DON'T WANNA SCARE THE PEOPLE FROM THE MAIN BASE.
...LIKE WHAT HAPPENED WITH THE TOWNSPEOPLE...
—I...
IT'S ALL RIGHT.

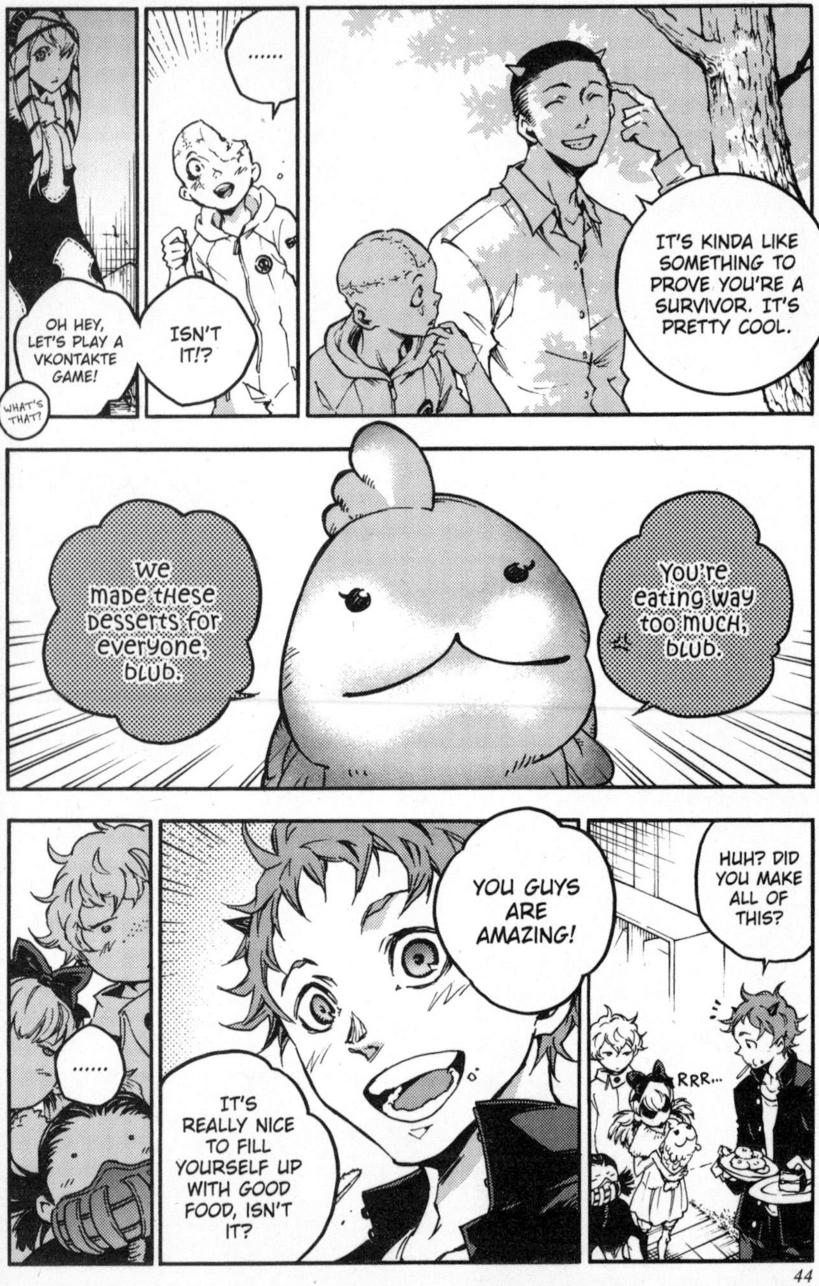
IT'S KINDA LIKE SOMETHING TO PROVE YOU'RE A SURVIVOR. IT'S PRETTY COOL.
......
ISN'T IT!?
OH HEY, LET'S PLAY A VKONTAKTE GAME!
WHAT'S THAT?
You're eating way too much, blub.
We made these desserts for everyone, blub.
HUH? DID YOU MAKE ALL OF THIS?
RRR...
YOU GUYS ARE AMAZING!
IT'S REALLY NICE TO FILL YOURSELF UP WITH GOOD FOOD, ISN'T IT?
......

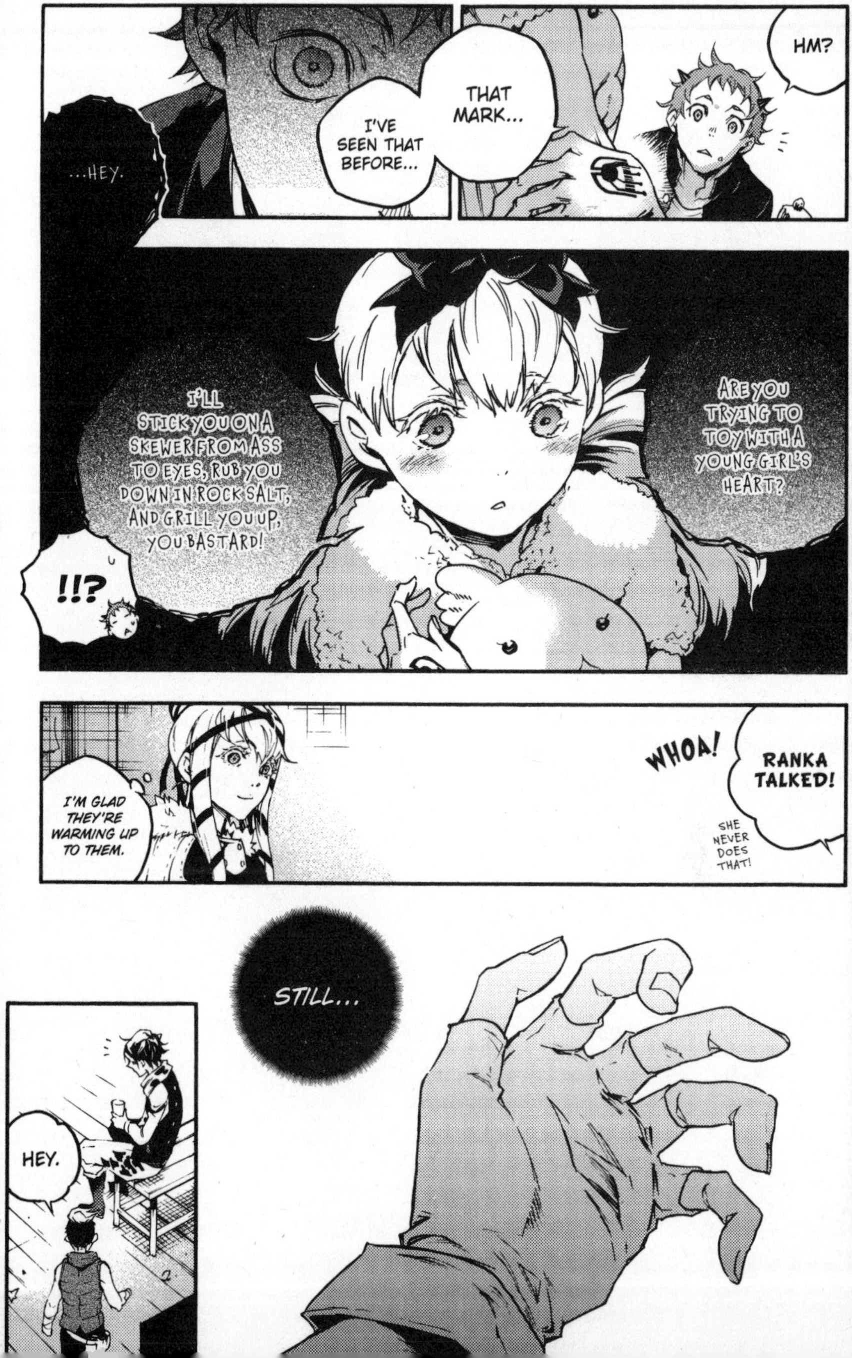
HM?
THAT MARK...
I'VE SEEN THAT BEFORE...
...HEY.
ARE YOU TRYING TO TOY WITH A YOUNG GIRL'S HEART?
I'LL STICK YOU ON A SKEWER FROM ASS TO EYES, RUB YOU DOWN IN ROCK SALT, AND GRILL YOU UP, YOU BASTARD!
!!?
WHOA!
RANKA TALKED!
SHE NEVER DOES THAT!
I'M GLAD THEY'RE WARMING UP TO THEM.
STILL...
HEY.

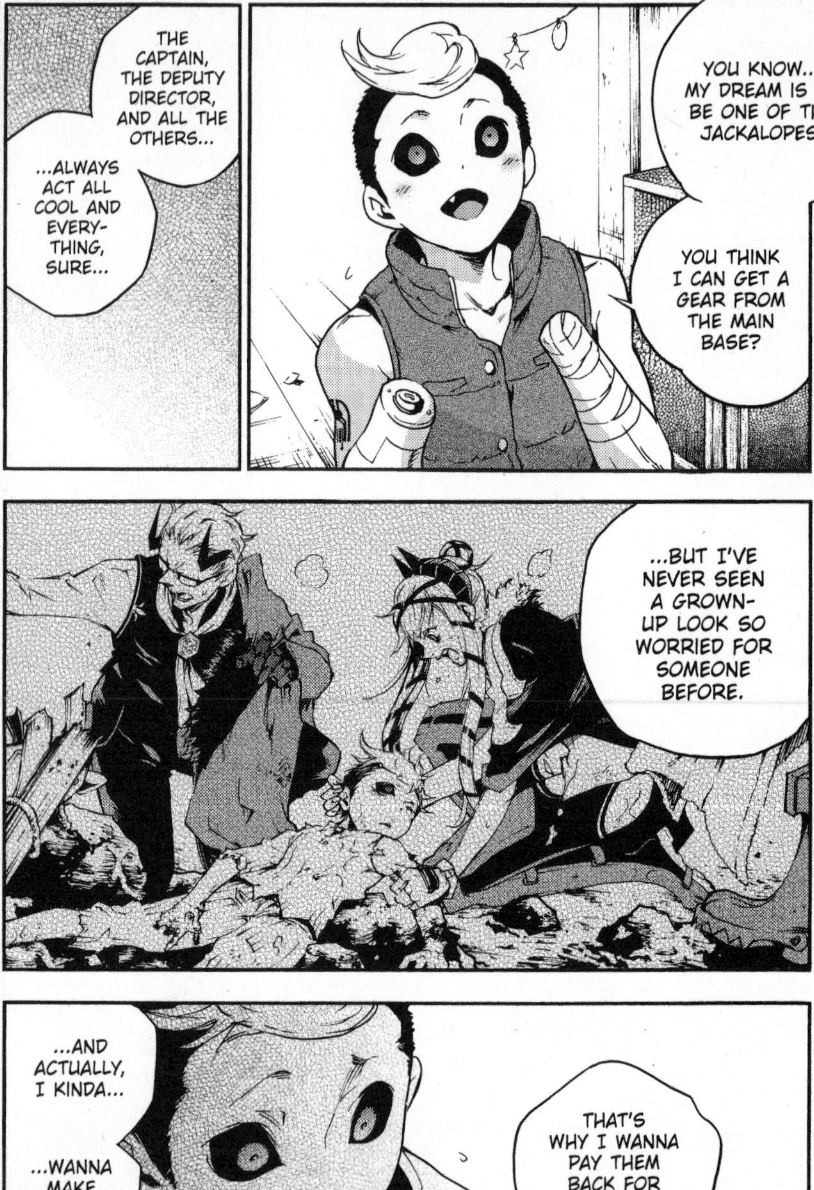
YOU KNOW... MY DREAM IS TO BE ONE OF THE JACKALOPES.
YOU THINK I CAN GET A GEAR FROM THE MAIN BASE?
THE CAPTAIN, THE DEPUTY DIRECTOR, AND ALL THE OTHERS...
...ALWAYS ACT ALL COOL AND EVERY-THING, SURE...
...BUT I'VE NEVER SEEN A GROWN-UP LOOK SO WORRIED FOR SOMEONE BEFORE.
THAT'S WHY I WANNA PAY THEM BACK FOR THAT, AT LEAST A LITTLE.
...AND ACTUALLY, I KINDA...
...WANNA MAKE THAT FACE MYSELF...

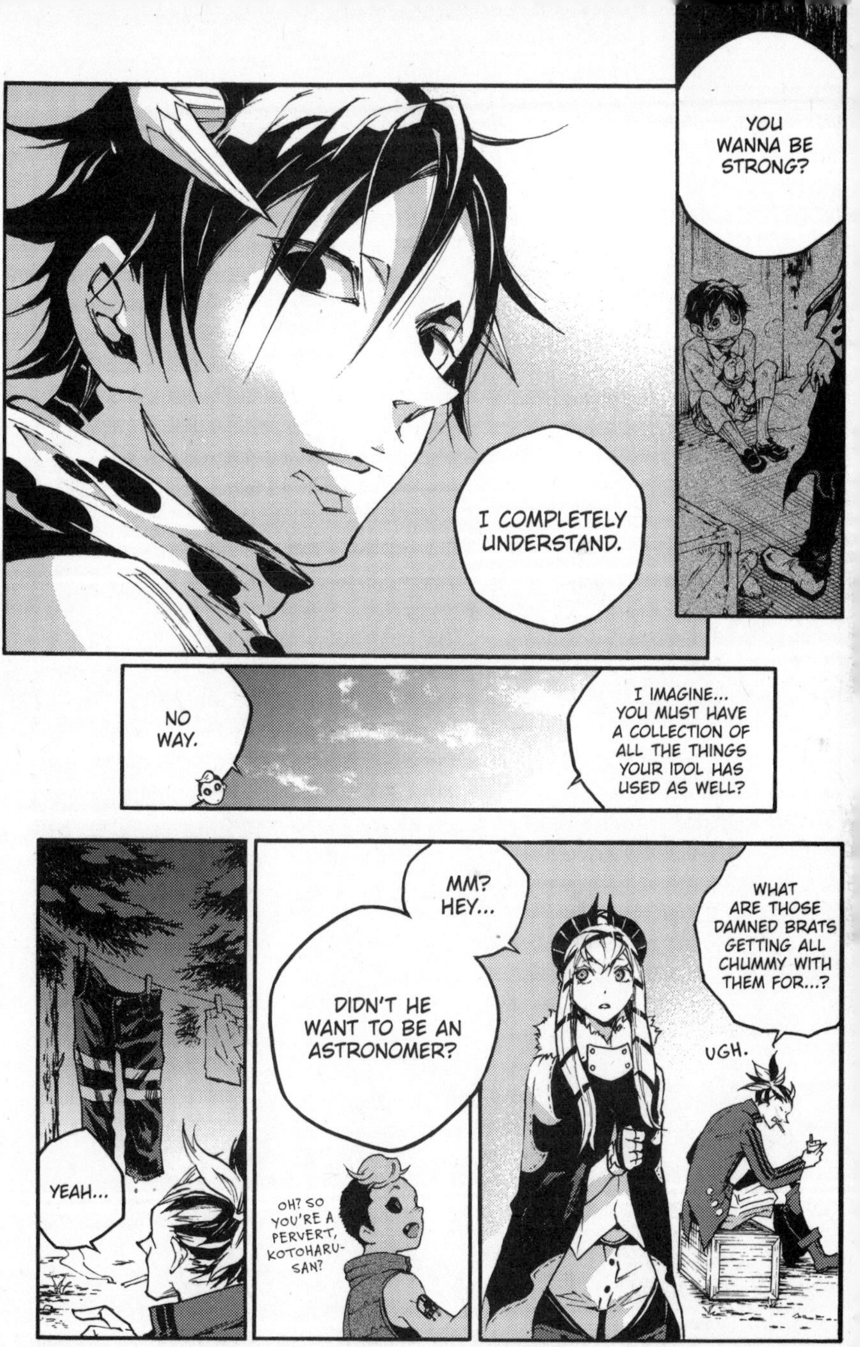

YOU WANNA BE STRONG?
I COMPLETELY UNDERSTAND.
I IMAGINE... YOU MUST HAVE A COLLECTION OF ALL THE THINGS YOUR IDOL HAS USED AS WELL?
NO WAY.
WHAT ARE THOSE DAMNED BRATS GETTING ALL CHUMMY WITH THEM FOR...?
UGH.
MM? HEY...
DIDN'T HE WANT TO BE AN ASTRONOMER?
OH? SO YOU'RE A PERVERT, KOTOHARU-SAN?
YEAH...

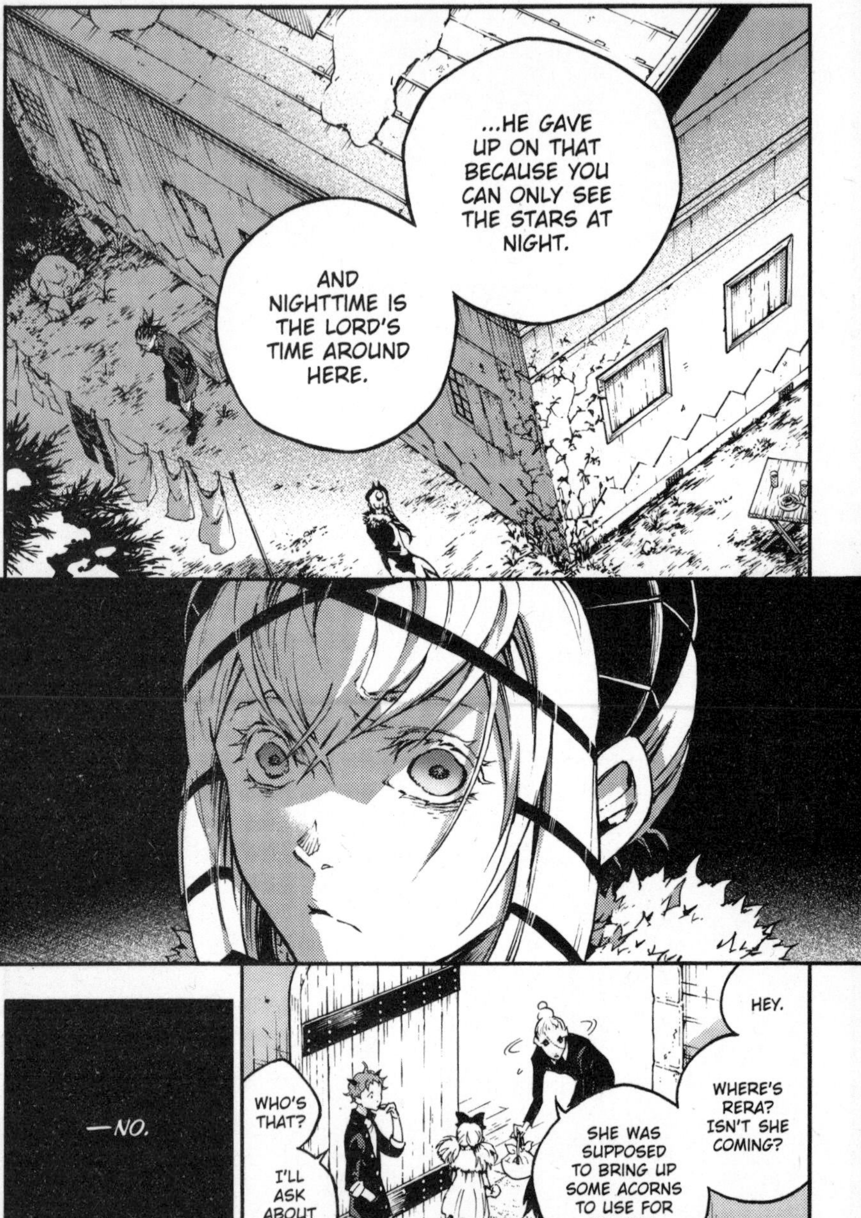
...HE GAVE UP ON THAT BECAUSE YOU CAN ONLY SEE THE STARS AT NIGHT.
AND NIGHTTIME IS THE LORD'S TIME AROUND HERE.
HEY.
WHERE'S RERA? ISN'T SHE COMING?
SHE WAS SUPPOSED TO BRING UP SOME ACORNS TO USE FOR COOKIES.
WHO'S THAT?
I'LL ASK ABOUT HER.
—NO.

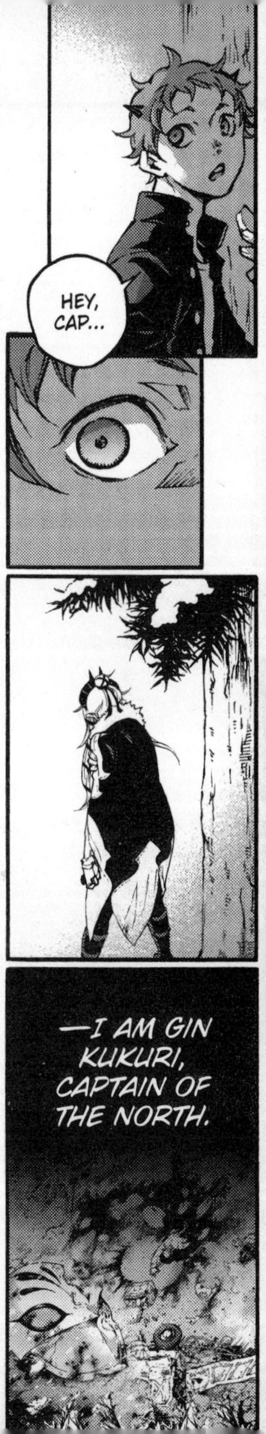
HEY, CAP...
—I AM GIN KUKURI, CAPTAIN OF THE NORTH.
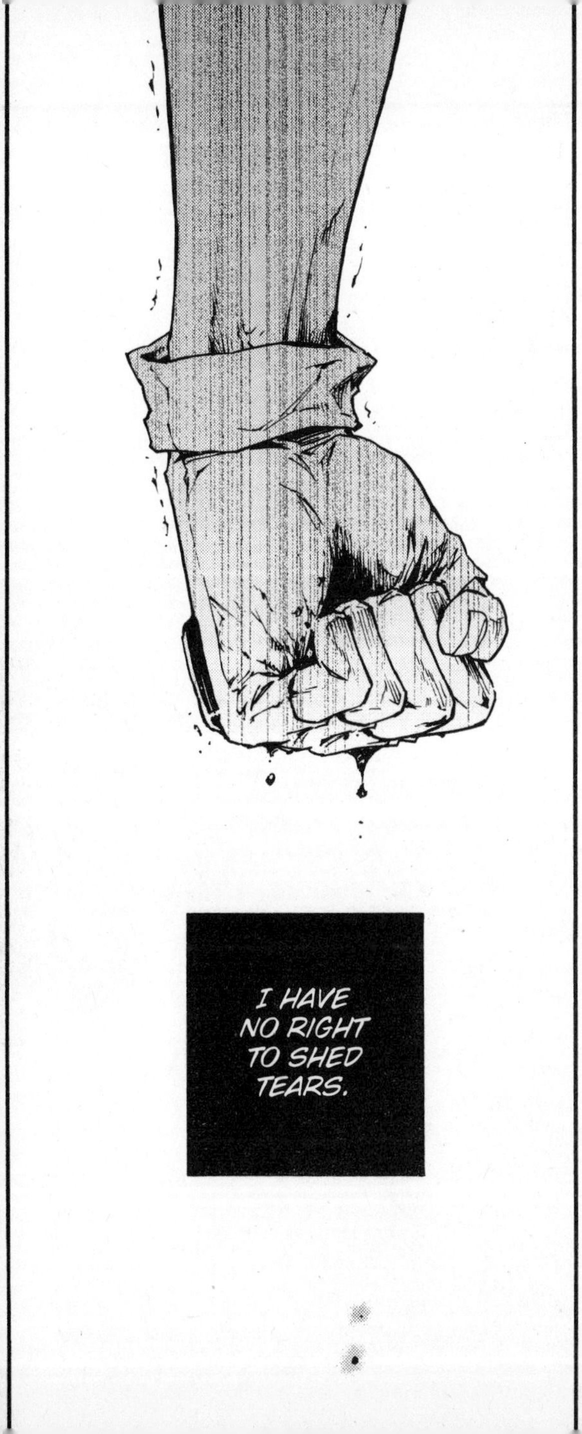
I HAVE NO RIGHT TO SHED TEARS.

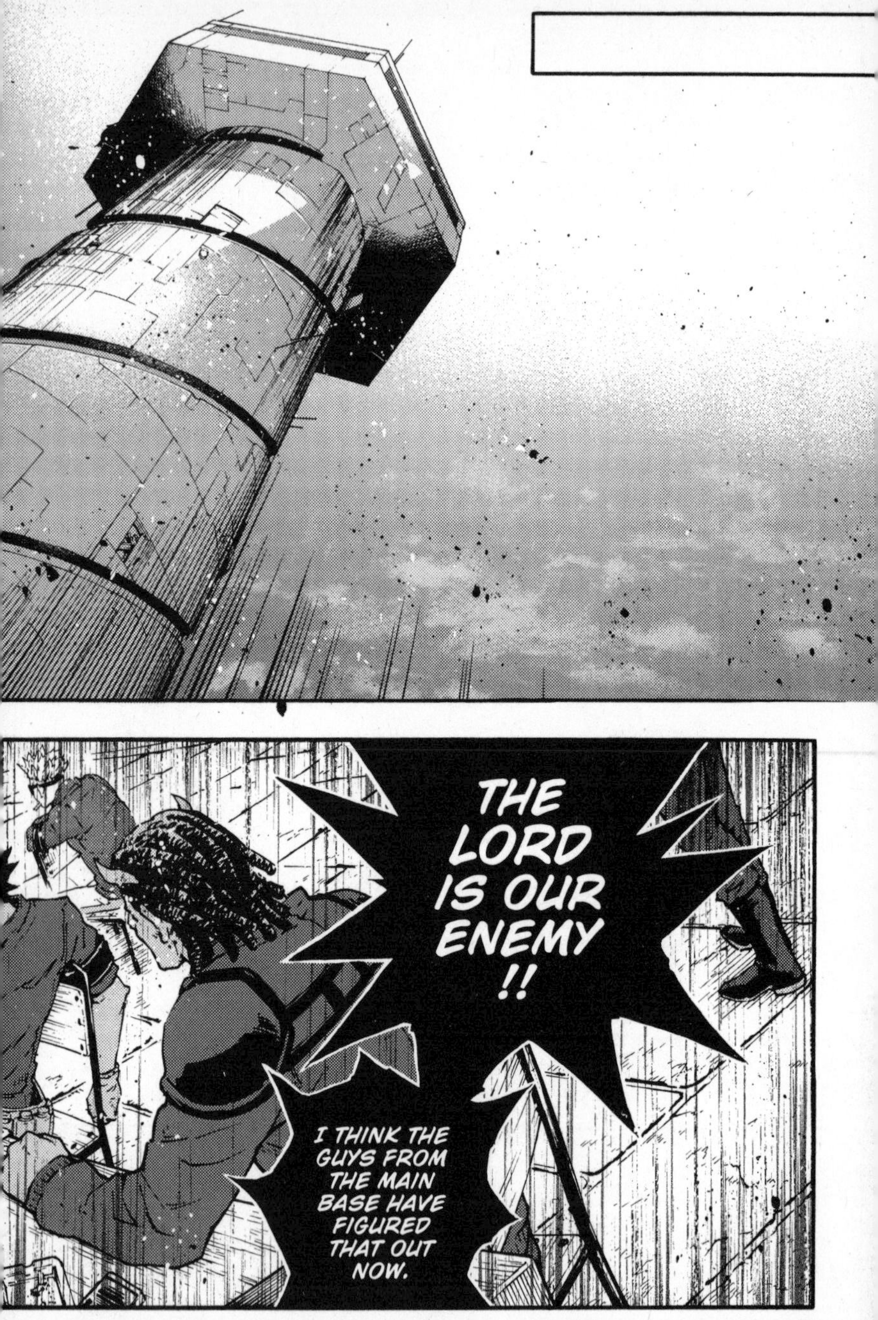
THE LORD IS OUR ENEMY !!
I THINK THE GUYS FROM THE MAIN BASE HAVE FIGURED THAT OUT NOW.

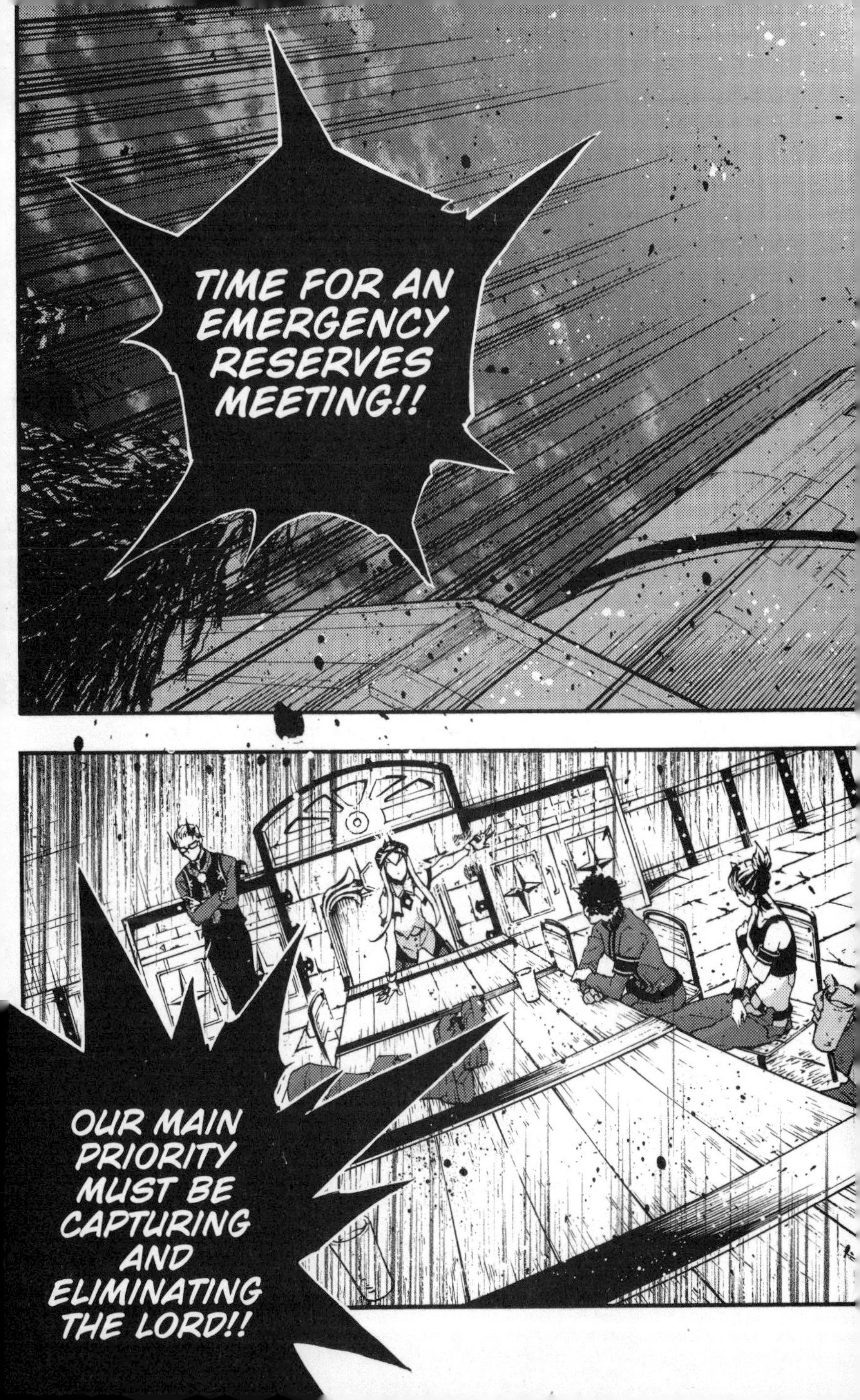
TIME FOR AN EMERGENCY RESERVES MEETING!!
OUR MAIN PRIORITY MUST BE CAPTURING AND ELIMINATING THE LORD!!

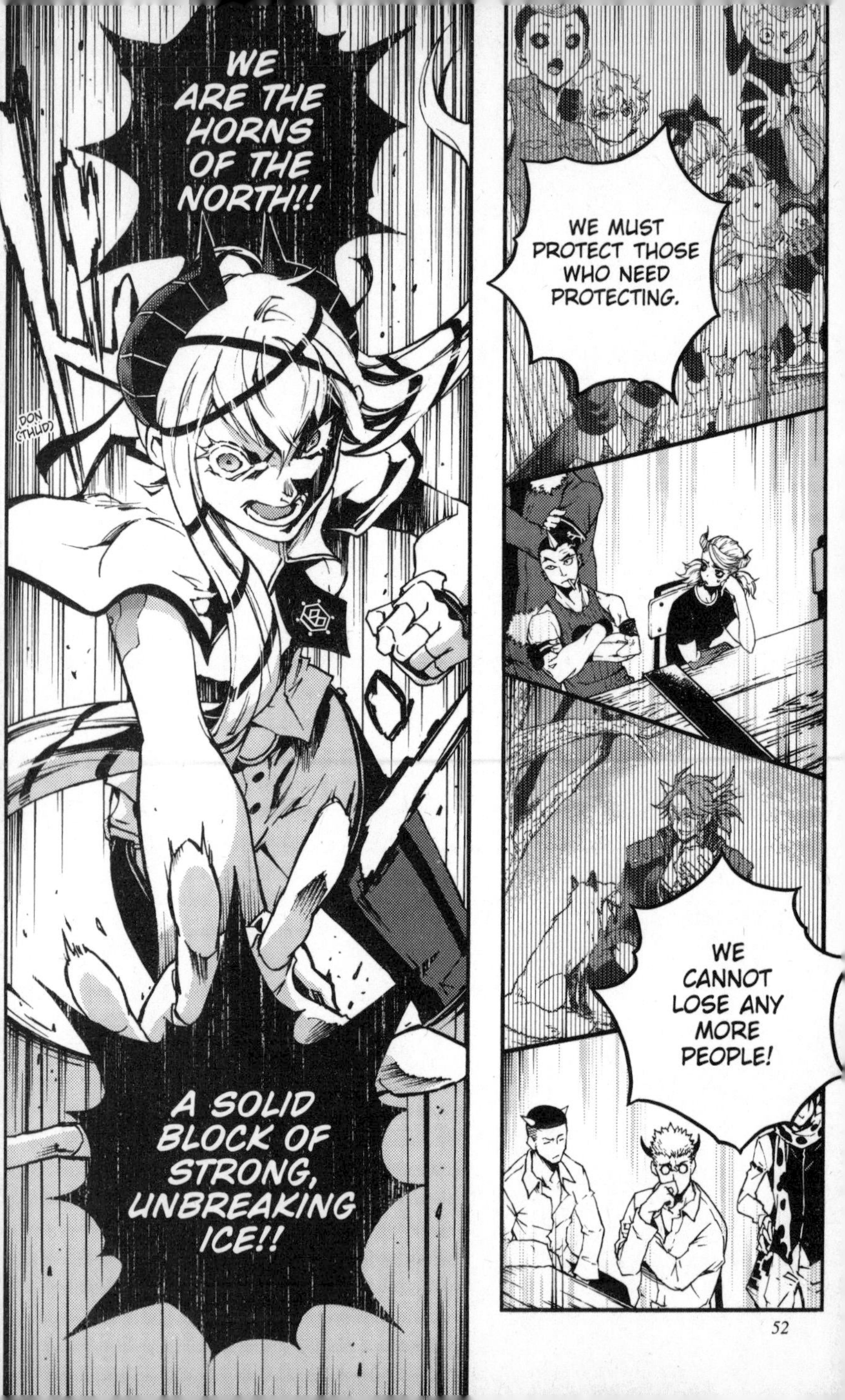
WE MUST PROTECT THOSE WHO NEED PROTECTING.
WE CANNOT LOSE ANY MORE PEOPLE!
WE ARE THE HORNS OF THE NORTH!!
DON (THUD)
A SOLID BLOCK OF STRONG, UNBREAKING ICE!!

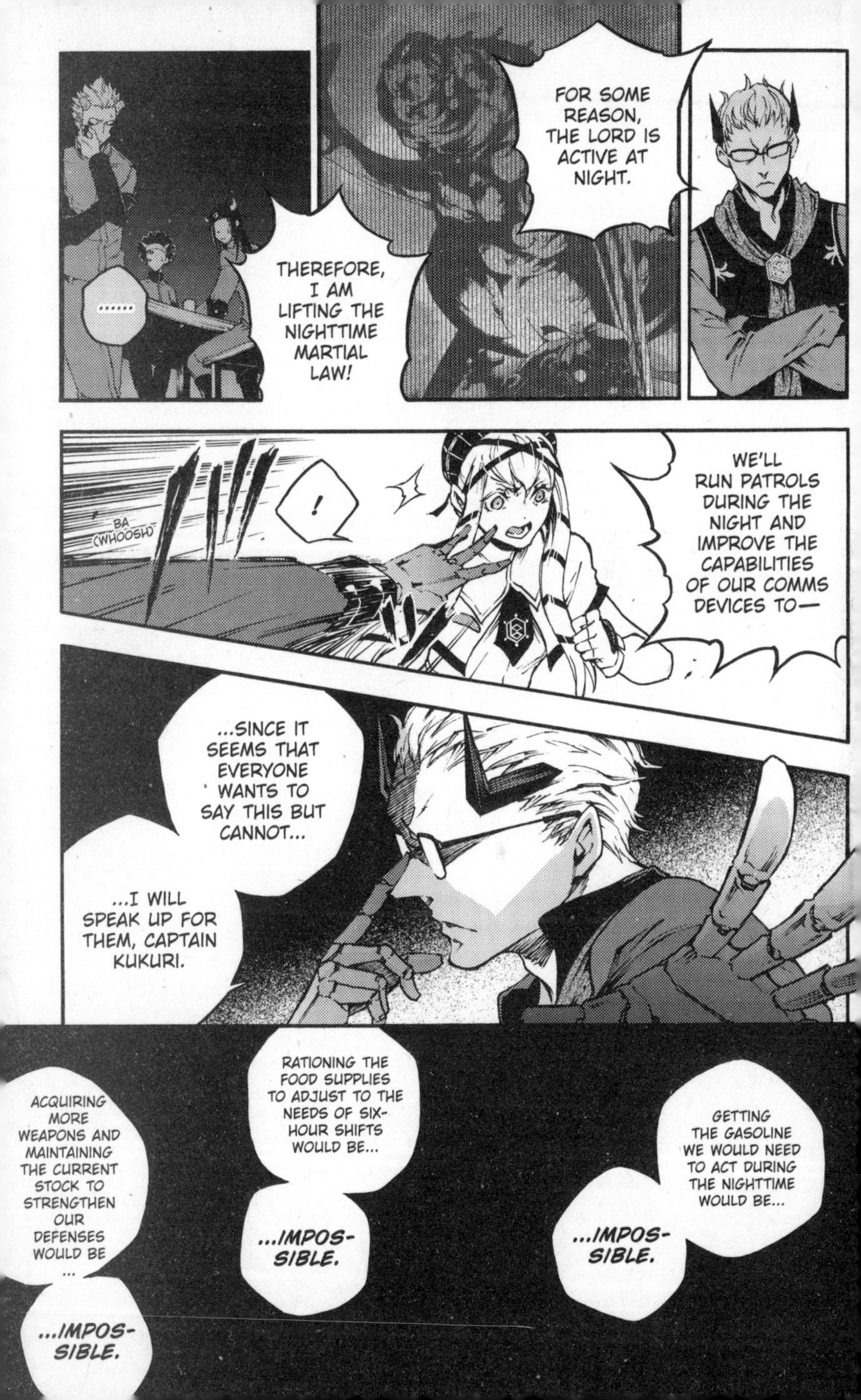
FOR SOME REASON, THE LORD IS ACTIVE AT NIGHT.
THEREFORE, I AM LIFTING THE NIGHTTIME MARTIAL LAW!
......
WE'LL RUN PATROLS DURING THE NIGHT AND IMPROVE THE CAPABILITIES OF OUR COMMS DEVICES TO—
!
BA (WHOOSH)
...SINCE IT SEEMS THAT EVERYONE WANTS TO SAY THIS BUT CANNOT...
...I WILL SPEAK UP FOR THEM, CAPTAIN KUKURI.
GETTING THE GASOLINE WE WOULD NEED TO ACT DURING THE NIGHTTIME WOULD BE...
...IMPOSSIBLE.
RATIONING THE FOOD SUPPLIES TO ADJUST TO THE NEEDS OF SIX-HOUR SHIFTS WOULD BE...
...IMPOSSIBLE.
ACQUIRING MORE WEAPONS AND MAINTAINING THE CURRENT STOCK TO STRENGTHEN OUR DEFENSES WOULD BE ...
...IMPOSSIBLE.

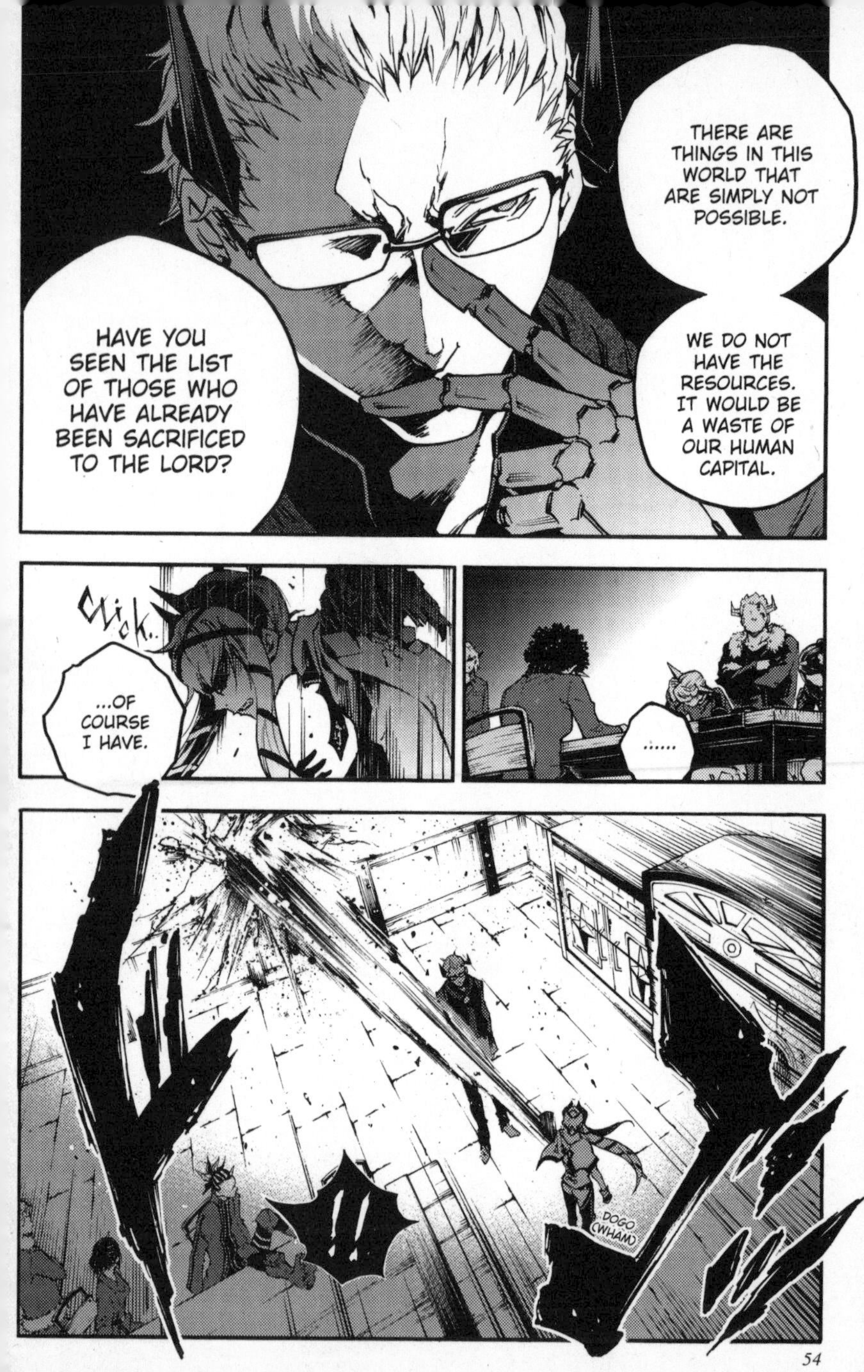
THERE ARE THINGS IN THIS WORLD THAT ARE SIMPLY NOT POSSIBLE.
WE DO NOT HAVE THE RESOURCES. IT WOULD BE A WASTE OF OUR HUMAN CAPITAL.
HAVE YOU SEEN THE LIST OF THOSE WHO HAVE ALREADY BEEN SACRIFICED TO THE LORD?
......
Click..
...OF COURSE I HAVE.
!!
DOGO (WHAM)

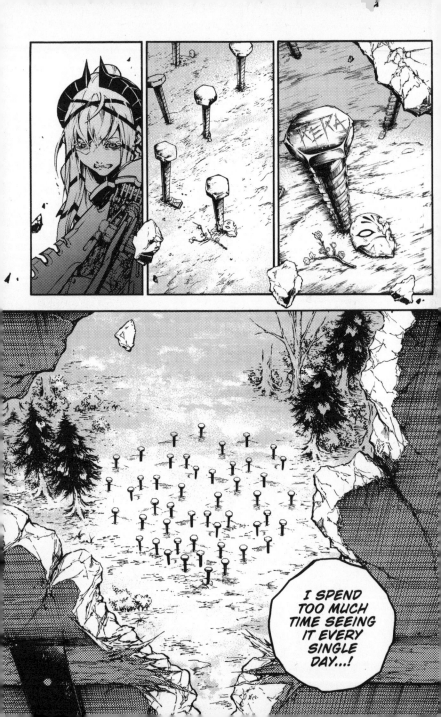

I SPEND
TOO MUCH
TIME SEEING
IT EVERY
SINGLE
DAY...!

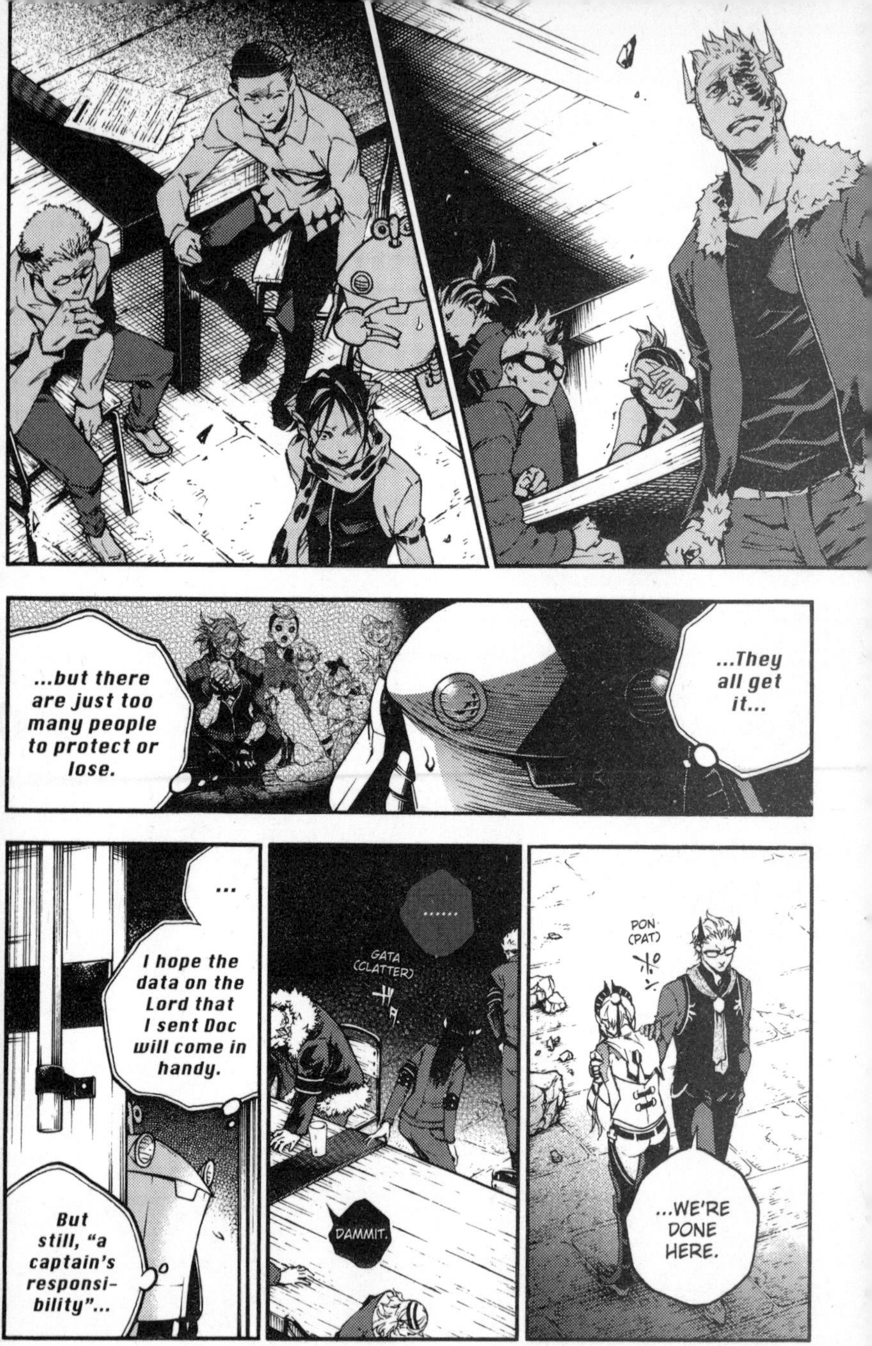
...They all get it...
...but there are just too many people to protect or lose.
PON (PAT)
...WE'RE DONE HERE.
......
GATA (CLATTER)
DAMMIT.
...
I hope the data on the Lord that I sent Doc will come in handy.
But still, "a captain's responsi-bility"...

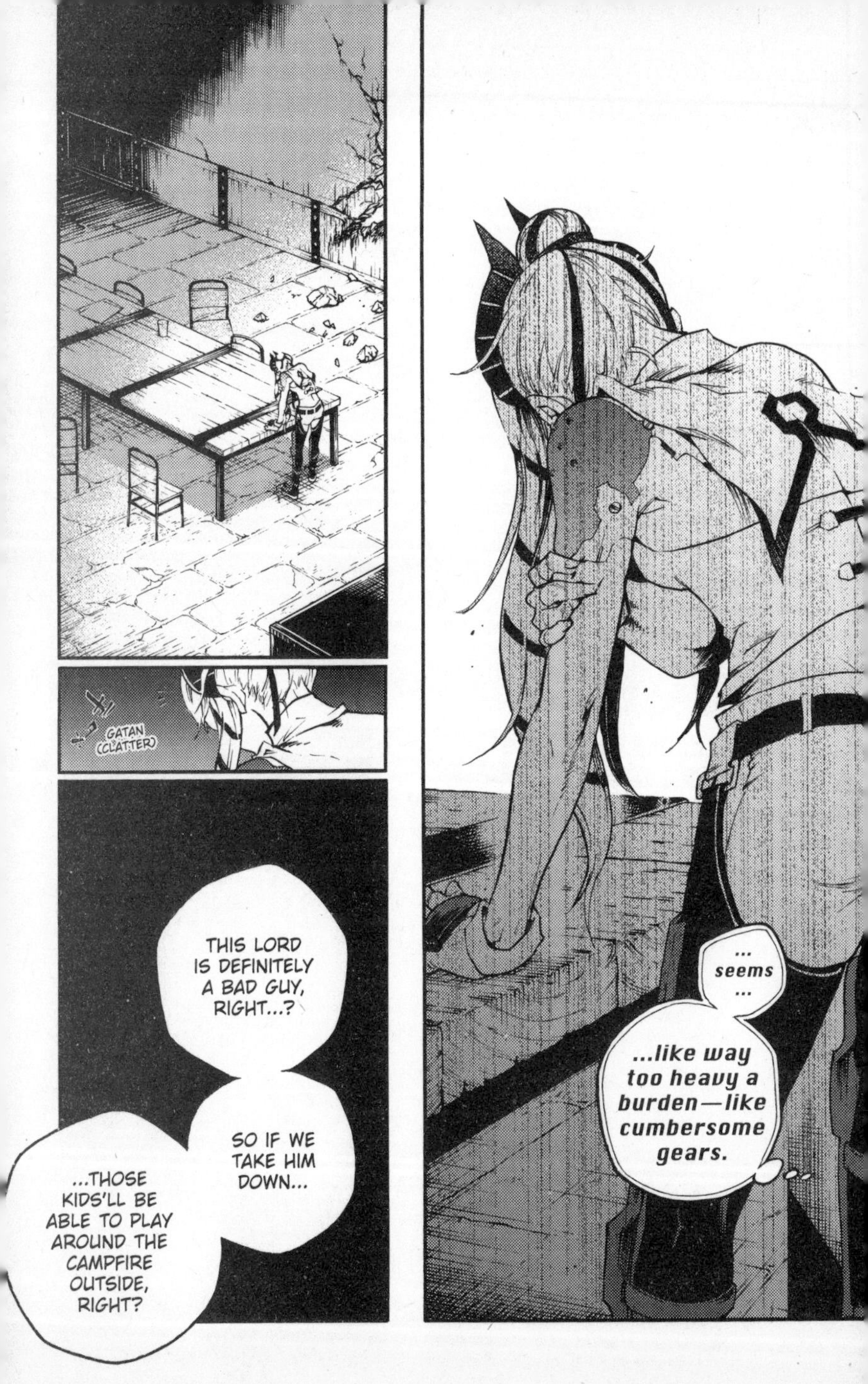
... seems ...
...like way too heavy a burden—like cumbersome gears.
GATAN (CLATTER)
THIS LORD IS DEFINITELY A BAD GUY, RIGHT...?
SO IF WE TAKE HIM DOWN...
...THOSE KIDS'LL BE ABLE TO PLAY AROUND THE CAMPFIRE OUTSIDE, RIGHT?

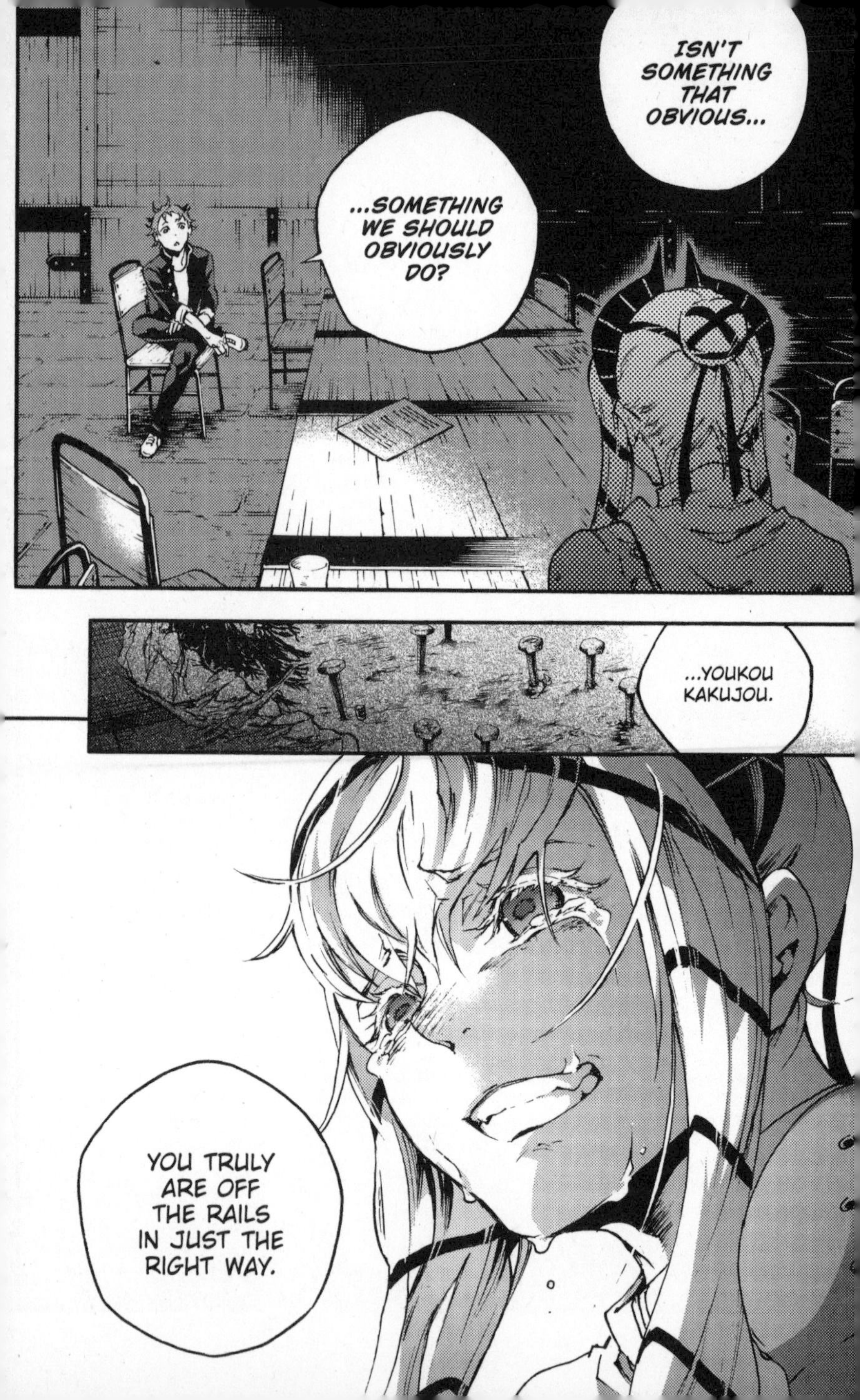
ISN'T SOMETHING THAT OBVIOUS...
...SOMETHING WE SHOULD OBVIOUSLY DO?
...YOUKOU KAKUJOU.
YOU TRULY ARE OFF THE RAILS IN JUST THE RIGHT WAY.

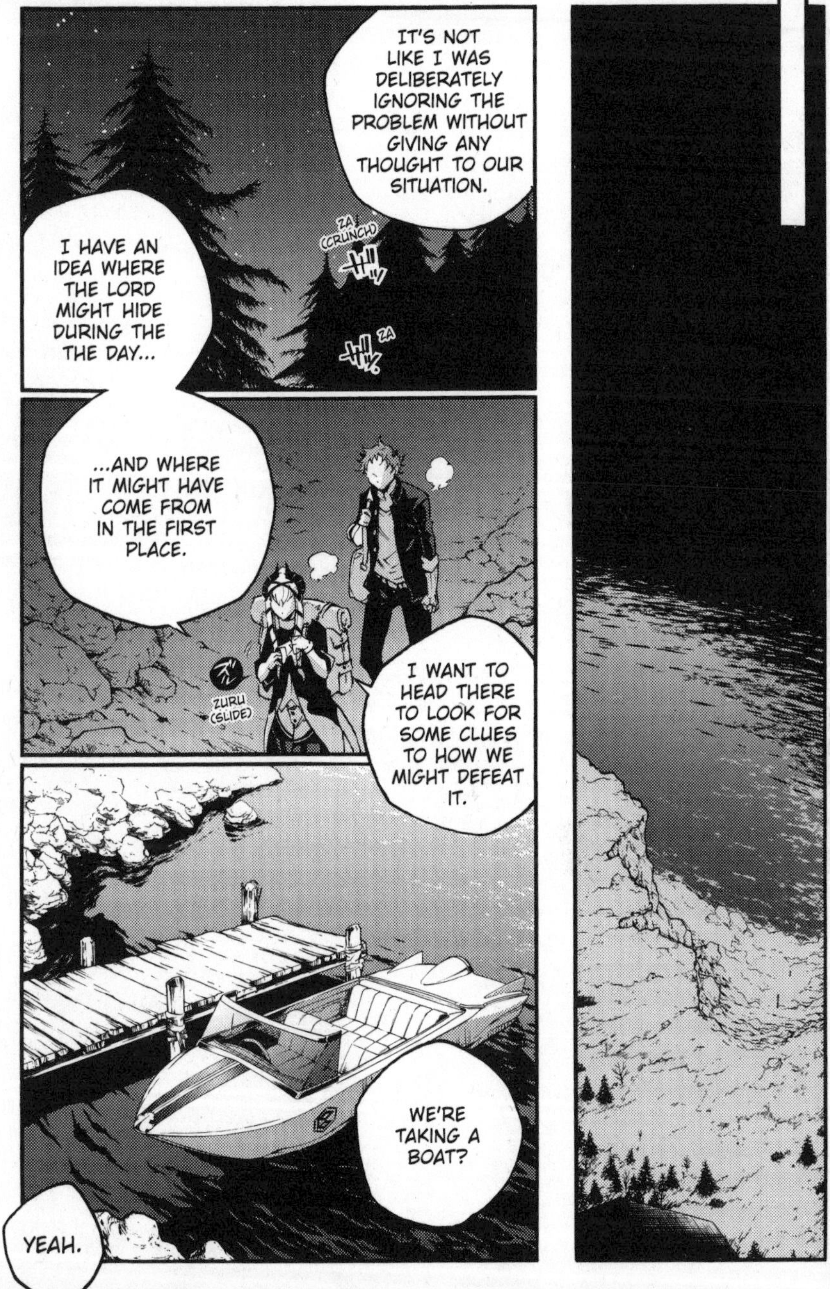
IT'S NOT LIKE I WAS DELIBERATELY IGNORING THE PROBLEM WITHOUT GIVING ANY THOUGHT TO OUR SITUATION.
ZA (CRUNCH)
I HAVE AN IDEA WHERE THE LORD MIGHT HIDE DURING THE THE DAY...
ZA
...AND WHERE IT MIGHT HAVE COME FROM IN THE FIRST PLACE.
I WANT TO HEAD THERE TO LOOK FOR SOME CLUES TO HOW WE MIGHT DEFEAT IT.
ZURU (SLIDE)
WE'RE TAKING A BOAT?
YEAH.

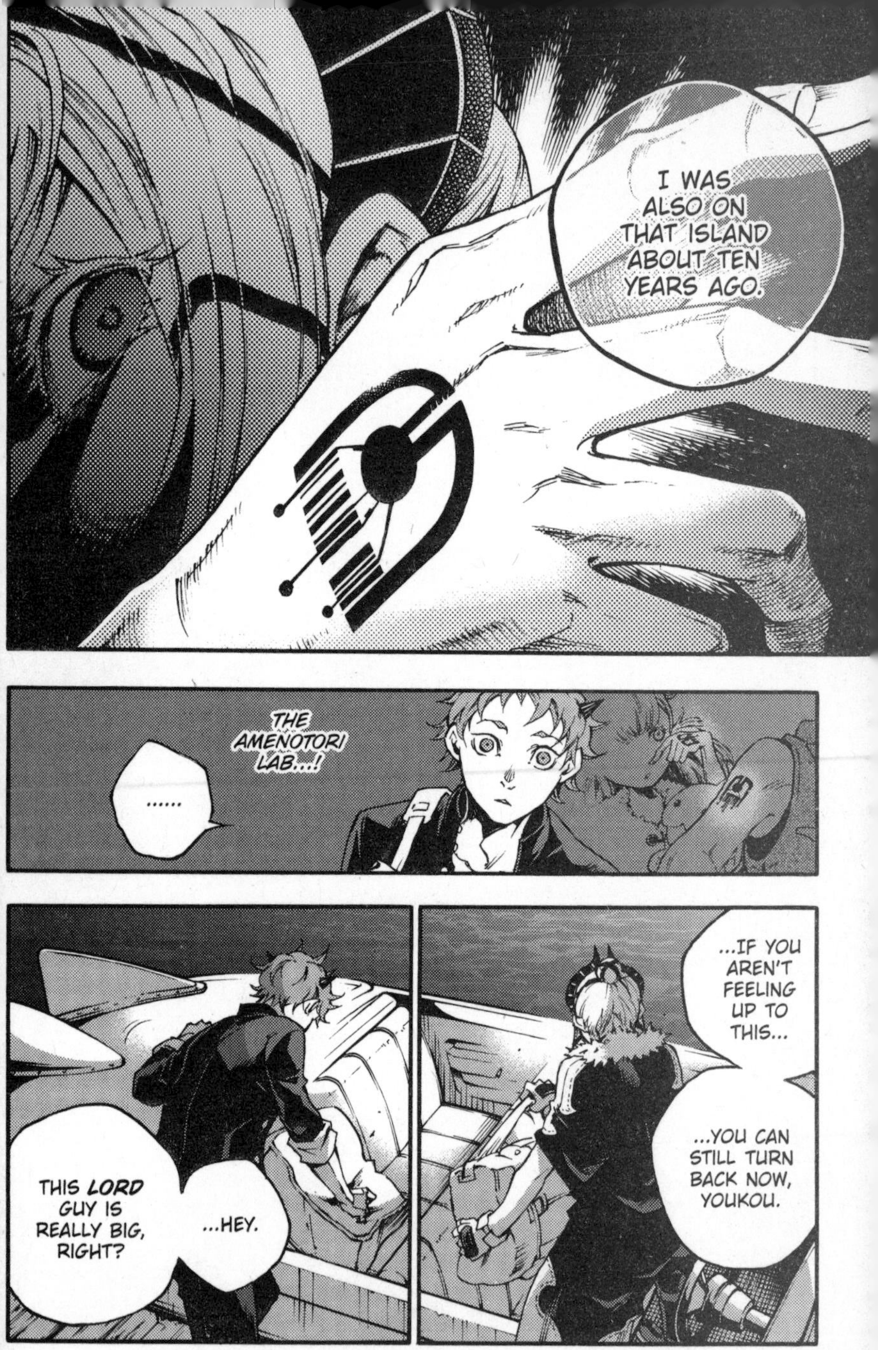
I WAS ALSO ON THAT ISLAND ABOUT TEN YEARS AGO.
THE AMENOTORI LAB...!
......
...IF YOU AREN'T FEELING UP TO THIS...
...YOU CAN STILL TURN BACK NOW, YOUKOU.
...HEY.
THIS LORD GUY IS REALLY BIG, RIGHT?

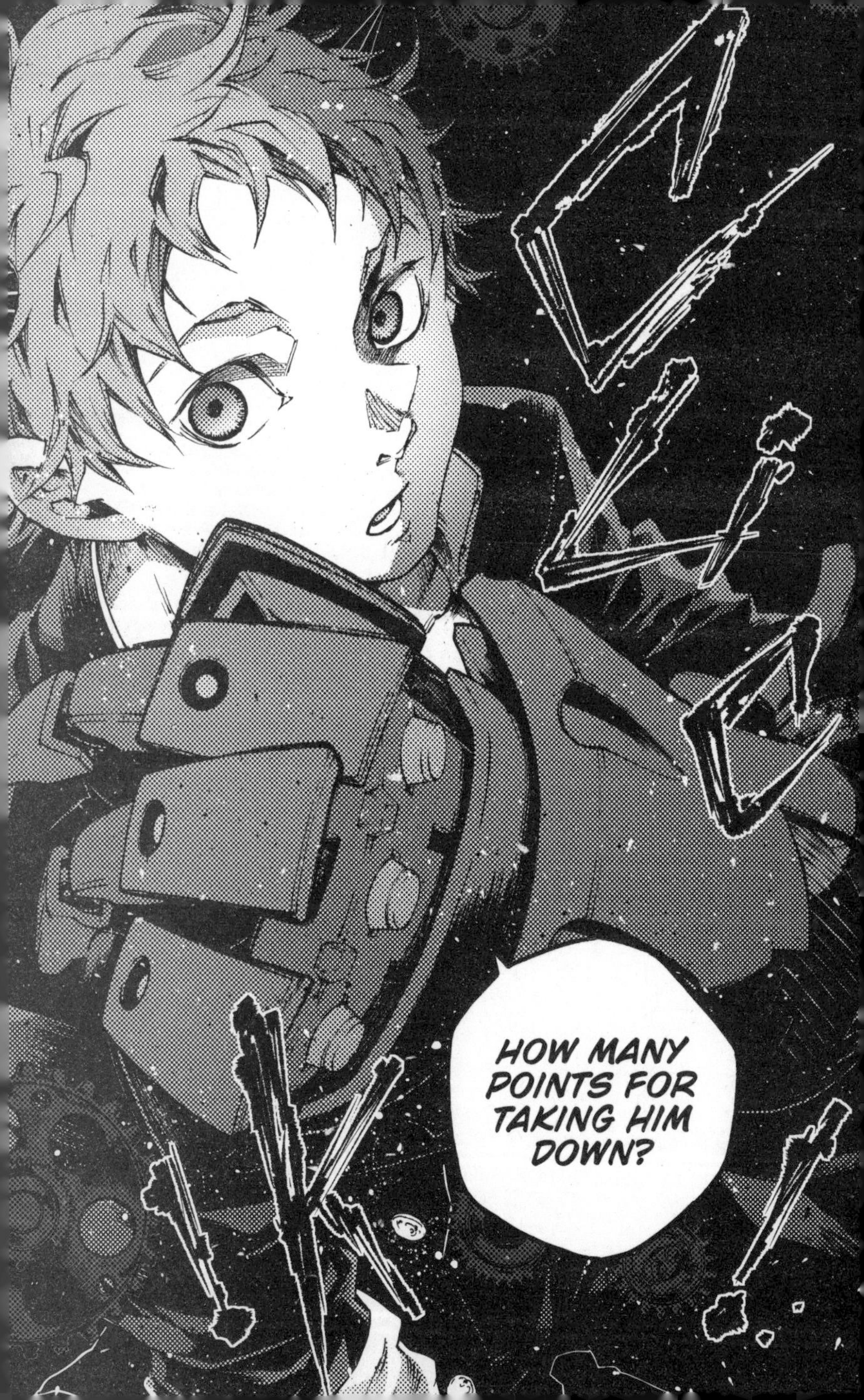
HOW MANY POINTS FOR TAKING HIM DOWN?

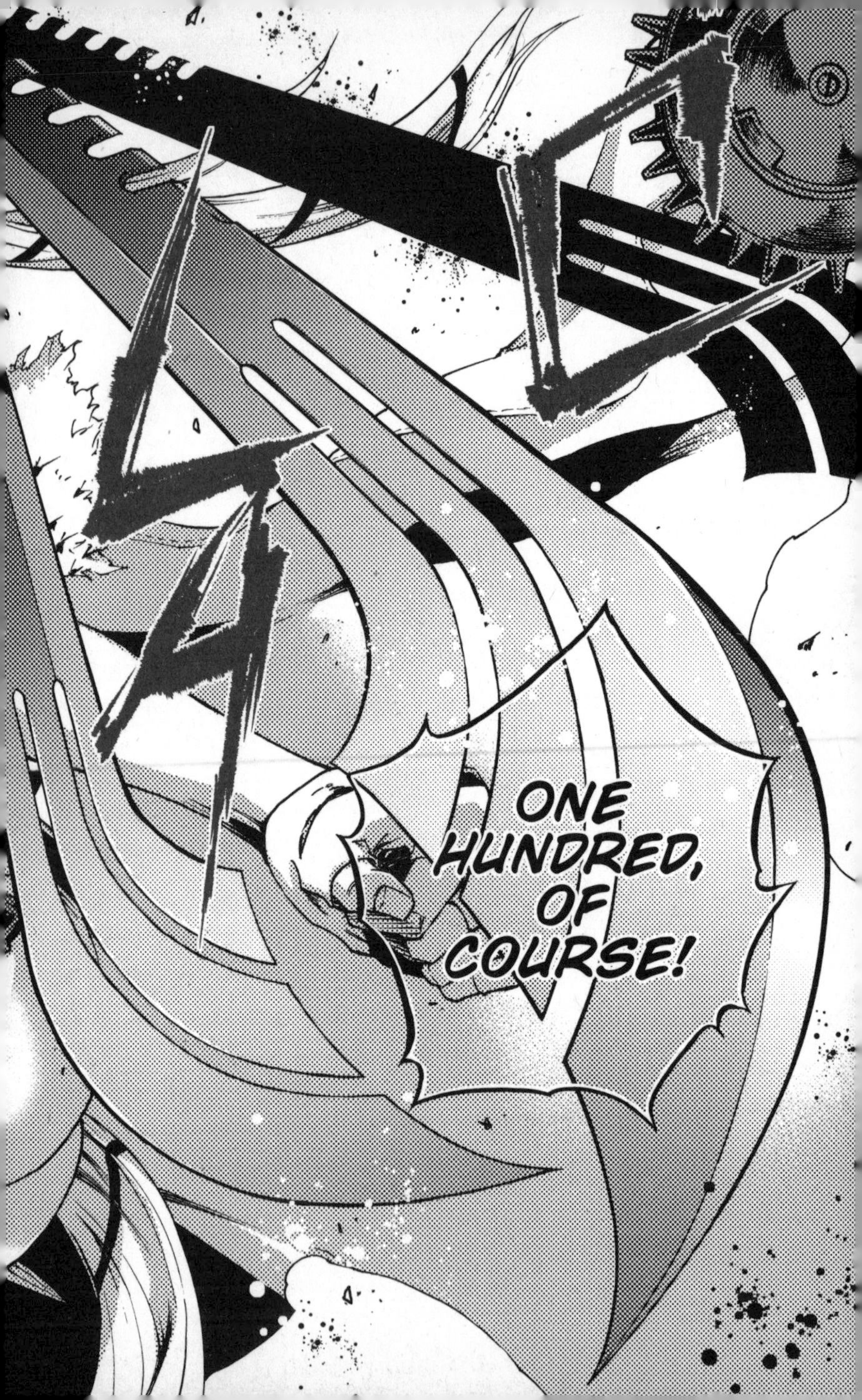
ONE HUNDRED, OF COURSE!

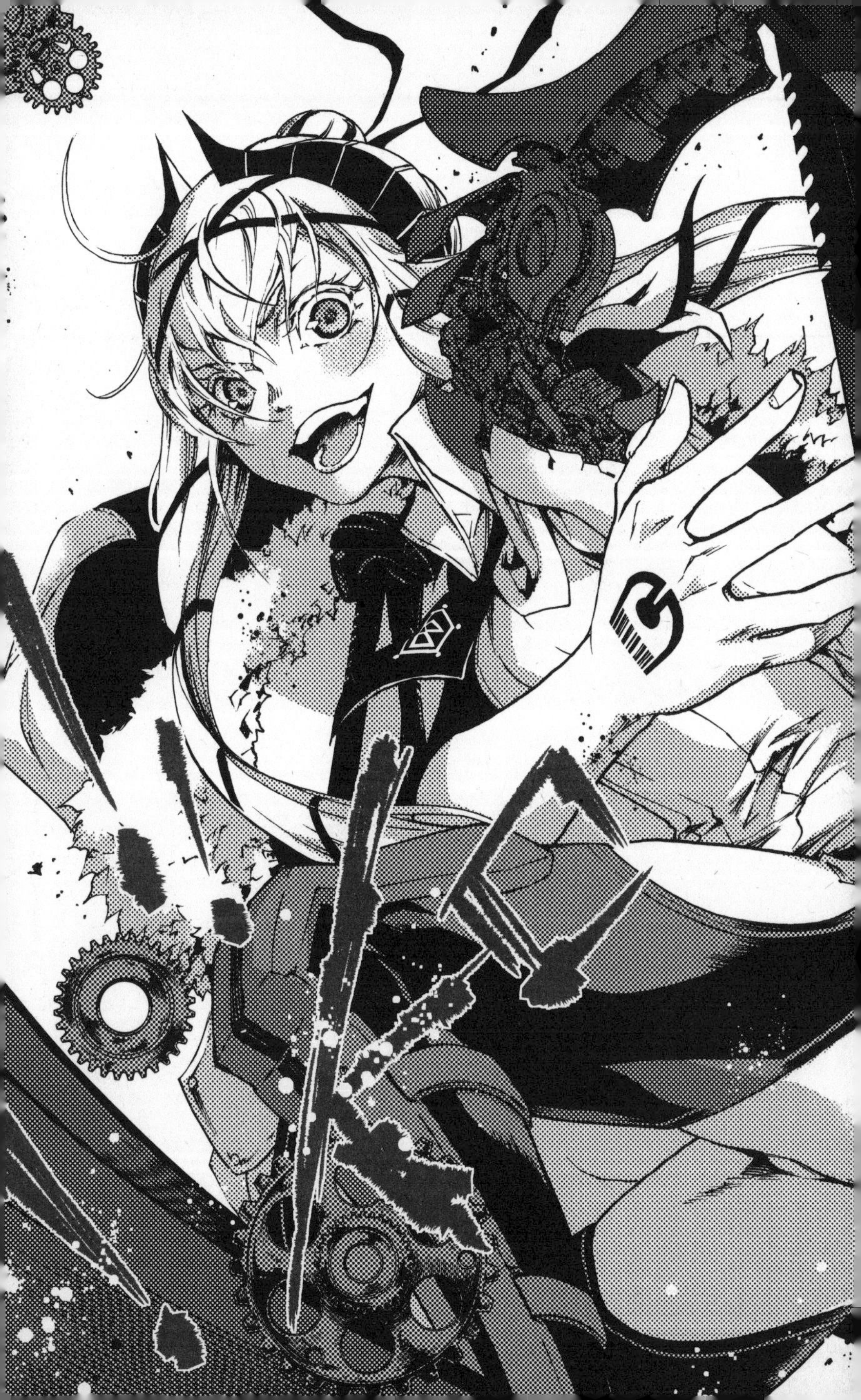

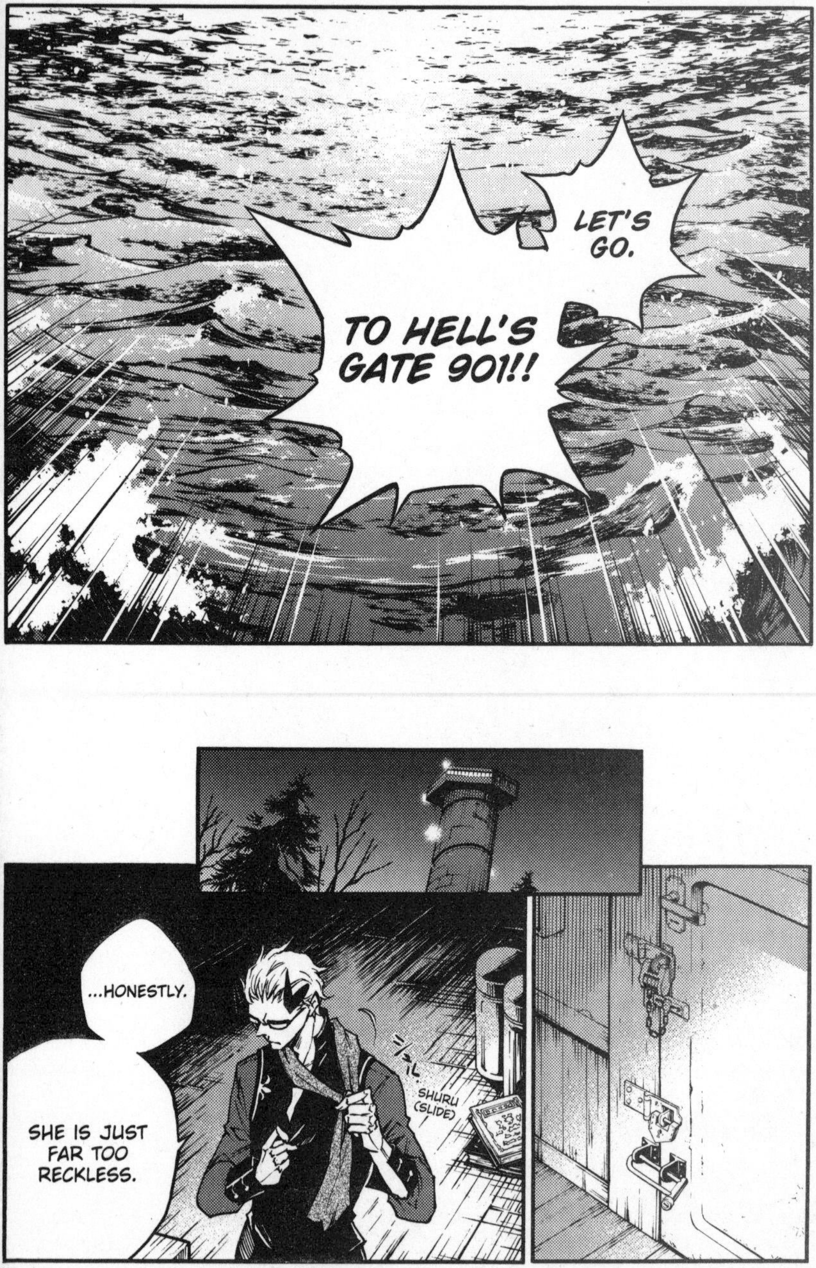
LET'S GO.
TO HELL'S GATE 901!!
...HONESTLY.
SHURU (SLIDE)
SHE IS JUST FAR TOO RECKLESS.

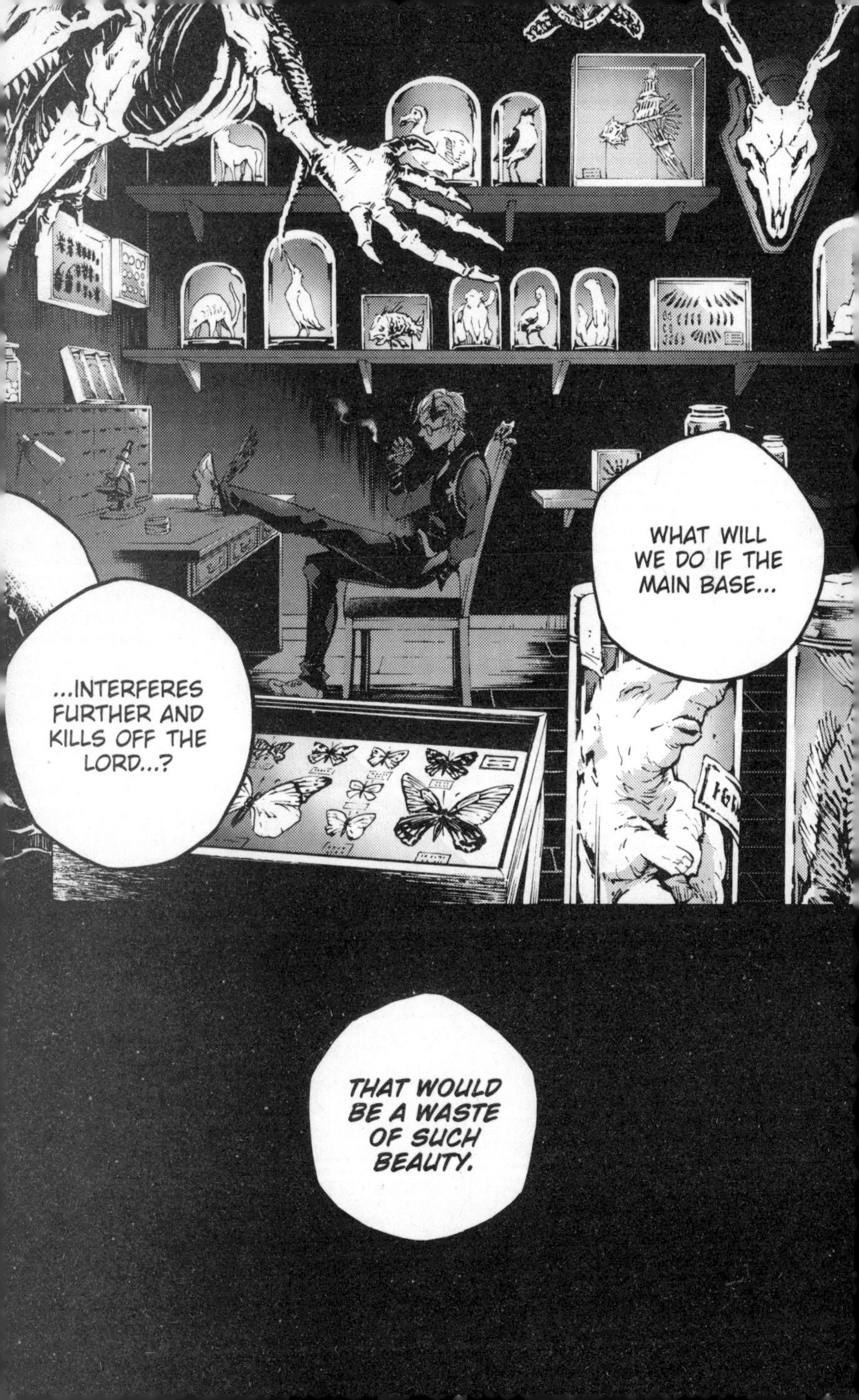
WHAT WILL WE DO IF THE MAIN BASE...
...INTERFERES FURTHER AND KILLS OFF THE LORD...?
THAT WOULD BE A WASTE OF SUCH BEAUTY.

SMOKIN'

THE WORLD IS DEAD,

PARADE

THE PARADE WILL START.

JINSEI KATAOKA

KAZUMA KONDOU

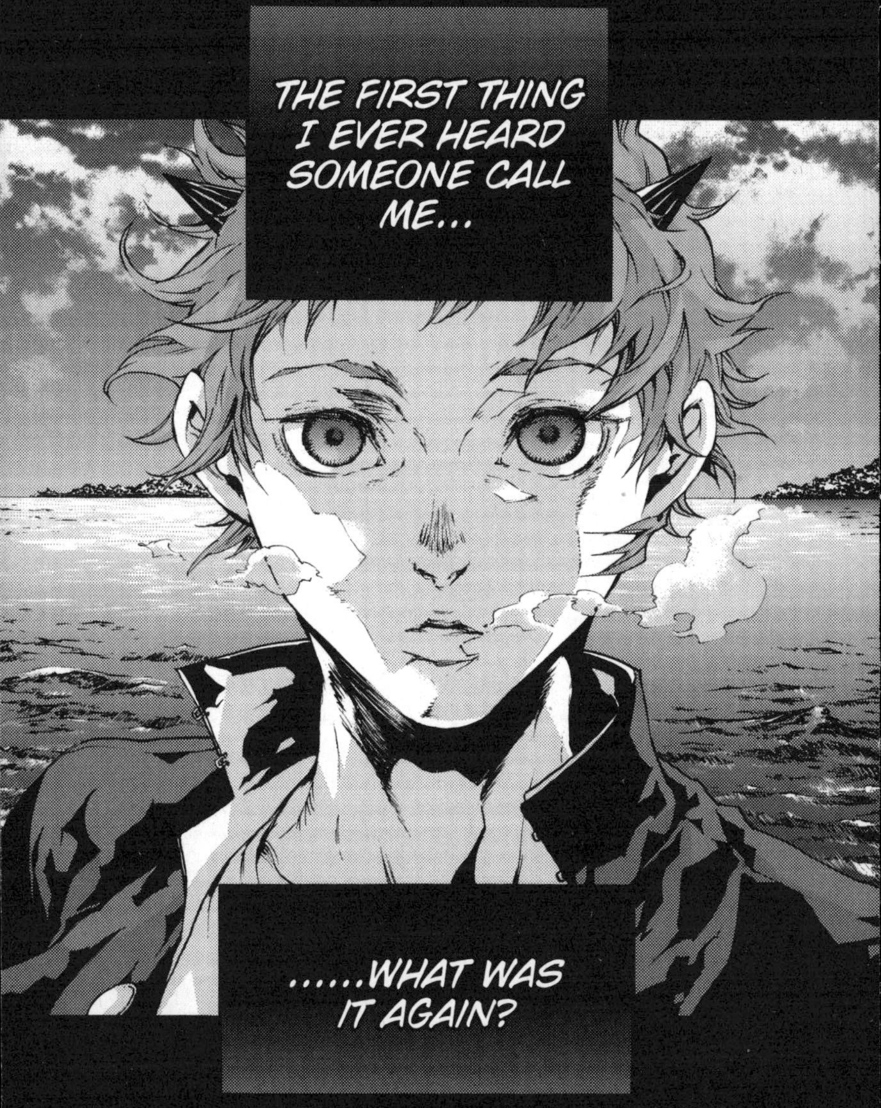
THE FIRST THING I EVER HEARD SOMEONE CALL ME...
......WHAT WAS IT AGAIN?

#26
THE PAIN OF FACING THE ENEMY

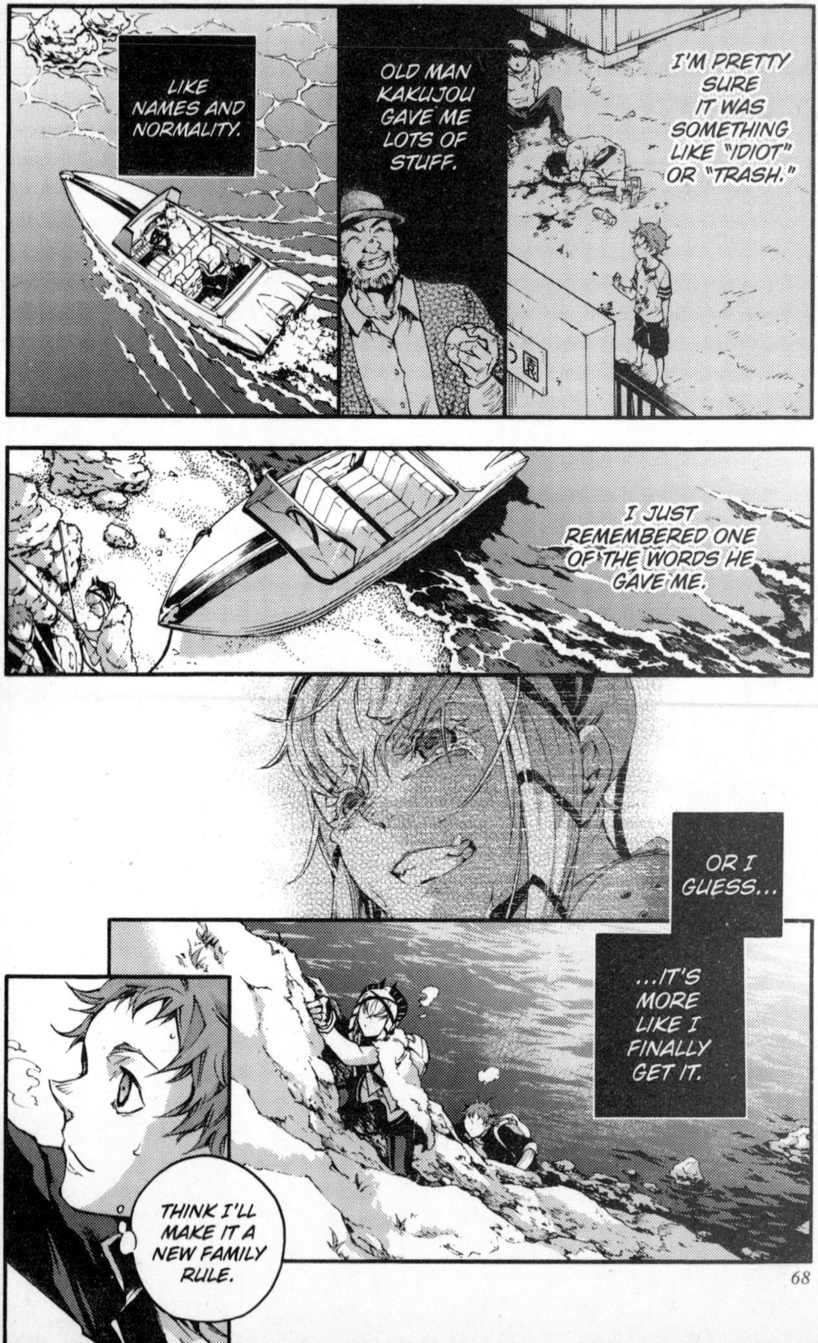
I'M PRETTY SURE IT WAS SOMETHING LIKE "IDIOT" OR "TRASH."
OLD MAN KAKUJOU GAVE ME LOTS OF STUFF.
LIKE NAMES AND NORMALITY.
I JUST REMEMBERED ONE OF THE WORDS HE GAVE ME.
OR I GUESS...
...IT'S MORE LIKE I FINALLY GET IT.
THINK I'LL MAKE IT A NEW FAMILY RULE.

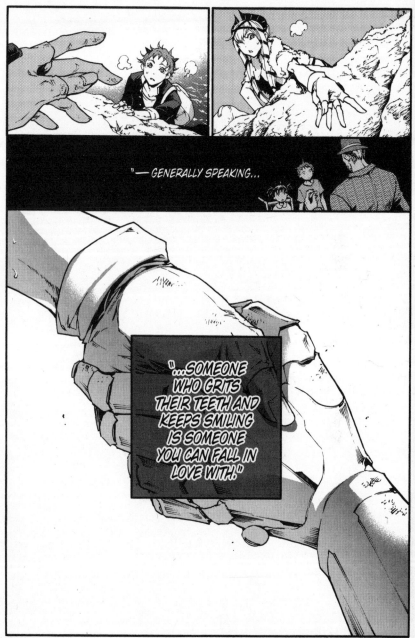

" — GENERALLY SPEAKING...

"...SOMEONE WHO GRITS THEIR TEETH AND KEEPS SMILING IS SOMEONE YOU CAN FALL IN LOVE WITH."

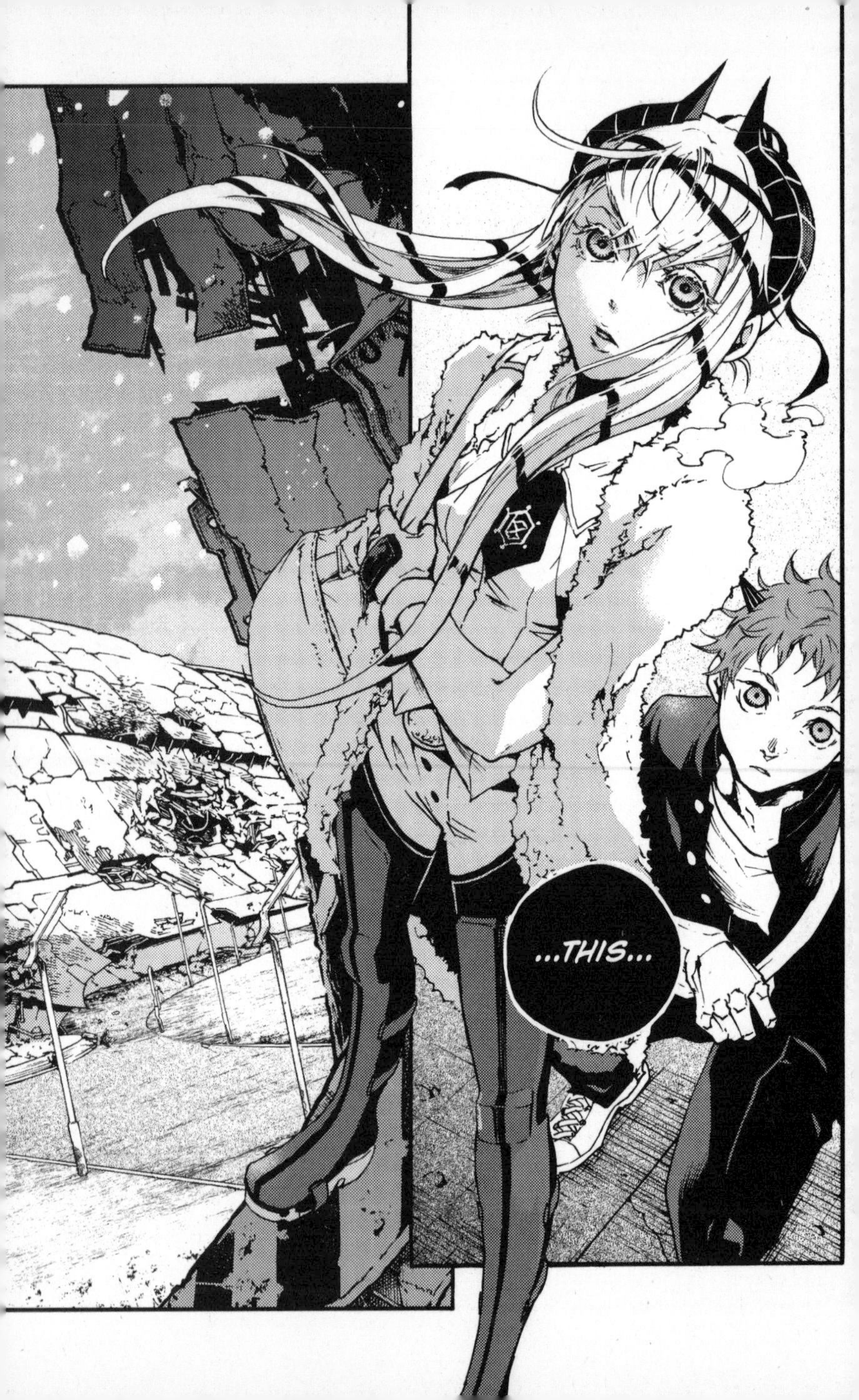
...THIS...

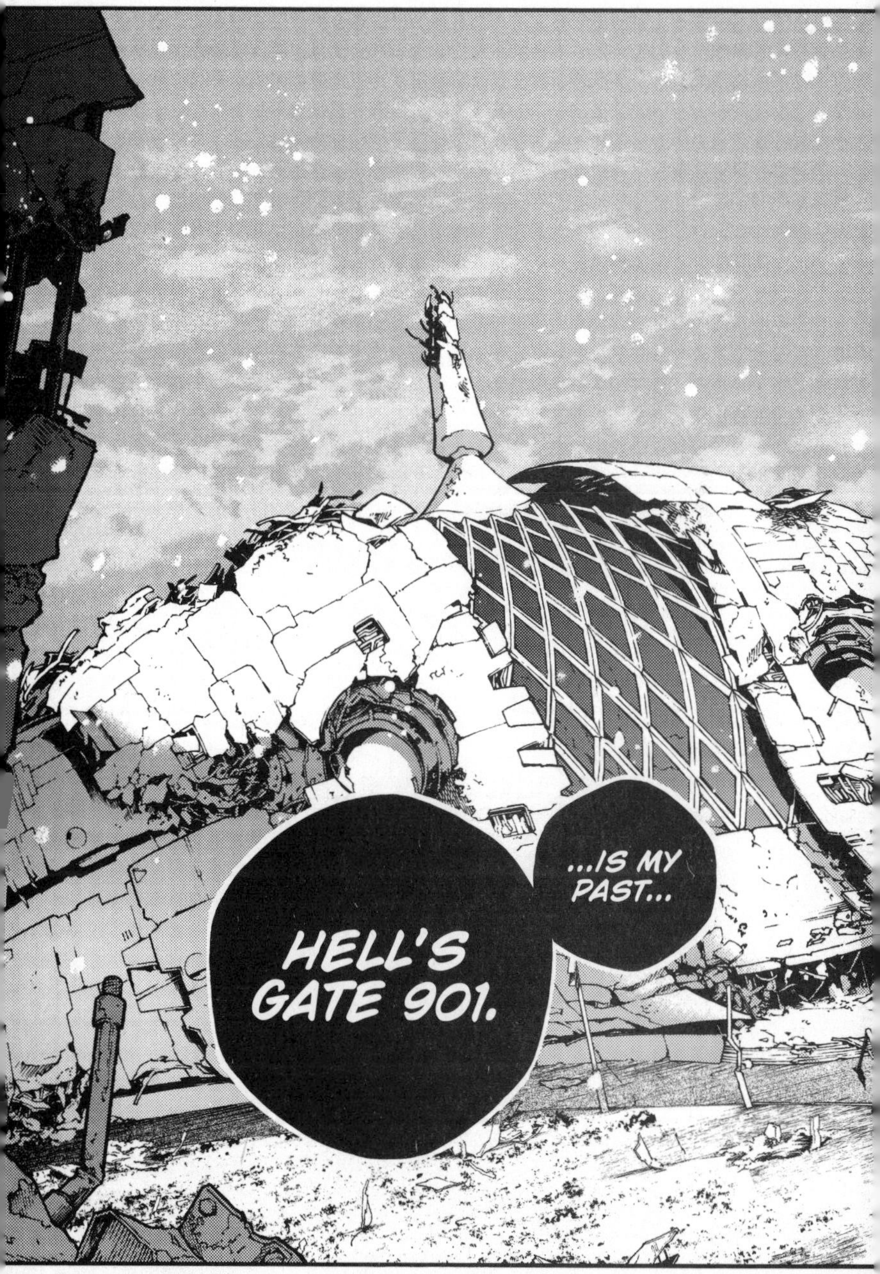
...IS MY PAST...
HELL'S GATE 901.

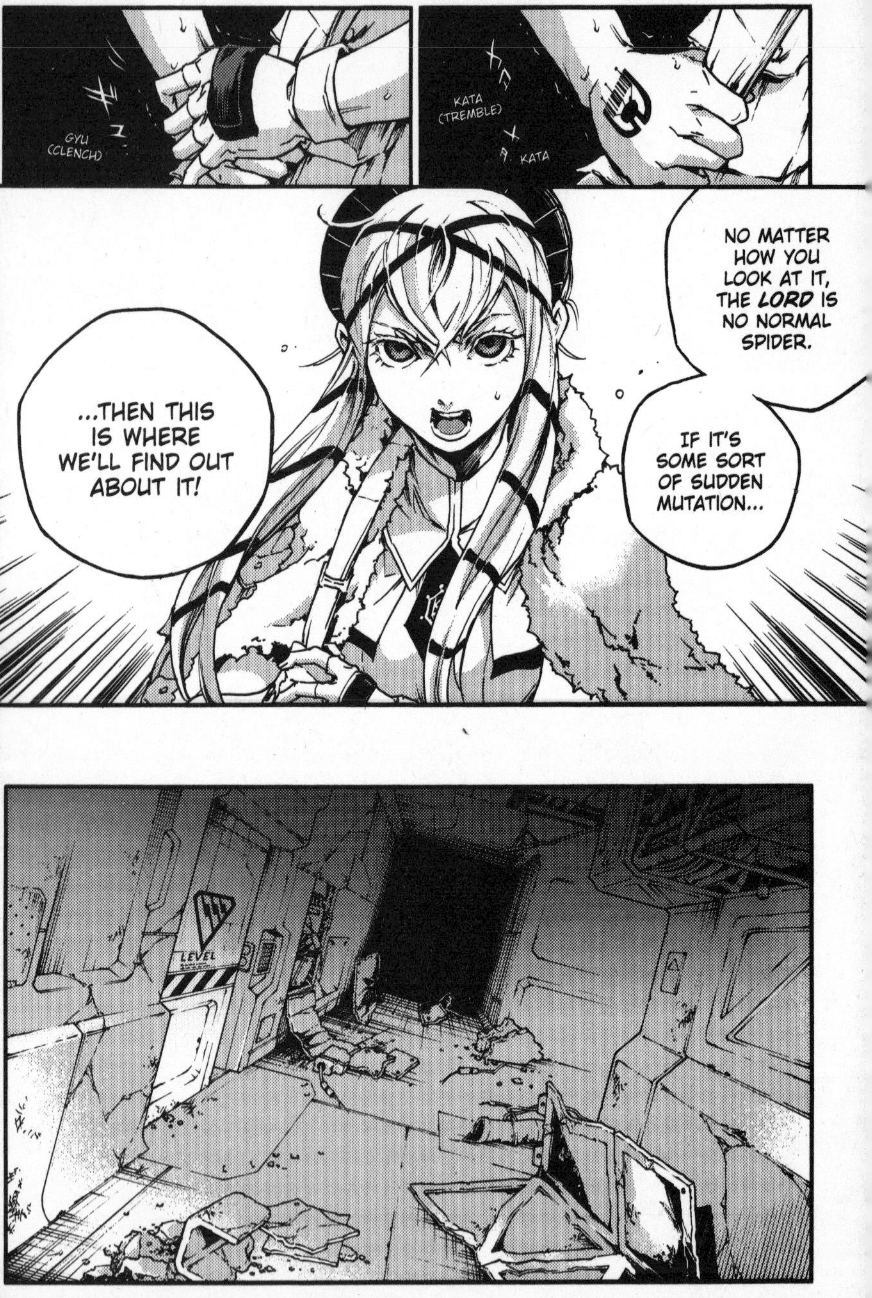
KATA (TREMBLE)
KATA
GYU (CLENCH)
NO MATTER HOW YOU LOOK AT IT, THE LORD IS NO NORMAL SPIDER.
IF IT'S SOME SORT OF SUDDEN MUTATION...
...THEN THIS IS WHERE WE'LL FIND OUT ABOUT IT!
LEVEL

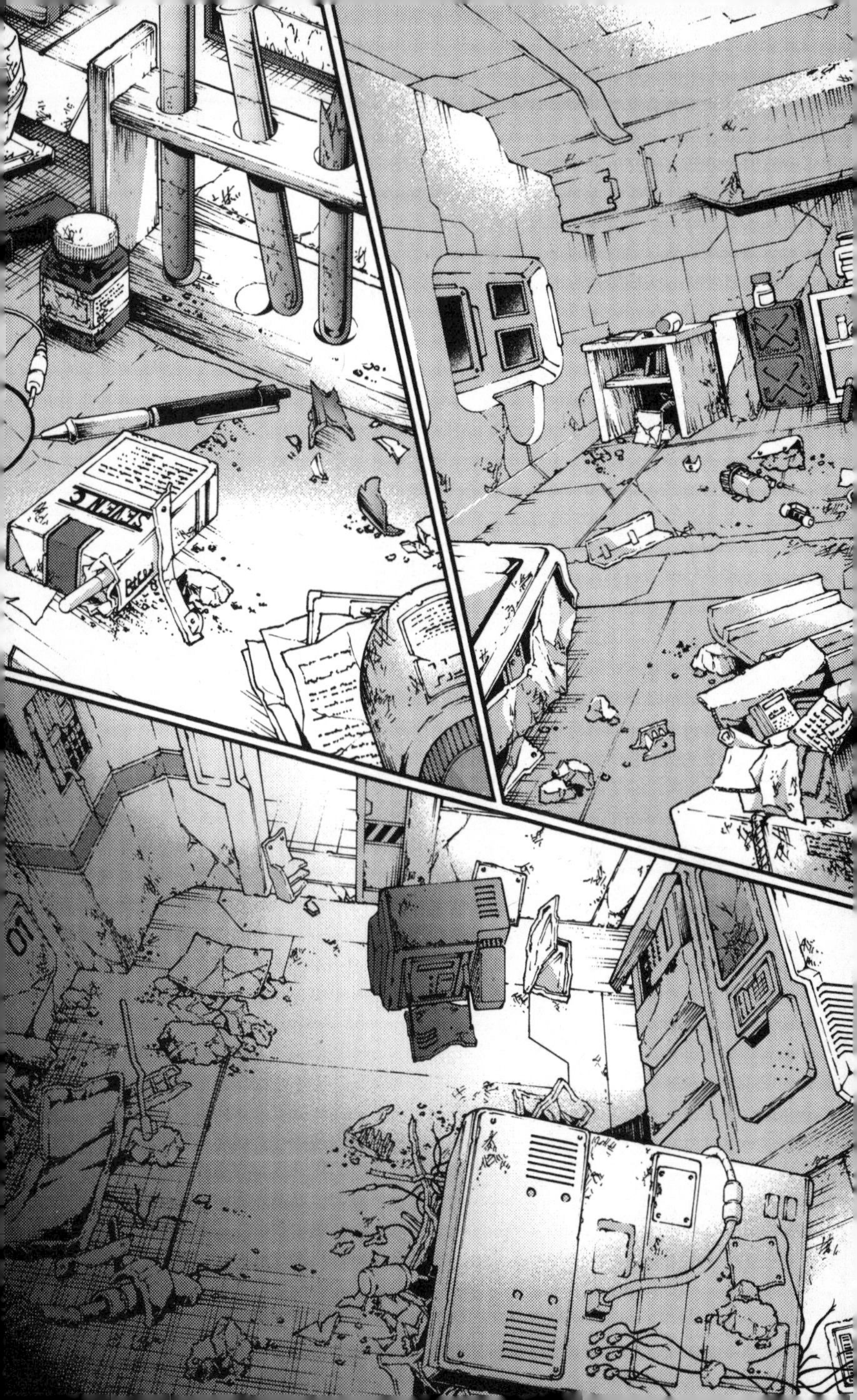

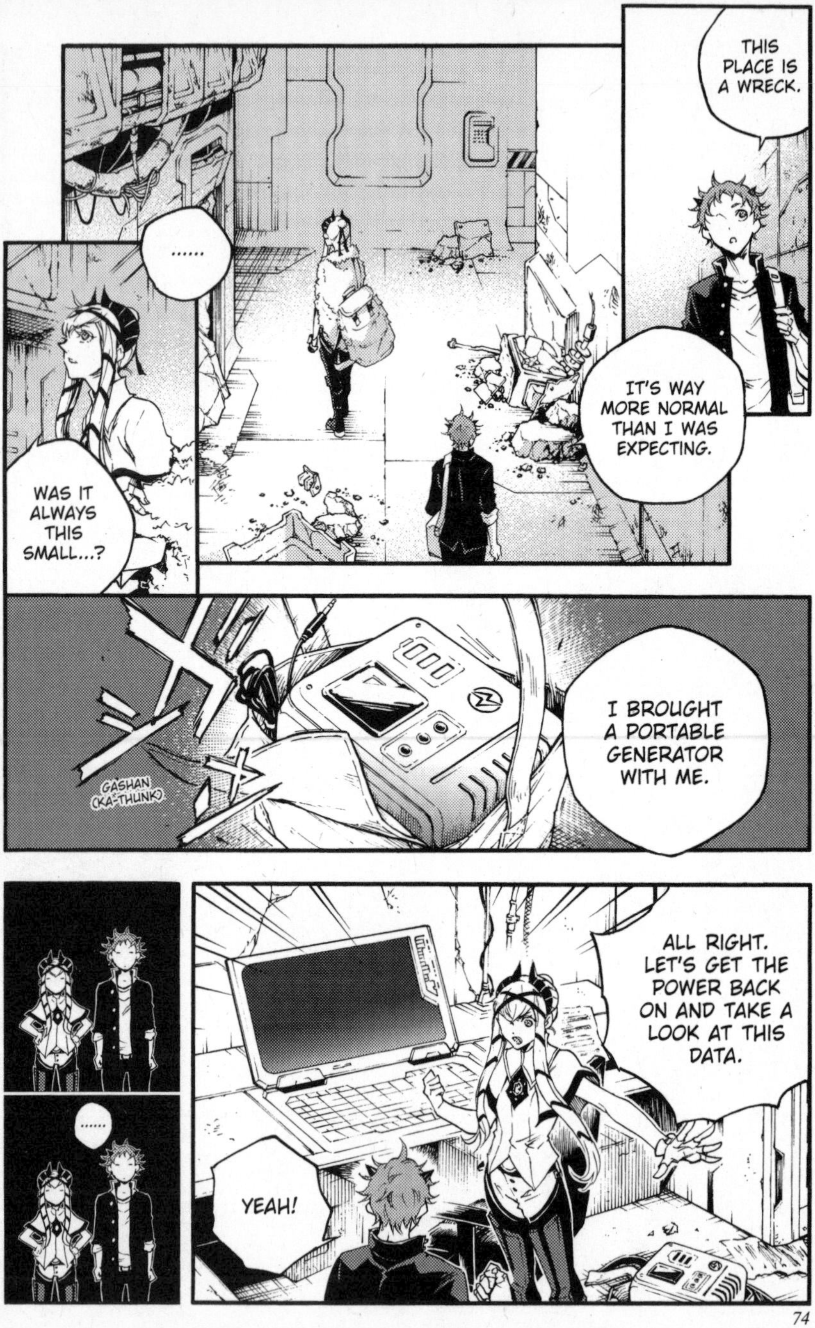
THIS PLACE IS A WRECK.
IT'S WAY MORE NORMAL THAN I WAS EXPECTING.
......
WAS IT ALWAYS THIS SMALL...?
I BROUGHT A PORTABLE GENERATOR WITH ME.
GASHAN (KA-THUNK)
ALL RIGHT. LET'S GET THE POWER BACK ON AND TAKE A LOOK AT THIS DATA.
YEAH!
......

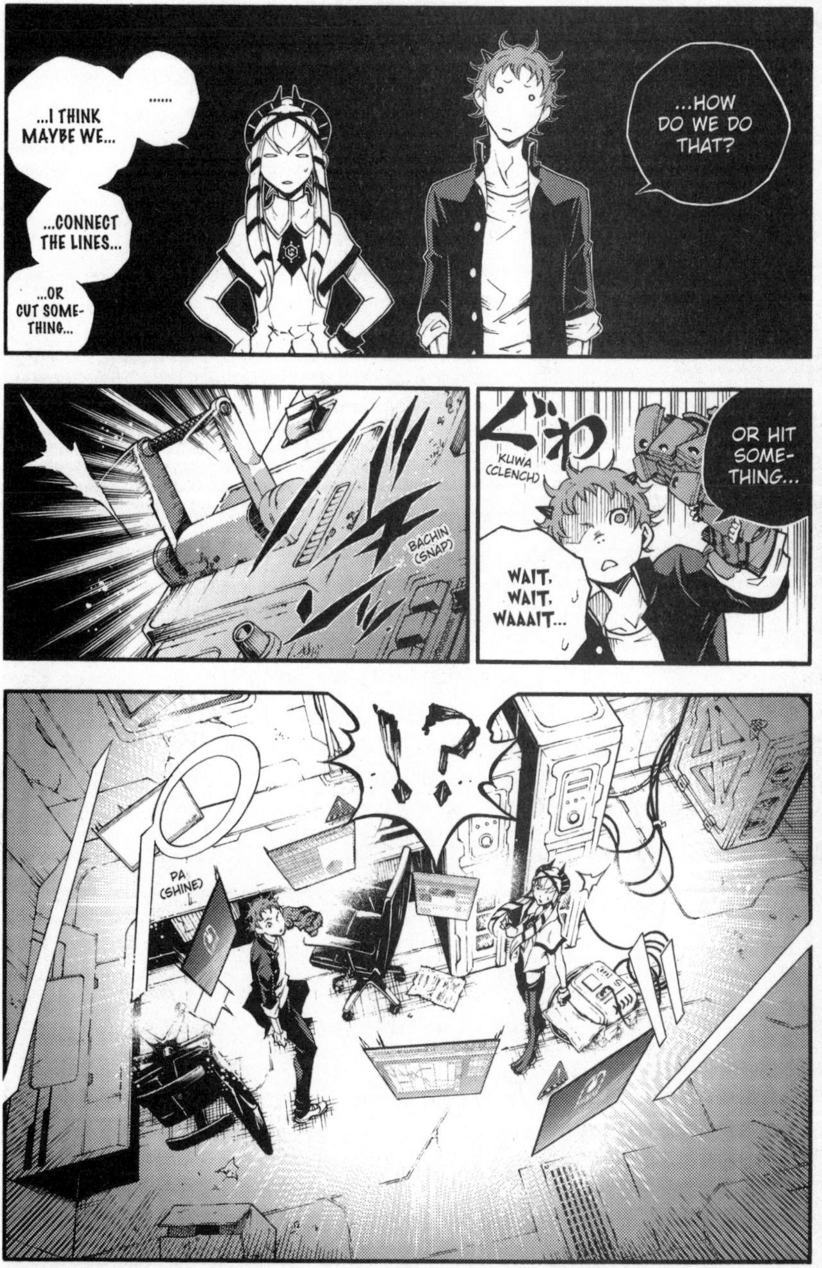
...HOW DO WE DO THAT?
......
...I THINK MAYBE WE...
...CONNECT THE LINES...
...OR CUT SOME-THING...
OR HIT SOME-THING...
くわ
KUWA (CLENCH)
WAIT, WAIT, WAAAIT...
BACHIN (SNAP)
!?
PA (SHINE)

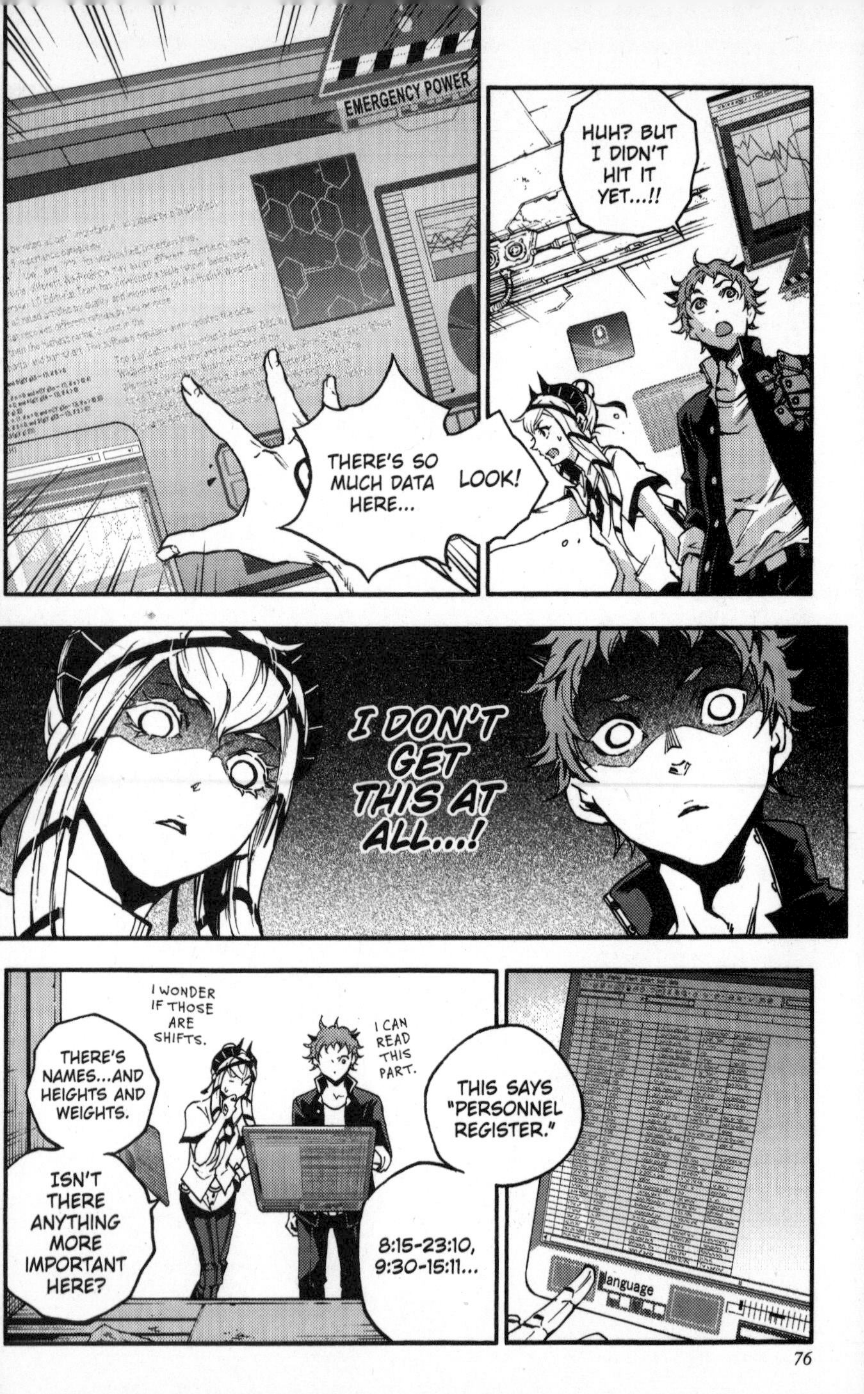
HUH? BUT I DIDN'T HIT IT YET...!!
LOOK!
EMERGENCY POWER
THERE'S SO MUCH DATA HERE...
I DON'T GET THIS AT ALL...!
Language
THIS SAYS "PERSONNEL REGISTER."
I CAN READ THIS PART.
8:15-23:10, 9:30-15:11...
I WONDER IF THOSE ARE SHIFTS.
THERE'S NAMES...AND HEIGHTS AND WEIGHTS.
ISN'T THERE ANYTHING MORE IMPORTANT HERE?

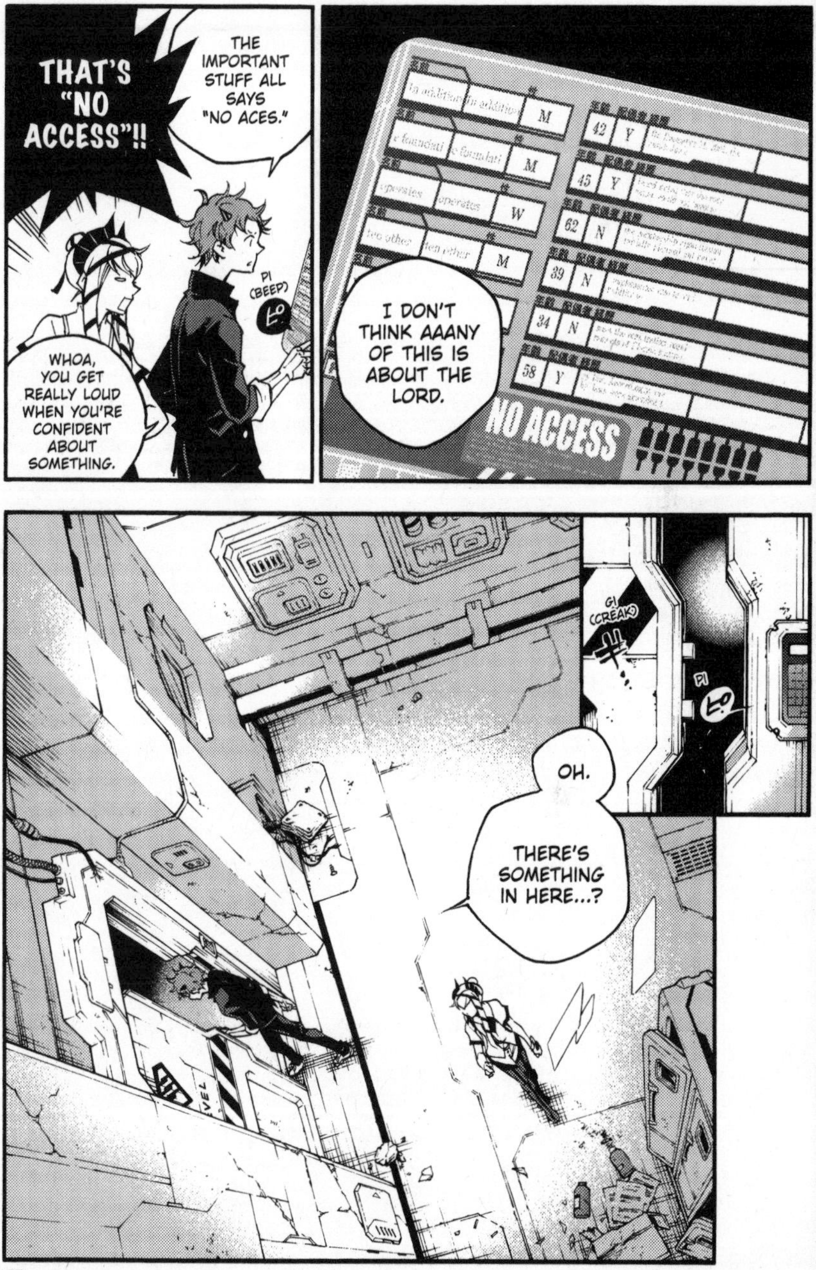
NO ACCESS
I DON'T THINK AAANY OF THIS IS ABOUT THE LORD.
THE IMPORTANT STUFF ALL SAYS "NO ACES."
THAT'S "NO ACCESS"!!
PI (BEEP)
WHOA, YOU GET REALLY LOUD WHEN YOU'RE CONFIDENT ABOUT SOMETHING.
GI (CREAK)
PI
OH.
THERE'S SOMETHING IN HERE...?

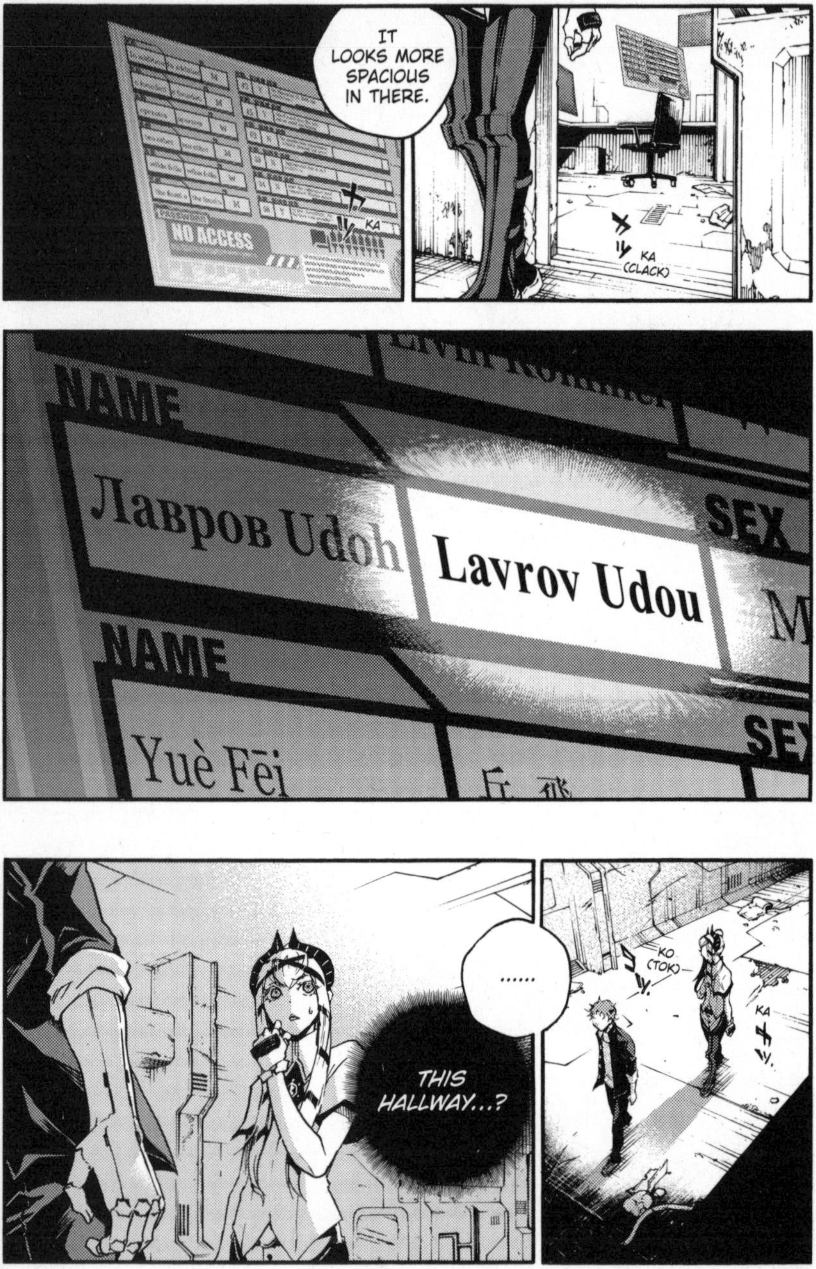
KA (CLACK)
IT LOOKS MORE SPACIOUS IN THERE.
NO ACCESS
KA
NAME
Лавров Udoh
Lavrov Udou
SEX
NAME
Yuè Fēi
KO (TOK)
KA
......
THIS HALLWAY...?

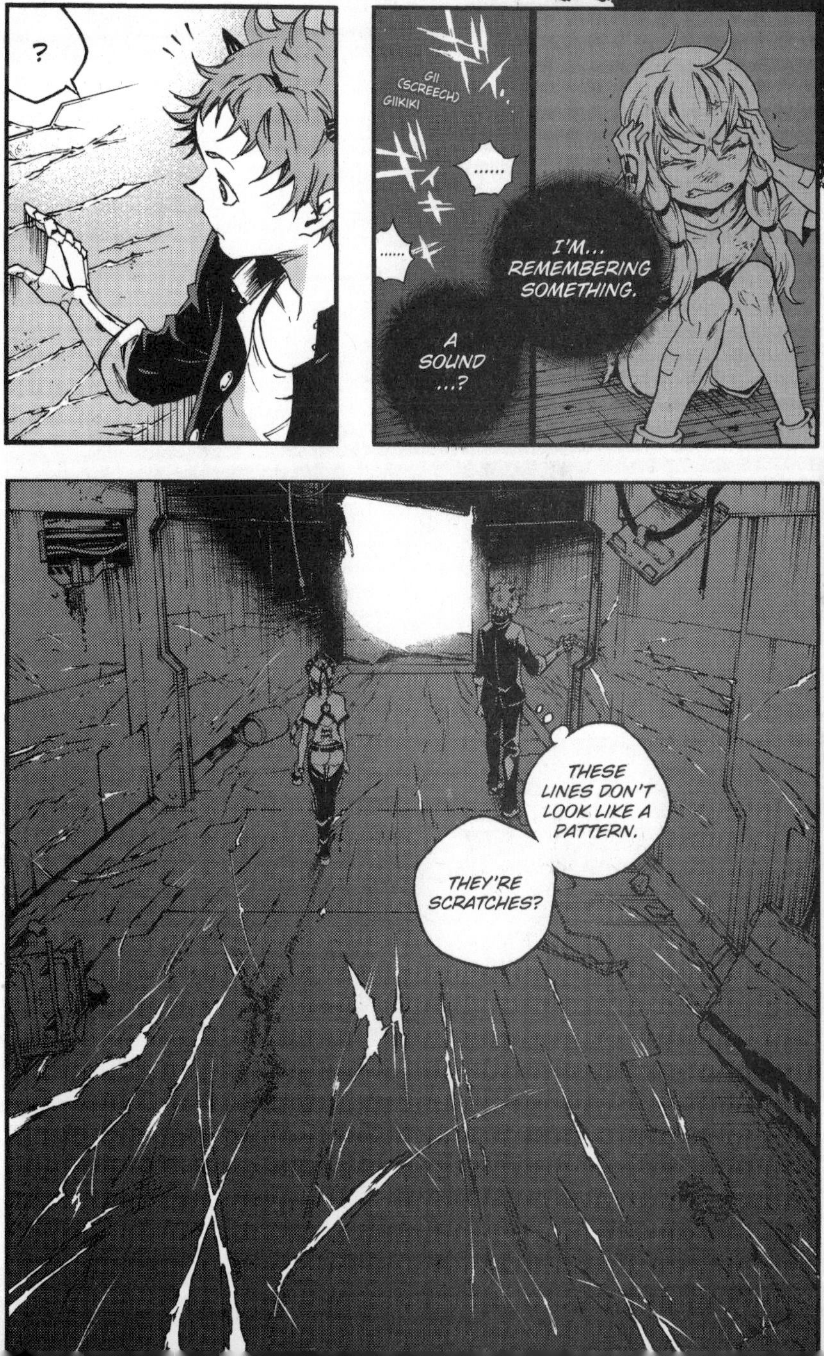
GII (SCREECH) GIIKIKI
......
......
I'M... REMEMBERING SOMETHING.
A SOUND ...?
?
THESE LINES DON'T LOOK LIKE A PATTERN.
THEY'RE SCRATCHES?

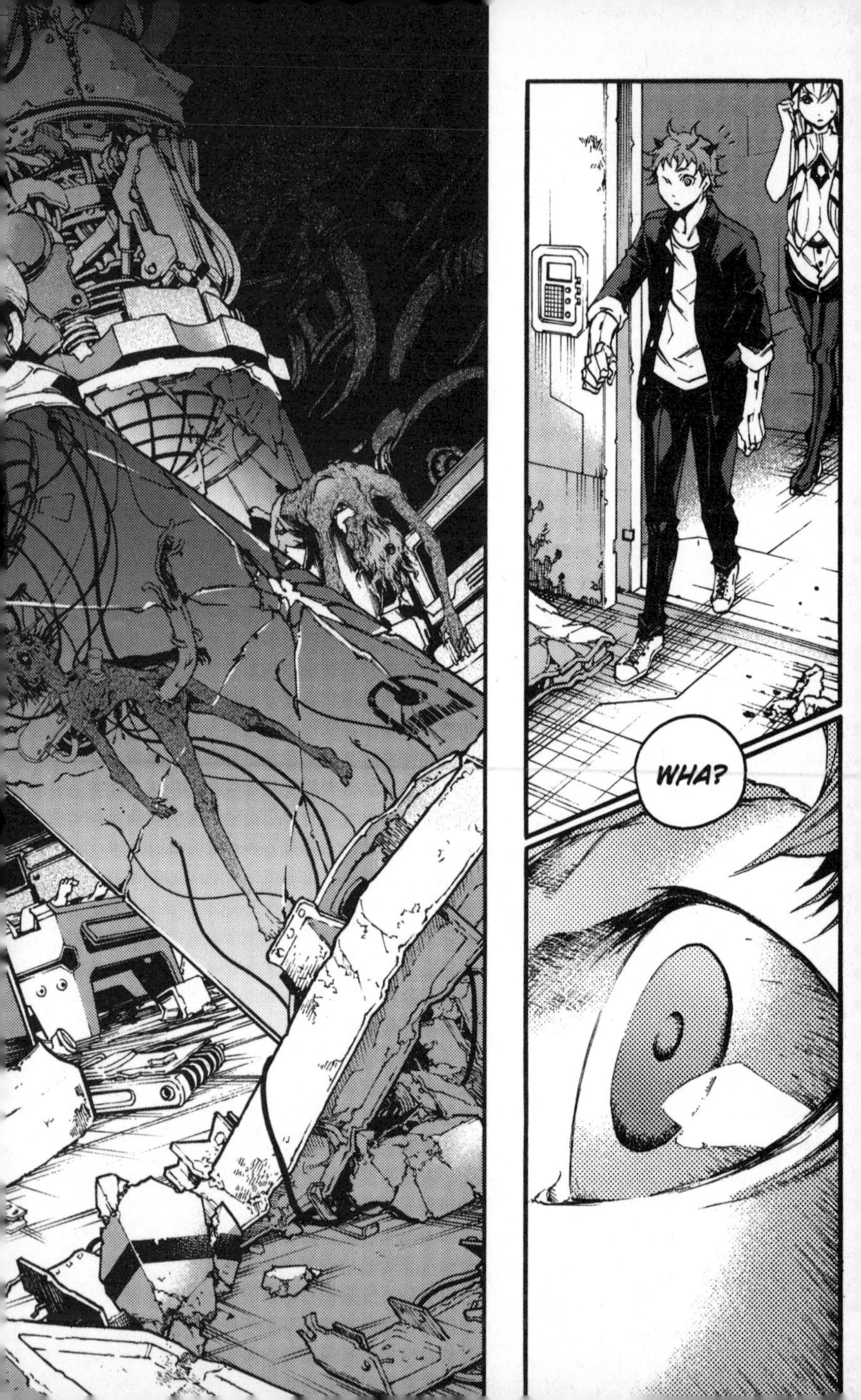
WHA?

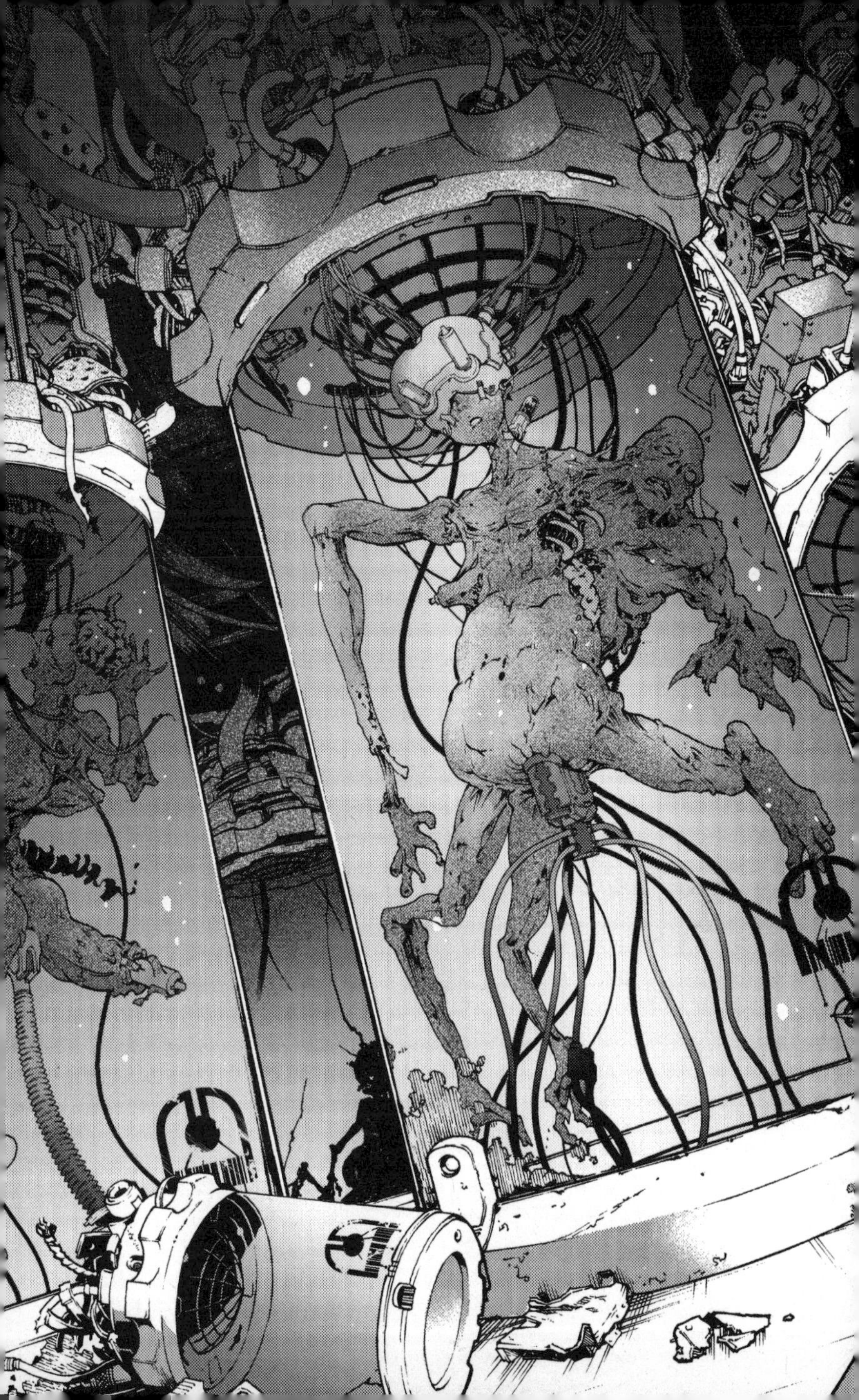

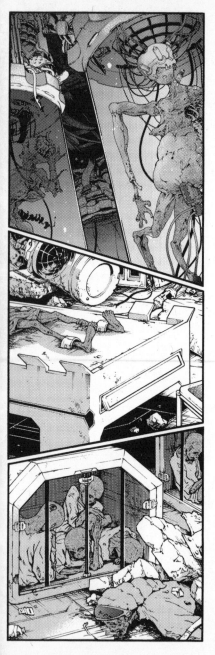

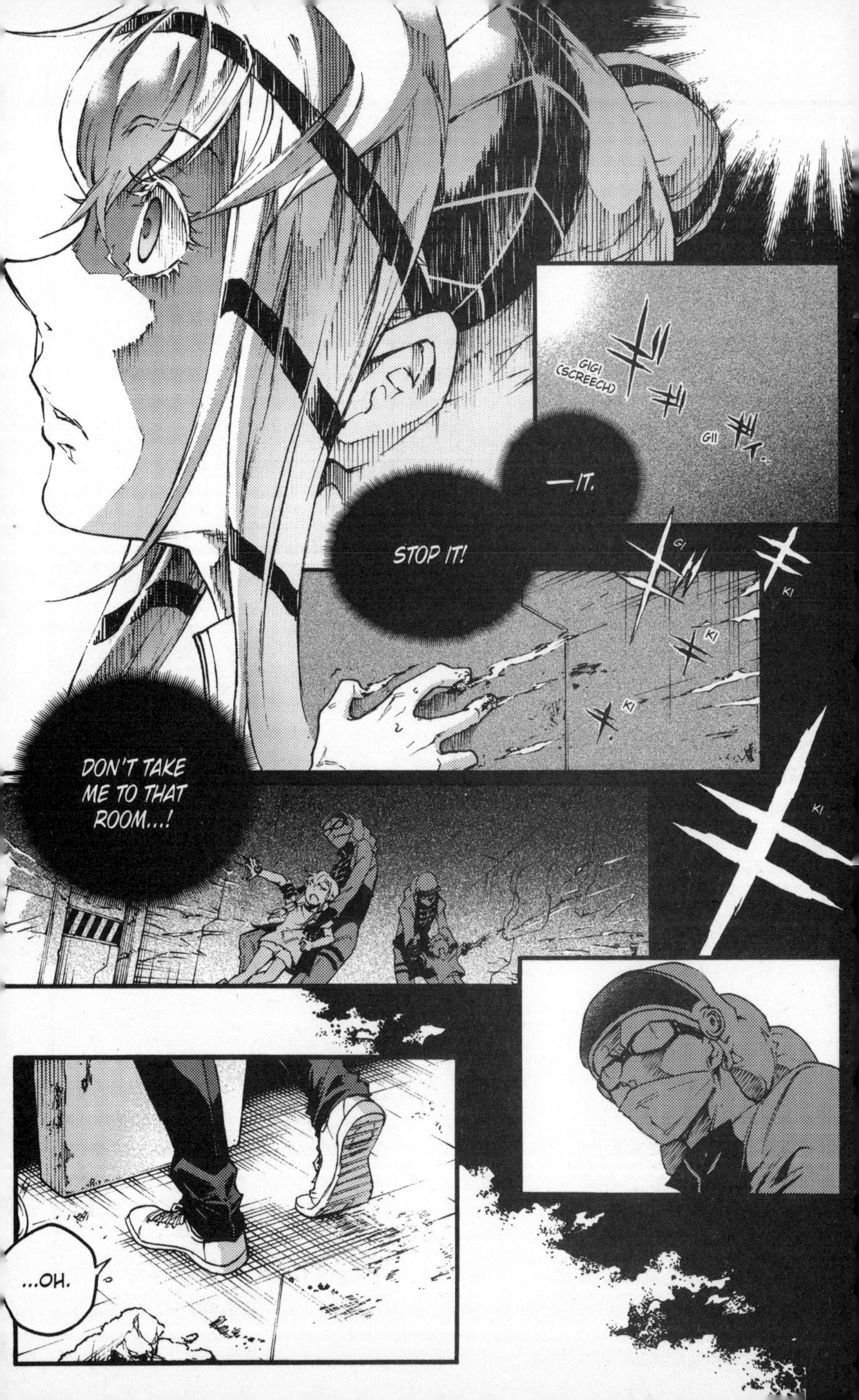
GIGI (SCREECH)
GII
—IT.
STOP IT!
GI
KI
KI
KI
DON'T TAKE ME TO THAT ROOM...!
KI
...OH.

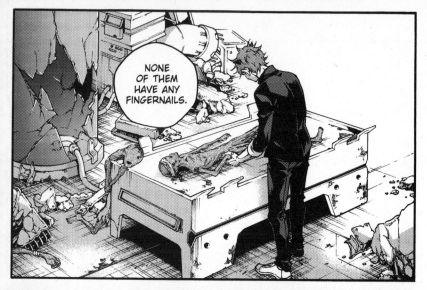

NONE OF THEM HAVE ANY FINGERNAILS.
...WE'RE LEAVING, YOUKOU-KUN.
...THIS IS JUST A GRAVE. THERE'S NOTHING HERE.
REALLY?
WE SHOULD LOOK AROUND A LITTLE...
GON (THUNK)

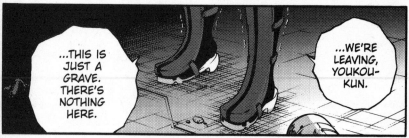

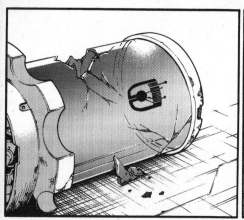

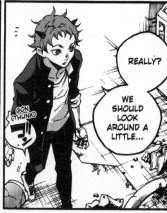

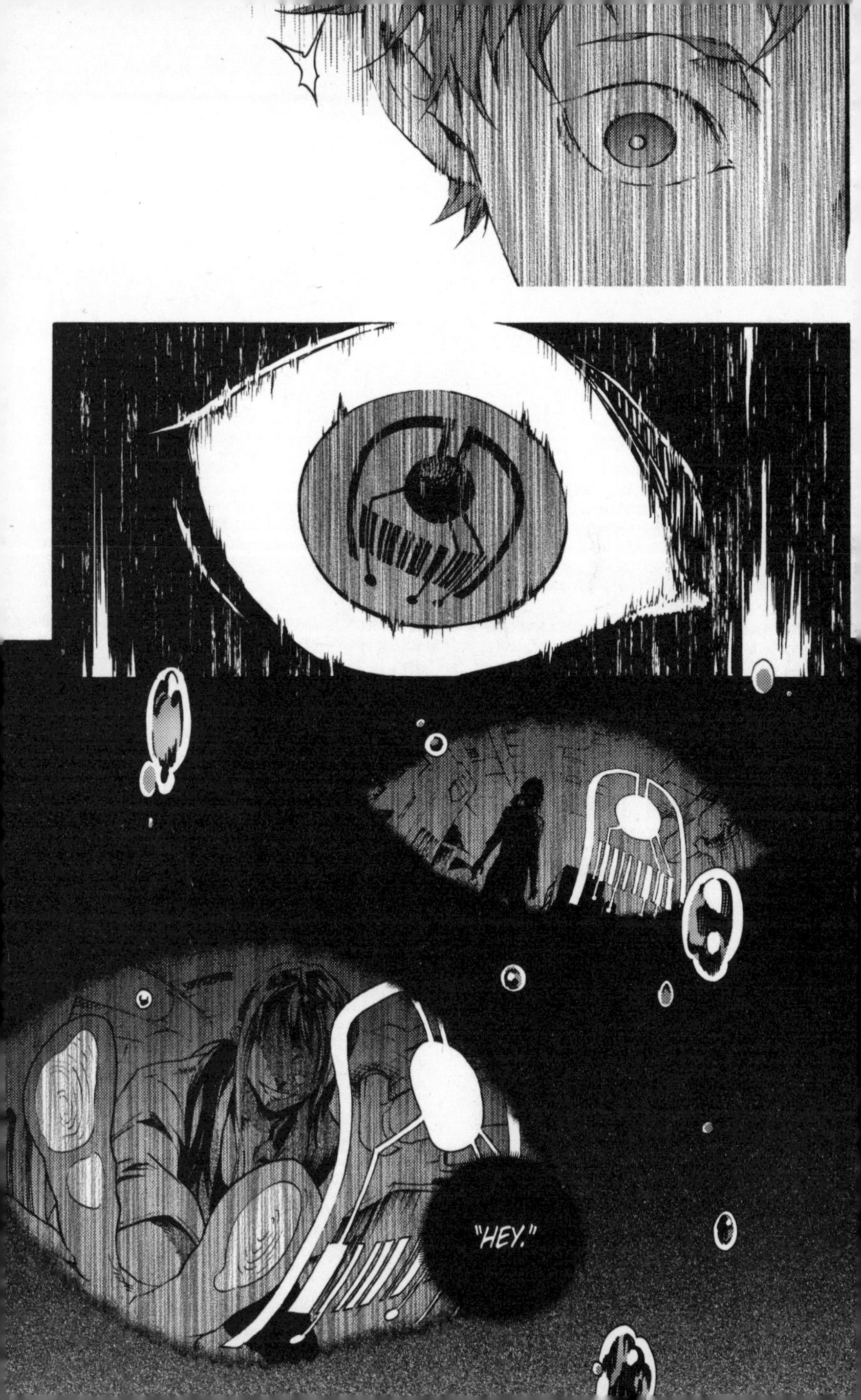
"HEY."

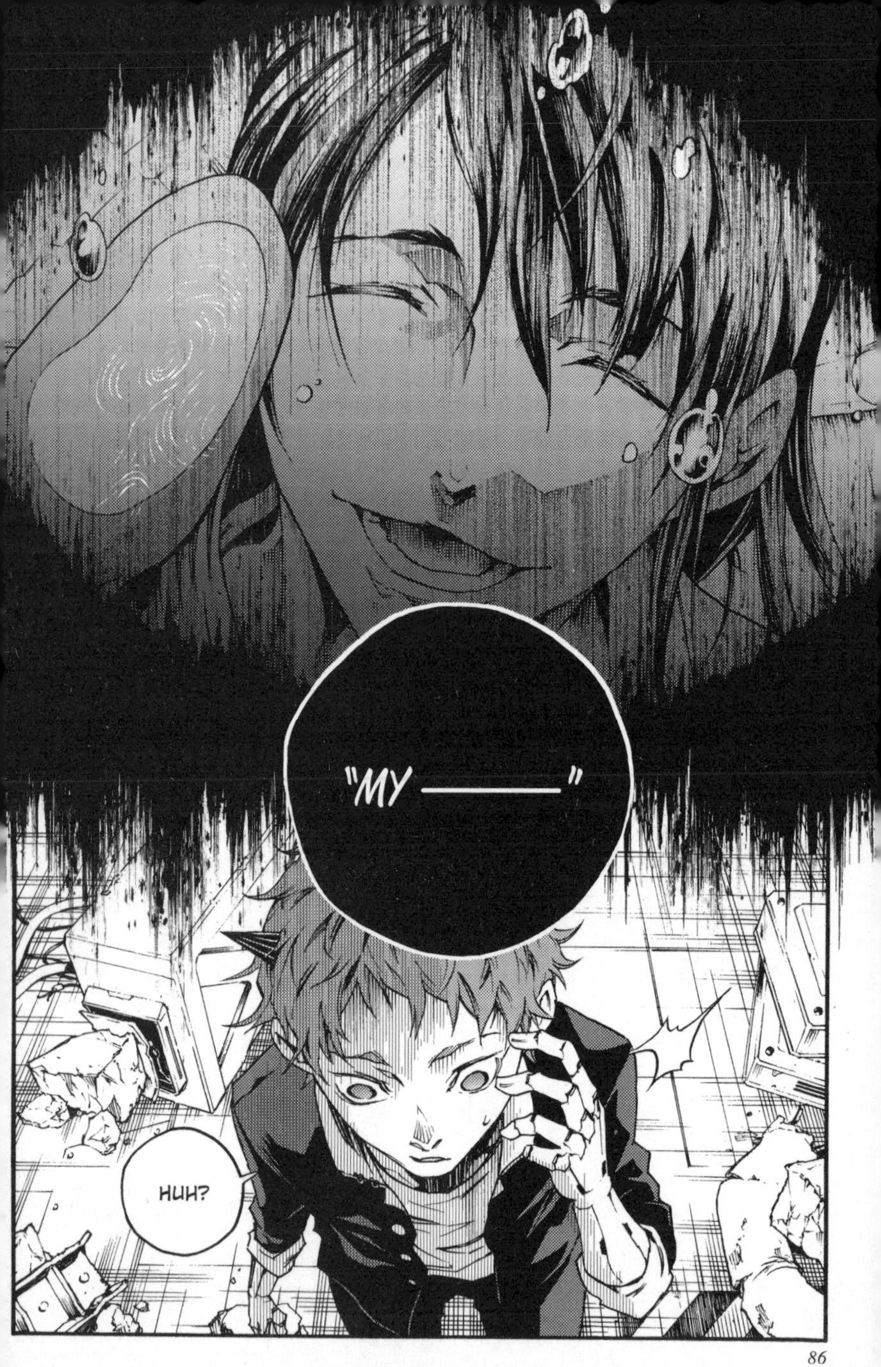
"MY ______"
HUH?

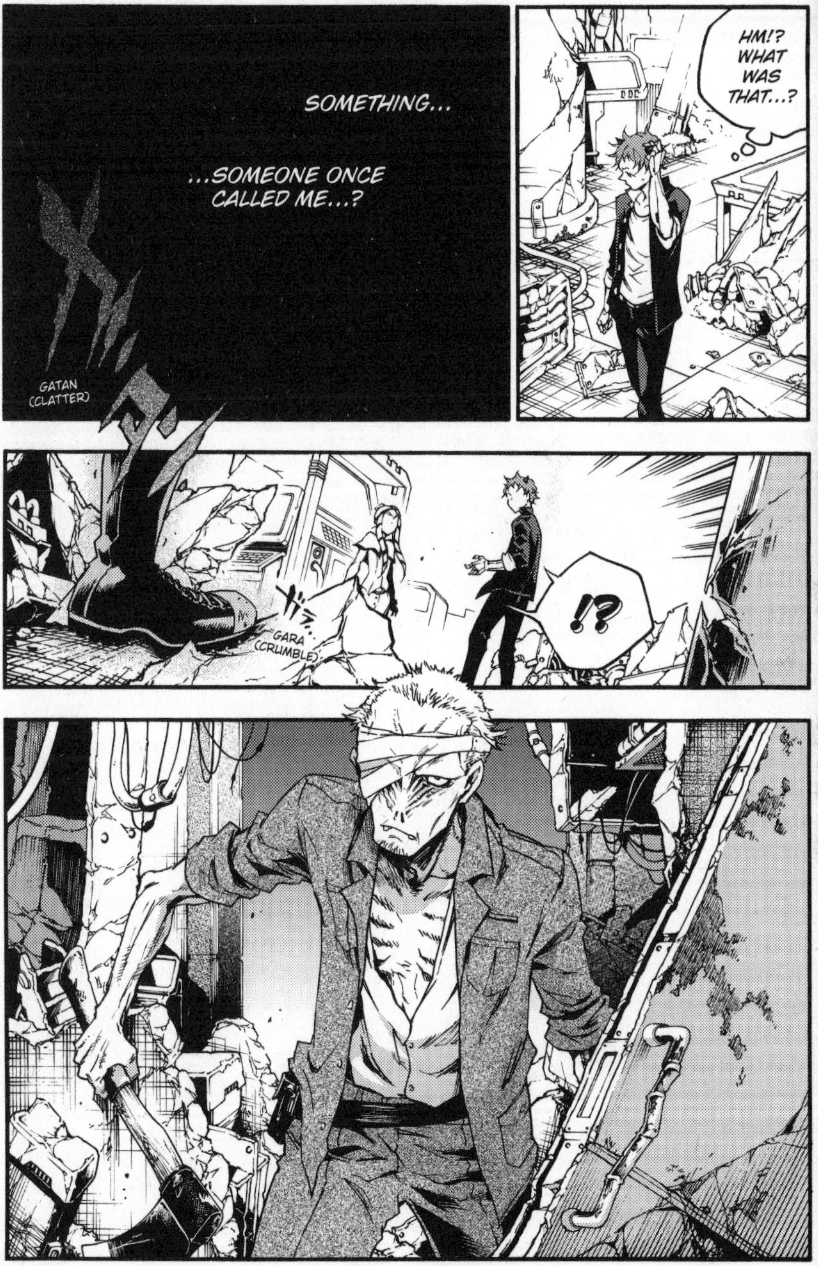
HM!? WHAT WAS THAT...?
SOMETHING...
...SOMEONE ONCE CALLED ME...?
GATAN (CLATTER)
!?
GARA (CRUMBLE)

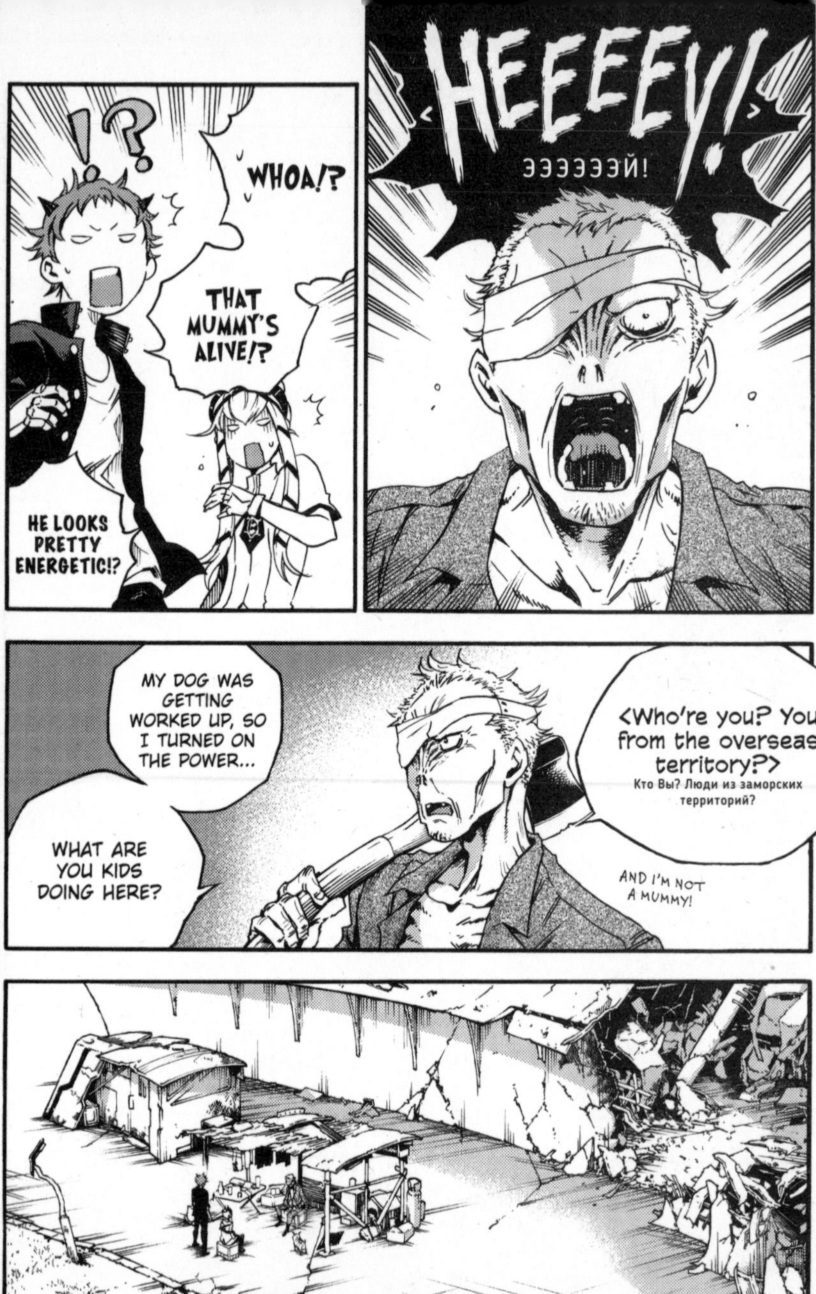

<HEEEEY!>
ЭЭЭЭЭЭЙ!
!?
WHOA!?
THAT MUMMY'S ALIVE!?
HE LOOKS PRETTY ENERGETIC!?
<Who're you? You from the overseas territory?>
Кто Вы? Люди из заморских территорий?
AND I'M NOT A MUMMY!
MY DOG WAS GETTING WORKED UP, SO I TURNED ON THE POWER...
WHAT ARE YOU KIDS DOING HERE?

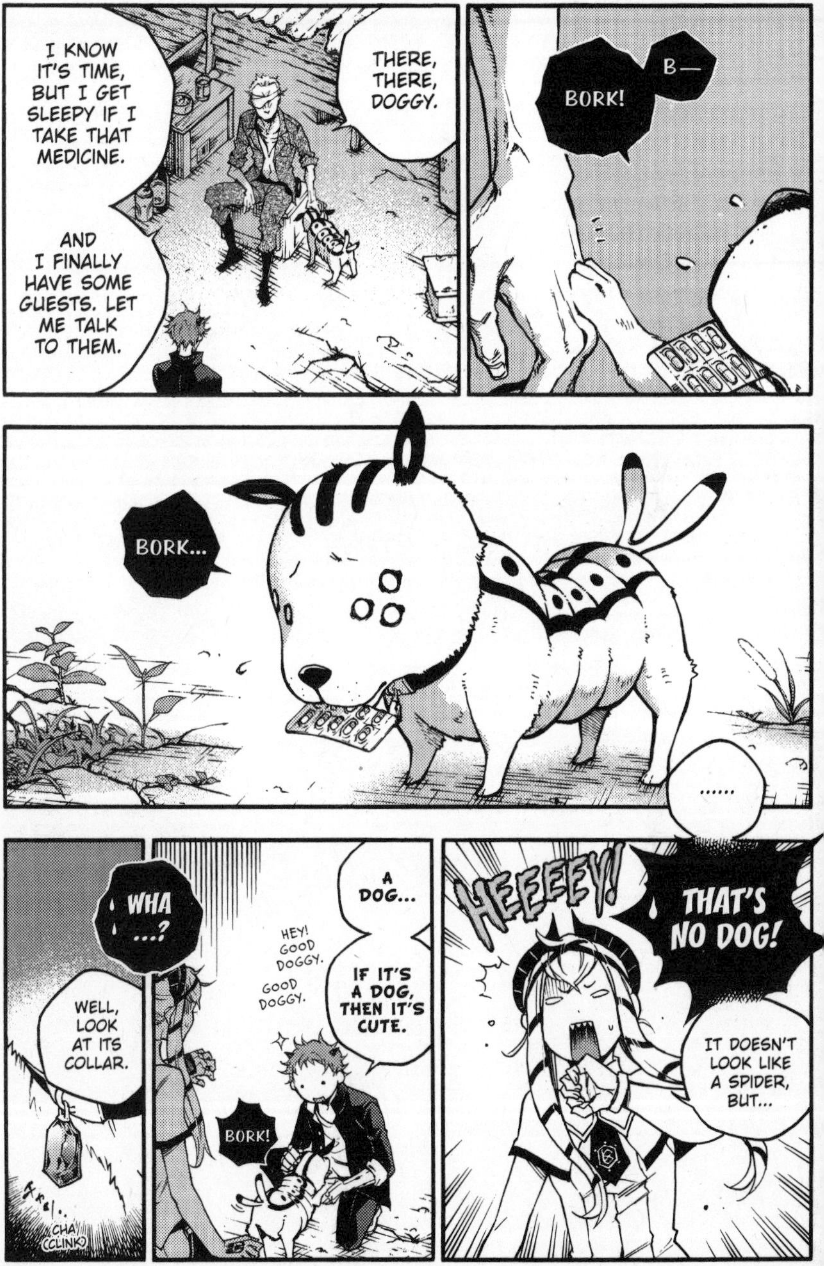
B—
BORK!
THERE, THERE, DOGGY.
I KNOW IT'S TIME, BUT I GET SLEEPY IF I TAKE THAT MEDICINE.
AND I FINALLY HAVE SOME GUESTS. LET ME TALK TO THEM.
BORK...
......
THAT'S NO DOG!
HEEEEY!
IT DOESN'T LOOK LIKE A SPIDER, BUT...
A DOG...
IF IT'S A DOG, THEN IT'S CUTE.
HEY! GOOD DOGGY.
GOOD DOGGY.
BORK!
WHA ...?
WELL, LOOK AT ITS COLLAR.
CHA (CLINK)

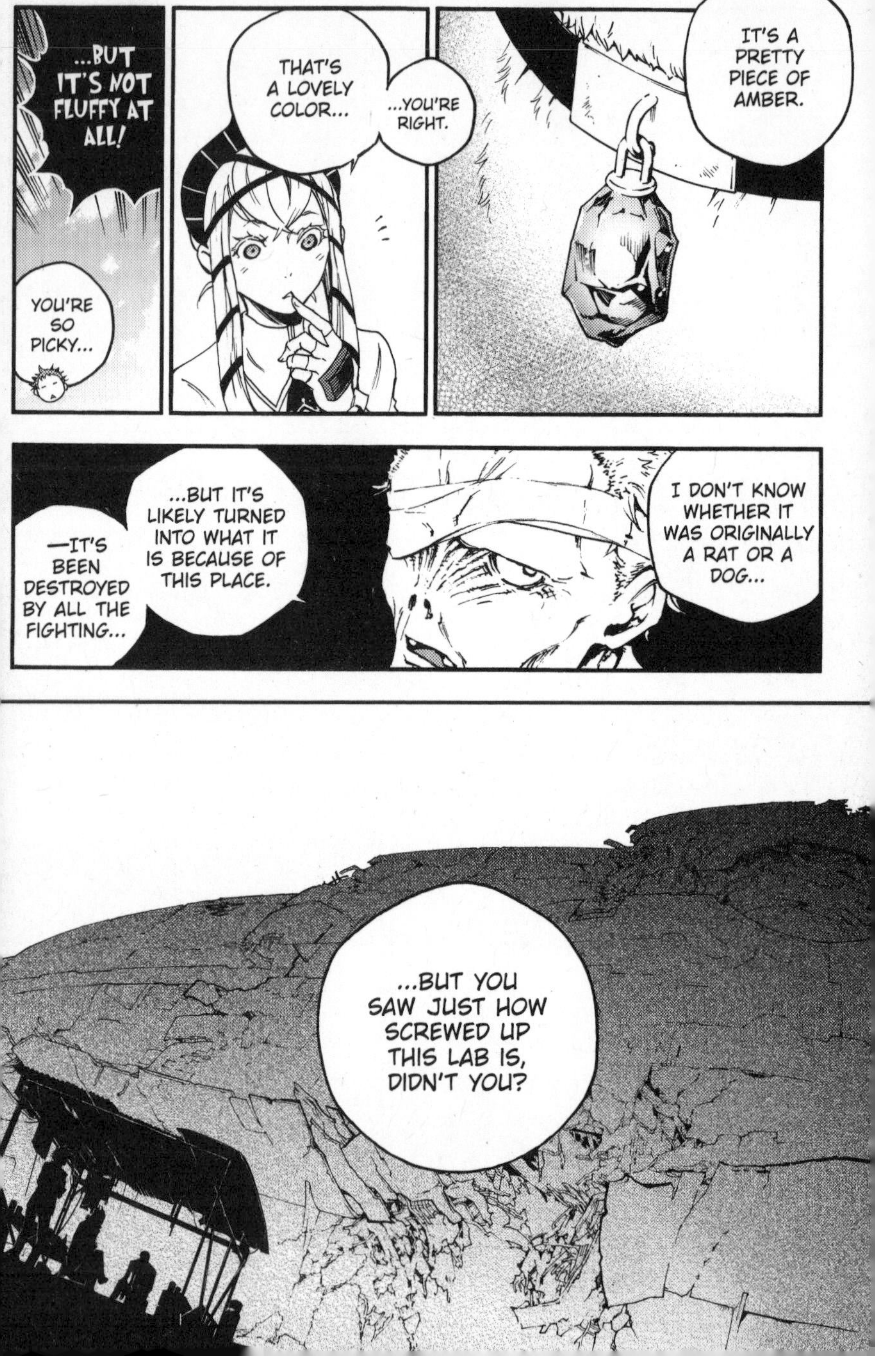
IT'S A PRETTY PIECE OF AMBER.
...YOU'RE RIGHT.
THAT'S A LOVELY COLOR...
...BUT IT'S NOT FLUFFY AT ALL!
YOU'RE SO PICKY...
I DON'T KNOW WHETHER IT WAS ORIGINALLY A RAT OR A DOG...
...BUT IT'S LIKELY TURNED INTO WHAT IT IS BECAUSE OF THIS PLACE.
—IT'S BEEN DESTROYED BY ALL THE FIGHTING...
...BUT YOU SAW JUST HOW SCREWED UP THIS LAB IS, DIDN'T YOU?

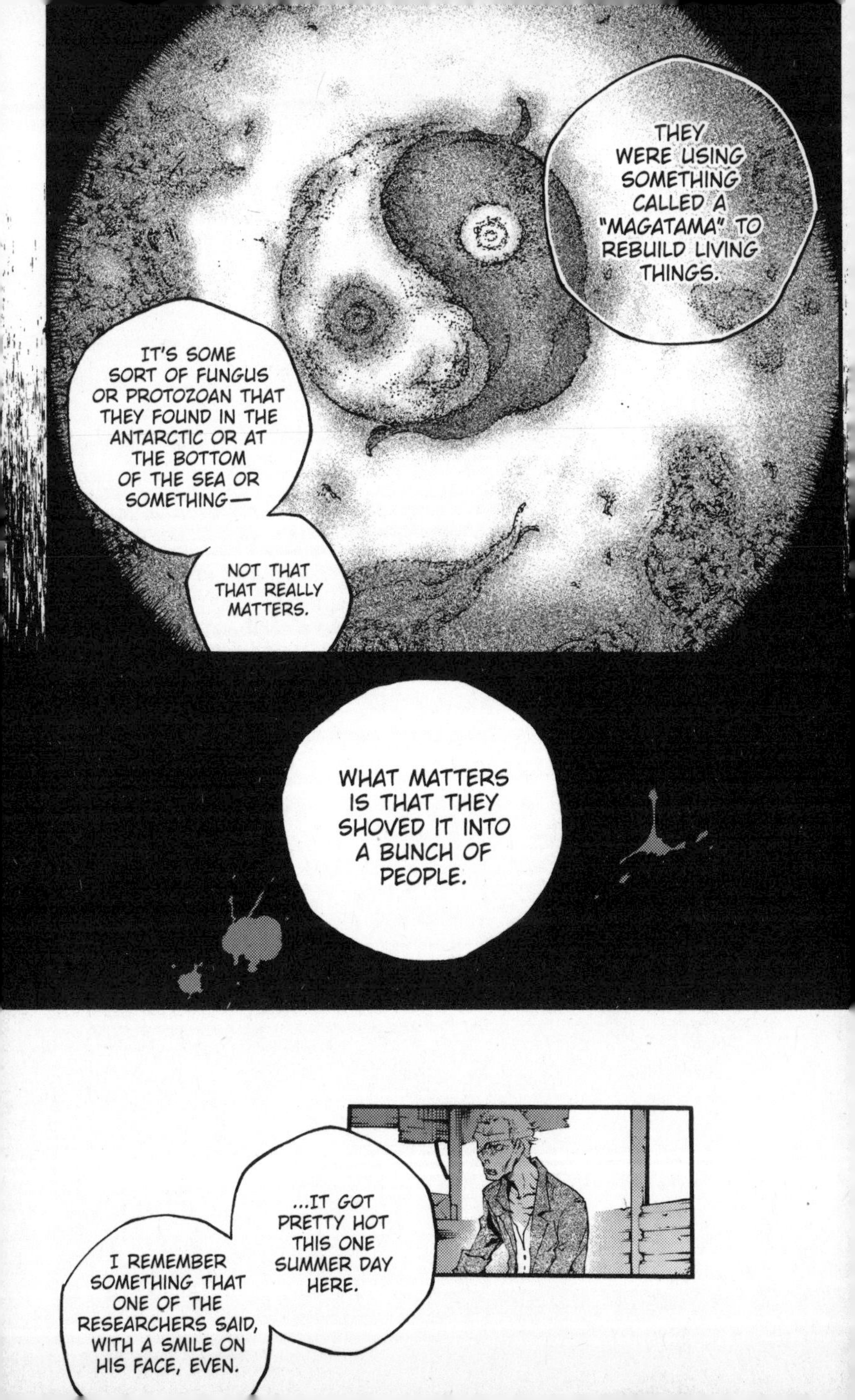
THEY WERE USING SOMETHING CALLED A "MAGATAMA" TO REBUILD LIVING THINGS.
IT'S SOME SORT OF FUNGUS OR PROTOZOAN THAT THEY FOUND IN THE ANTARCTIC OR AT THE BOTTOM OF THE SEA OR SOMETHING—
NOT THAT THAT REALLY MATTERS.
WHAT MATTERS IS THAT THEY SHOVED IT INTO A BUNCH OF PEOPLE.
...IT GOT PRETTY HOT THIS ONE SUMMER DAY HERE.
I REMEMBER SOMETHING THAT ONE OF THE RESEARCHERS SAID, WITH A SMILE ON HIS FACE, EVEN.

"IF WE USE THE MAGATAMA, PEOPLE ARE BASICALLY LIKE CLAY IN OUR HANDS.

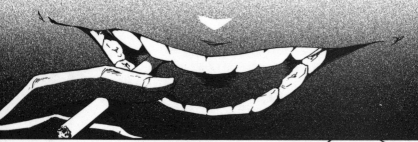

"IT MAKES A MAN FEEL LIKE A GOD."

REMEMBERING THAT...

...CHILLS ME DOWN TO THE BONE.

AFTER AMENOTORI BOUGHT THIS PLACE, ALL THE DECENT RESEARCHERS WERE DRIVEN AWAY.

...OLD MAN.

IT BECAME SUCH A HELL THAT IT ALMOST MADE AN OLD DESERTER LIKE ME WANT TO GO BACK TO THE BATTLEFIELD.

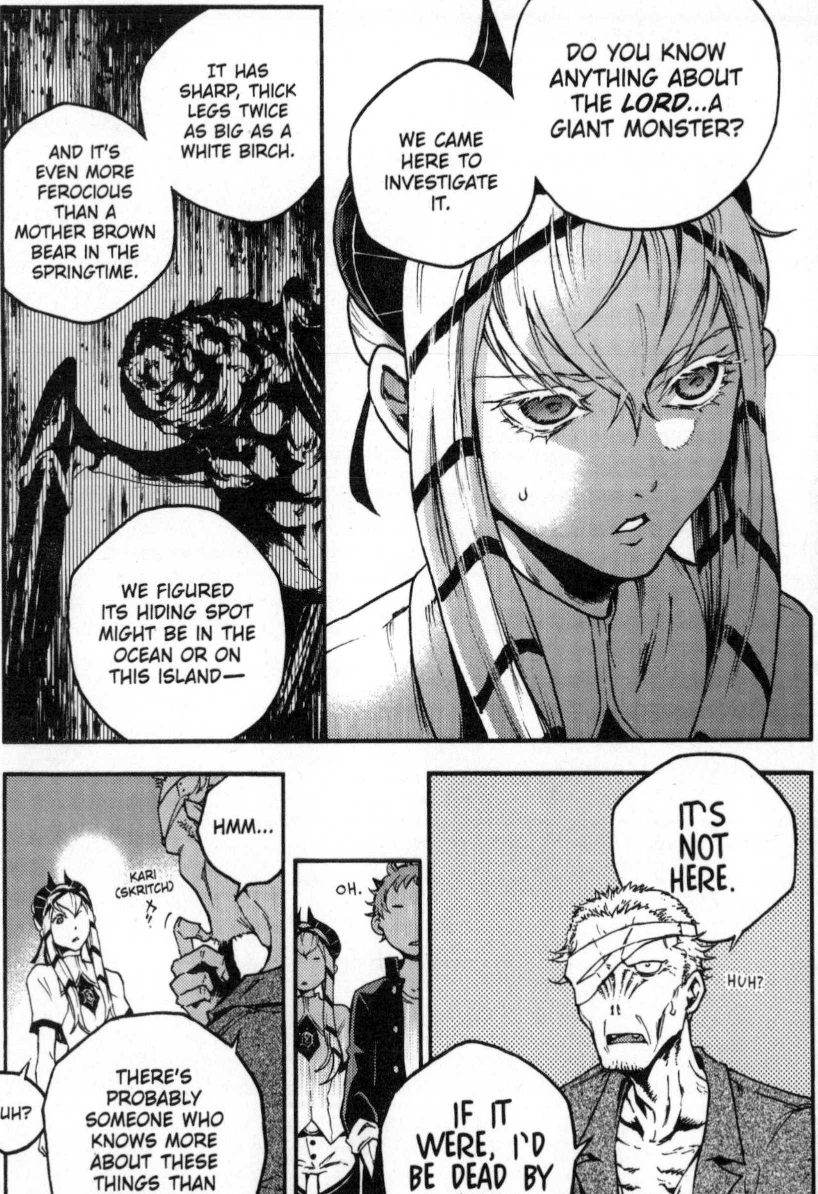
DO YOU KNOW ANYTHING ABOUT THE ***LORD***...A GIANT MONSTER?
WE CAME HERE TO INVESTIGATE IT.
IT HAS SHARP, THICK LEGS TWICE AS BIG AS A WHITE BIRCH.
AND IT'S EVEN MORE FEROCIOUS THAN A MOTHER BROWN BEAR IN THE SPRINGTIME.
WE FIGURED ITS HIDING SPOT MIGHT BE IN THE OCEAN OR ON THIS ISLAND—
IT'S NOT HERE.
HUH?
IF IT WERE, I'D BE DEAD BY NOW.
OH.
HMM...
KARI (SKRITCH)
THERE'S PROBABLY SOMEONE WHO KNOWS MORE ABOUT THESE THINGS THAN ME, THOUGH.
HUH?

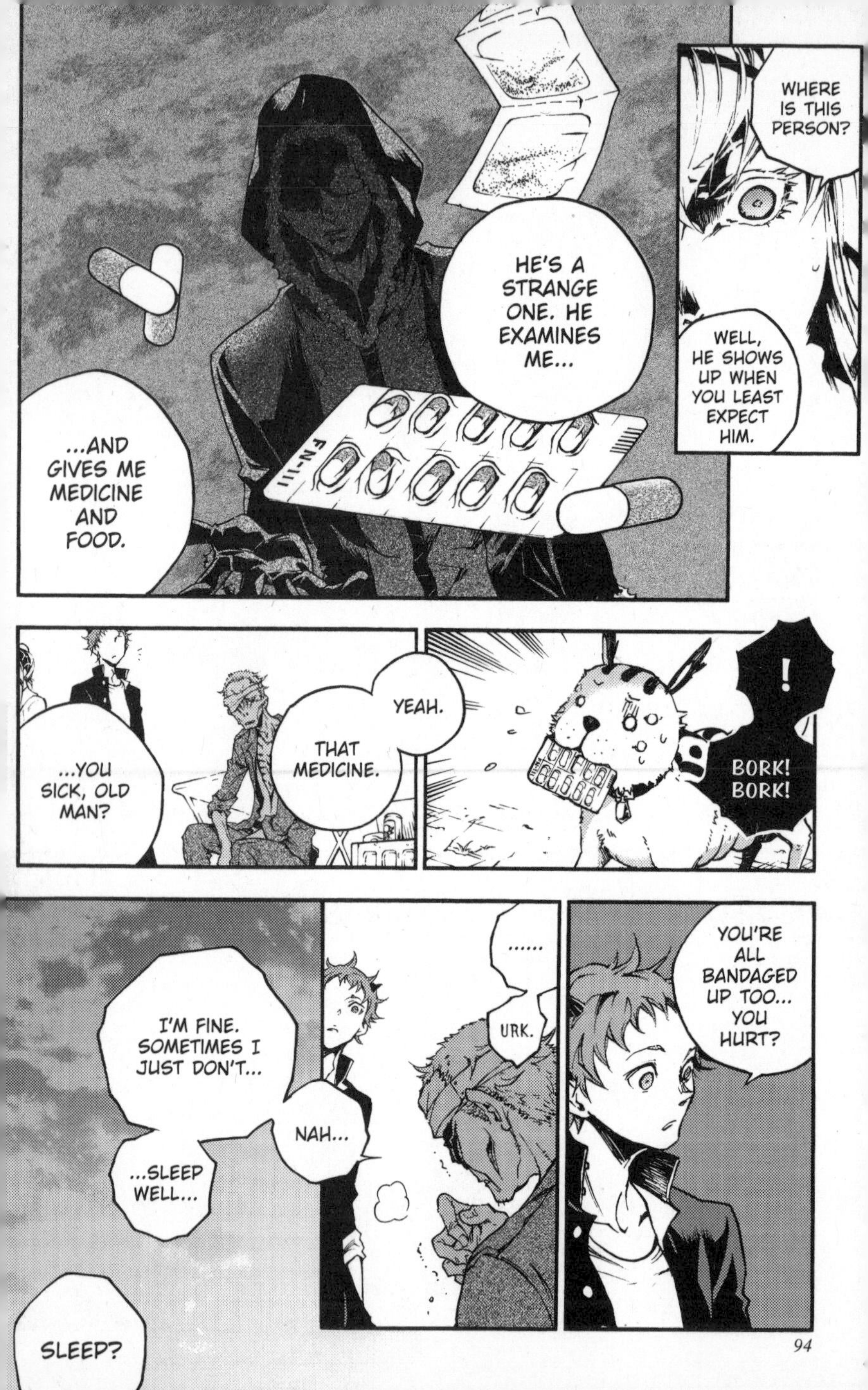
WHERE IS THIS PERSON?
WELL, HE SHOWS UP WHEN YOU LEAST EXPECT HIM.
HE'S A STRANGE ONE. HE EXAMINES ME...
FN-111
...AND GIVES ME MEDICINE AND FOOD.
!
BORK! BORK!
YEAH.
THAT MEDICINE.
...YOU SICK, OLD MAN?
YOU'RE ALL BANDAGED UP TOO... YOU HURT?
......
URK.
NAH...
I'M FINE. SOMETIMES I JUST DON'T...
...SLEEP WELL...
SLEEP?

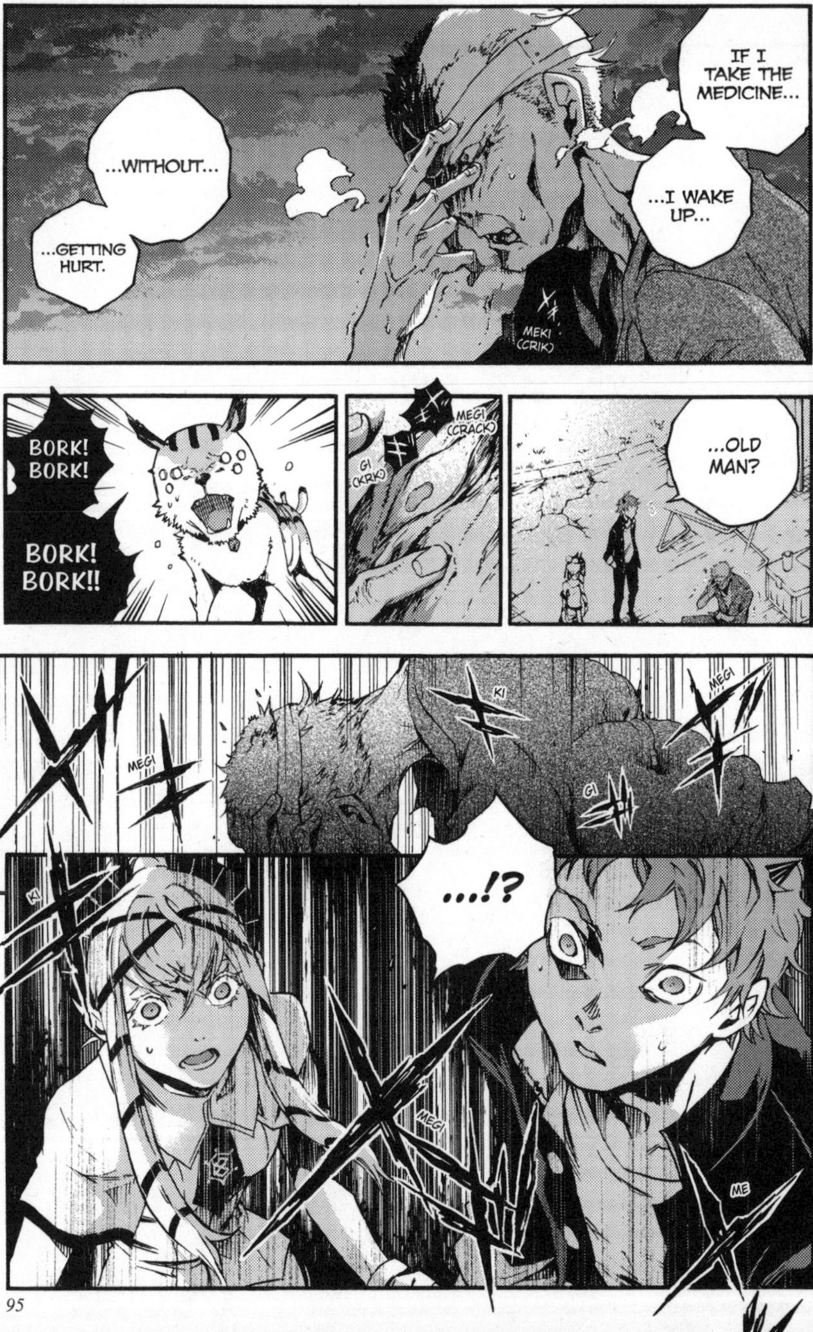
IF I TAKE THE MEDICINE...
...I WAKE UP...
...WITHOUT...
...GETTING HURT.
MEKI (CRIK)
...OLD MAN?
MEGI (CRACK)
GI (KRK)
BORK! BORK!
BORK! BORK!!
MEGI
KI
GI
MEGI
...!?
KI
MEGI
ME

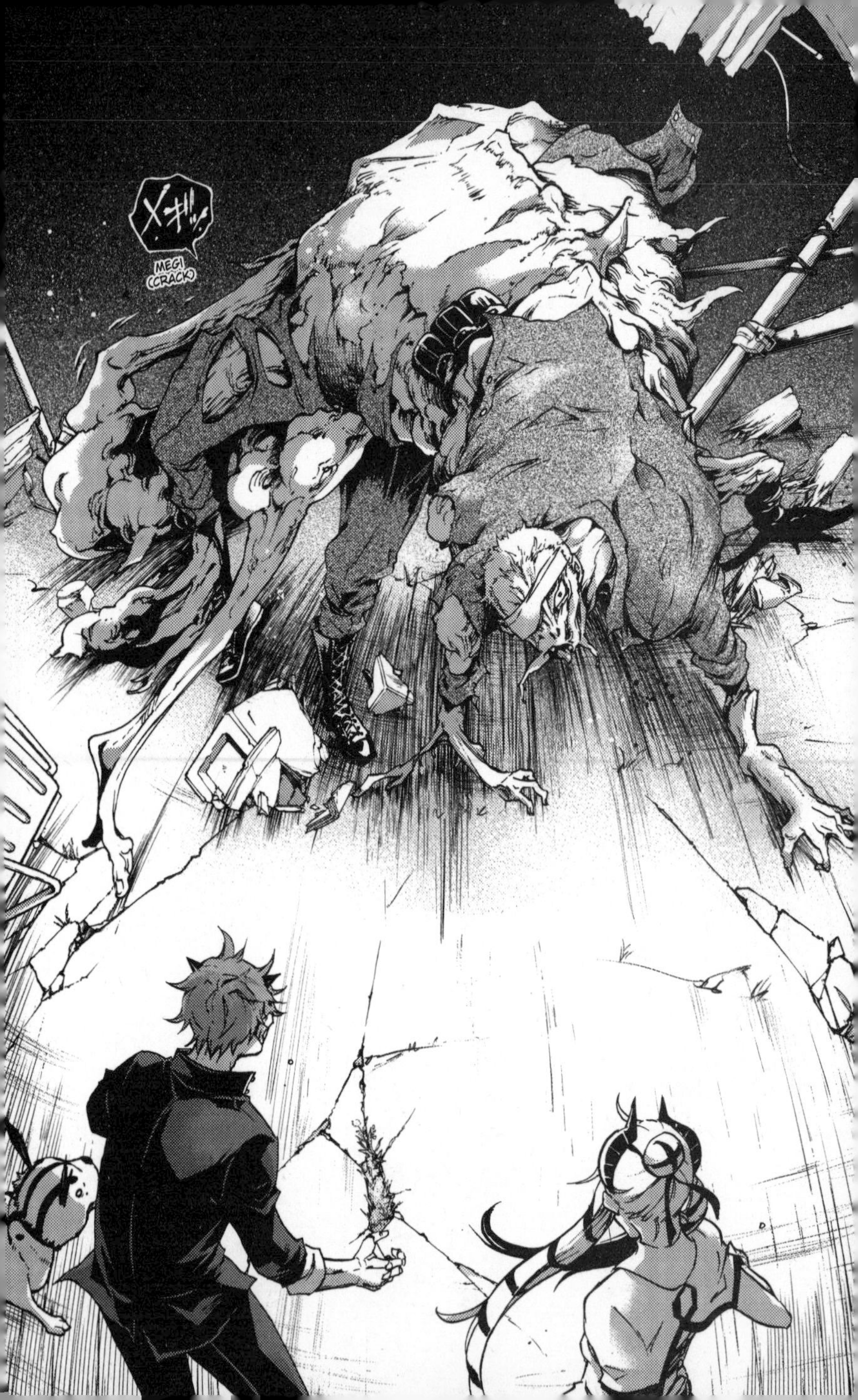
メギッ
MEGI
(CRACK)

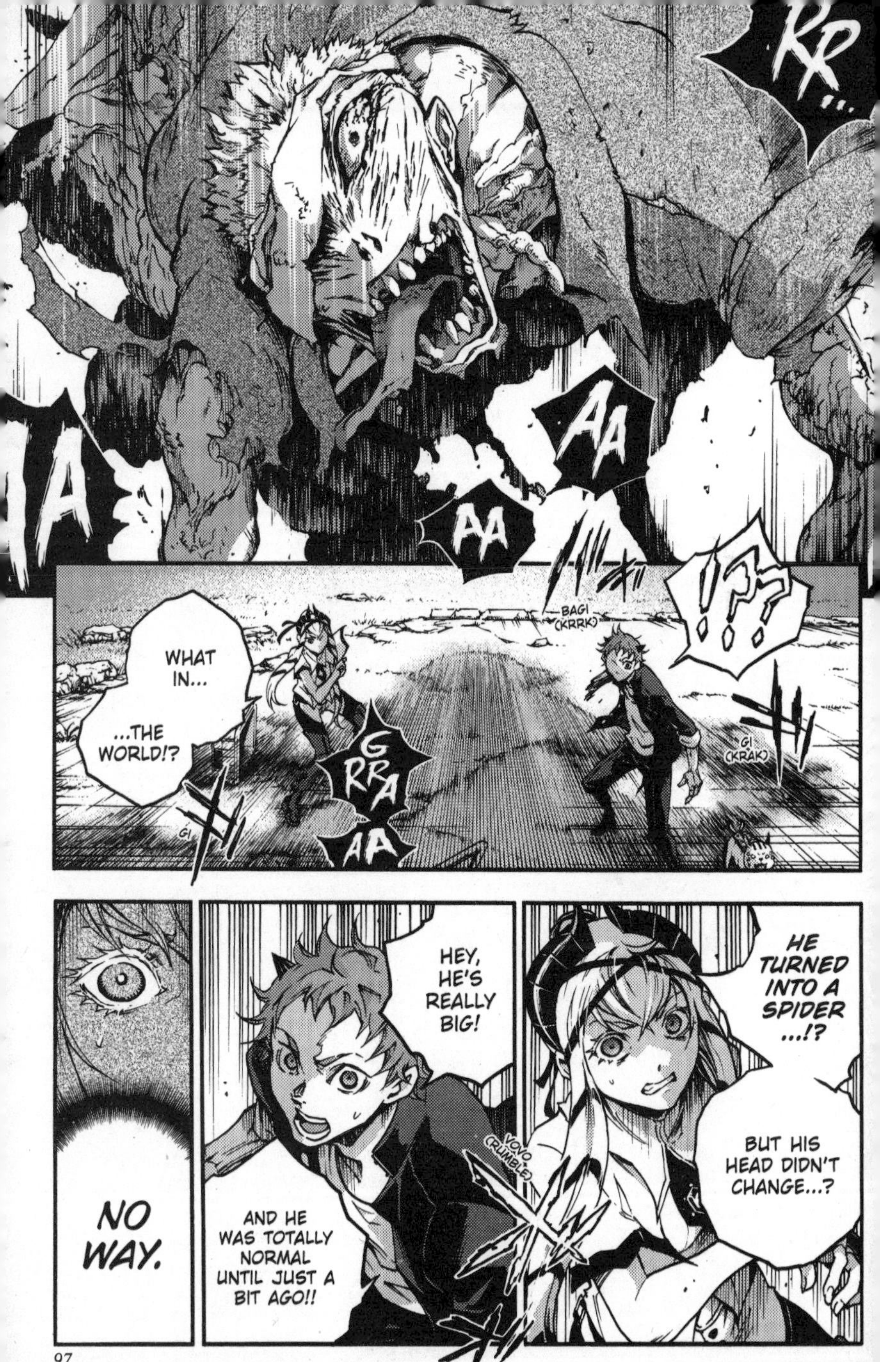
KR...
AA
AA
A
!?
BAGI (KRRK)
GI (KRAK)
WHAT IN... ...THE WORLD!?
GRRAAA
GI
HE TURNED INTO A SPIDER...!?
BUT HIS HEAD DIDN'T CHANGE...?
HEY, HE'S REALLY BIG!
VOVO (RUMBLE)
AND HE WAS TOTALLY NORMAL UNTIL JUST A BIT AGO!!
NO WAY.

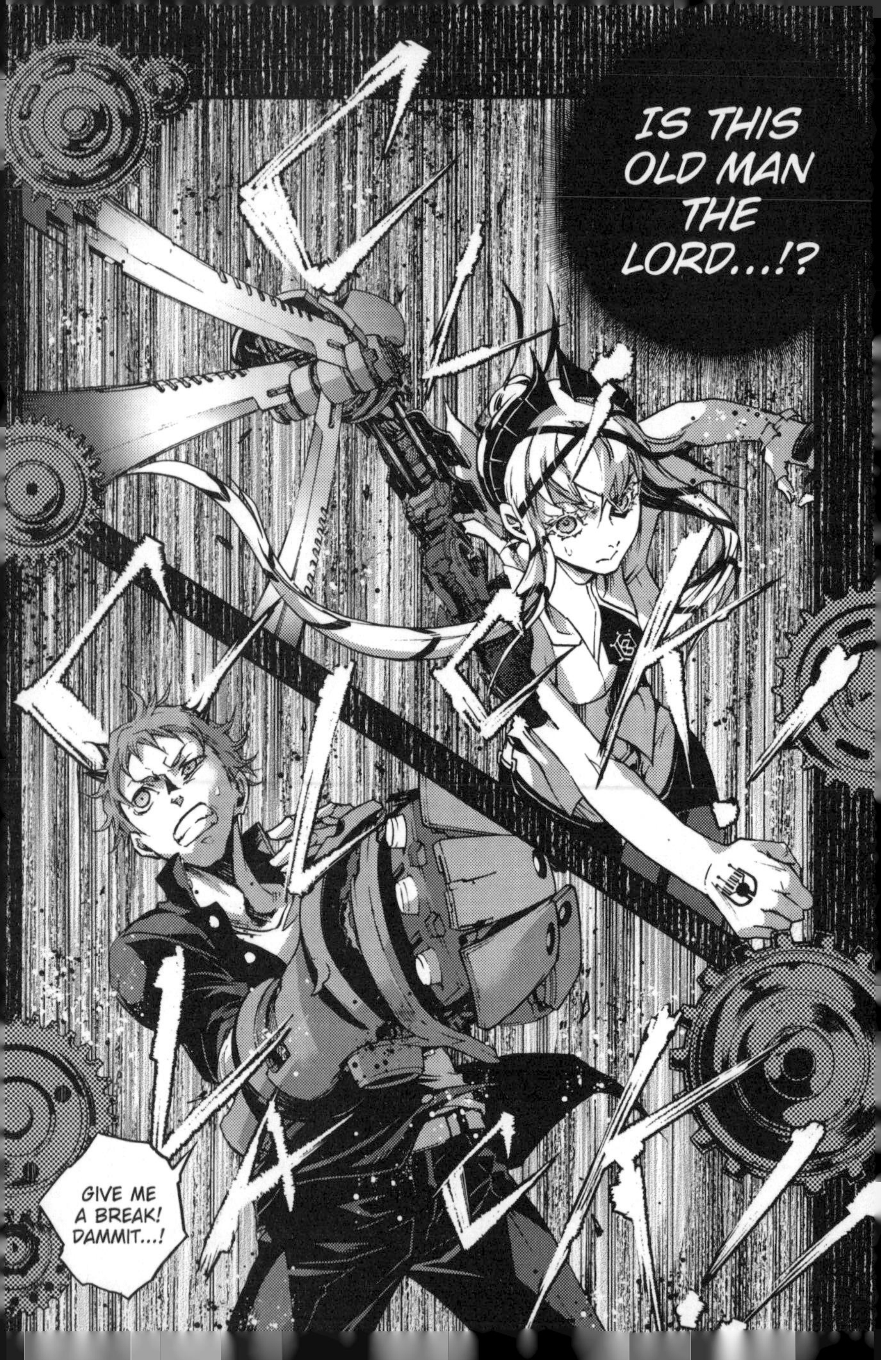
IS THIS OLD MAN THE LORD...!?
GIVE ME A BREAK! DAMMIT...!

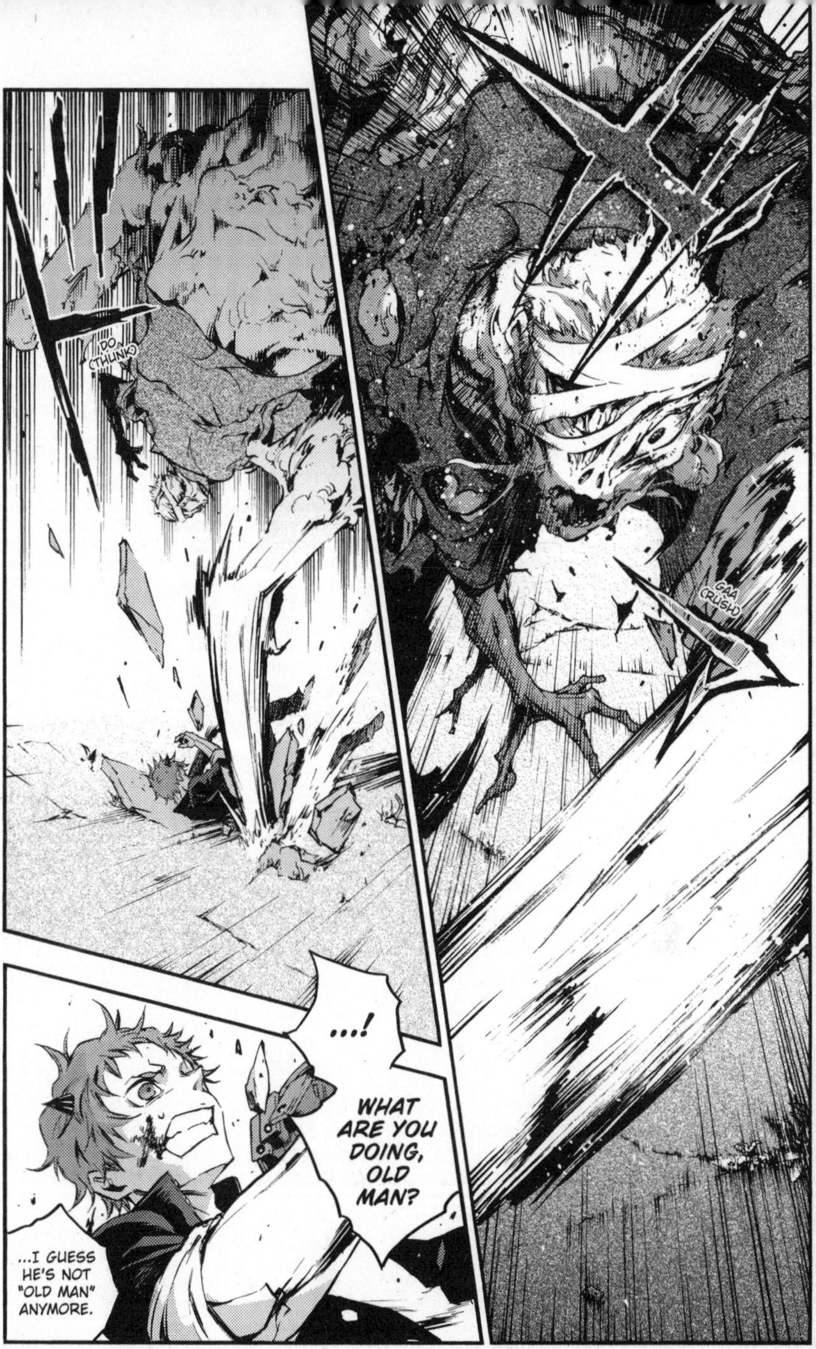
GAA (RUSH)
DO (THUNK)
...!
WHAT ARE YOU DOING, OLD MAN?
...I GUESS HE'S NOT "OLD MAN" ANYMORE.

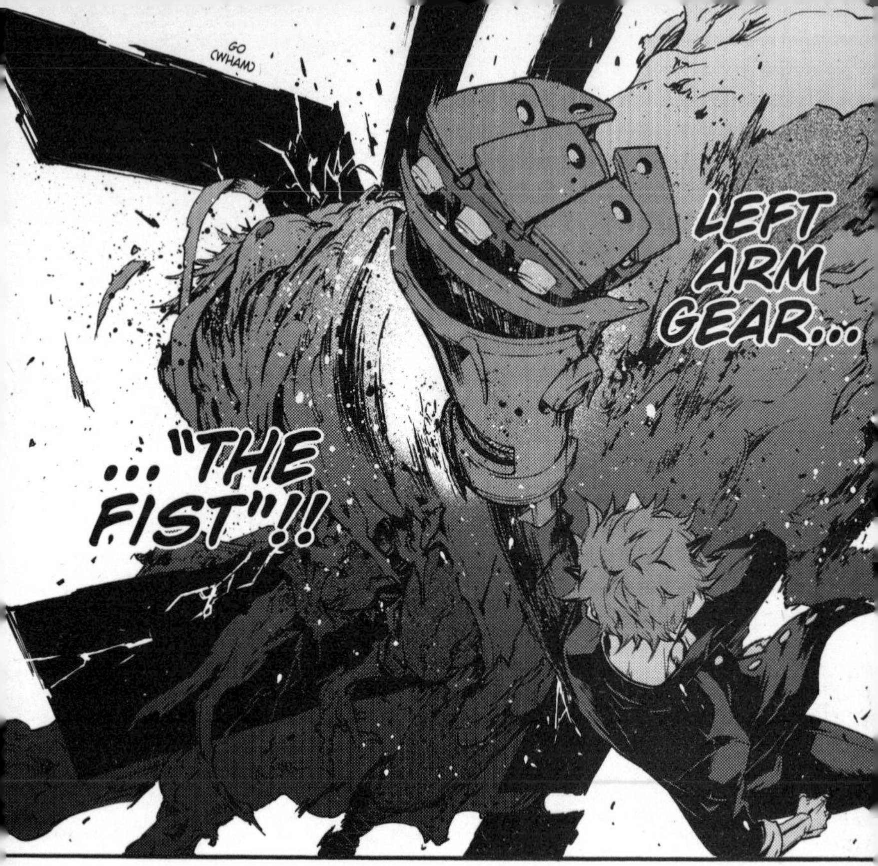
LEFT ARM GEAR...
GO (WHAM)
..."THE FIST"!!

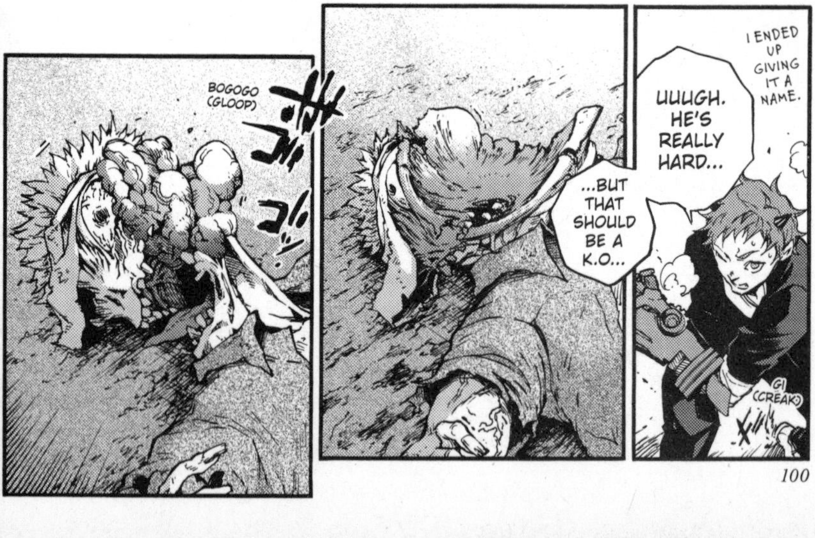
I ENDED UP GIVING IT A NAME.
UUUGH. HE'S REALLY HARD...
...BUT THAT SHOULD BE A K.O...
GI (CREAK)
BOGOGO (GLOOP)

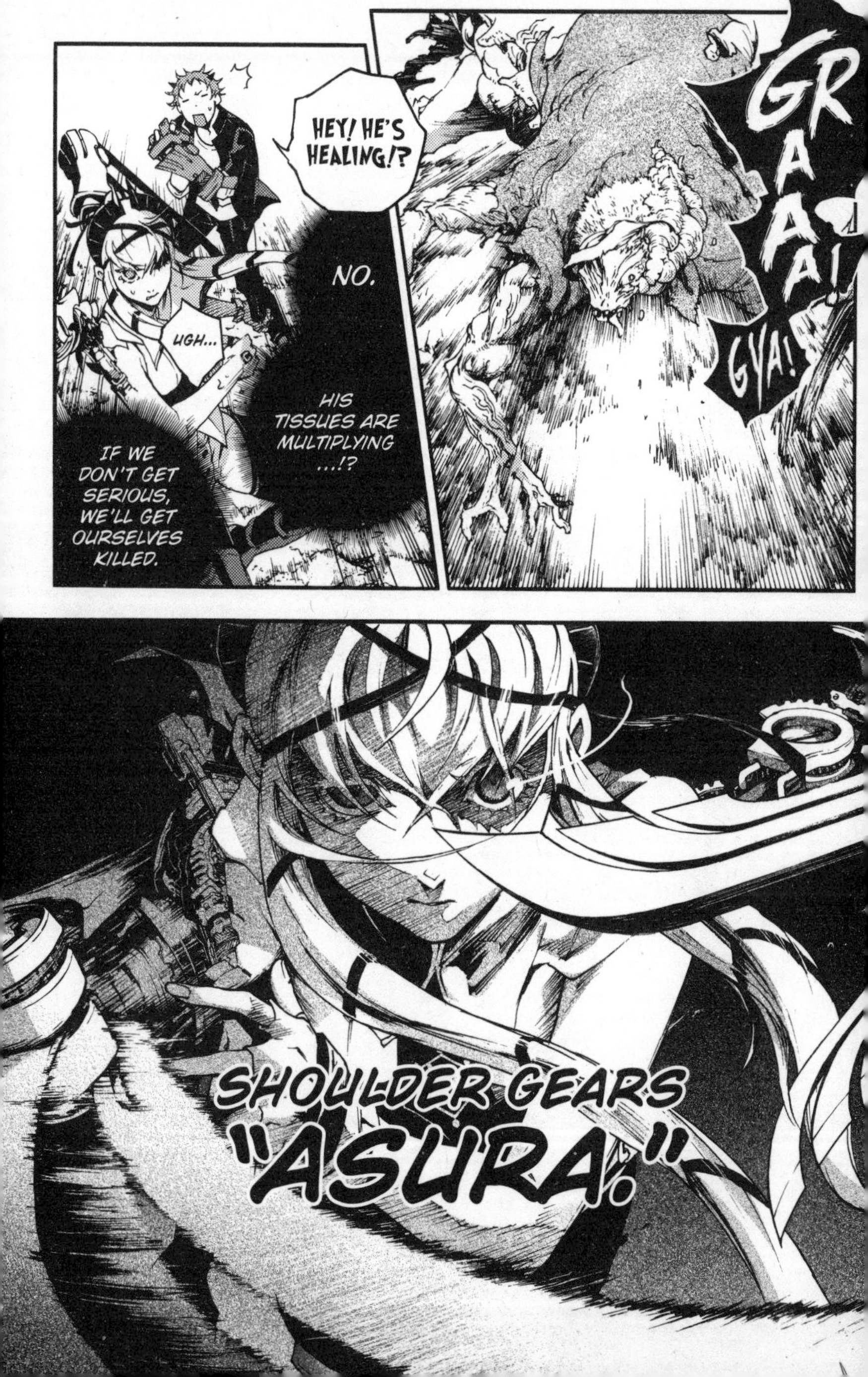
GRAAA!
GYA!
HEY! HE'S HEALING!?
NO.
HIS TISSUES ARE MULTIPLYING ...!?
UGH...
IF WE DON'T GET SERIOUS, WE'LL GET OURSELVES KILLED.
SHOULDER GEARS "ASURA."

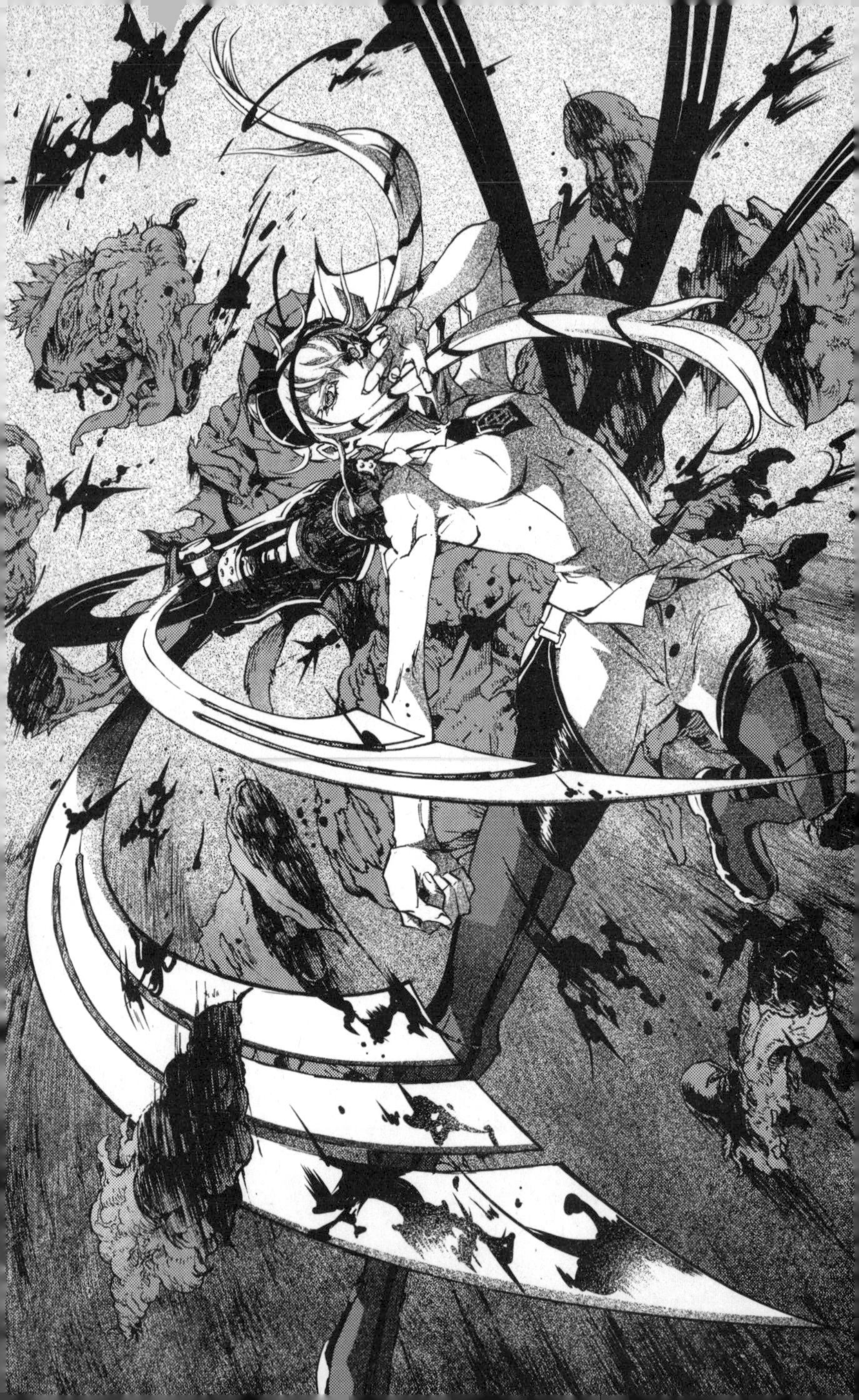

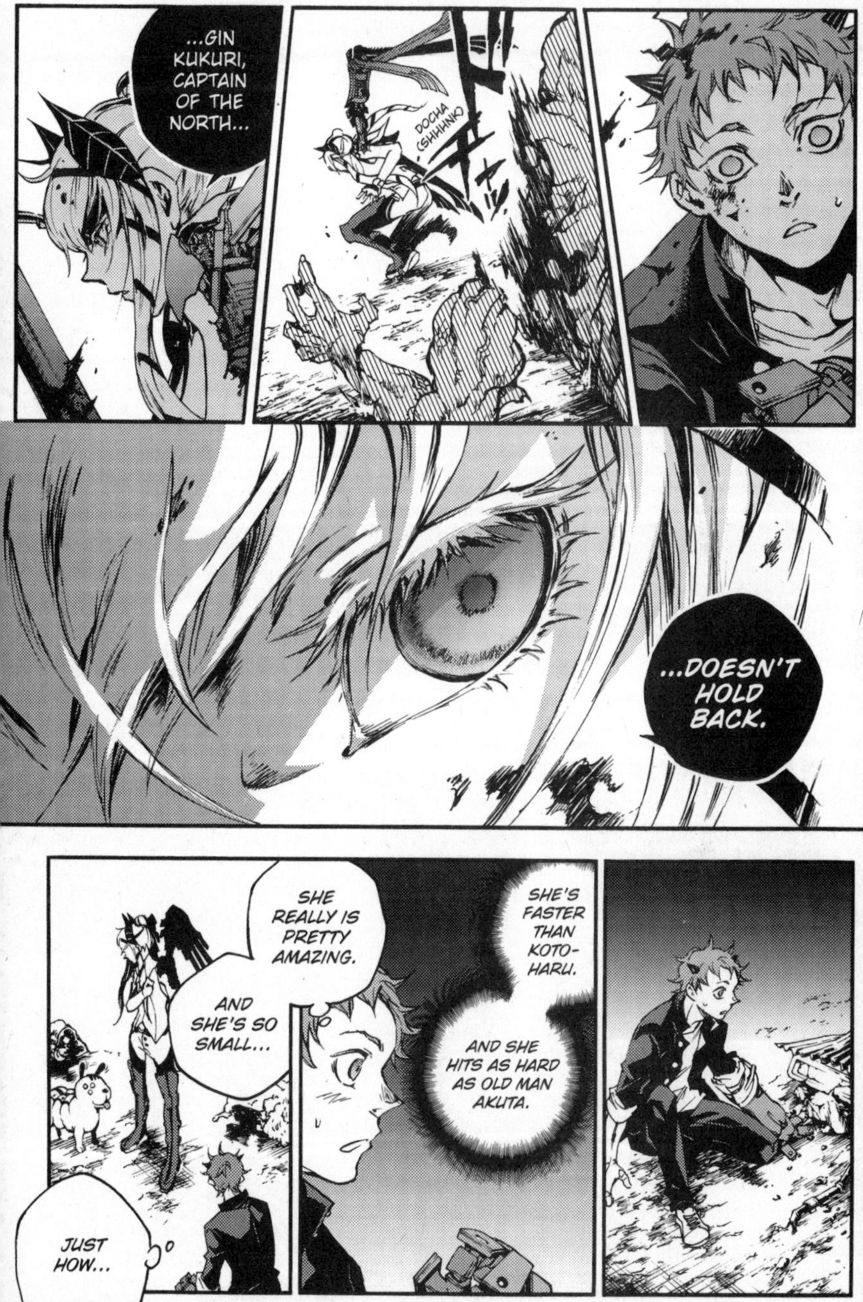
DOCHA (SHHHNK)
...GIN KUKURI, CAPTAIN OF THE NORTH...
...DOESN'T HOLD BACK.
SHE REALLY IS PRETTY AMAZING.
SHE'S FASTER THAN KOTO-HARU.
AND SHE HITS AS HARD AS OLD MAN AKUTA.
AND SHE'S SO SMALL...
JUST HOW...

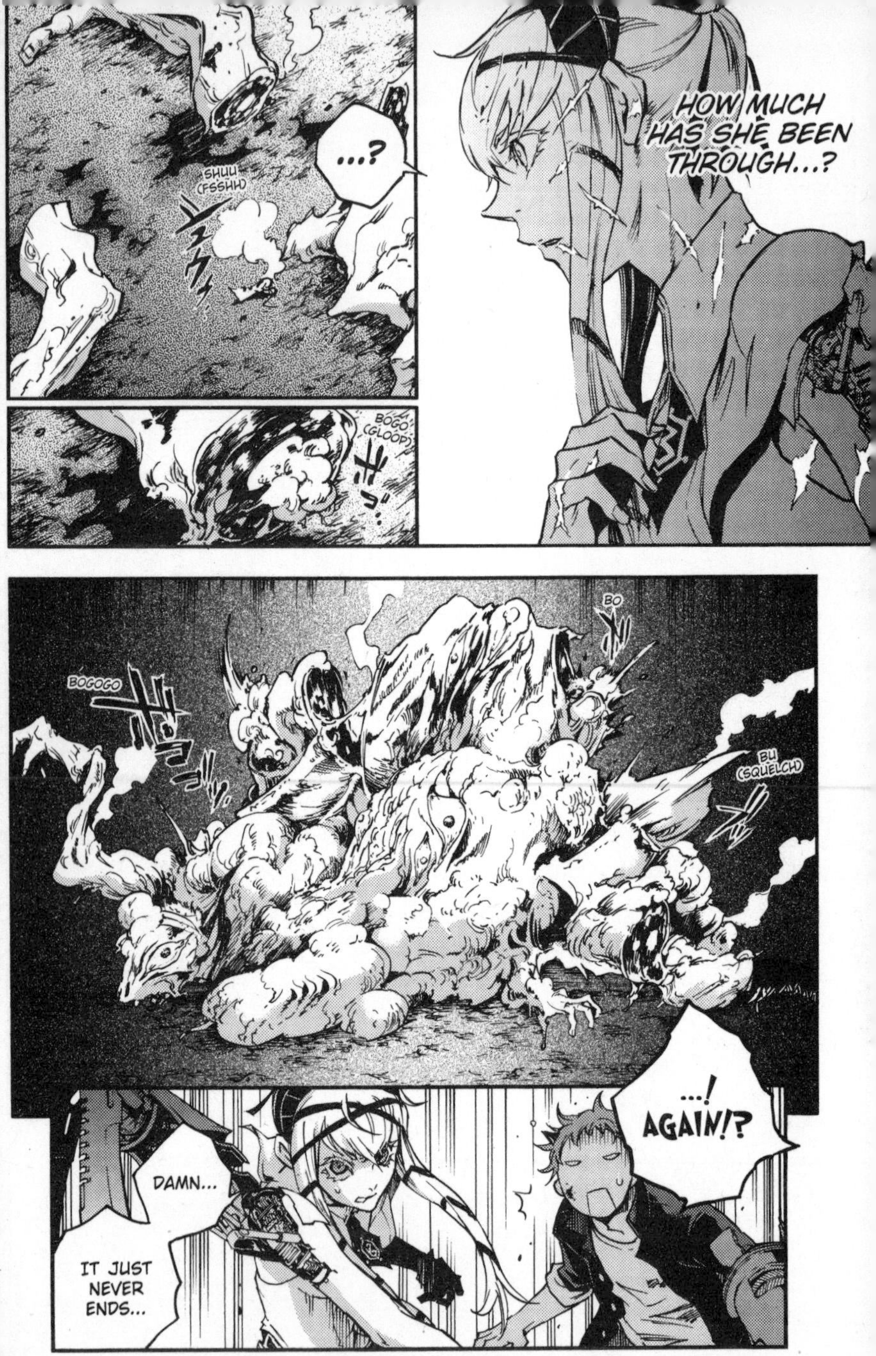
HOW MUCH HAS SHE BEEN THROUGH...?
...?
SHUU (FSSHH)
BOGO (GLOOP)
BO
BU (SQUELCH)
BOGOGO
...! AGAIN!?
DAMN...
IT JUST NEVER ENDS...

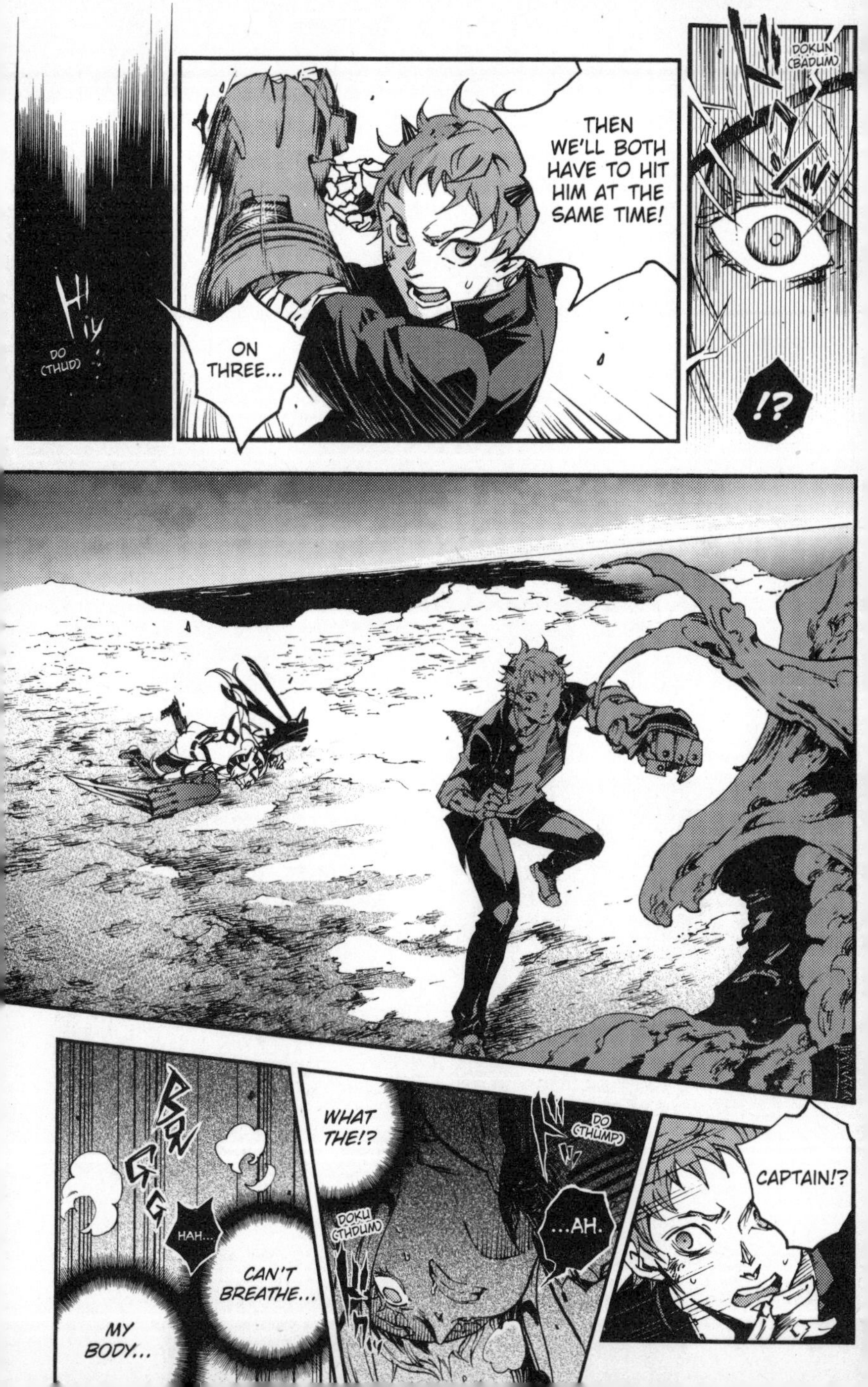
DOKUN (BADUM)
!?
THEN WE'LL BOTH HAVE TO HIT HIM AT THE SAME TIME!
ON THREE...
DO (THUD)
CAPTAIN!?
DO (THUMP)
WHAT THE!?
...AH.
DOKU (THDUM)
HAH...
CAN'T BREATHE...
MY BODY...

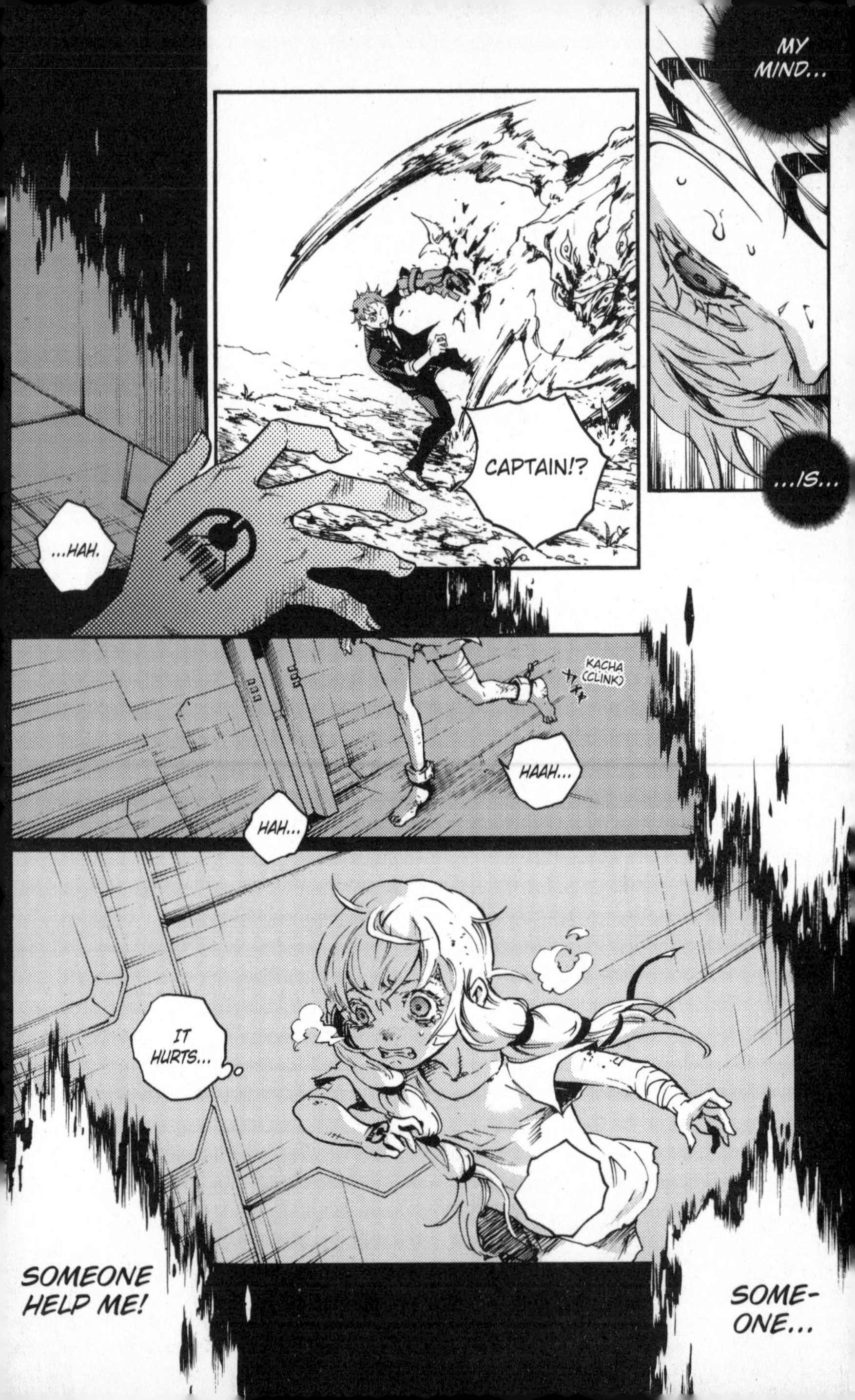
MY MIND...
...IS...
CAPTAIN!?
...HAH.
KACHA (CLINK)
HAAH...
HAH...
IT HURTS...
SOME-ONE...
SOMEONE HELP ME!

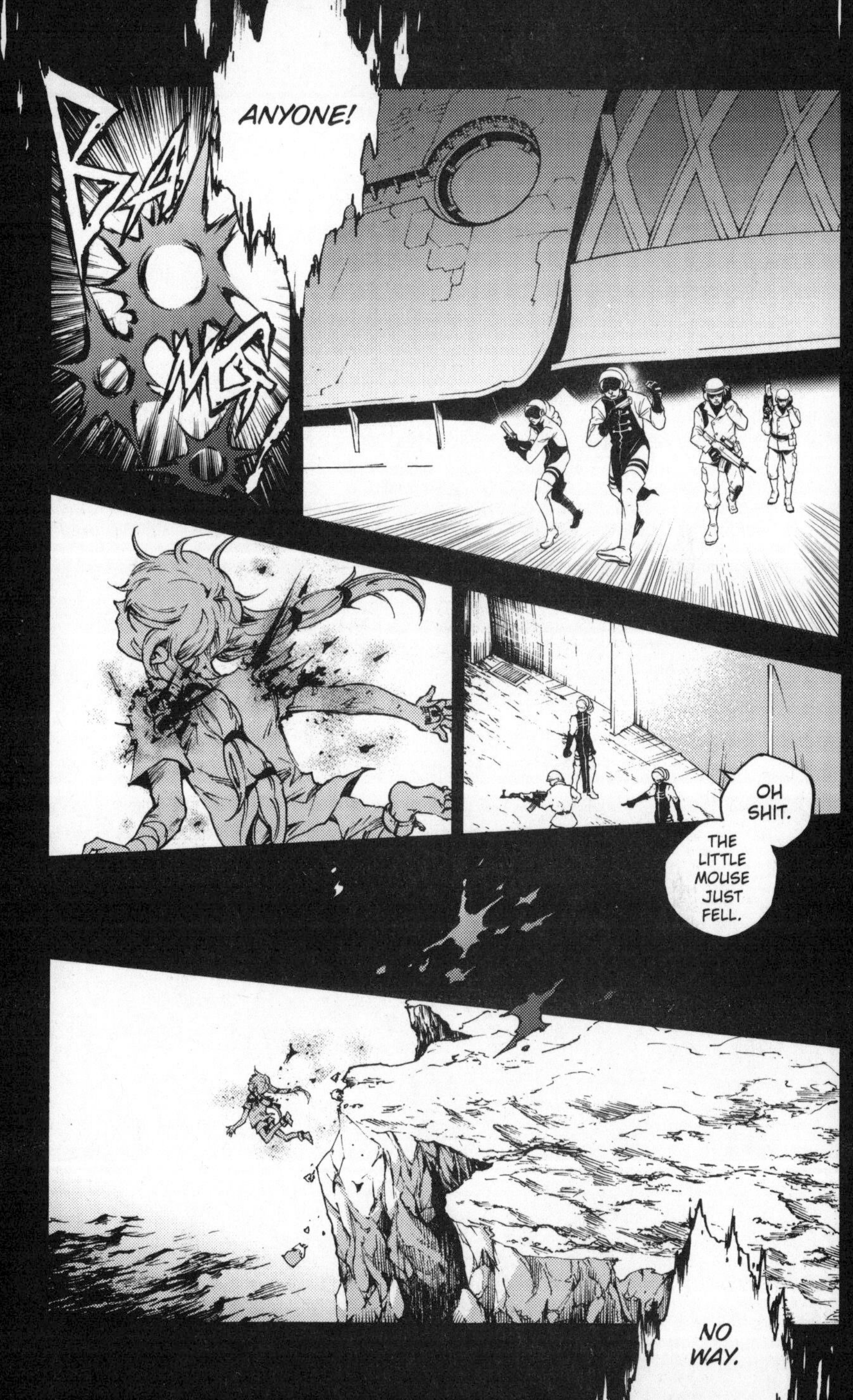
ANYONE!
BAM
BANG
OH SHIT.
THE LITTLE MOUSE JUST FELL.
NO WAY.

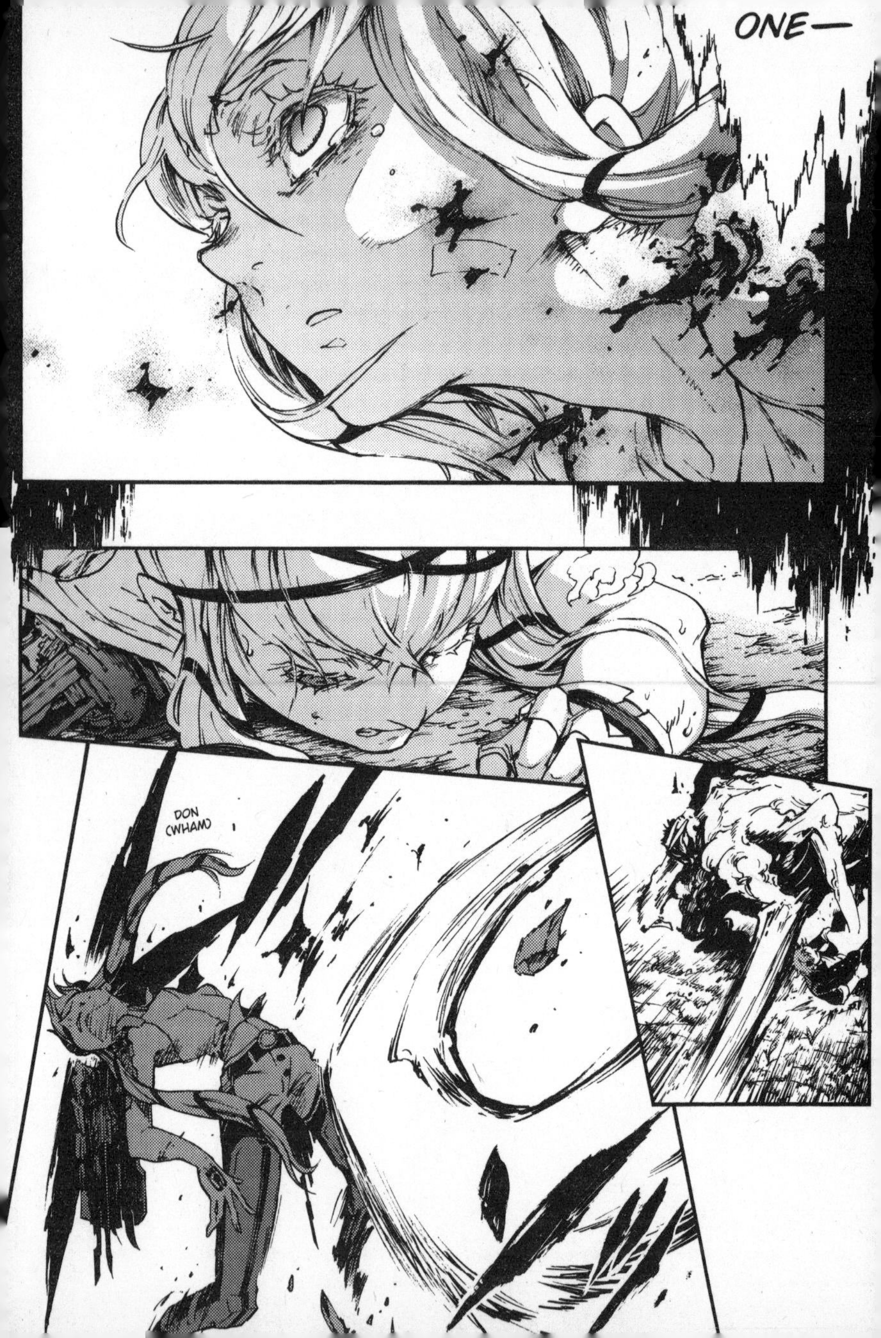
ONE—
DON
(WHAM)

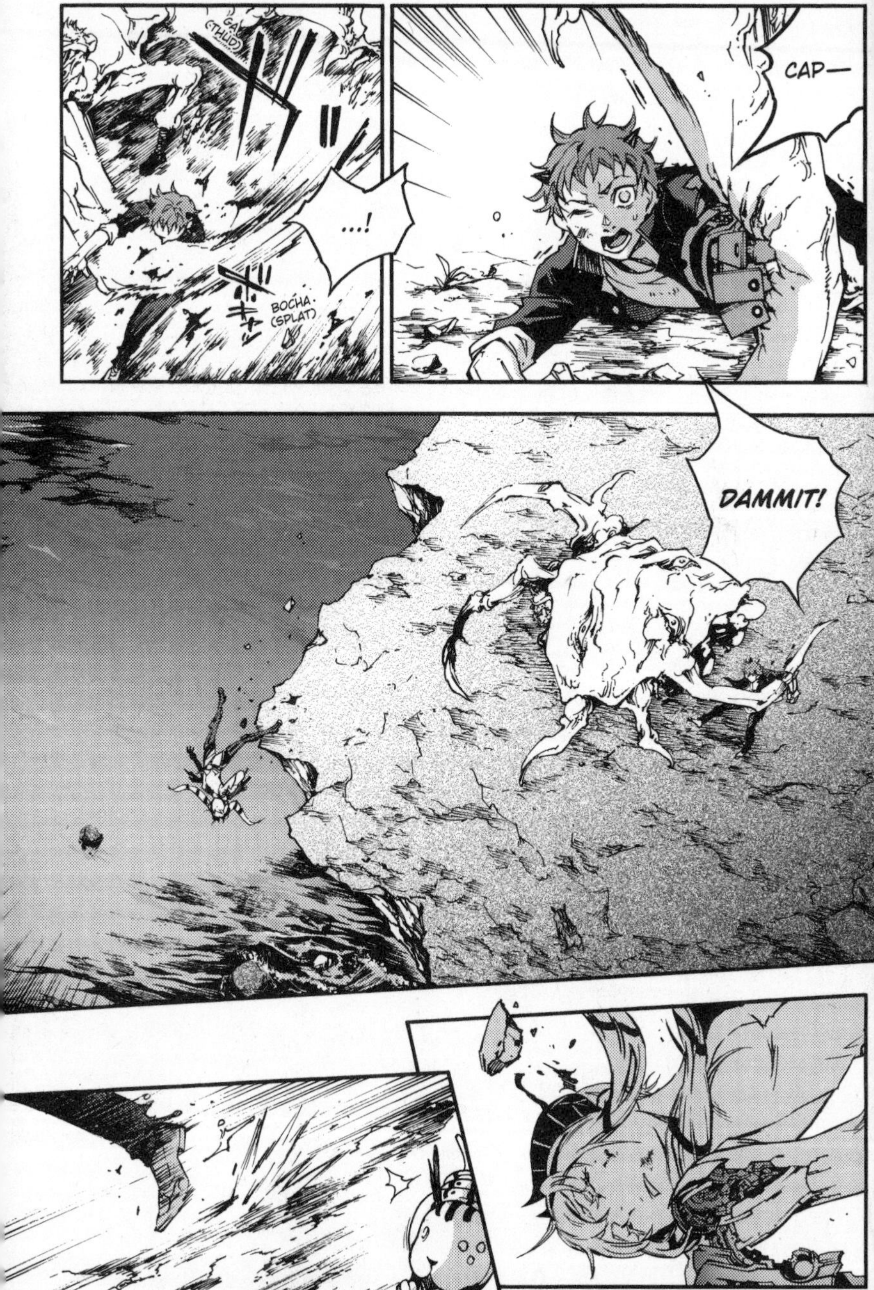
CAP—
GA (THUD)
...!
BOCHA (SPLAT)
DAMMIT!

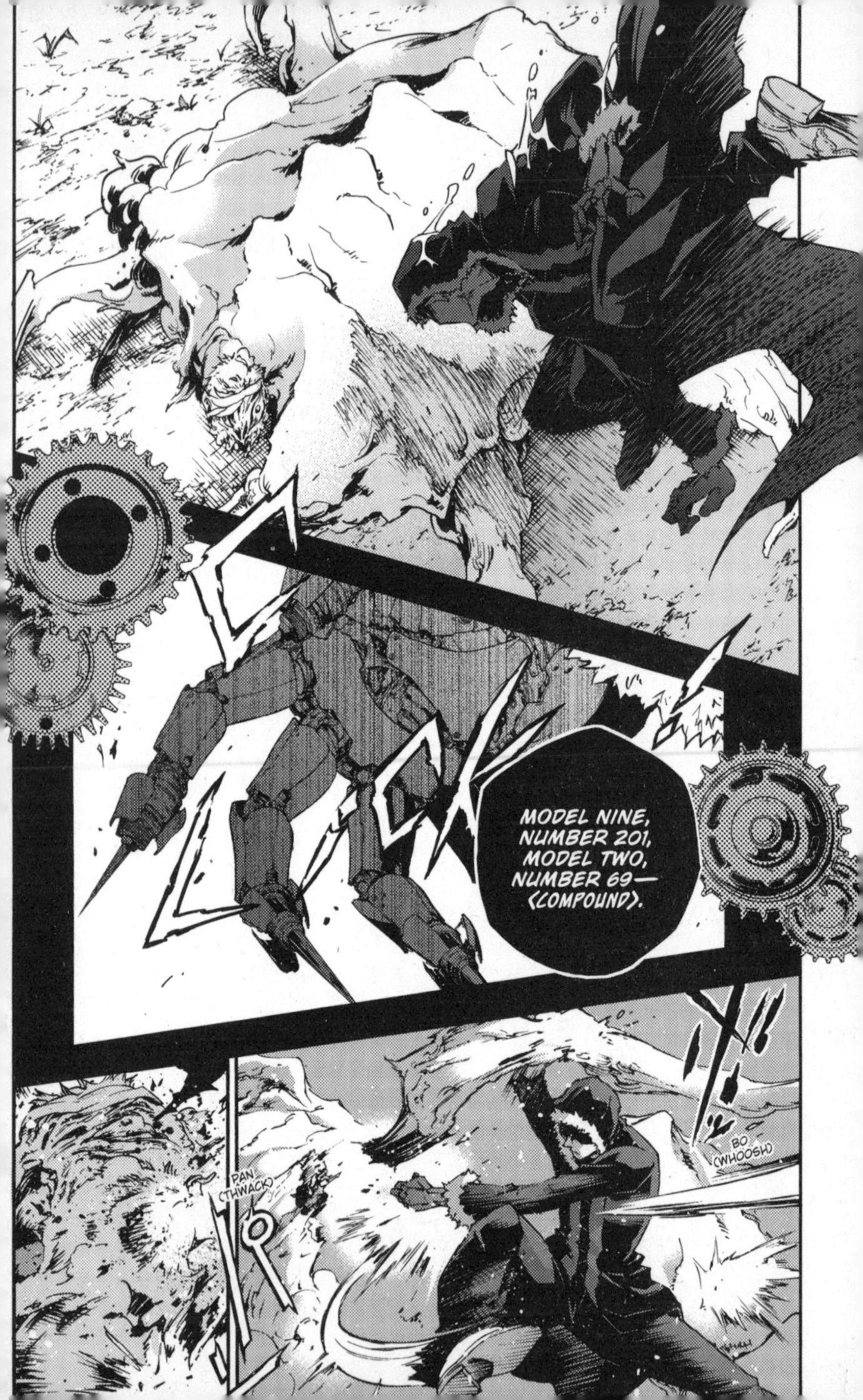
MODEL NINE,
NUMBER 201,
MODEL TWO,
NUMBER 69—
⟨COMPOUND⟩.
BO
(WHOOSH)
PAN
(THWACK)

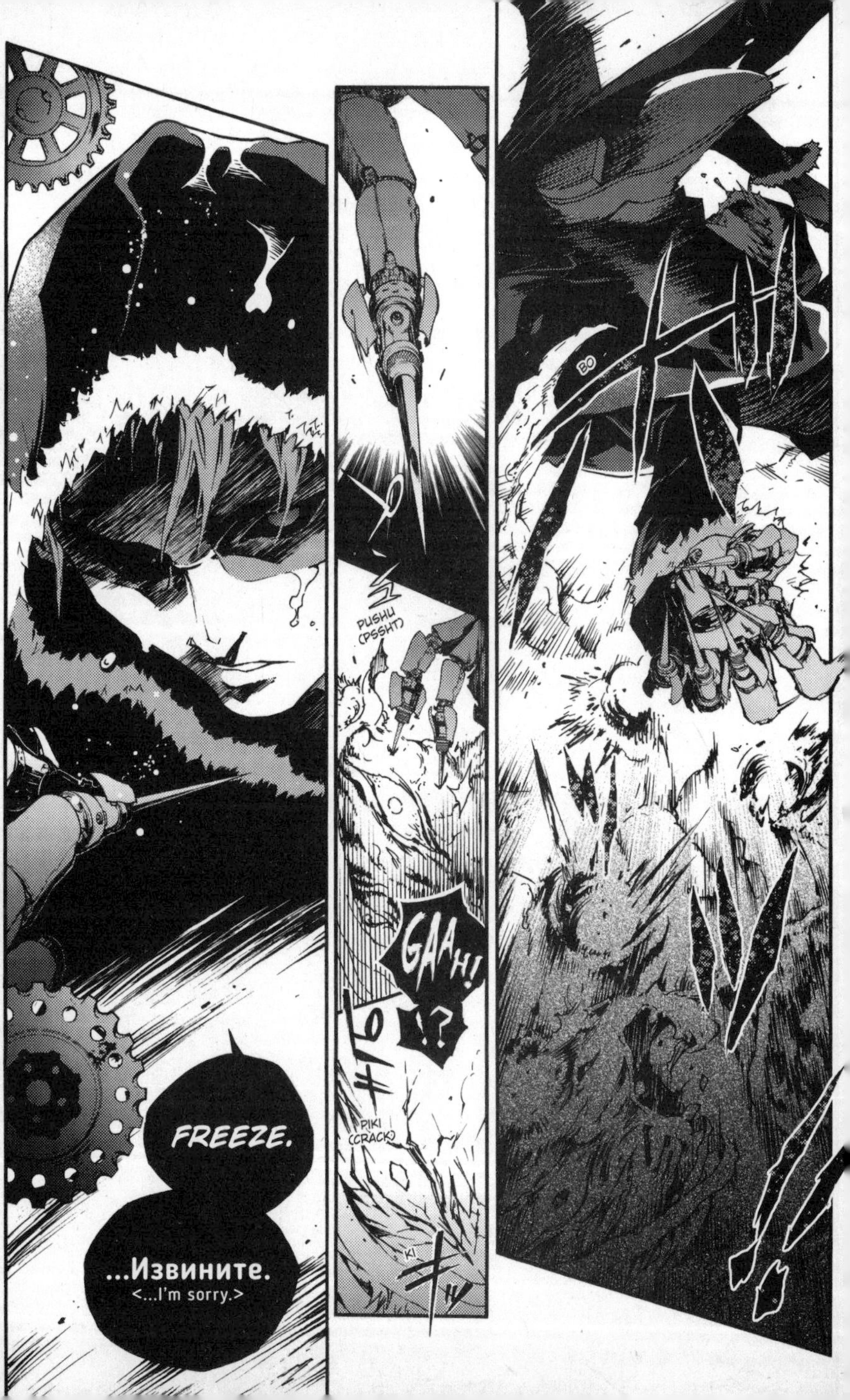
BO
PUSHU
(PSSHT)
GAAH!
!?
PIKI
(CRACK)
KI
FREEZE.
...Извините.
<...I'm sorry.>

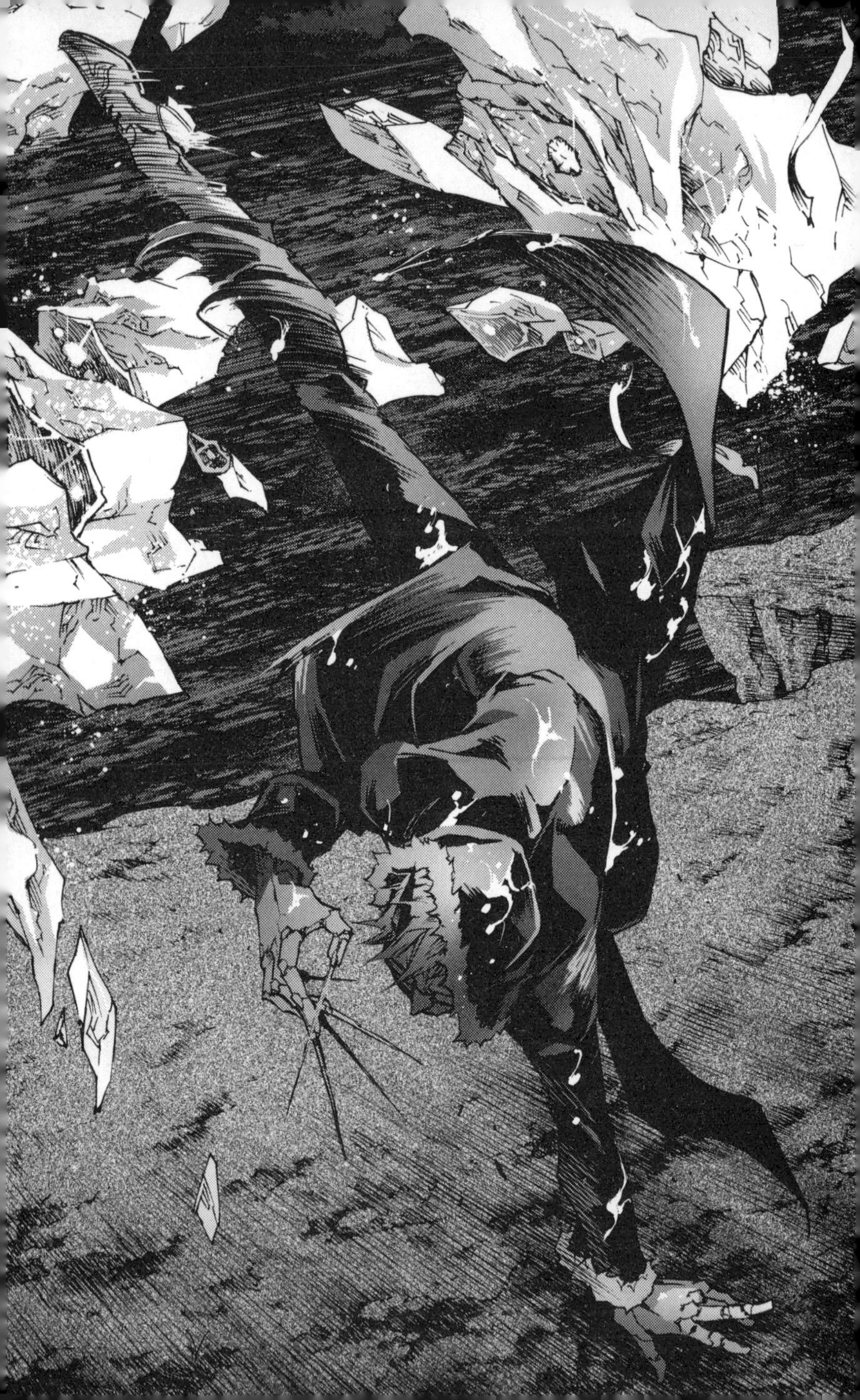

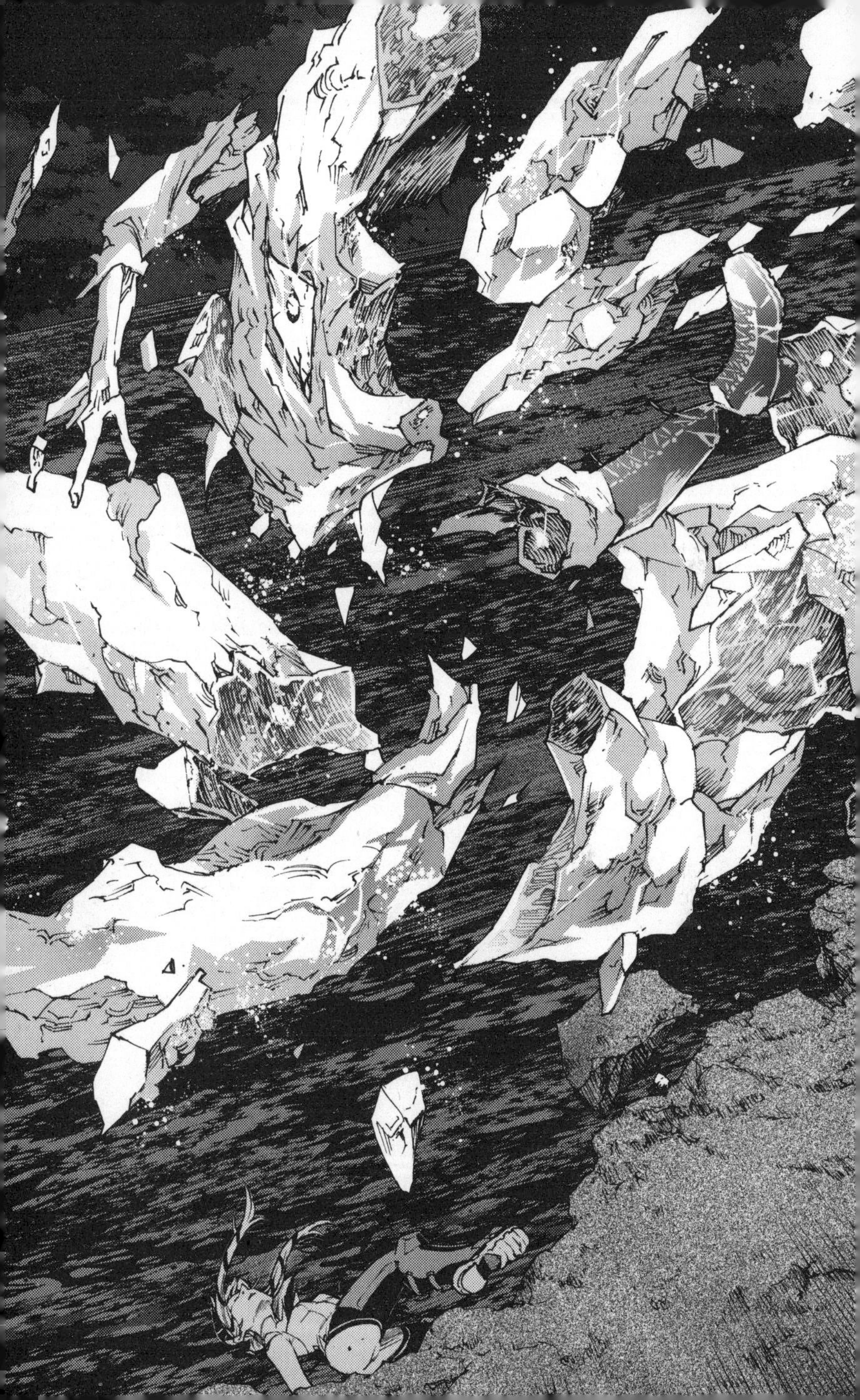

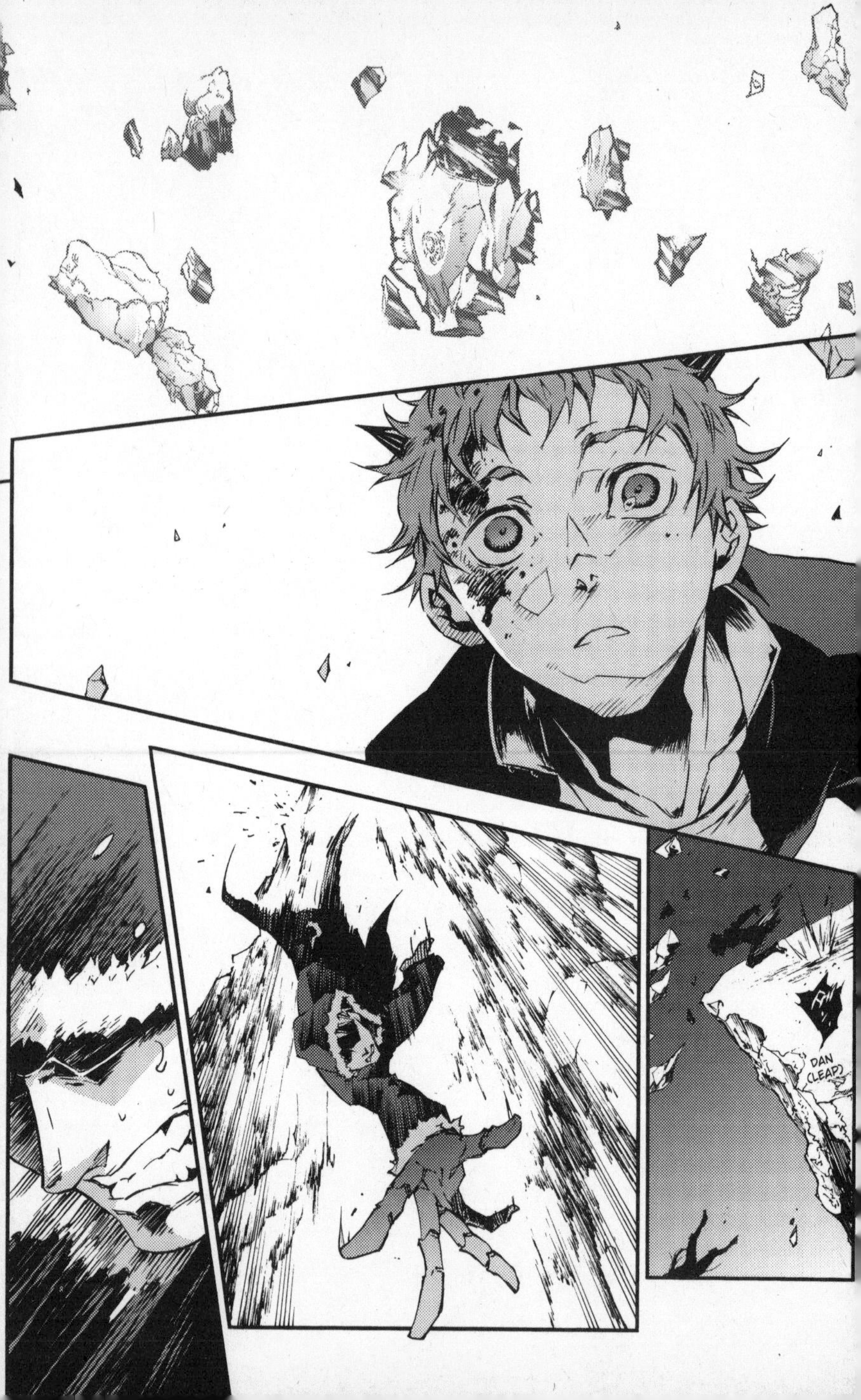

DAN
(LEAP)

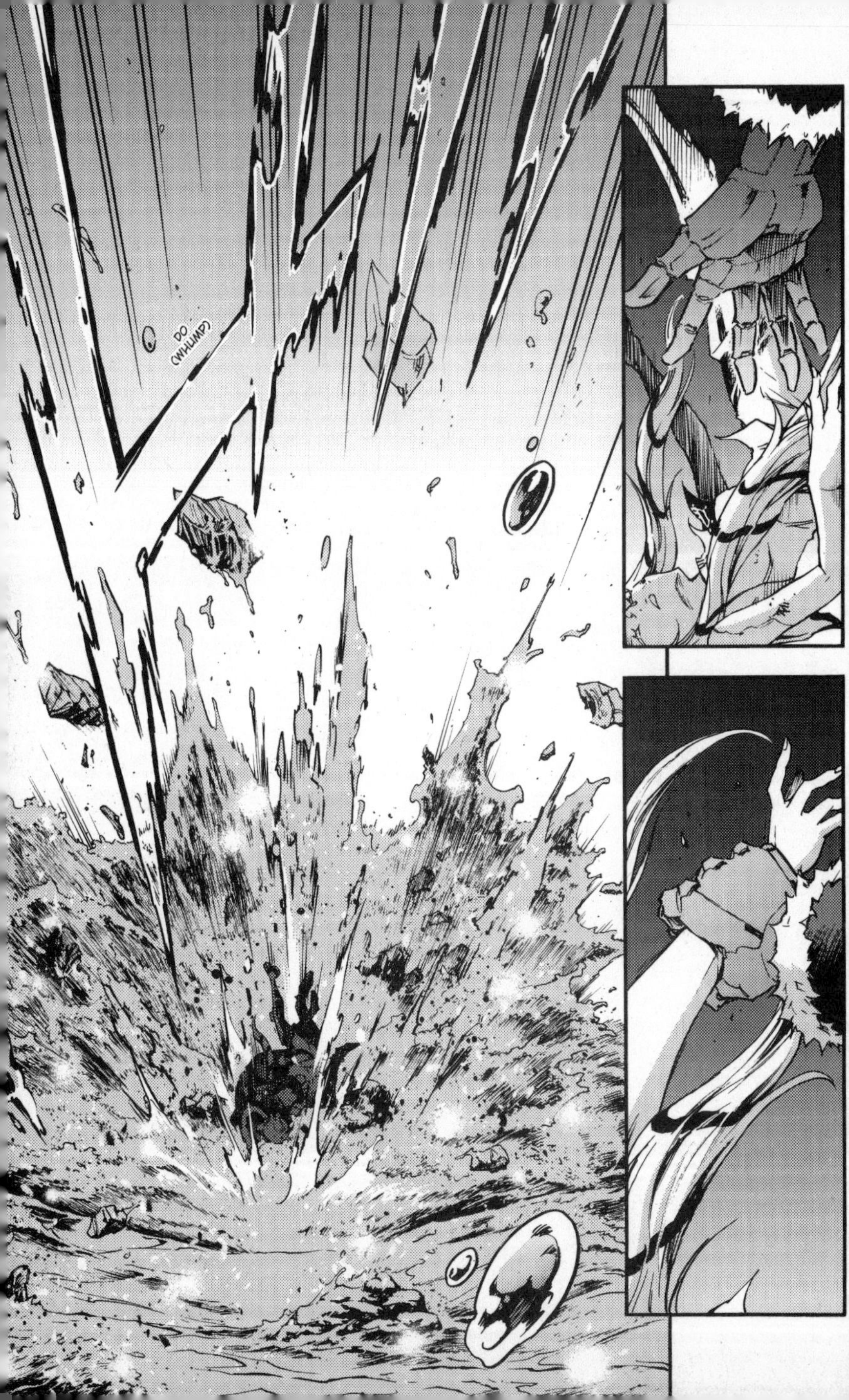
DO
(WHUMP)

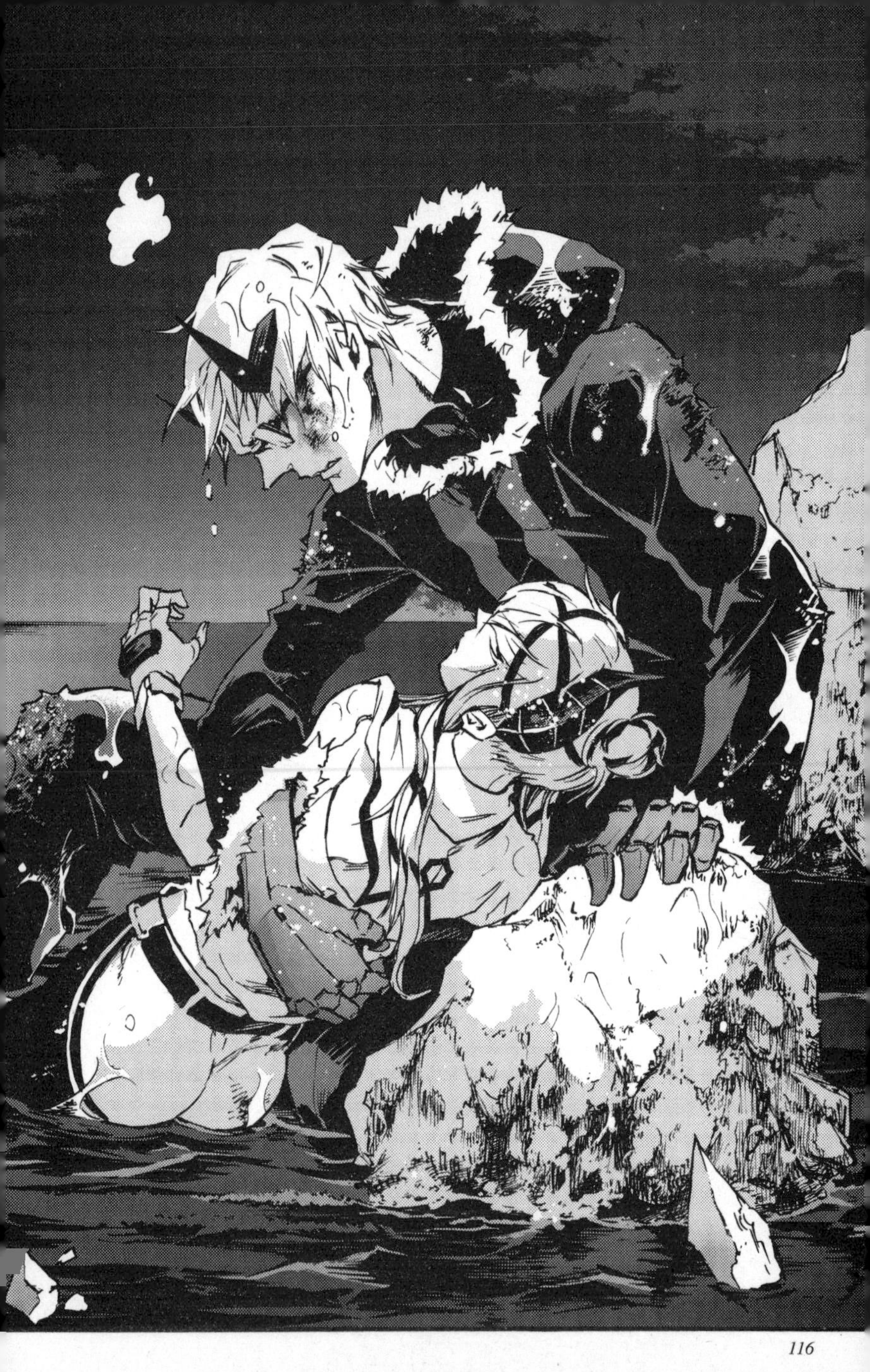

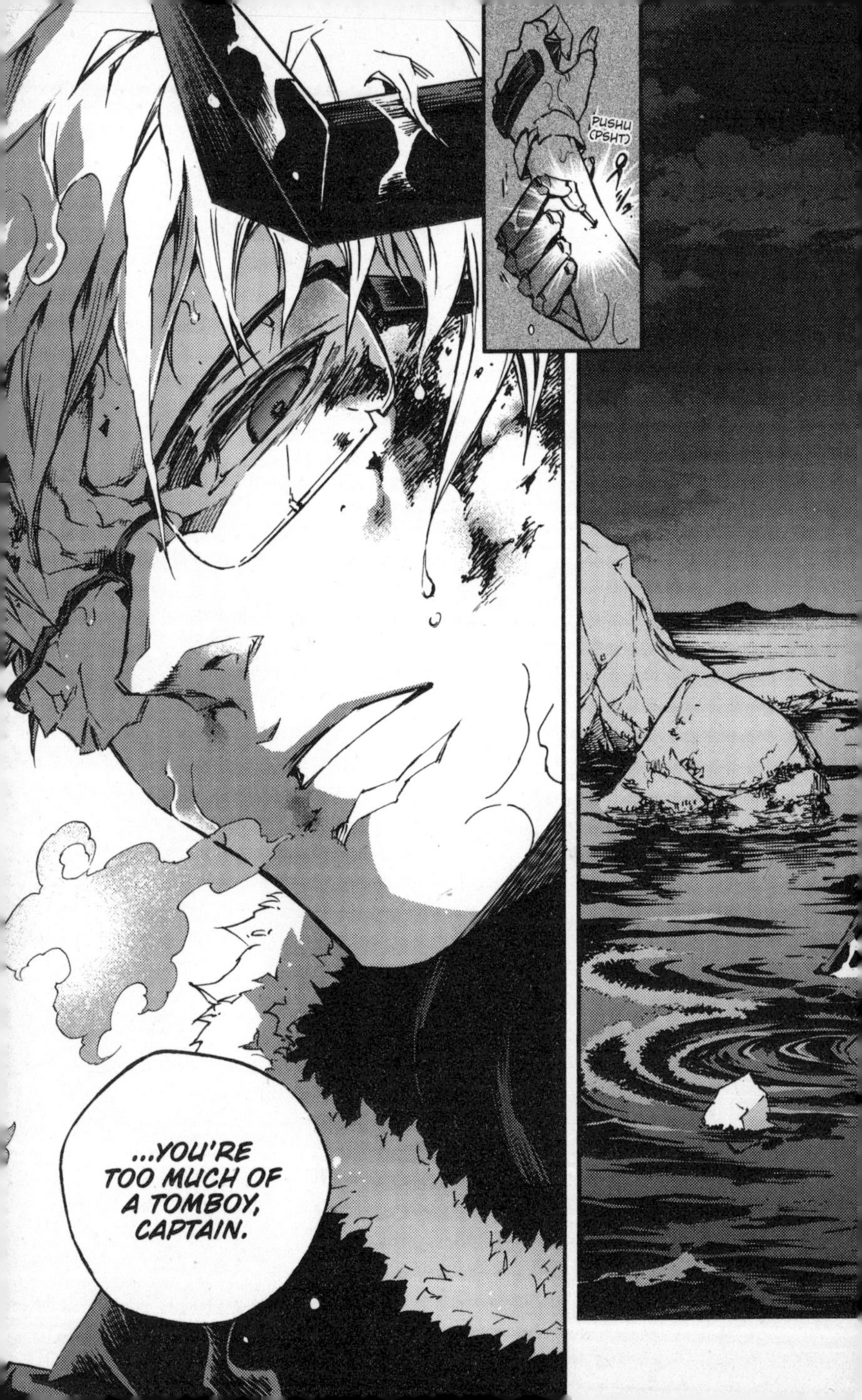
PUSHU
(PSHT)
...YOU'RE TOO MUCH OF A TOMBOY, CAPTAIN.

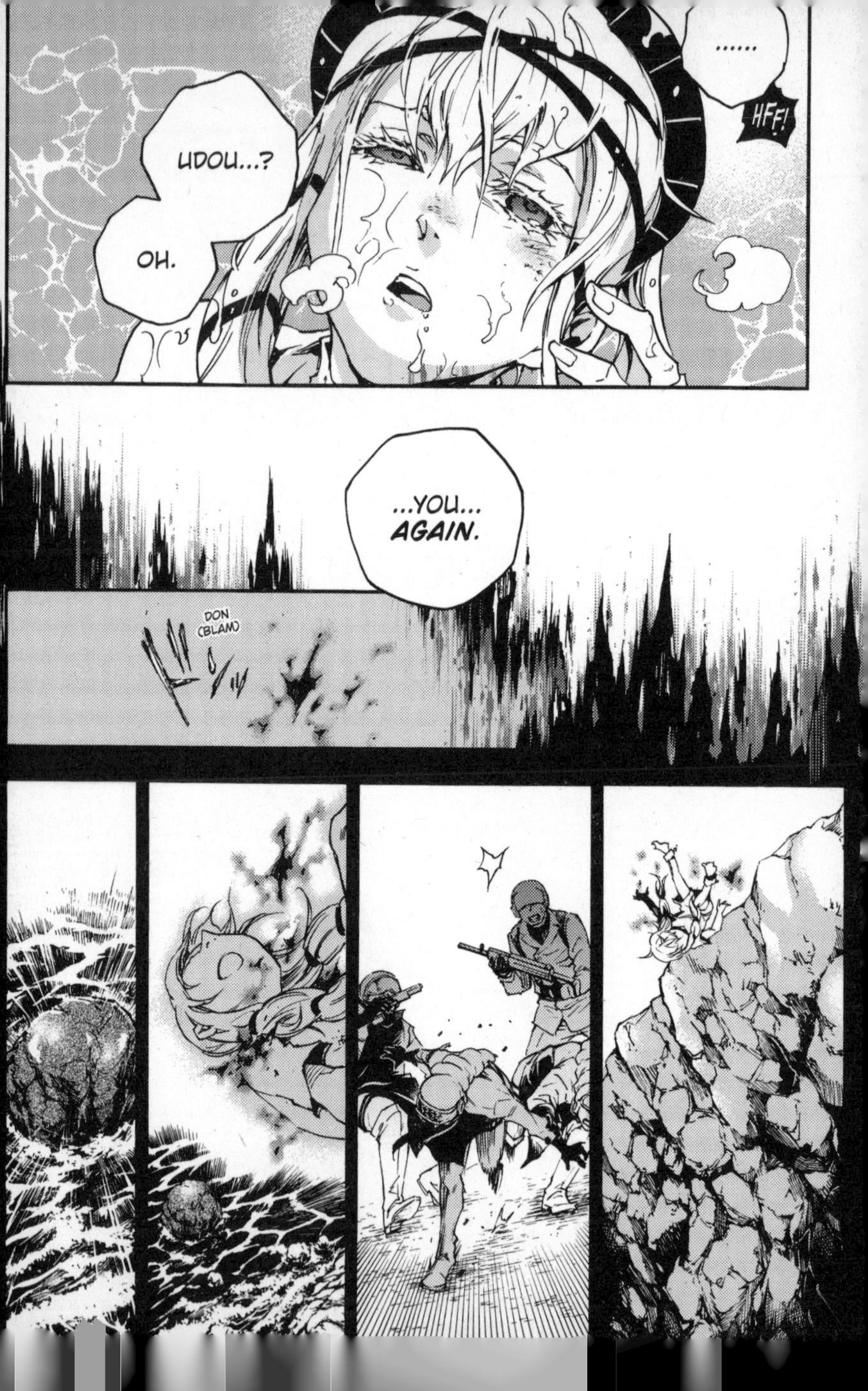
......
HFF!
UDOU...?
OH.
...YOU... AGAIN.
DON
(BLAM)

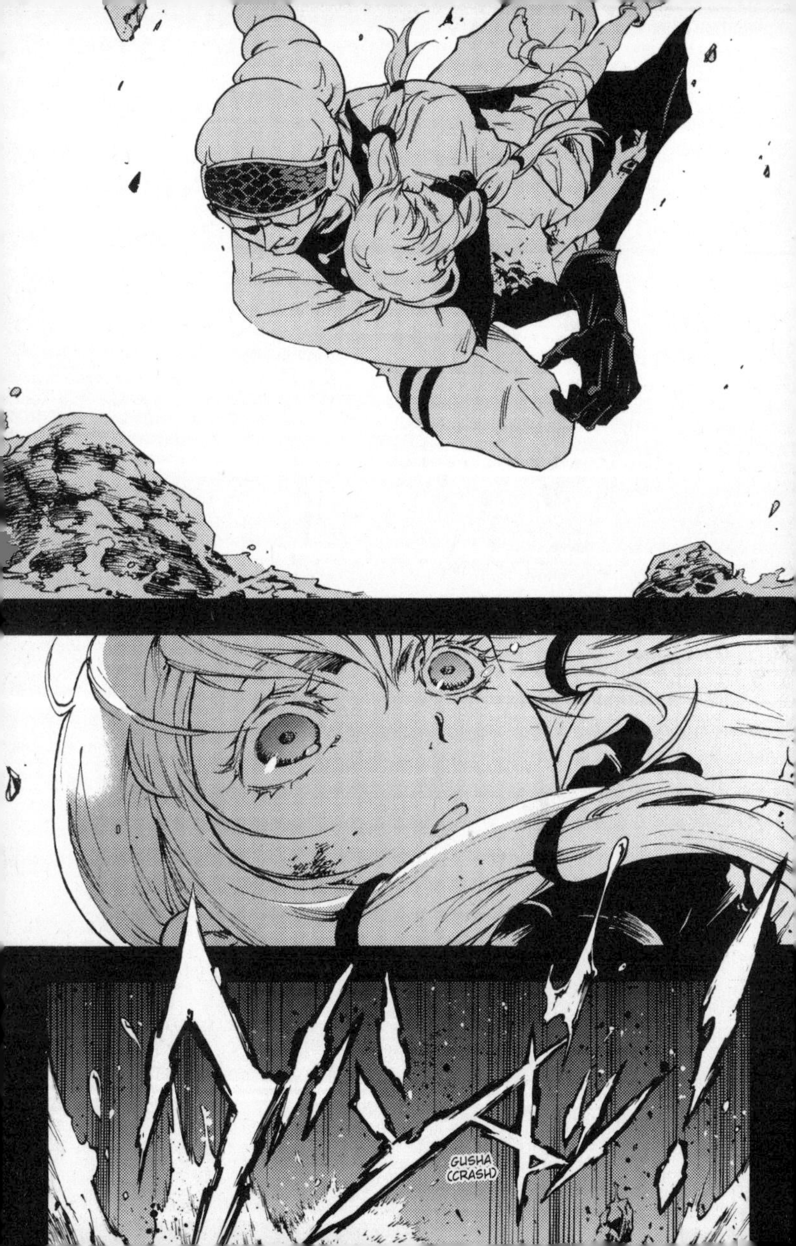
GUSHA
(CRASH)

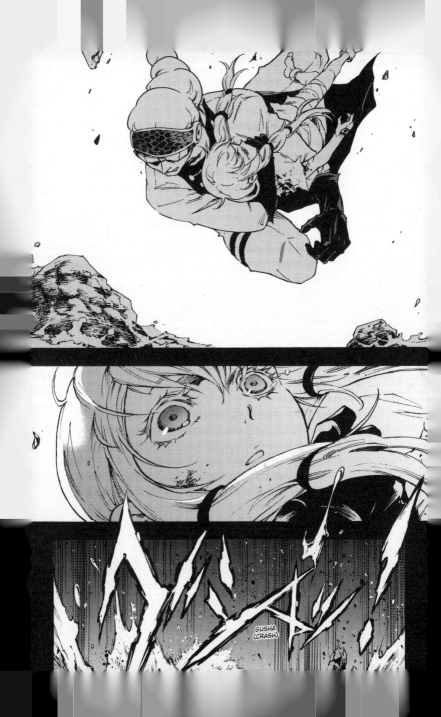

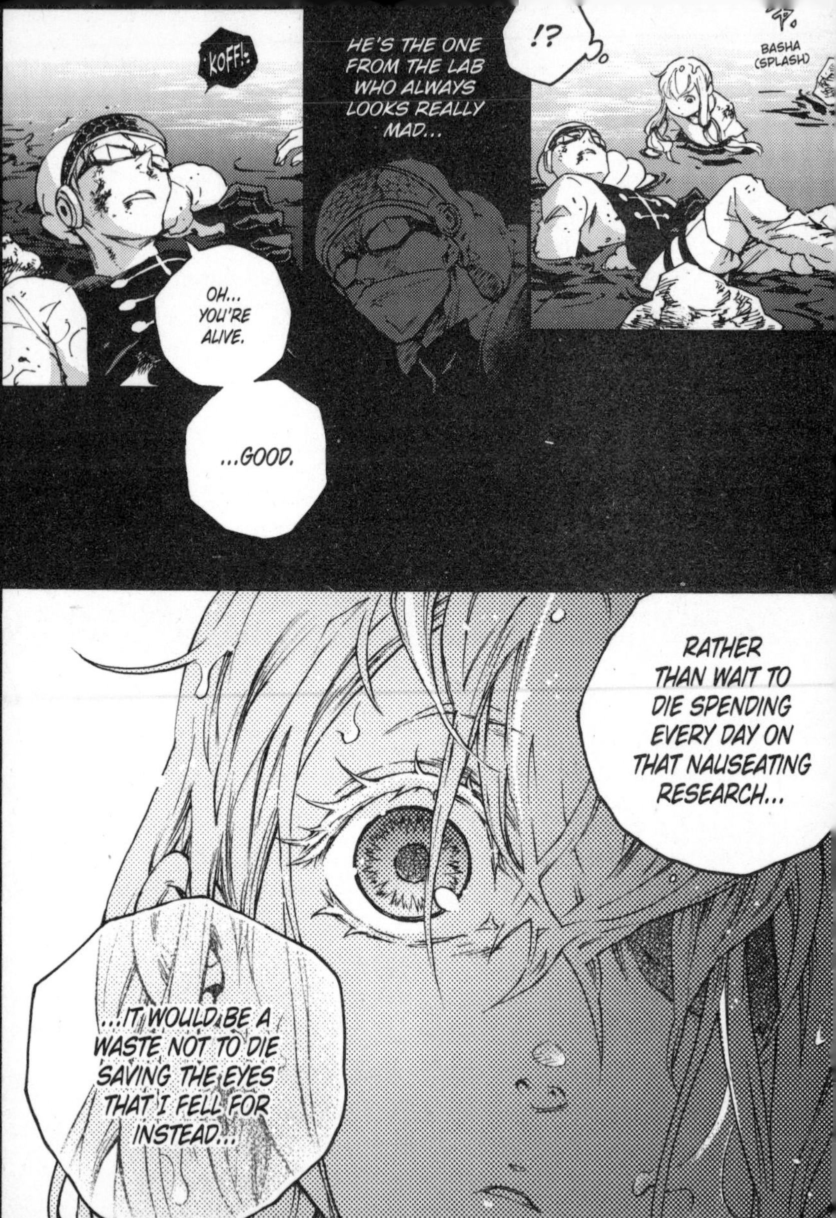
!?
BASHA (SPLASH)
HE'S THE ONE FROM THE LAB WHO ALWAYS LOOKS REALLY MAD...
KOFF!
OH... YOU'RE ALIVE.
...GOOD.
RATHER THAN WAIT TO DIE SPENDING EVERY DAY ON THAT NAUSEATING RESEARCH...
...IT WOULD BE A WASTE NOT TO DIE SAVING THE EYES THAT I FELL FOR INSTEAD...

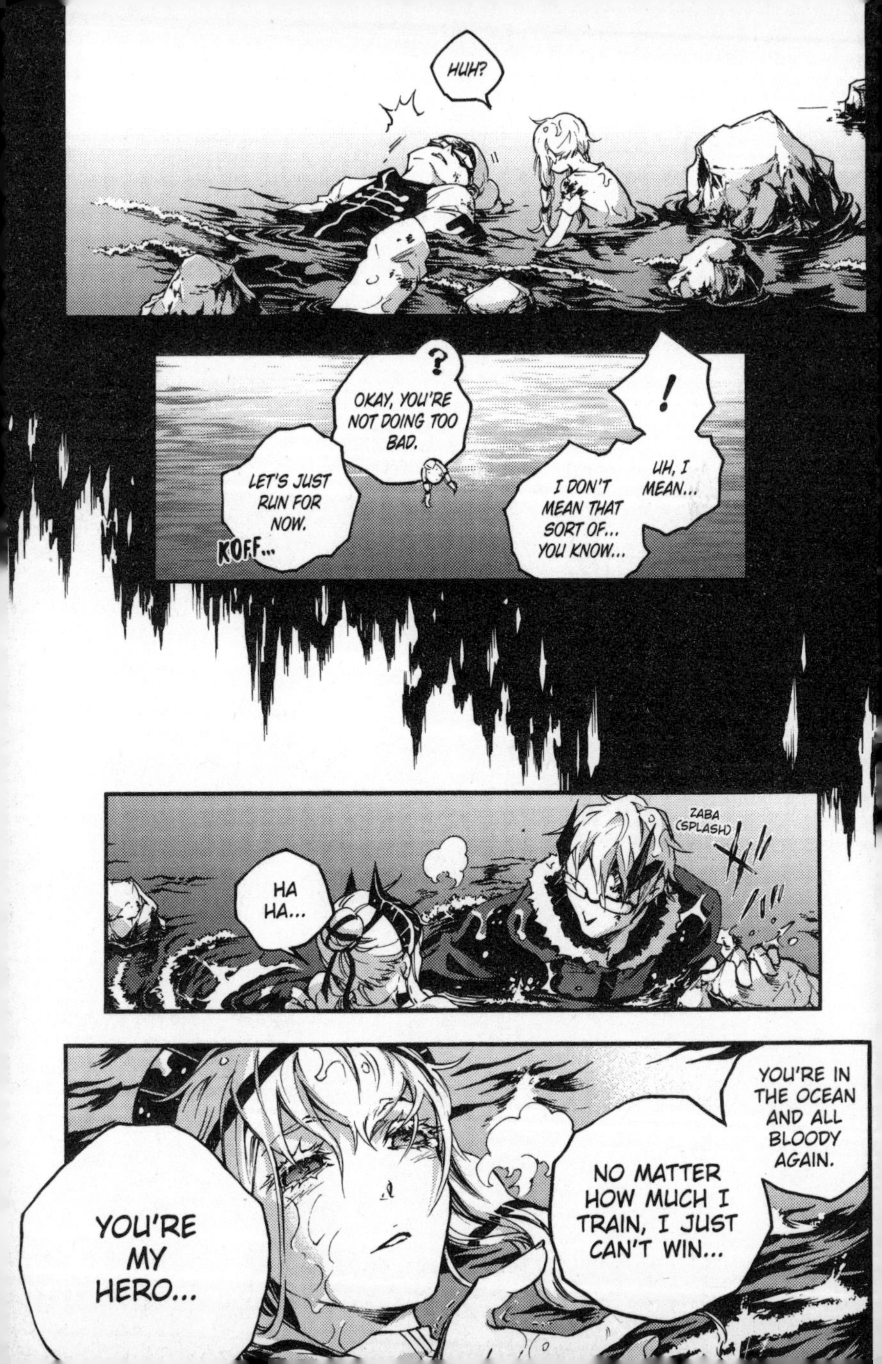
HUH?
!
UH, I MEAN...
I DON'T MEAN THAT SORT OF... YOU KNOW...
?
OKAY, YOU'RE NOT DOING TOO BAD.
LET'S JUST RUN FOR NOW.
KOFF...
ZABA (SPLASH)
HA HA...
YOU'RE IN THE OCEAN AND ALL BLOODY AGAIN.
NO MATTER HOW MUCH I TRAIN, I JUST CAN'T WIN...
YOU'RE MY HERO...

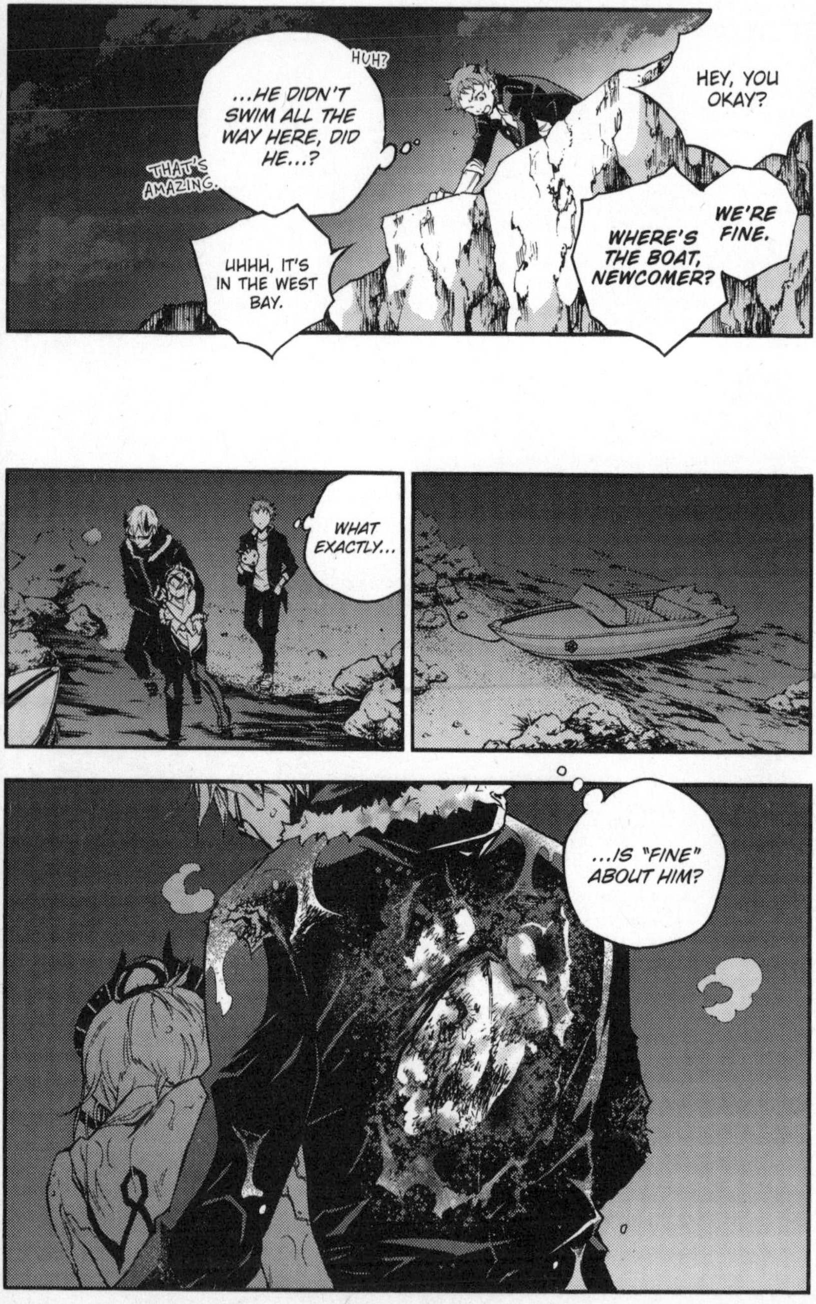
HEY, YOU OKAY?
WE'RE FINE.
WHERE'S THE BOAT, NEWCOMER?
HUH?
...HE DIDN'T SWIM ALL THE WAY HERE, DID HE...?
THAT'S AMAZING.
UHHH, IT'S IN THE WEST BAY.
WHAT EXACTLY...
...IS "FINE" ABOUT HIM?

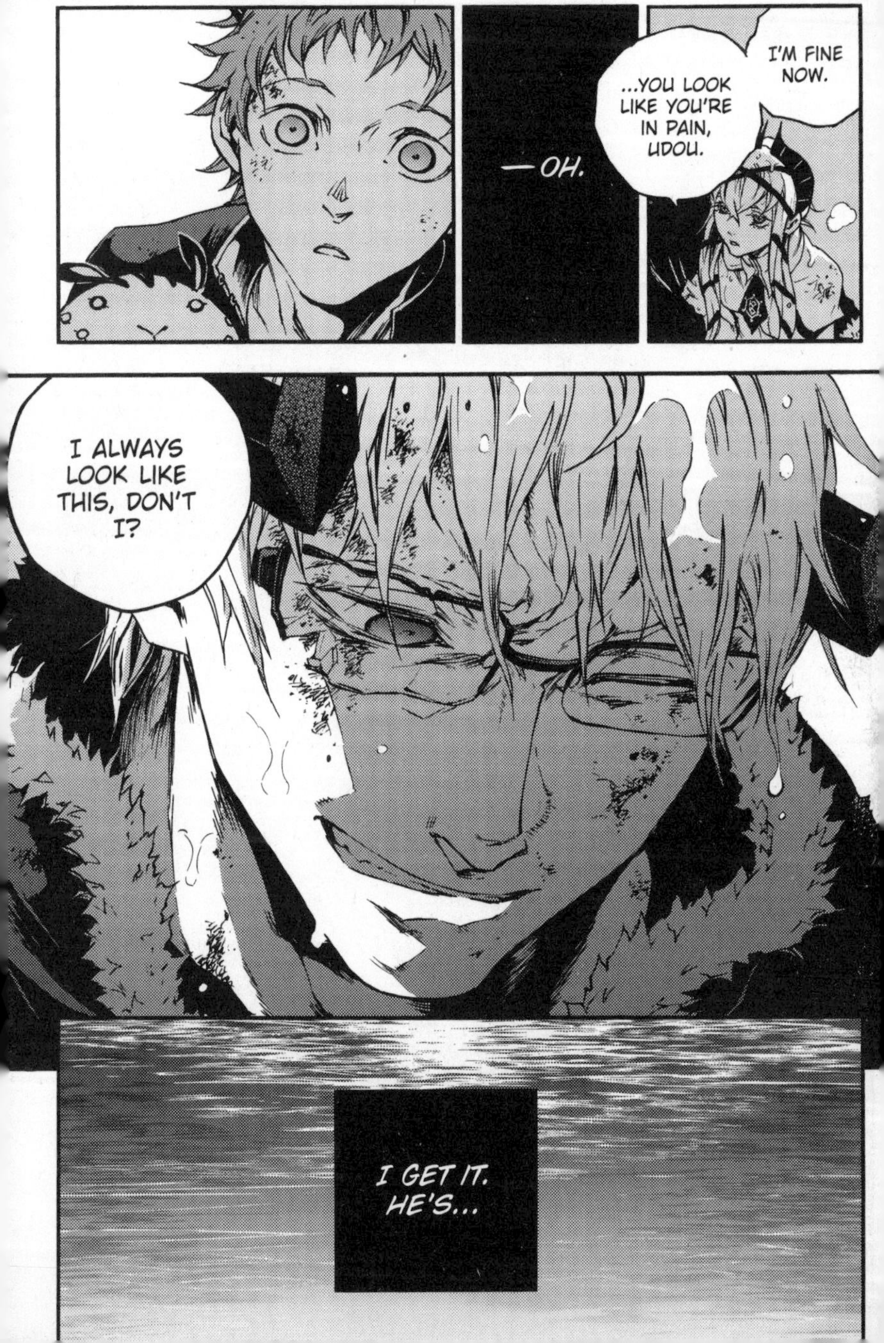
I'M FINE NOW.
...YOU LOOK LIKE YOU'RE IN PAIN, UDOU.
—OH.
I ALWAYS LOOK LIKE THIS, DON'T I?
I GET IT. HE'S...

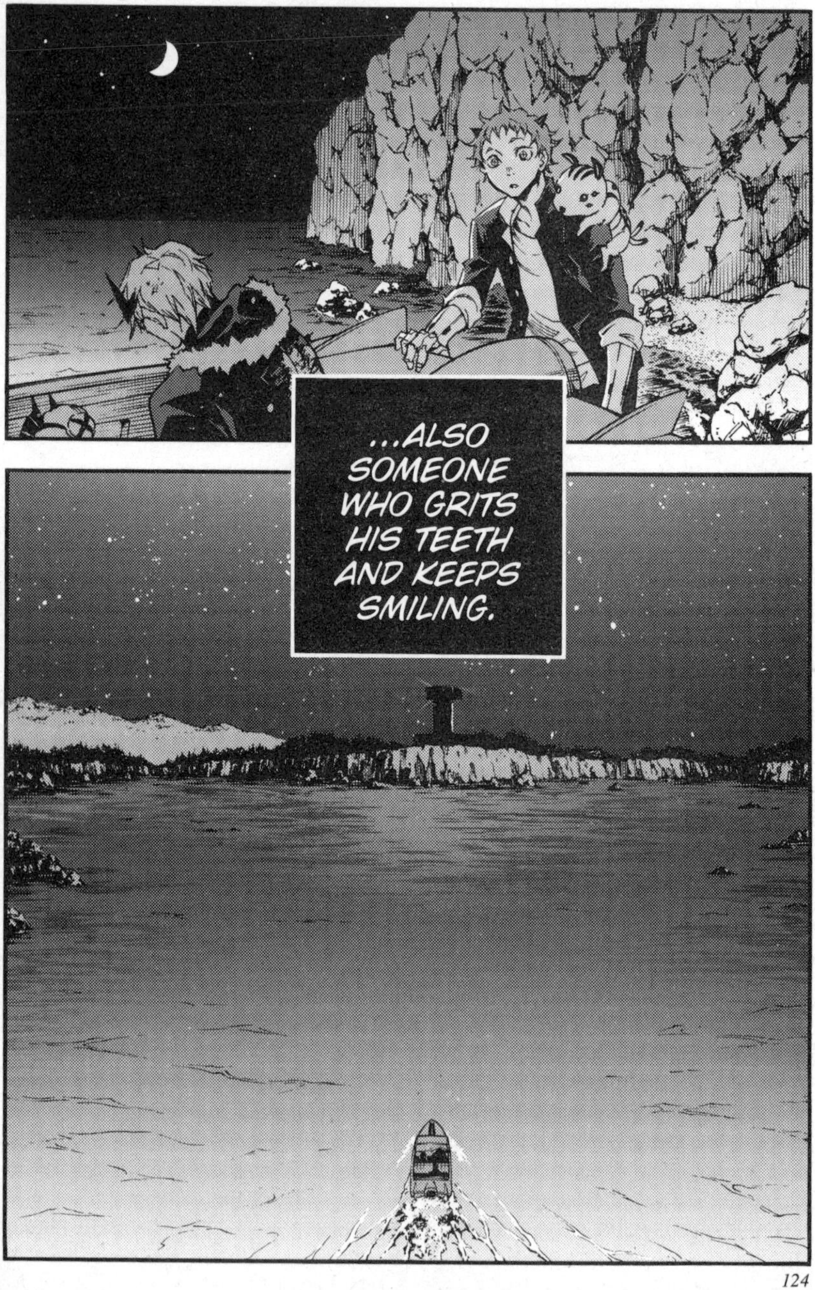
...ALSO SOMEONE WHO GRITS HIS TEETH AND KEEPS SMILING.

SMOKIN' PARADE

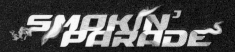

THE

WORLD

SMOKIN'PARADE

DEAD,

JINSEI KATAOKA
KAZUMA KONDOU

THE

PARAD

WILL

START

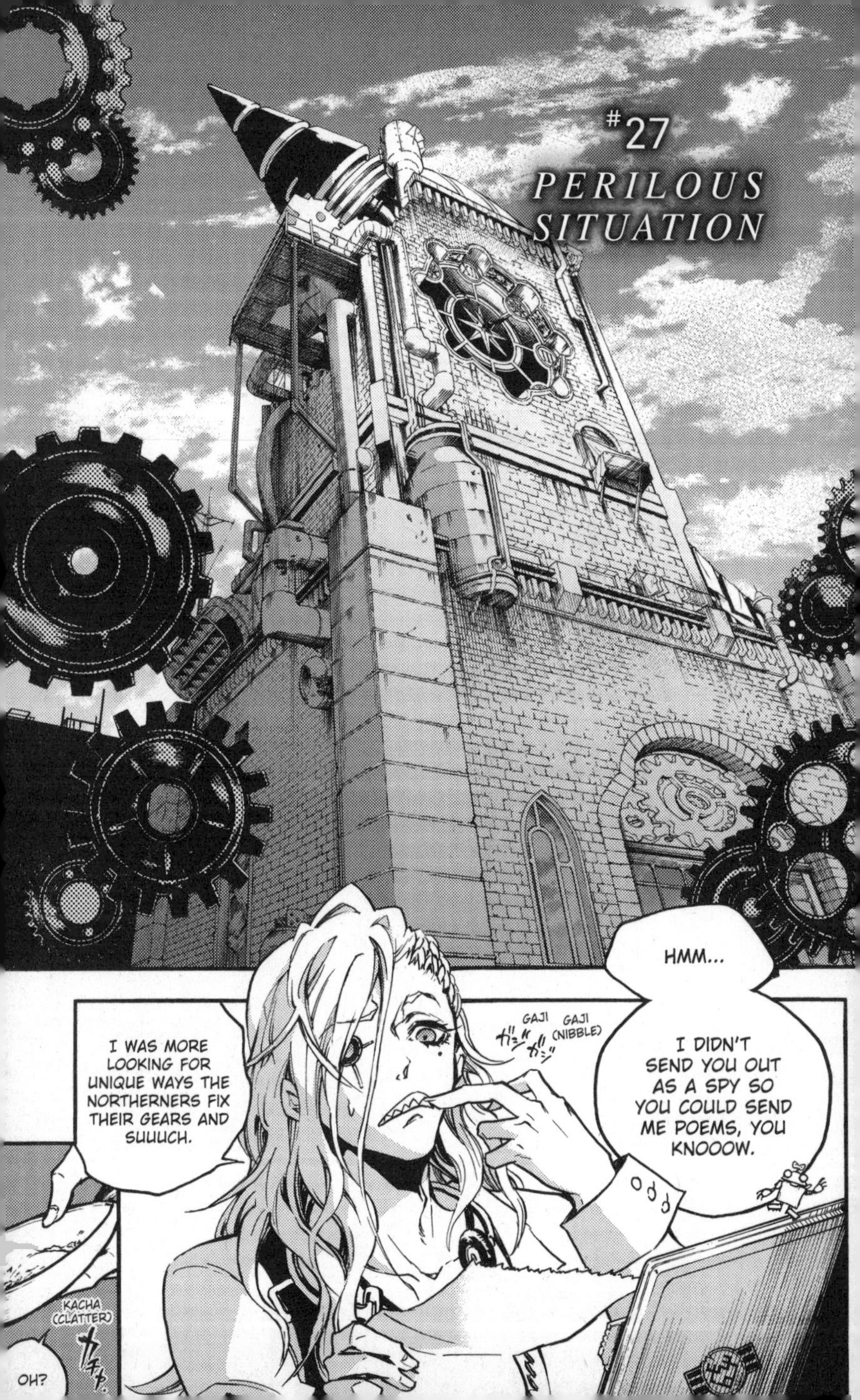
#27
PERILOUS SITUATION
HMM...
I DIDN'T SEND YOU OUT AS A SPY SO YOU COULD SEND ME POEMS, YOU KNOOOW.
GAJI GAJI (NIBBLE)
I WAS MORE LOOKING FOR UNIQUE WAYS THE NORTHERNERS FIX THEIR GEARS AND SUUUCH.
KACHA (CLATTER)
OH?

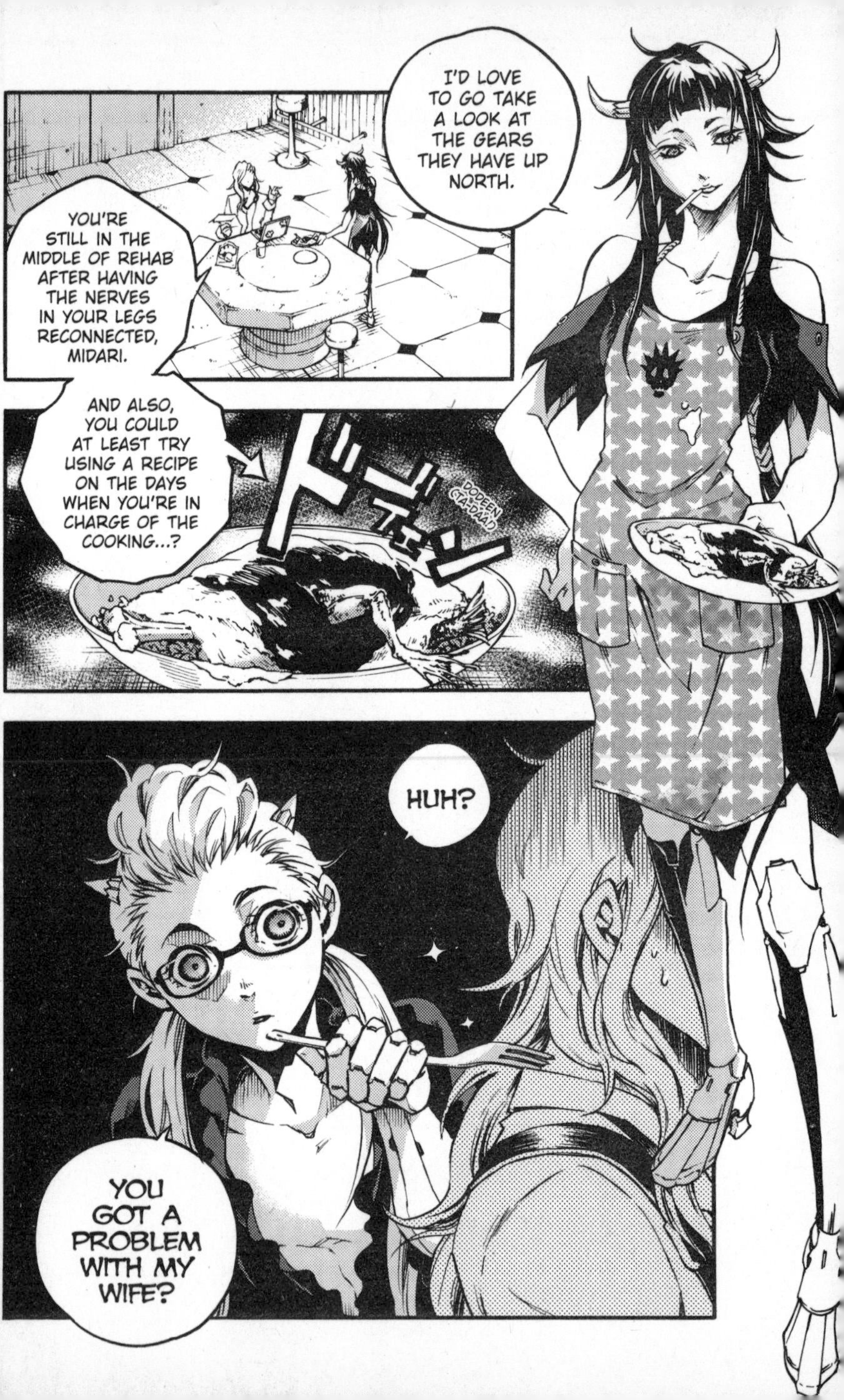
I'D LOVE TO GO TAKE A LOOK AT THE GEARS THEY HAVE UP NORTH.
YOU'RE STILL IN THE MIDDLE OF REHAB AFTER HAVING THE NERVES IN YOUR LEGS RECONNECTED, MIDARI.
AND ALSO, YOU COULD AT LEAST TRY USING A RECIPE ON THE DAYS WHEN YOU'RE IN CHARGE OF THE COOKING...?
DODEEN
(TA-DAA!)
HUH?
YOU GOT A PROBLEM WITH MY WIFE?

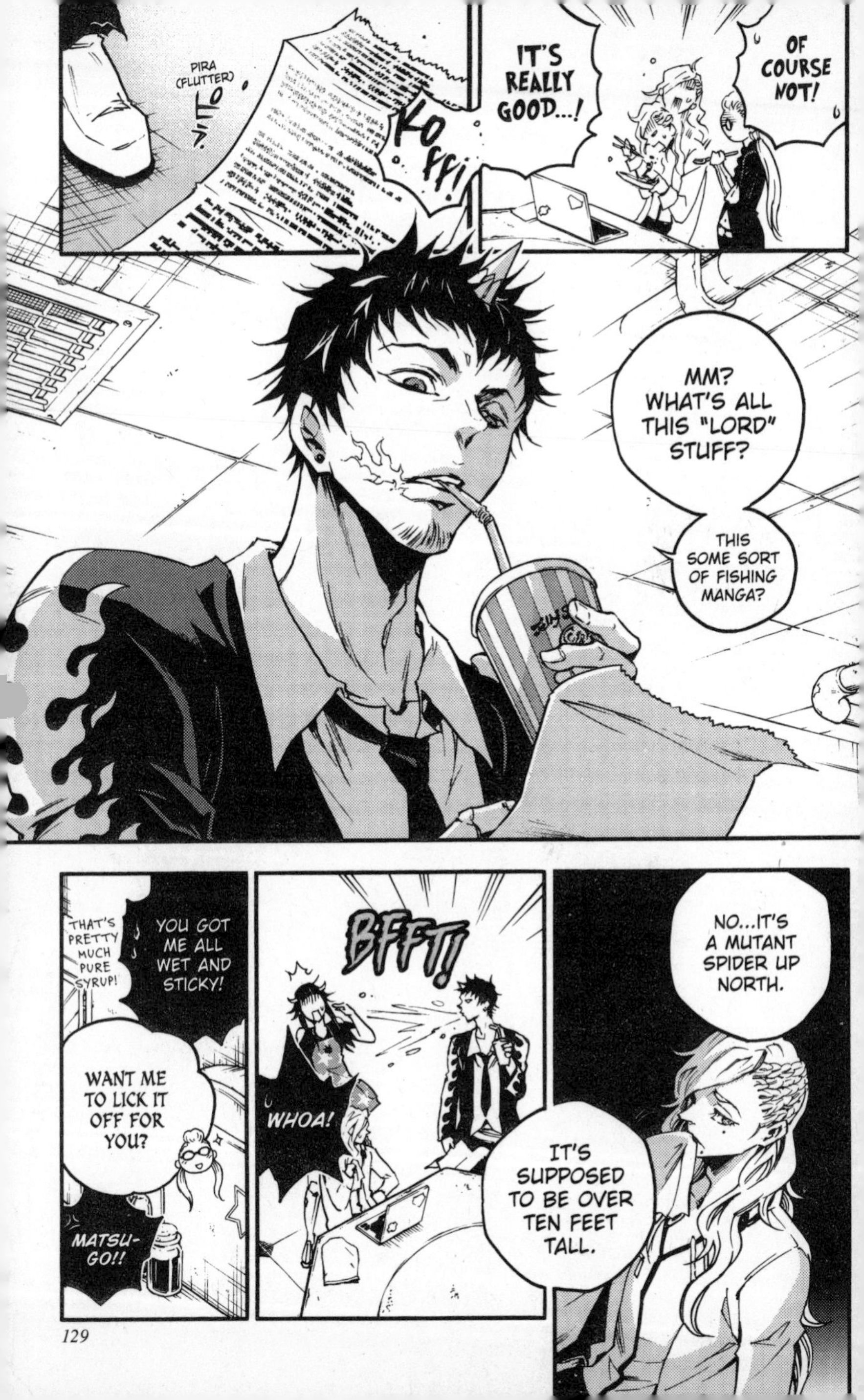
OF COURSE NOT!
IT'S REALLY GOOD...!
PIRA (FLUTTER)
KOSS!
MM? WHAT'S ALL THIS "LORD" STUFF?
THIS SOME SORT OF FISHING MANGA?
NO...IT'S A MUTANT SPIDER UP NORTH.
IT'S SUPPOSED TO BE OVER TEN FEET TALL.
BFFT!
WHOA!
YOU GOT ME ALL WET AND STICKY!
THAT'S PRETTY MUCH PURE SYRUP!
WANT ME TO LICK IT OFF FOR YOU?
MATSU-GO!!

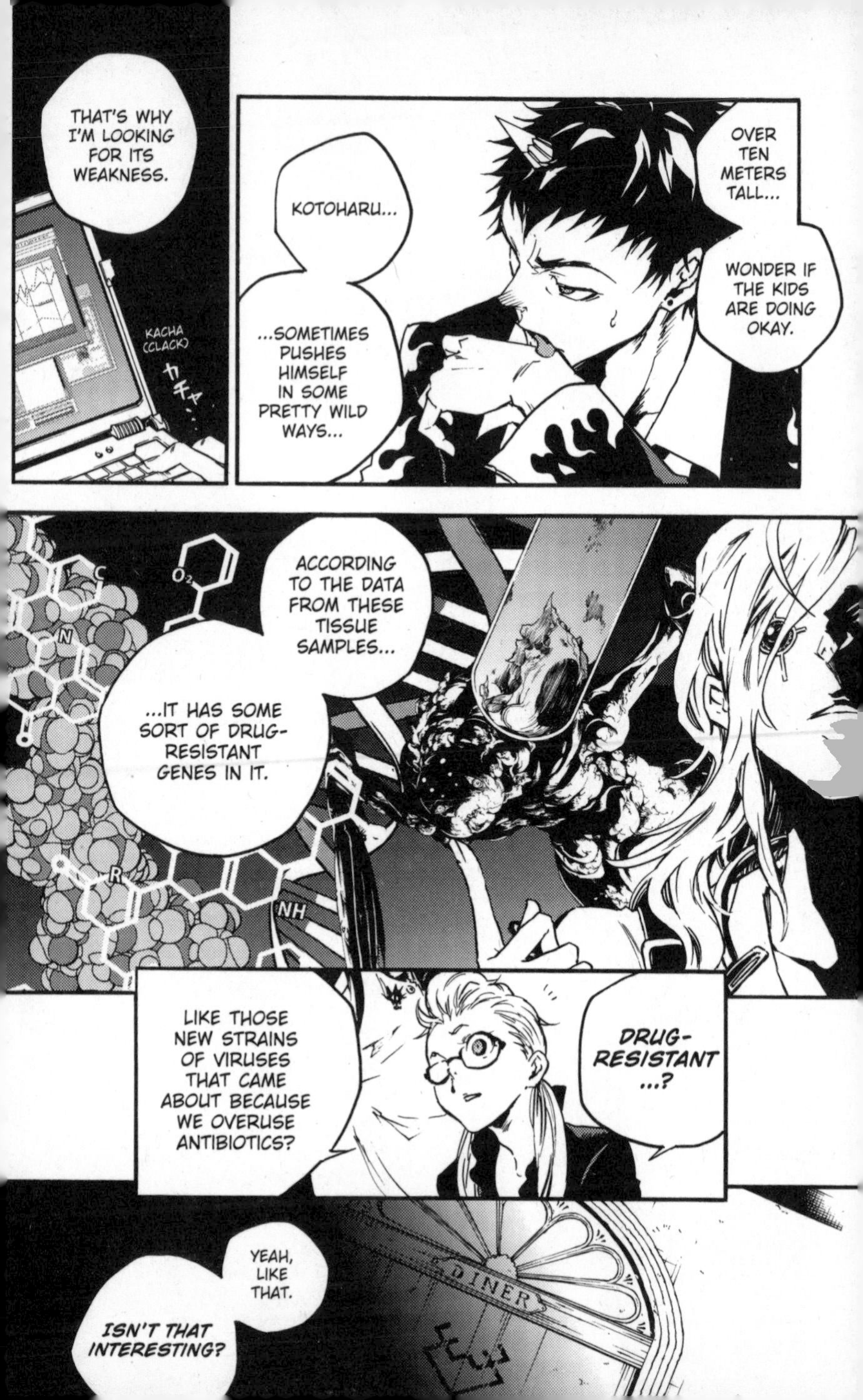
OVER TEN METERS TALL...
WONDER IF THE KIDS ARE DOING OKAY.
KOTOHARU...
...SOMETIMES PUSHES HIMSELF IN SOME PRETTY WILD WAYS...
THAT'S WHY I'M LOOKING FOR ITS WEAKNESS.
KACHA (CLACK)
カチャ
ACCORDING TO THE DATA FROM THESE TISSUE SAMPLES...
...IT HAS SOME SORT OF DRUG-RESISTANT GENES IN IT.
DRUG-RESISTANT ...?
LIKE THOSE NEW STRAINS OF VIRUSES THAT CAME ABOUT BECAUSE WE OVERUSE ANTIBIOTICS?
DINER
YEAH, LIKE THAT.
ISN'T THAT INTERESTING?

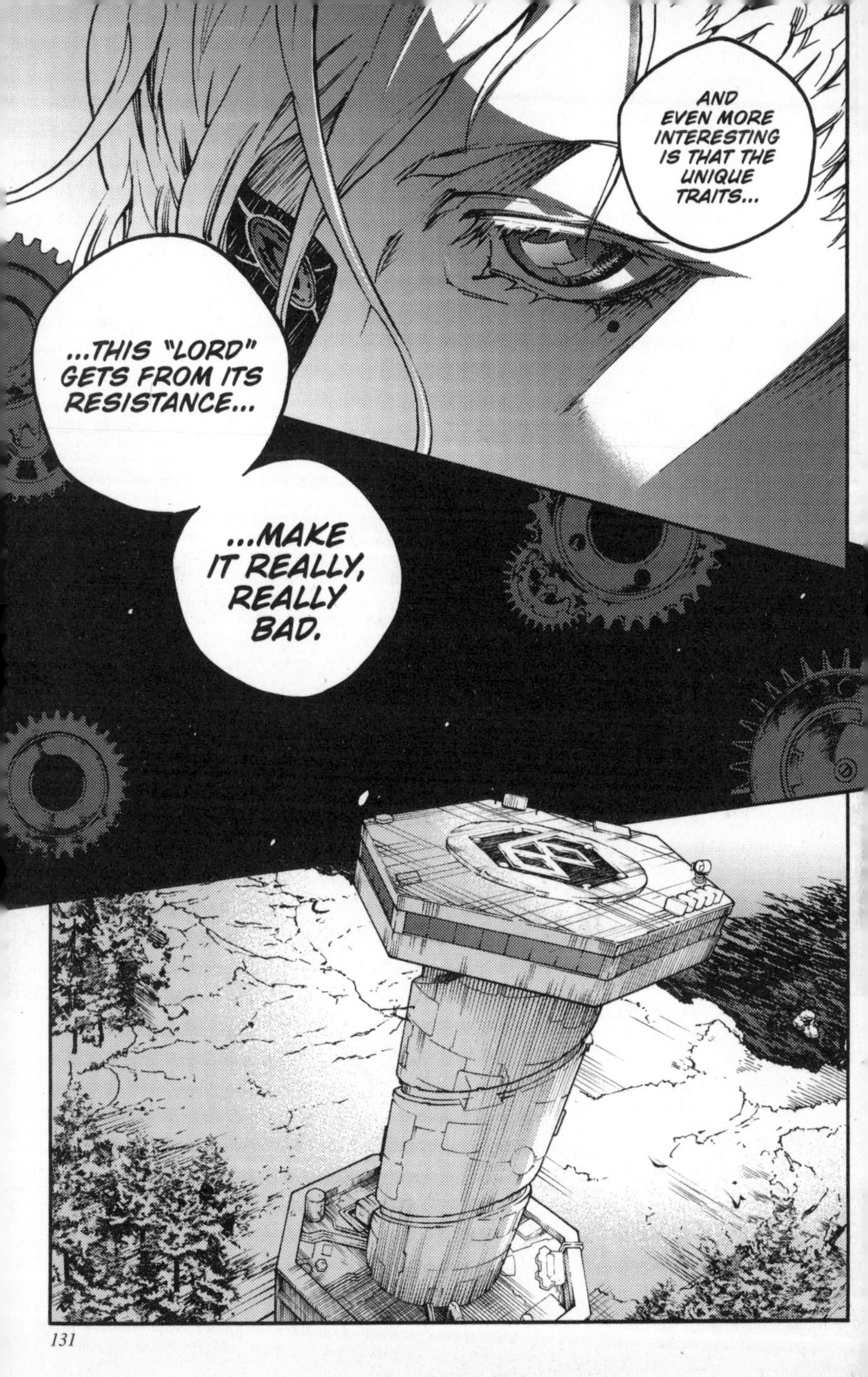
AND EVEN MORE INTERESTING IS THAT THE UNIQUE TRAITS...
...THIS "LORD" GETS FROM ITS RESISTANCE...
...MAKE IT REALLY, REALLY BAD.

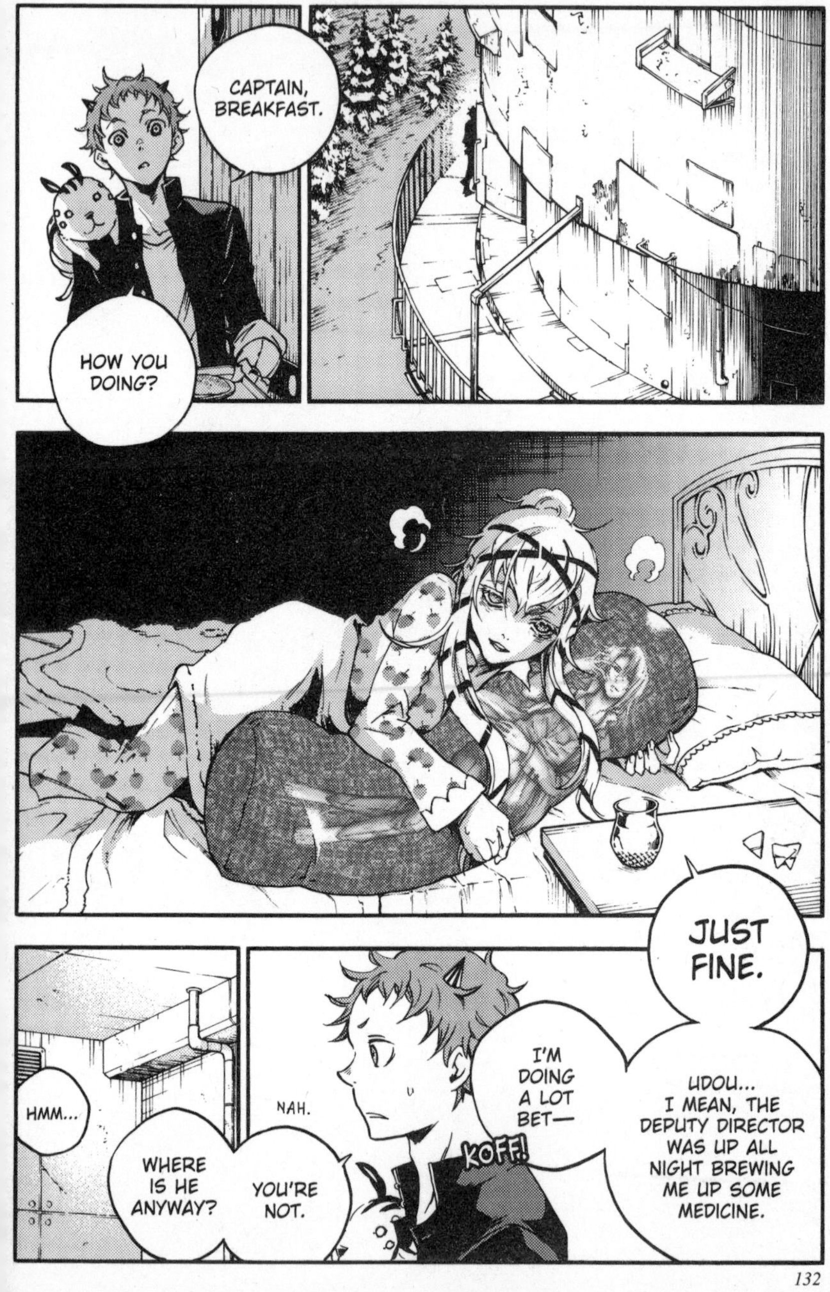
CAPTAIN, BREAKFAST.
HOW YOU DOING?
JUST FINE.
UDOU... I MEAN, THE DEPUTY DIRECTOR WAS UP ALL NIGHT BREWING ME UP SOME MEDICINE.
I'M DOING A LOT BET—
KOFF!
NAH.
YOU'RE NOT.
WHERE IS HE ANYWAY?
HMM...

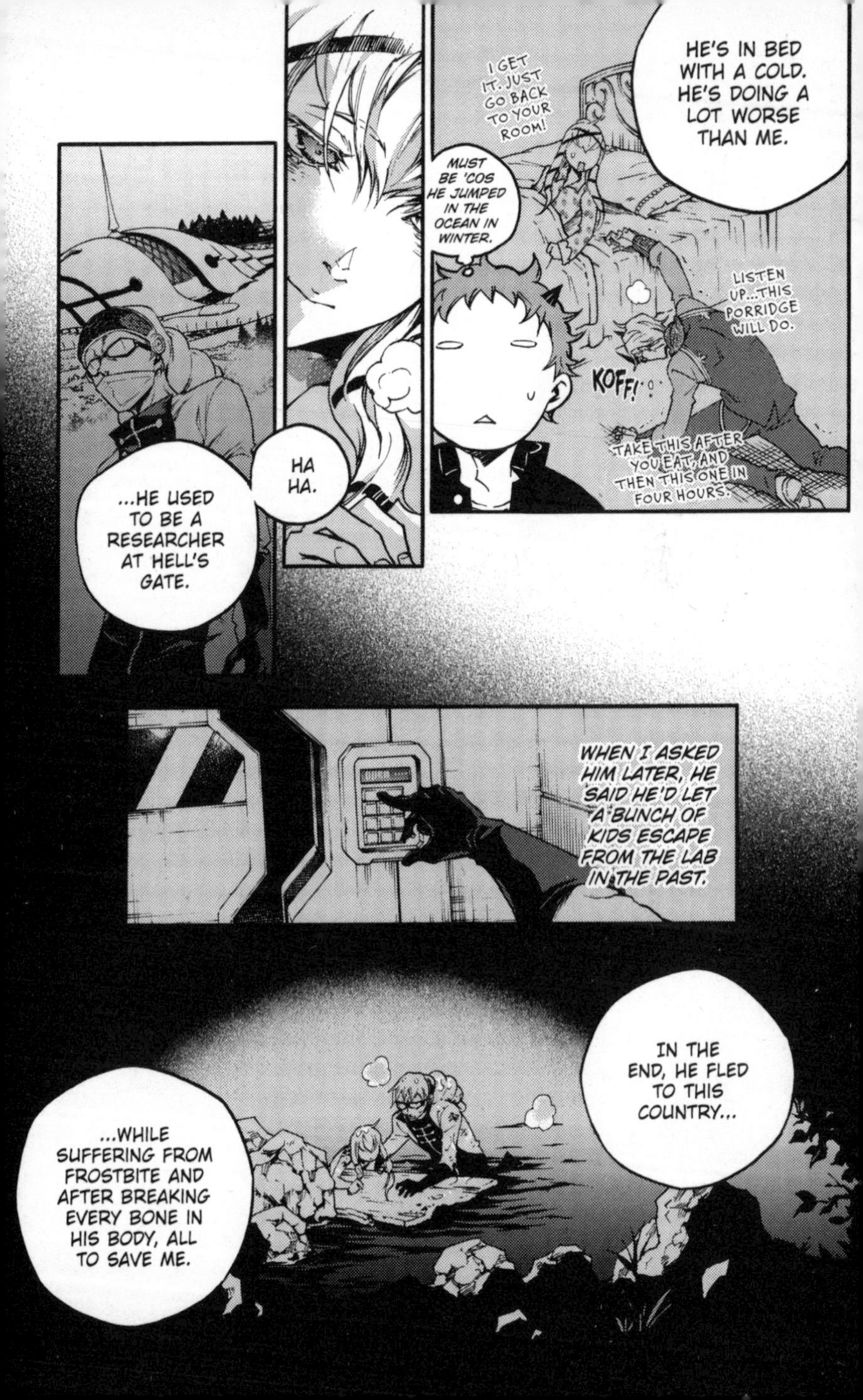
HE'S IN BED WITH A COLD. HE'S DOING A LOT WORSE THAN ME.
I GET IT. JUST GO BACK TO YOUR ROOM!
MUST BE 'COS HE JUMPED IN THE OCEAN IN WINTER.
LISTEN UP...THIS PORRIDGE WILL DO.
KOFF!
TAKE THIS AFTER YOU EAT, AND THEN THIS ONE IN FOUR HOURS.
HA HA.
...HE USED TO BE A RESEARCHER AT HELL'S GATE.
WHEN I ASKED HIM LATER, HE SAID HE'D LET A BUNCH OF KIDS ESCAPE FROM THE LAB IN THE PAST.
IN THE END, HE FLED TO THIS COUNTRY...
...WHILE SUFFERING FROM FROSTBITE AND AFTER BREAKING EVERY BONE IN HIS BODY, ALL TO SAVE ME.

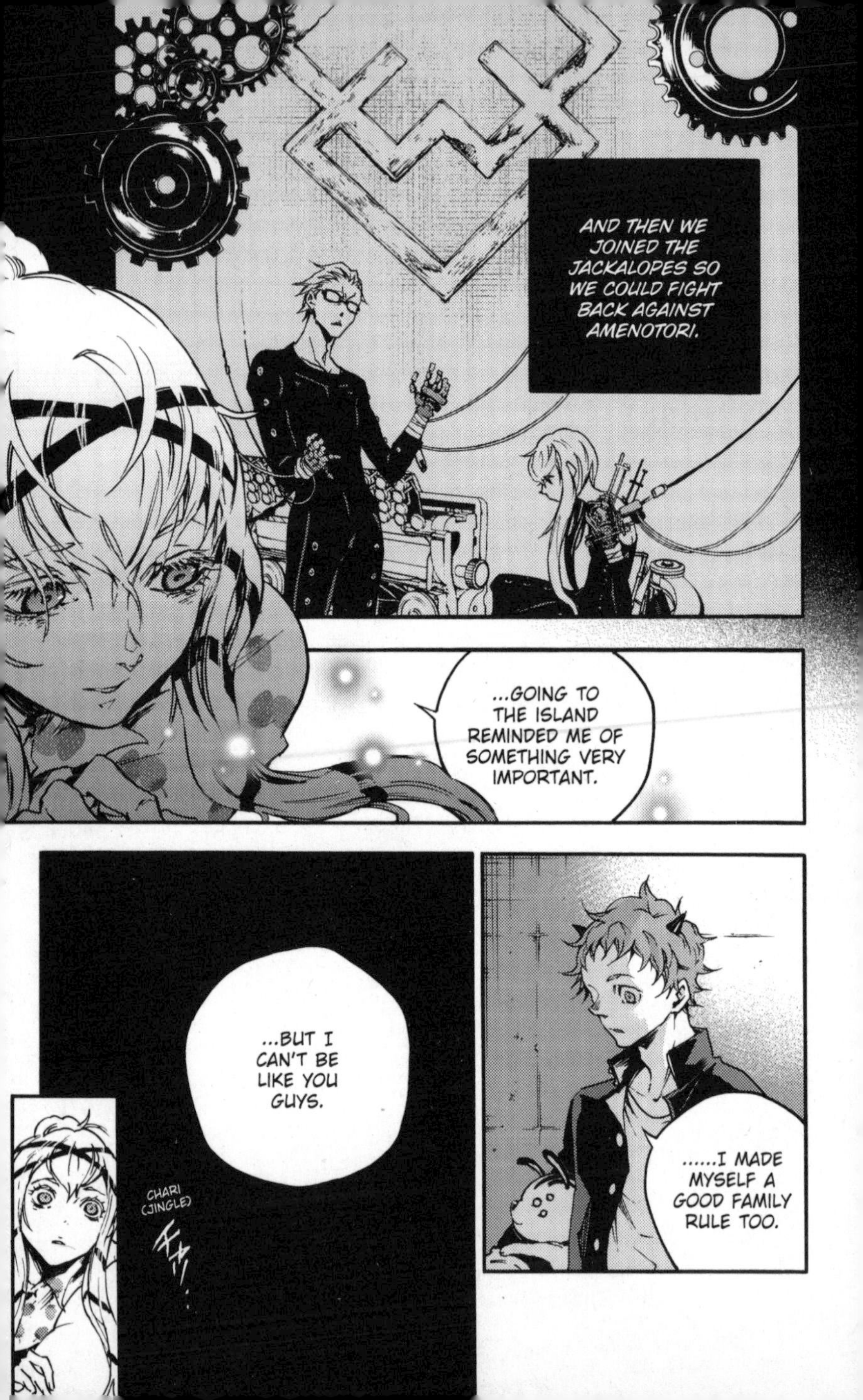
AND THEN WE JOINED THE JACKALOPES SO WE COULD FIGHT BACK AGAINST AMENOTORI.
...GOING TO THE ISLAND REMINDED ME OF SOMETHING VERY IMPORTANT.
......I MADE MYSELF A GOOD FAMILY RULE TOO.
...BUT I CAN'T BE LIKE YOU GUYS.
CHARI (JINGLE)

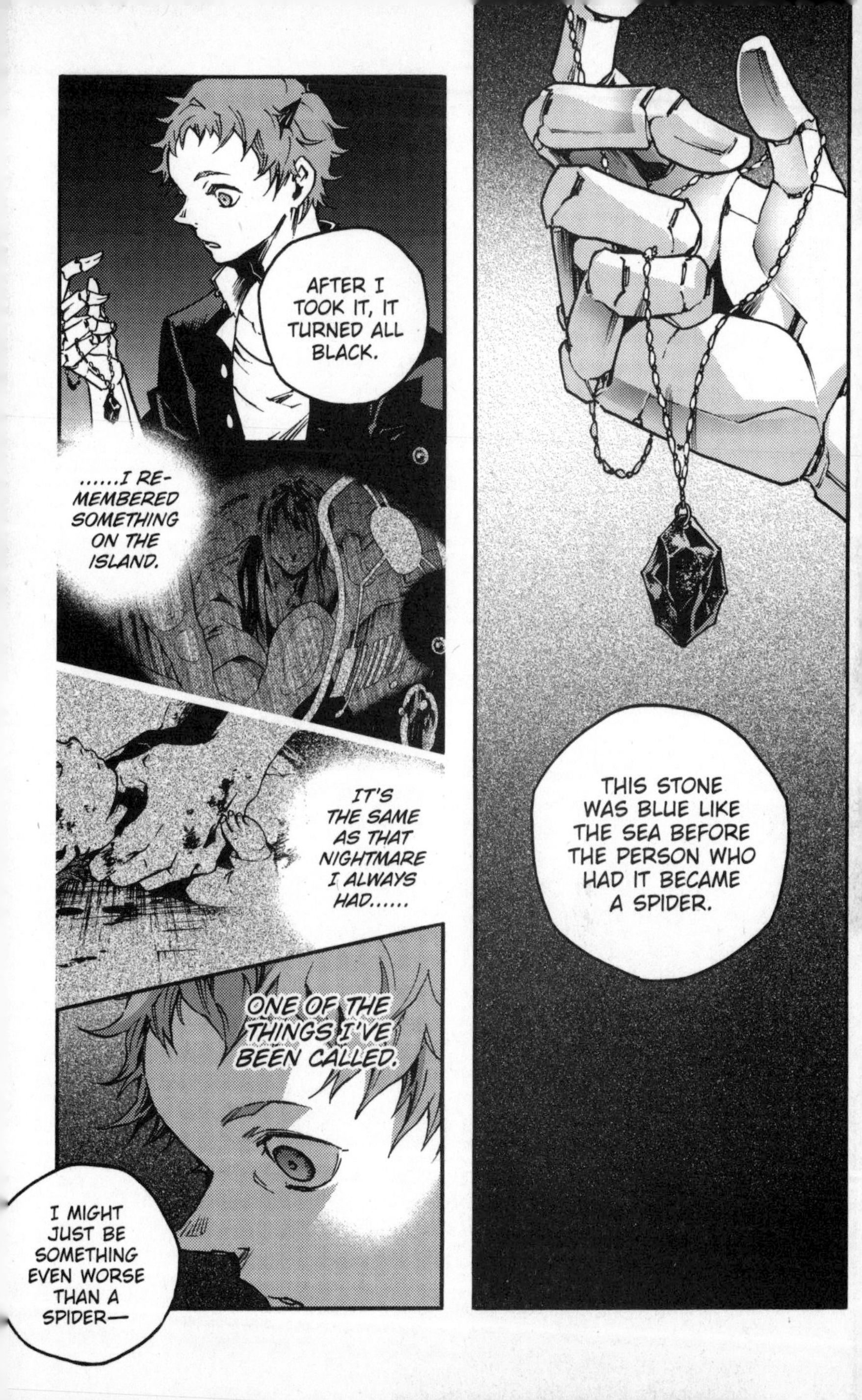
THIS STONE WAS BLUE LIKE THE SEA BEFORE THE PERSON WHO HAD IT BECAME A SPIDER.
AFTER I TOOK IT, IT TURNED ALL BLACK.
......I REMEMBERED SOMETHING ON THE ISLAND.
IT'S THE SAME AS THAT NIGHTMARE I ALWAYS HAD......
ONE OF THE THINGS I'VE BEEN CALLED.
I MIGHT JUST BE SOMETHING EVEN WORSE THAN A SPIDER—

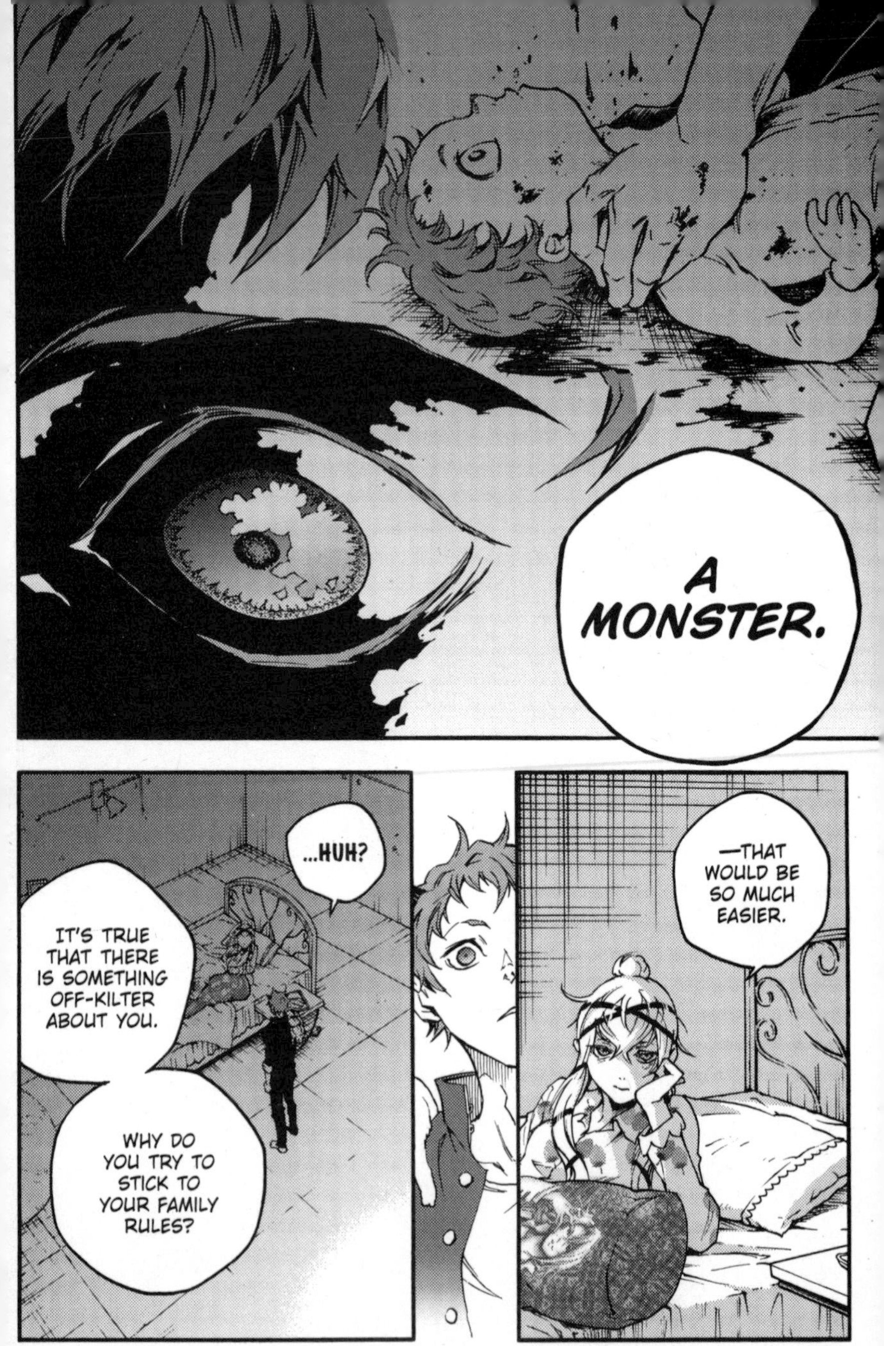
A MONSTER.
—THAT WOULD BE SO MUCH EASIER.
...HUH?
IT'S TRUE THAT THERE IS SOMETHING OFF-KILTER ABOUT YOU.
WHY DO YOU TRY TO STICK TO YOUR FAMILY RULES?

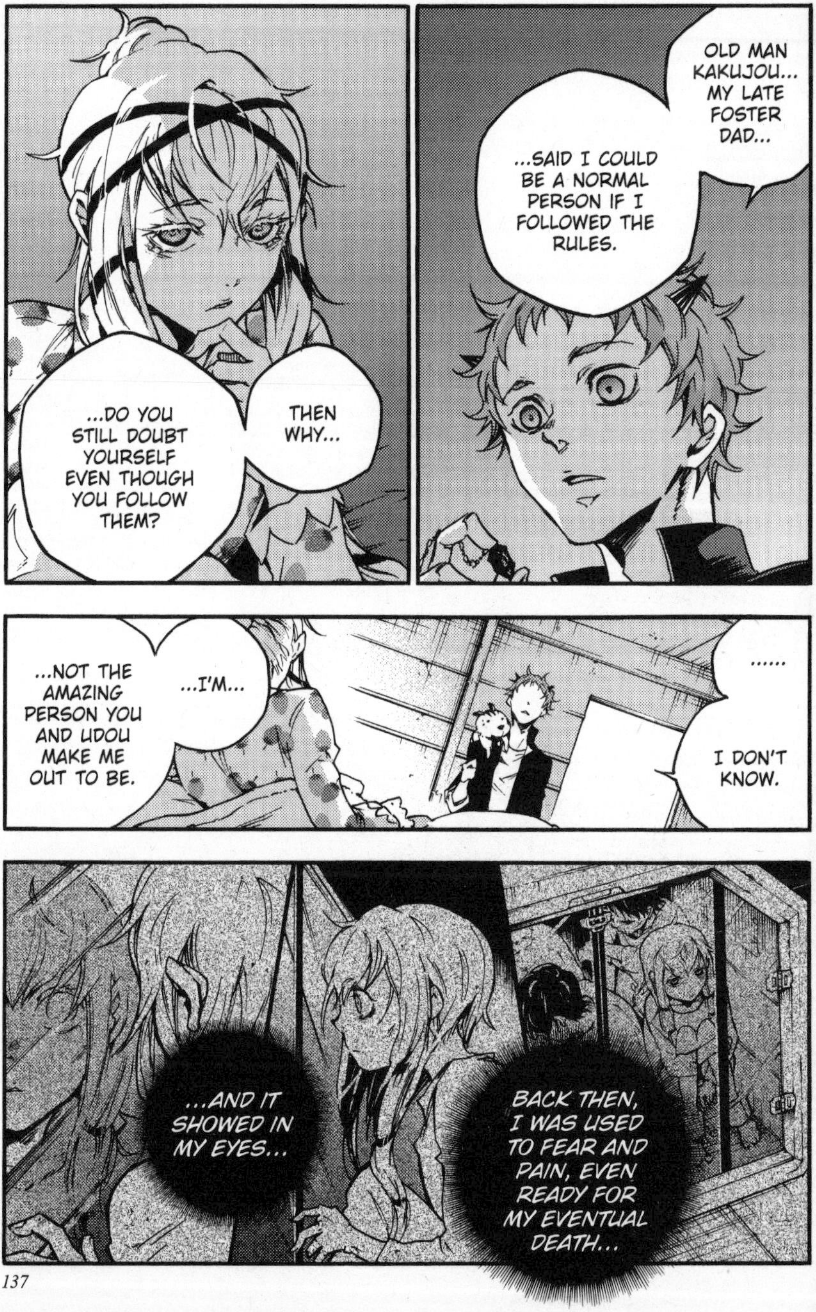
OLD MAN KAKUJOU... MY LATE FOSTER DAD...
...SAID I COULD BE A NORMAL PERSON IF I FOLLOWED THE RULES.
THEN WHY...
...DO YOU STILL DOUBT YOURSELF EVEN THOUGH YOU FOLLOW THEM?
......
I DON'T KNOW.
...I'M...
...NOT THE AMAZING PERSON YOU AND UDOU MAKE ME OUT TO BE.
BACK THEN, I WAS USED TO FEAR AND PAIN, EVEN READY FOR MY EVENTUAL DEATH...
...AND IT SHOWED IN MY EYES...

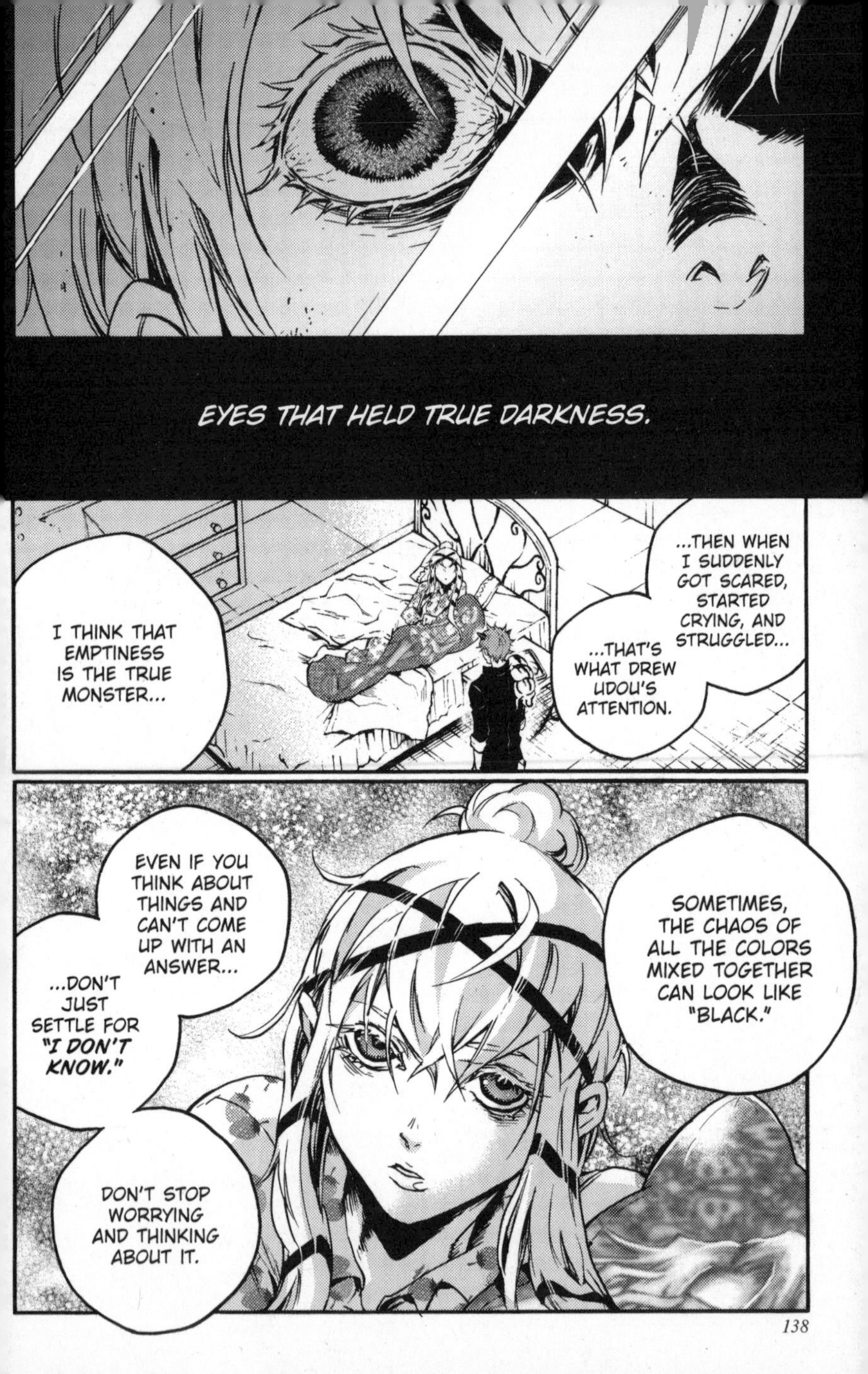
EYES THAT HELD TRUE DARKNESS.
...THEN WHEN I SUDDENLY GOT SCARED, STARTED CRYING, AND STRUGGLED...
...THAT'S WHAT DREW UDOU'S ATTENTION.
I THINK THAT EMPTINESS IS THE TRUE MONSTER...
SOMETIMES, THE CHAOS OF ALL THE COLORS MIXED TOGETHER CAN LOOK LIKE "BLACK."
EVEN IF YOU THINK ABOUT THINGS AND CAN'T COME UP WITH AN ANSWER...
...DON'T JUST SETTLE FOR ***"I DON'T KNOW."***
DON'T STOP WORRYING AND THINKING ABOUT IT.

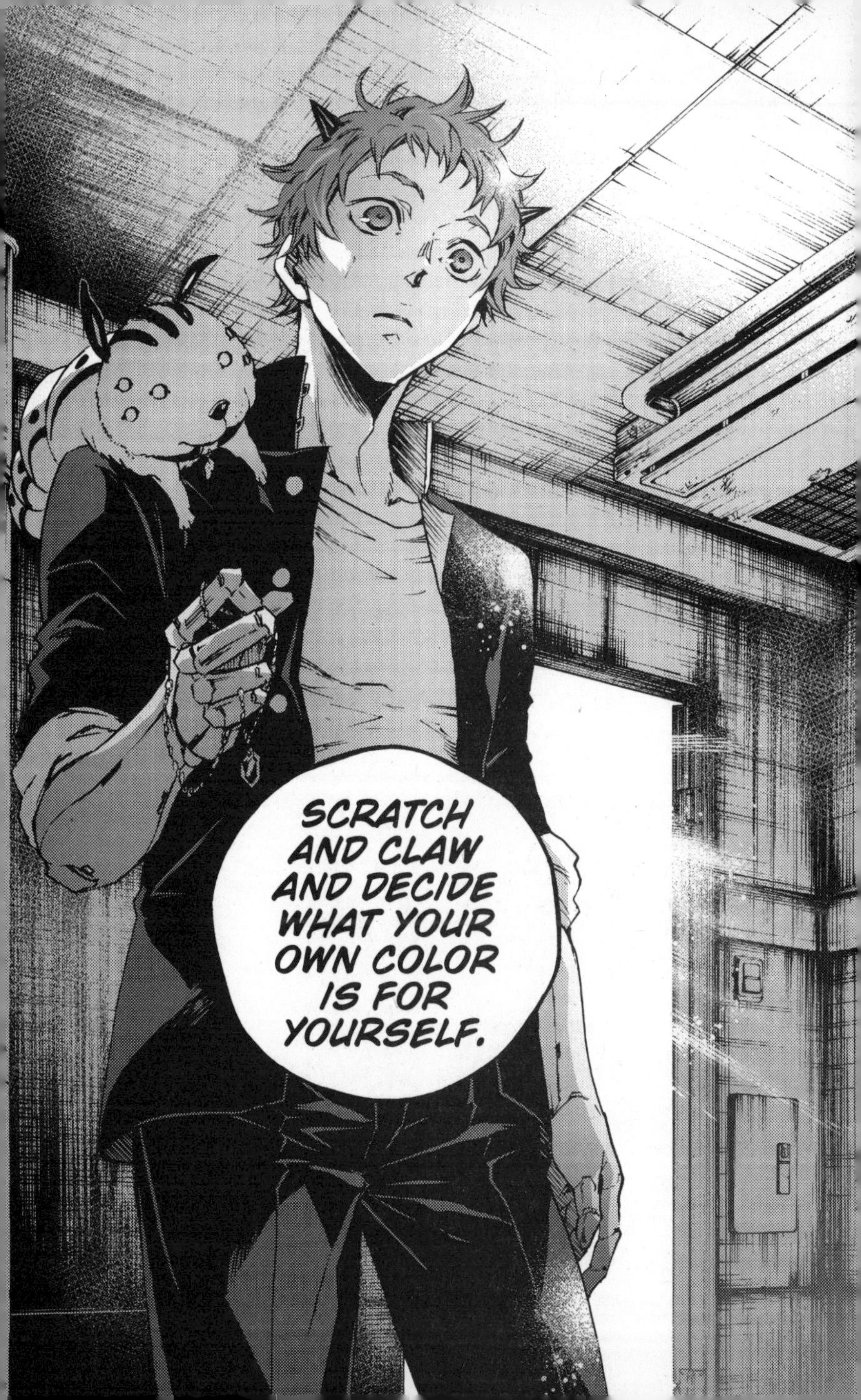
SCRATCH AND CLAW AND DECIDE WHAT YOUR OWN COLOR IS FOR YOURSELF.

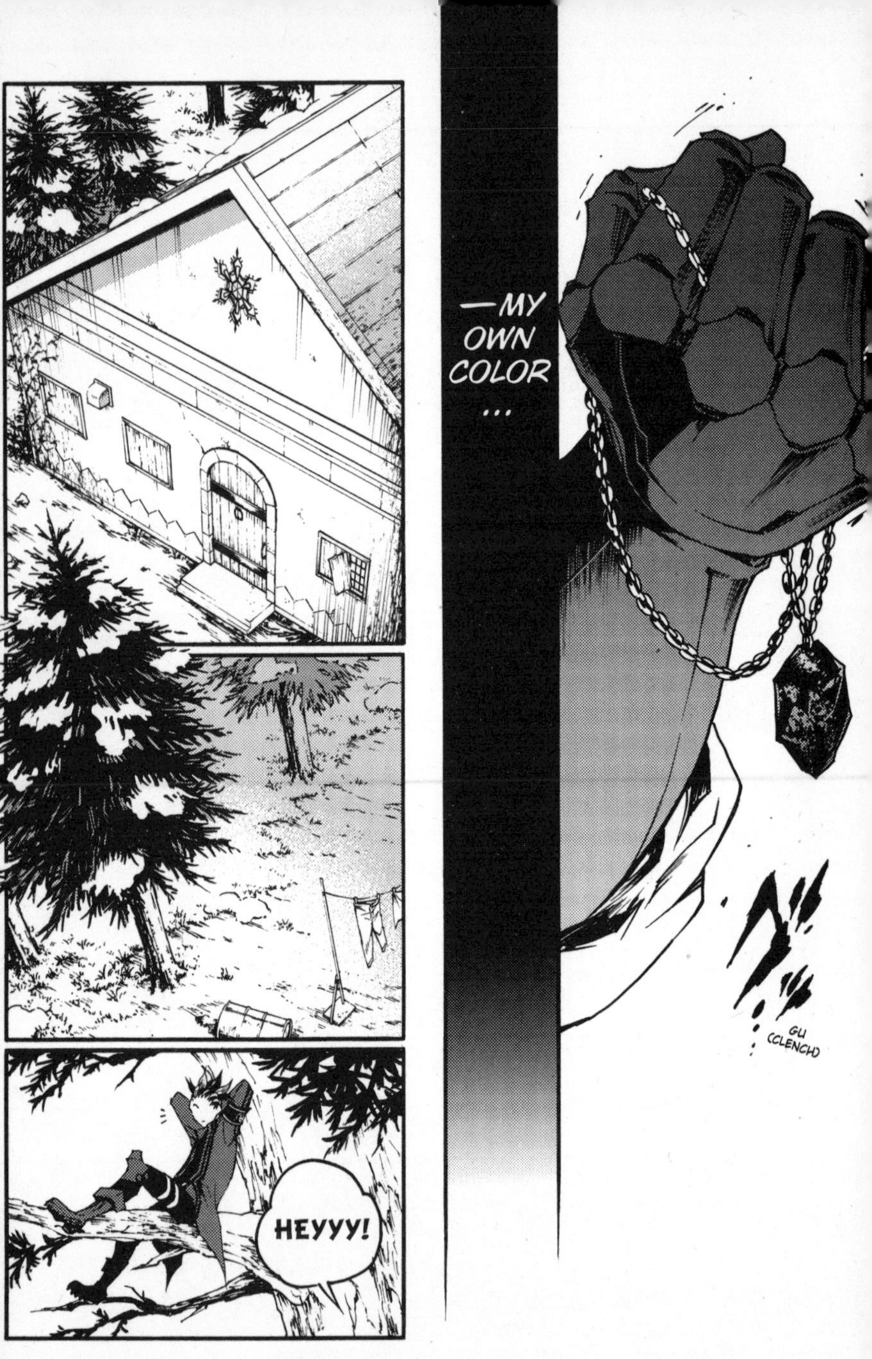
—MY OWN COLOR ...
GU (CLENCH)
HEYYY!

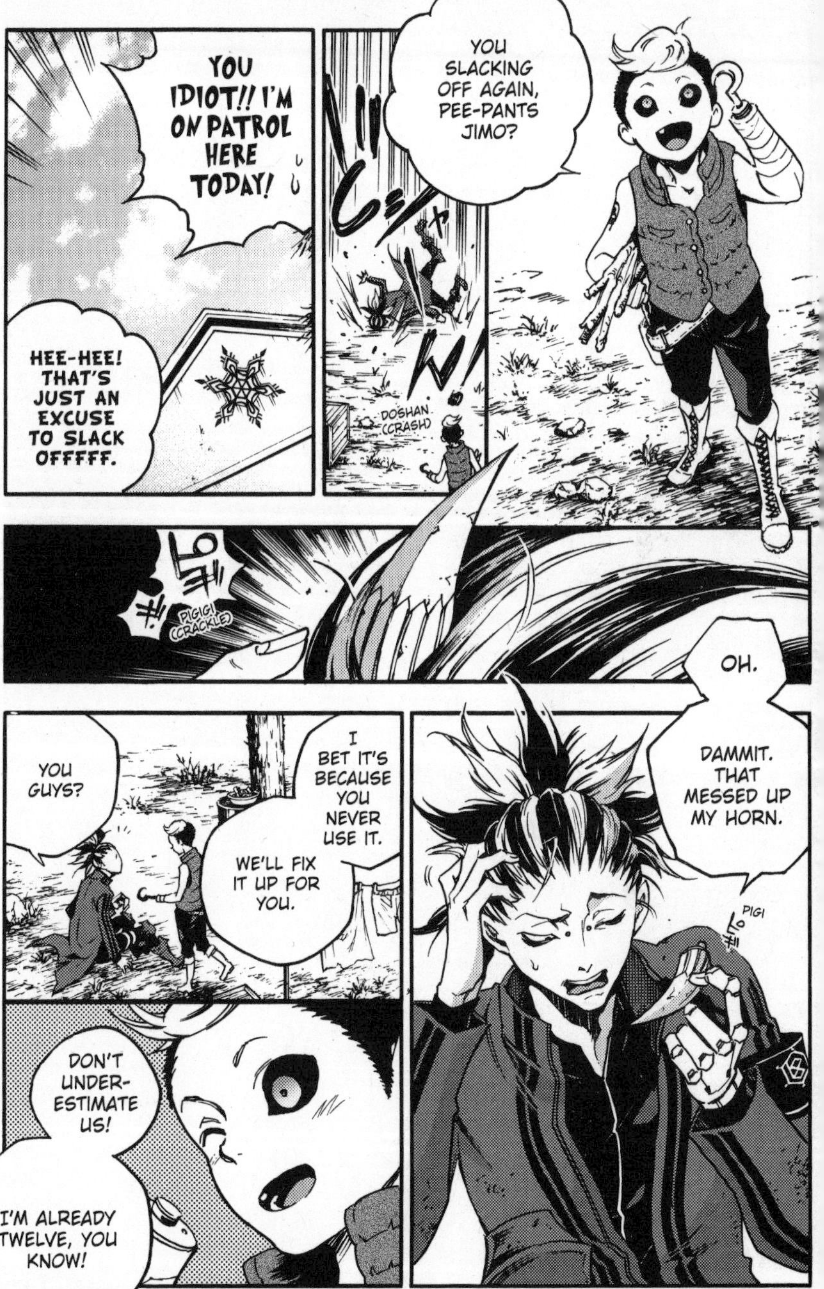
YOU SLACKING OFF AGAIN, PEE-PANTS JIMO?
DOSHAN (CRASH)
YOU IDIOT!! I'M ON PATROL HERE TODAY!
HEE-HEE! THAT'S JUST AN EXCUSE TO SLACK OFFFFF.
PIGIGI (CRACKLE)
OH.
DAMMIT. THAT MESSED UP MY HORN.
PIGI
I BET IT'S BECAUSE YOU NEVER USE IT.
WE'LL FIX IT UP FOR YOU.
YOU GUYS?
DON'T UNDER-ESTIMATE US!
I'M ALREADY TWELVE, YOU KNOW!

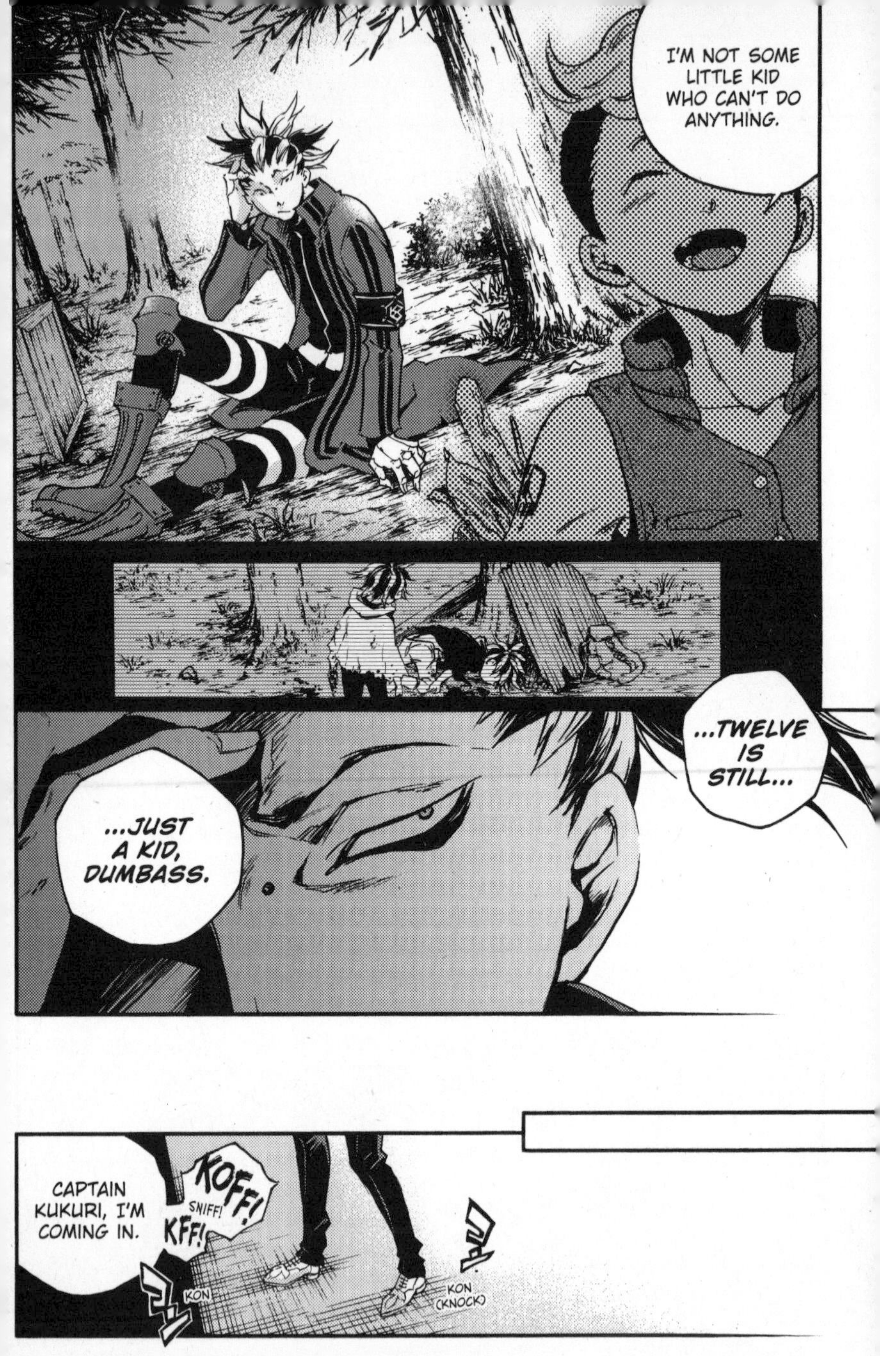
I'M NOT SOME LITTLE KID WHO CAN'T DO ANYTHING.
...TWELVE IS STILL...
...JUST A KID, DUMBASS.
KON (KNOCK)
KOFF!
SNIFF!
KFF!
CAPTAIN KUKURI, I'M COMING IN.
KON

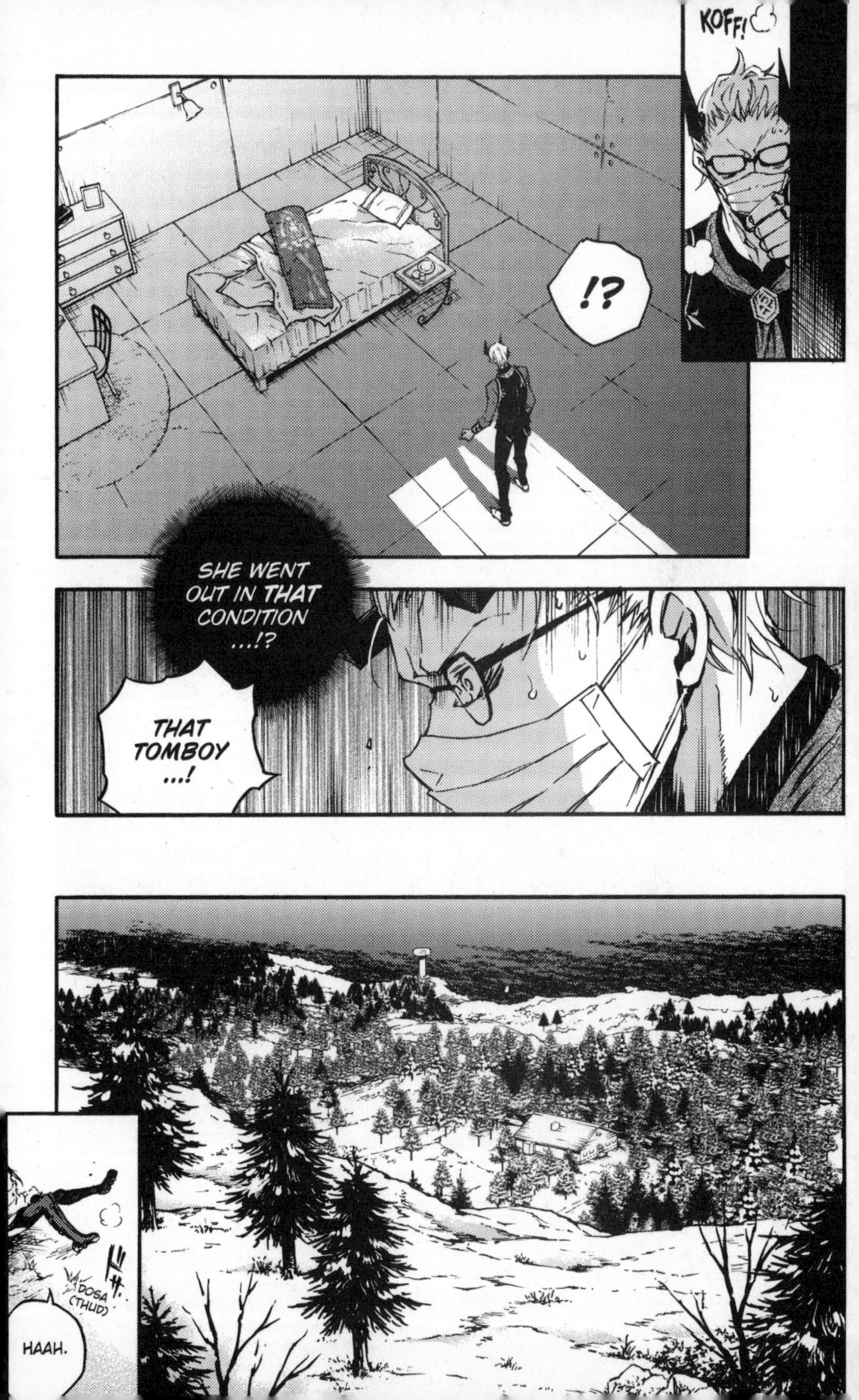
KOFF!
!?
SHE WENT OUT IN THAT CONDITION ...!?
THAT TOMBOY ...!
DOSA (THUD)
HAAH.

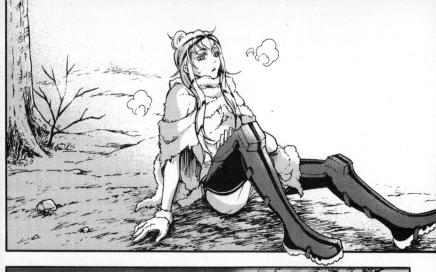

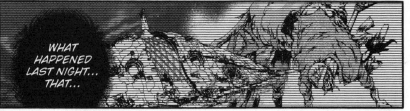

WHAT HAPPENED LAST NIGHT... THAT...
...WASN'T JUST A NORMAL SPIDER...
...BUT IT ALSO DIDN'T EVEN COMPARE TO THE SIZE OF THE LORD'S FOOTPRINTS.
SO THAT WASN'T THE SAME LORD THAT'S BEEN TERRORIZING US.
...IT HAS TO BE RELATED.
IN THAT CASE, WHAT IF...?

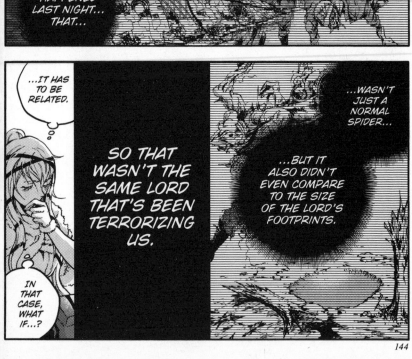

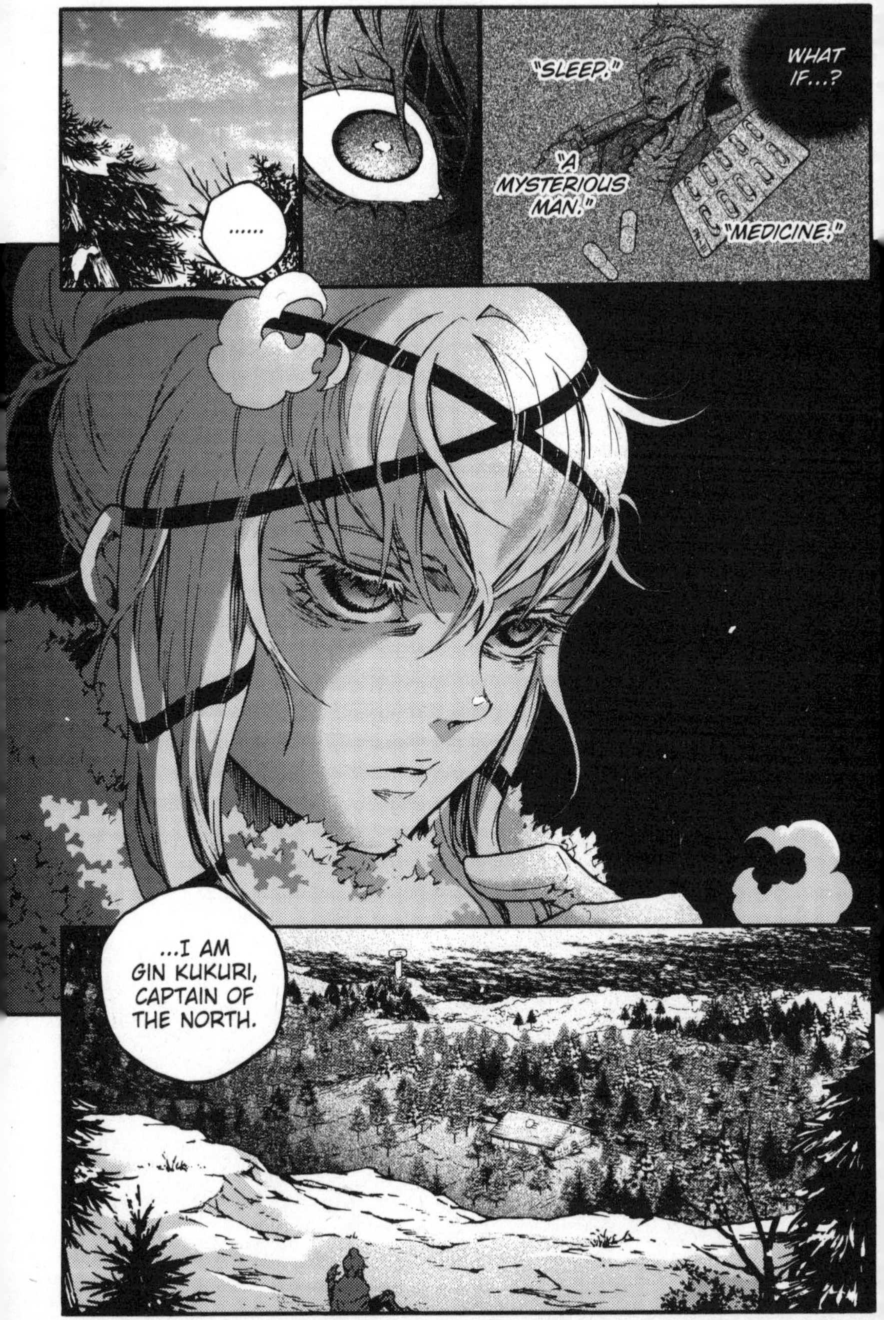
WHAT IF...?
"SLEEP."
"A MYSTERIOUS MAN."
"MEDICINE."
......
...I AM GIN KUKURI, CAPTAIN OF THE NORTH.

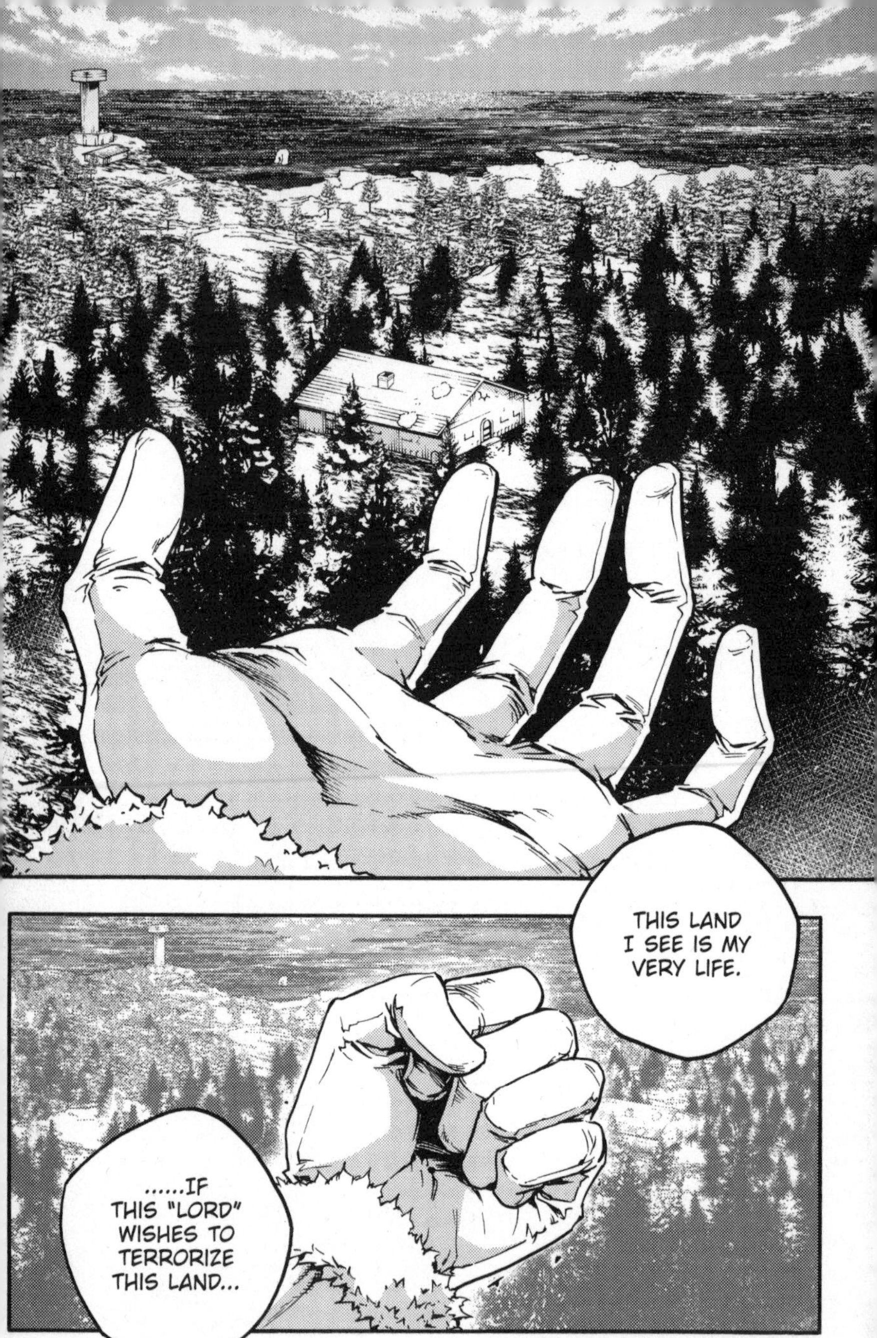
THIS LAND I SEE IS MY VERY LIFE.
......IF THIS "LORD" WISHES TO TERRORIZE THIS LAND...

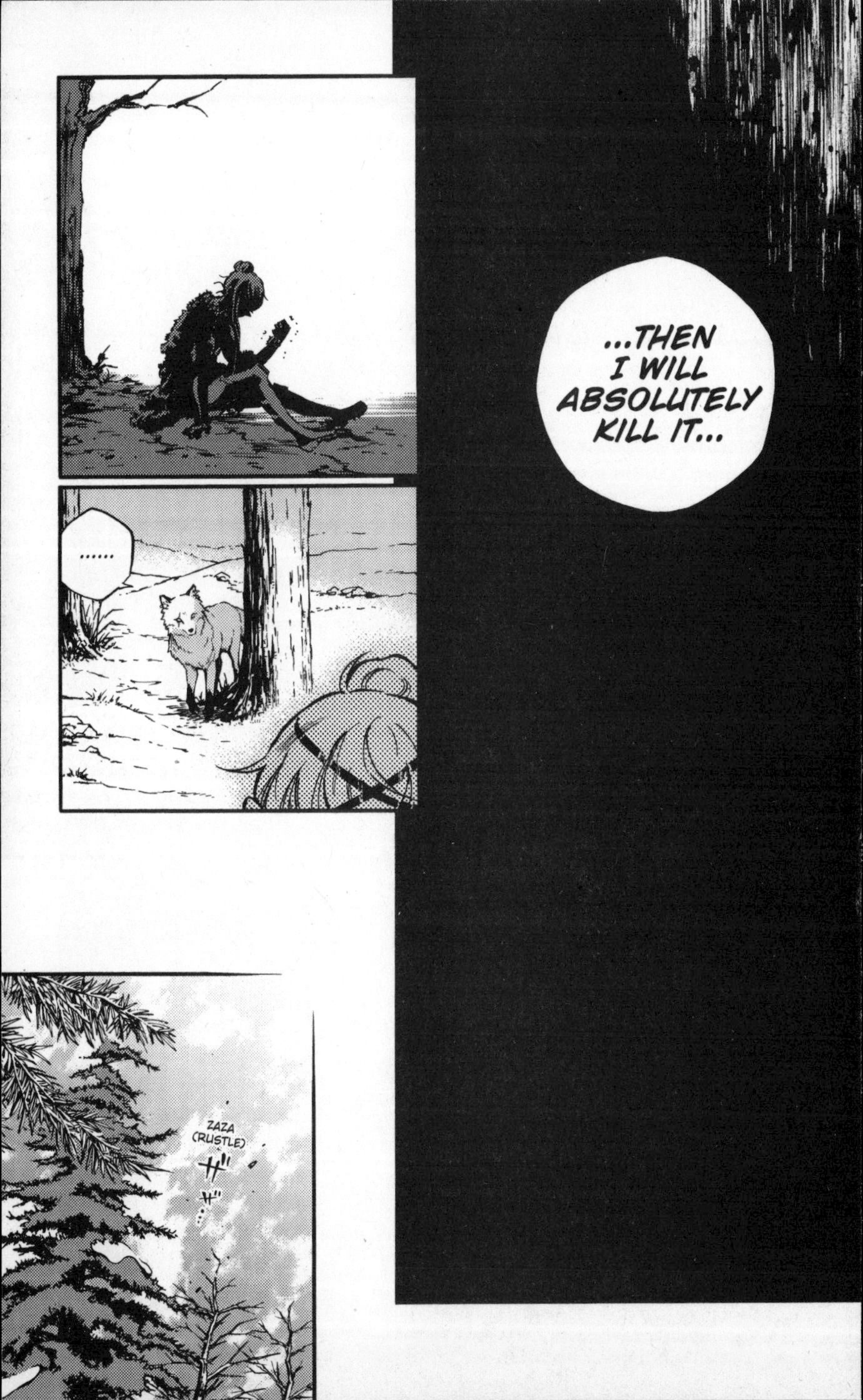
...THEN I WILL ABSOLUTELY KILL IT...
......
ZAZA (RUSTLE)

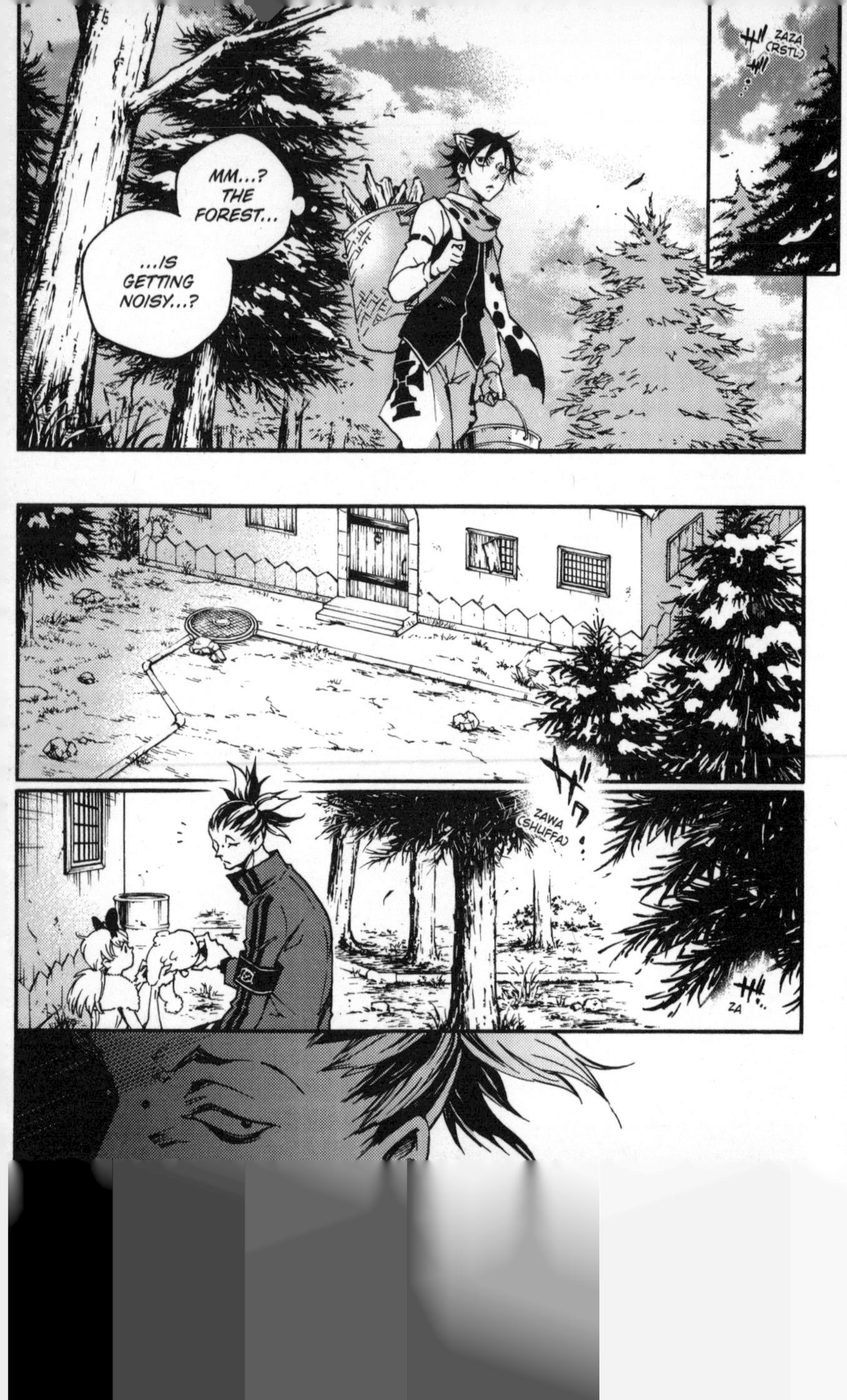
ZAZA (RSTL)
MM...? THE FOREST...
...IS GETTING NOISY...?
ZAWA (SHUFFA)
ZA

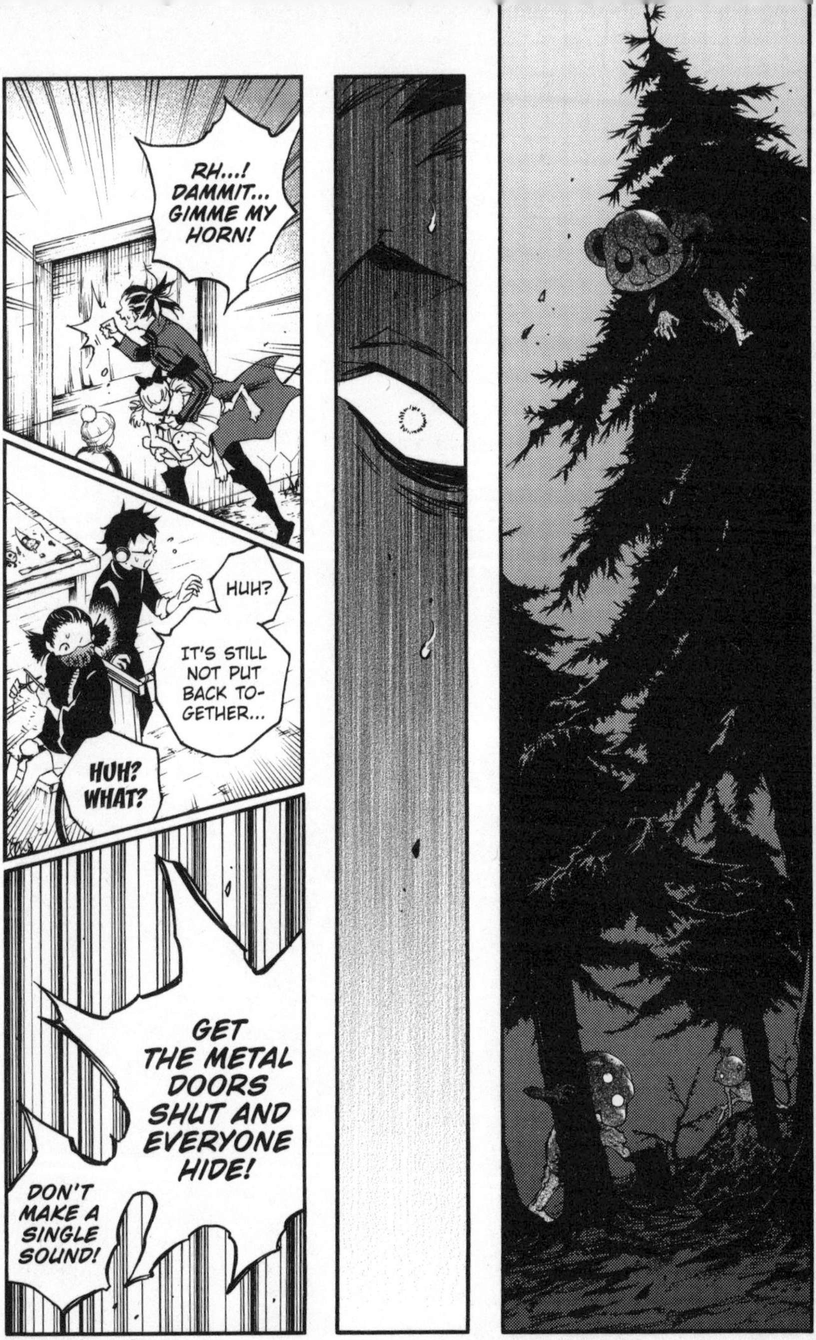
RH...! DAMMIT... GIMME MY HORN!
HUH?
IT'S STILL NOT PUT BACK TO-GETHER...
HUH? WHAT?
GET THE METAL DOORS SHUT AND EVERYONE HIDE!
DON'T MAKE A SINGLE SOUND!

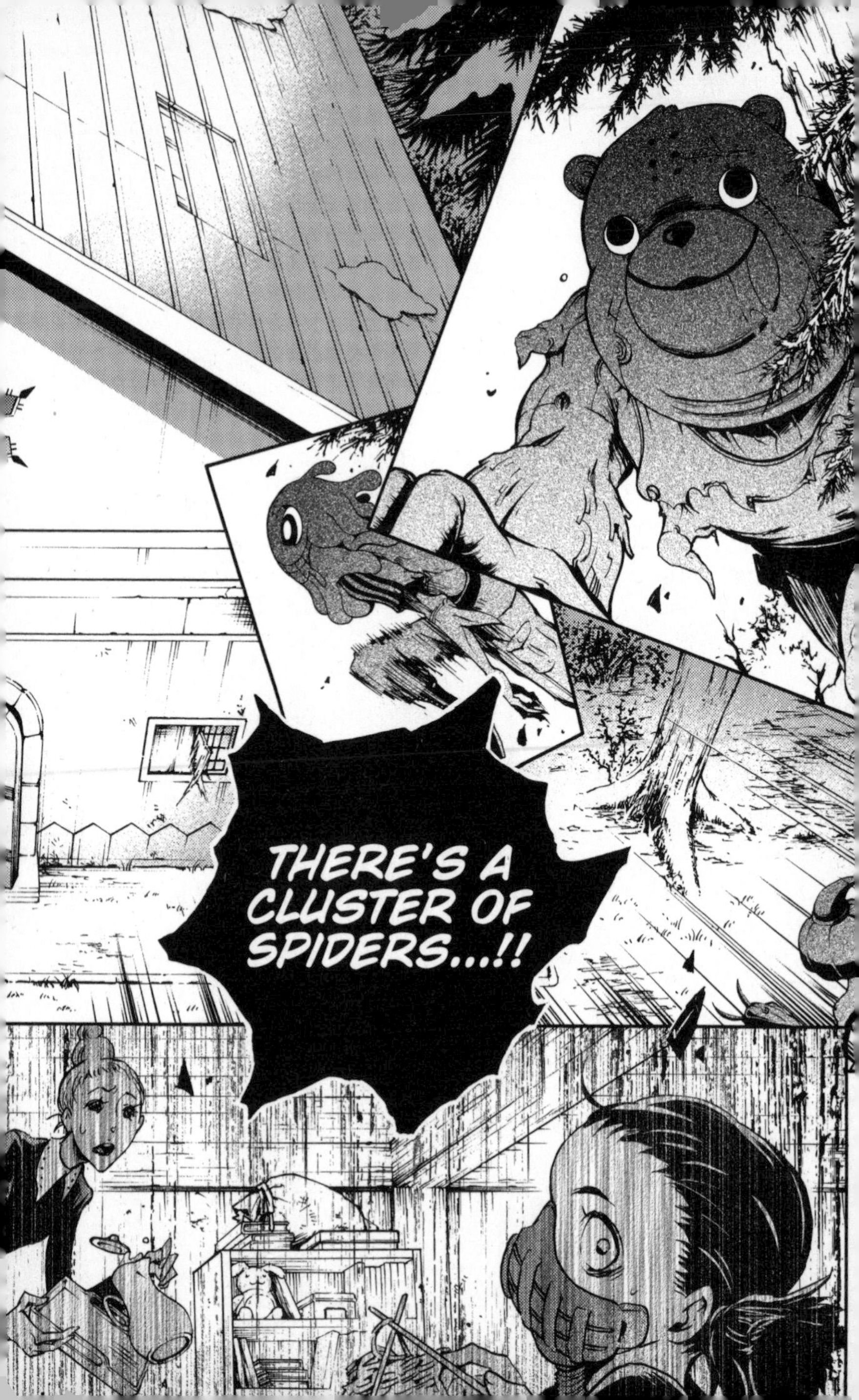
THERE'S A CLUSTER OF SPIDERS...!!

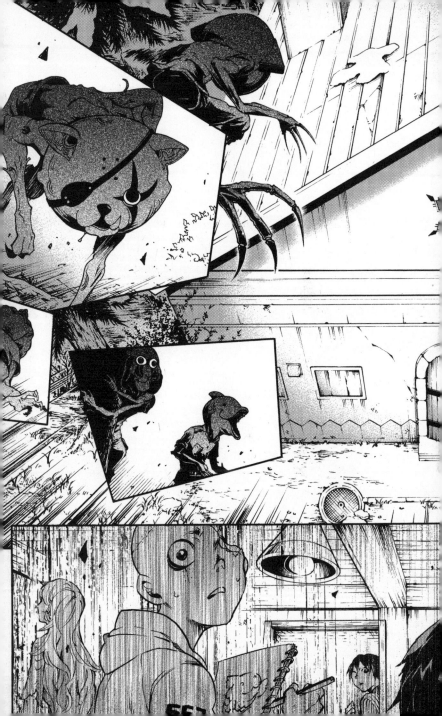

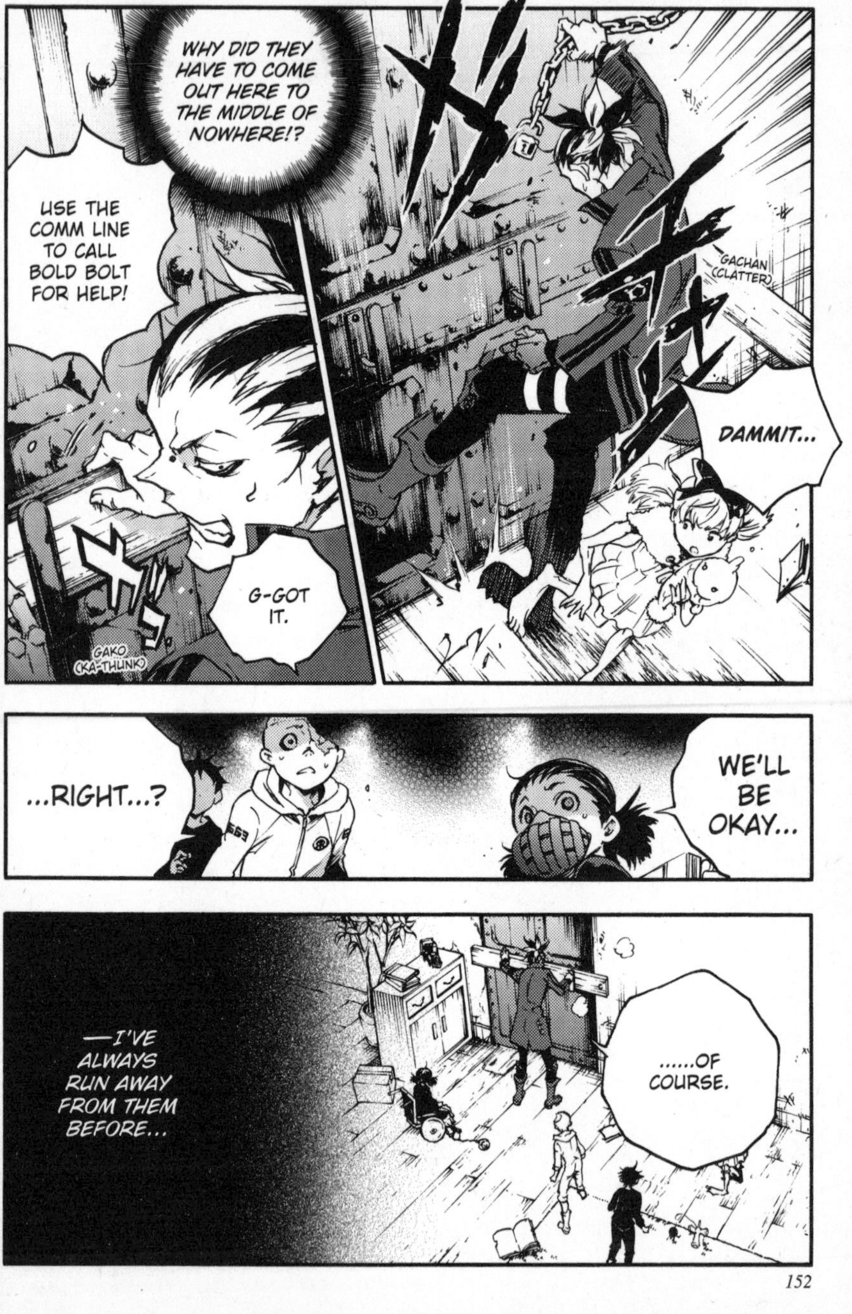
GACHAN (CLATTER)
DAMMIT...
WHY DID THEY HAVE TO COME OUT HERE TO THE MIDDLE OF NOWHERE!?
USE THE COMM LINE TO CALL BOLD BOLT FOR HELP!
G-GOT IT.
GAKO (KA-THUNK)
WE'LL BE OKAY...
...RIGHT...?
......OF COURSE.
—I'VE ALWAYS RUN AWAY FROM THEM BEFORE...

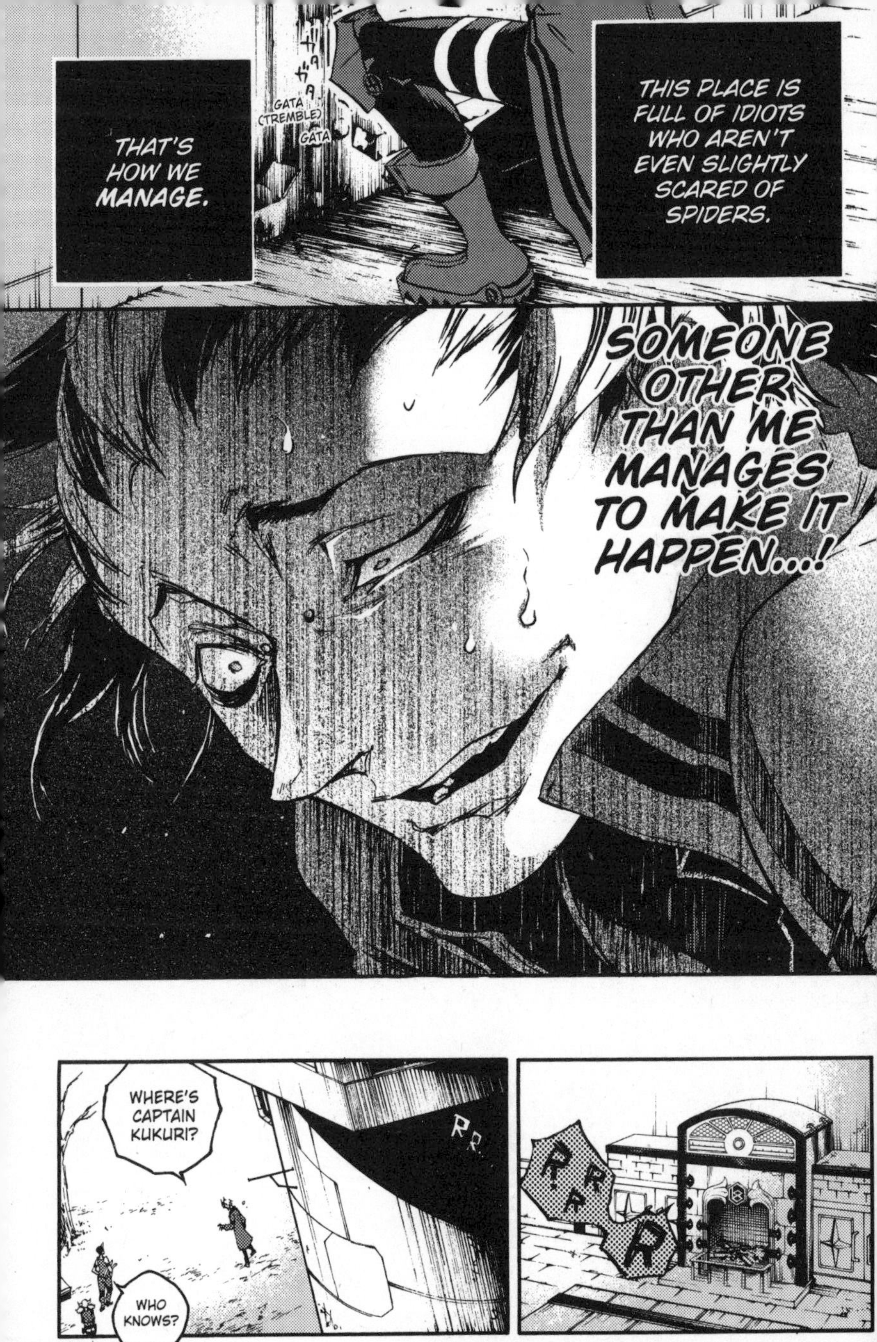
THIS PLACE IS FULL OF IDIOTS WHO AREN'T EVEN SLIGHTLY SCARED OF SPIDERS.
GATA (TREMBLE) GATA
THAT'S HOW WE MANAGE.
SOMEONE OTHER THAN ME MANAGES TO MAKE IT HAPPEN...!
RRRRR
RR
WHERE'S CAPTAIN KUKURI?
WHO KNOWS?

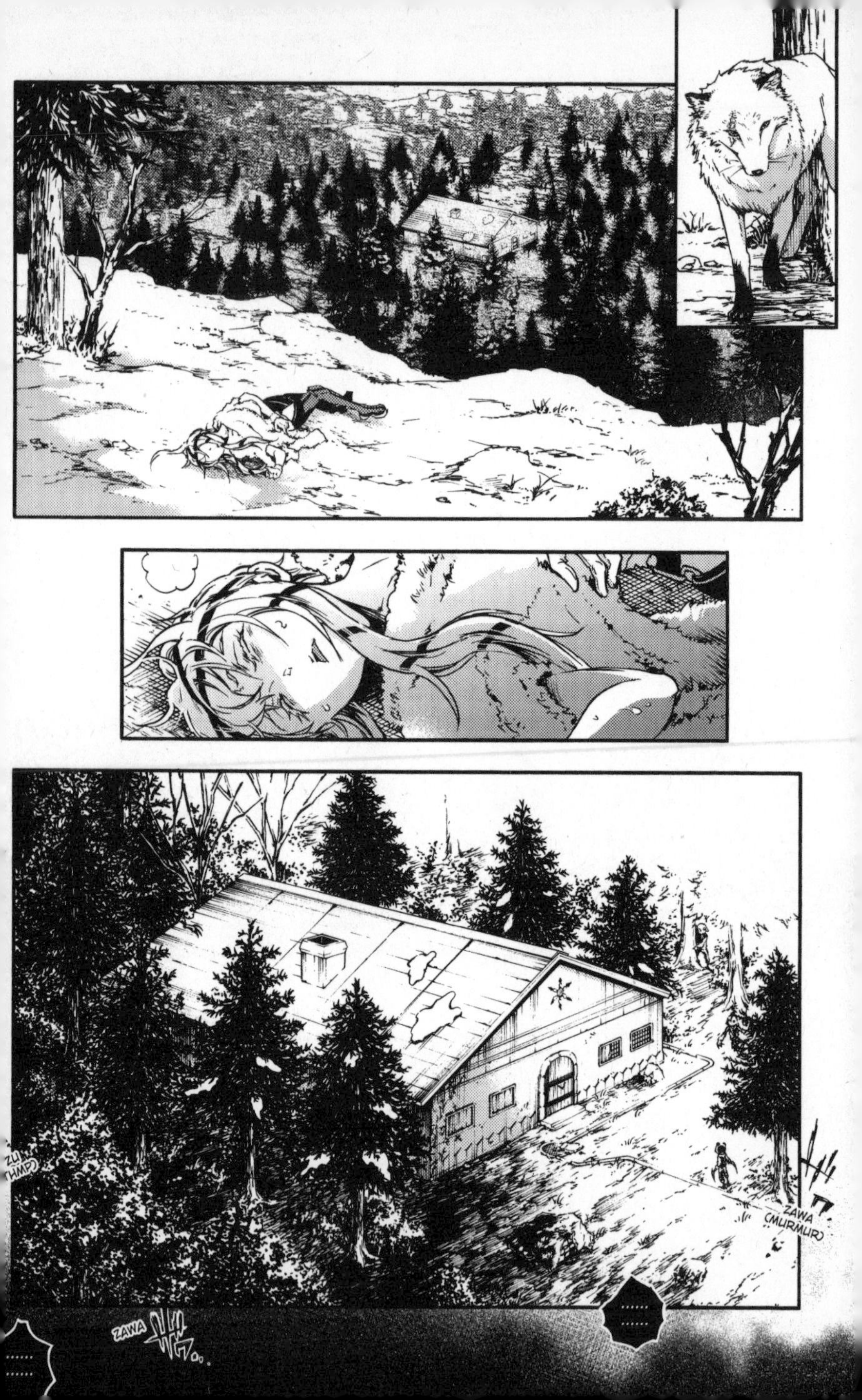
ZAWA (MURMUR)
ZU (THMP)
......
......
ZAWA
......
......

What's that noise I've been hearing...?

Pi

GAPA (POP)

JIII (BZZ)

BIRORORO (WHIRR)

!

IT'S DOC'S ANALYSIS OF THE LORD.

RRRR

R

R

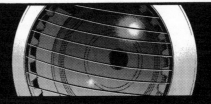

The Lord...

...attracts Spiders to it...?

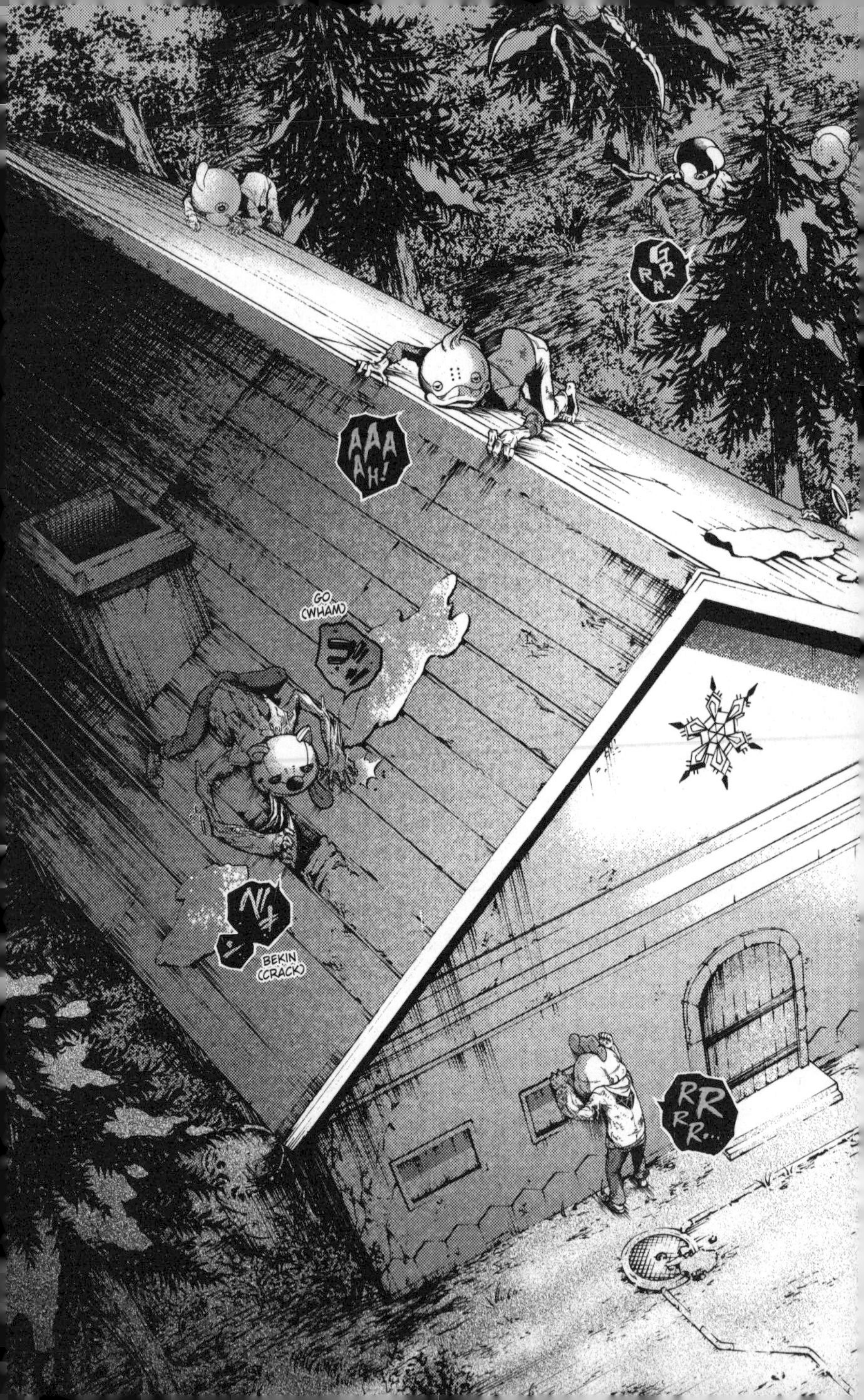
GRRR.
AAAAH!
GO (WHAM)
RRRR...
BEKIN (CRACK)

SMOKIN' PARADE

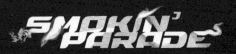

THE WORLD IS DEAD, THE PARADE WILL START.

JINSEI KATAOKA, KAZUMA KONDOU

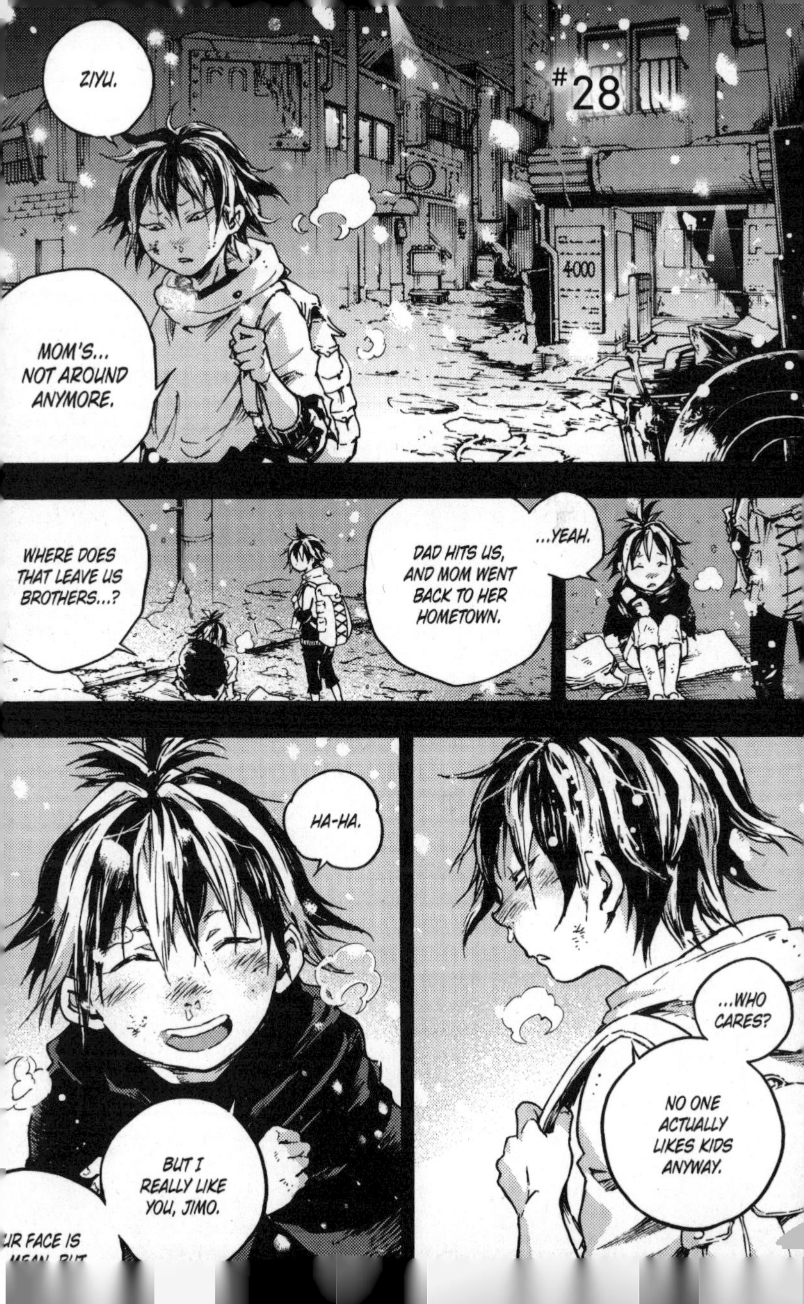
#28
ZIYU.
MOM'S... NOT AROUND ANYMORE.
...YEAH.
DAD HITS US, AND MOM WENT BACK TO HER HOMETOWN.
WHERE DOES THAT LEAVE US BROTHERS...?
...WHO CARES?
NO ONE ACTUALLY LIKES KIDS ANYWAY.
HA-HA.
BUT I REALLY LIKE YOU, JIMO.
UR FACE IS

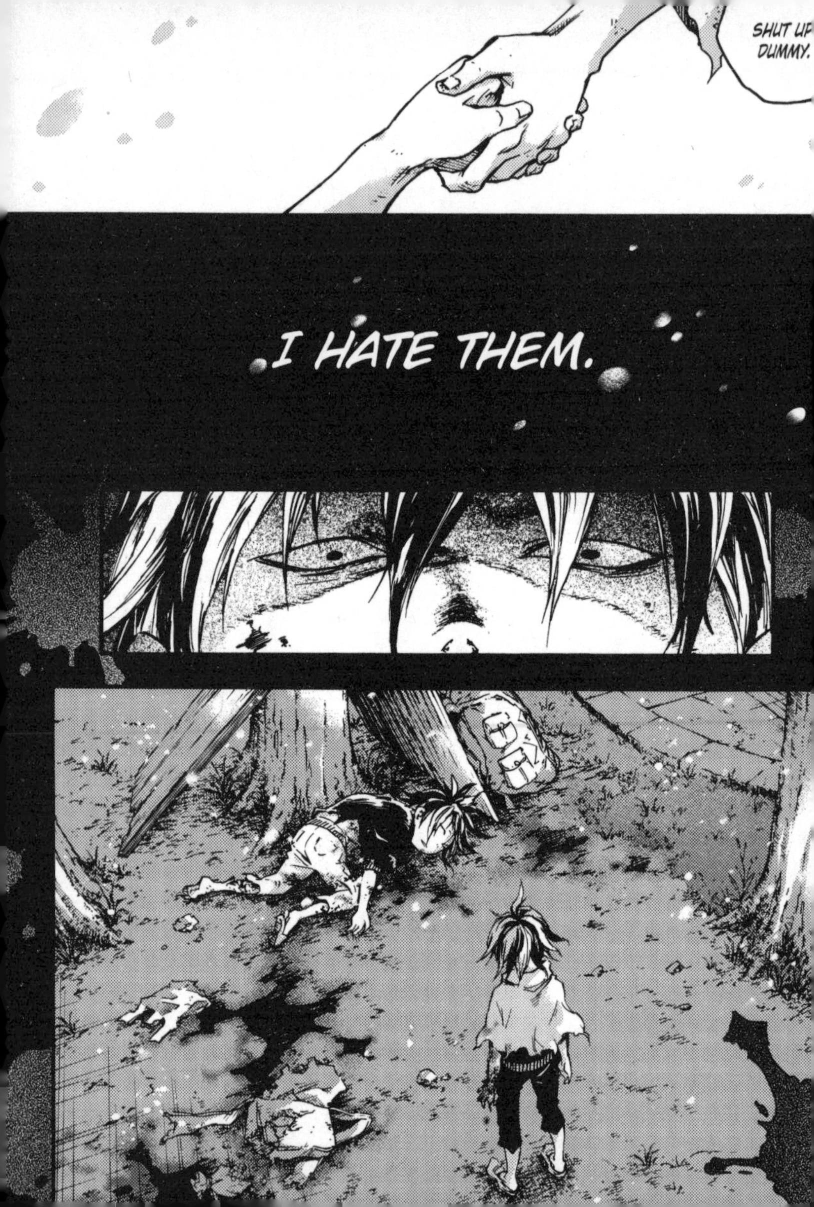
SHUT UP
DUMMY.
I HATE THEM.

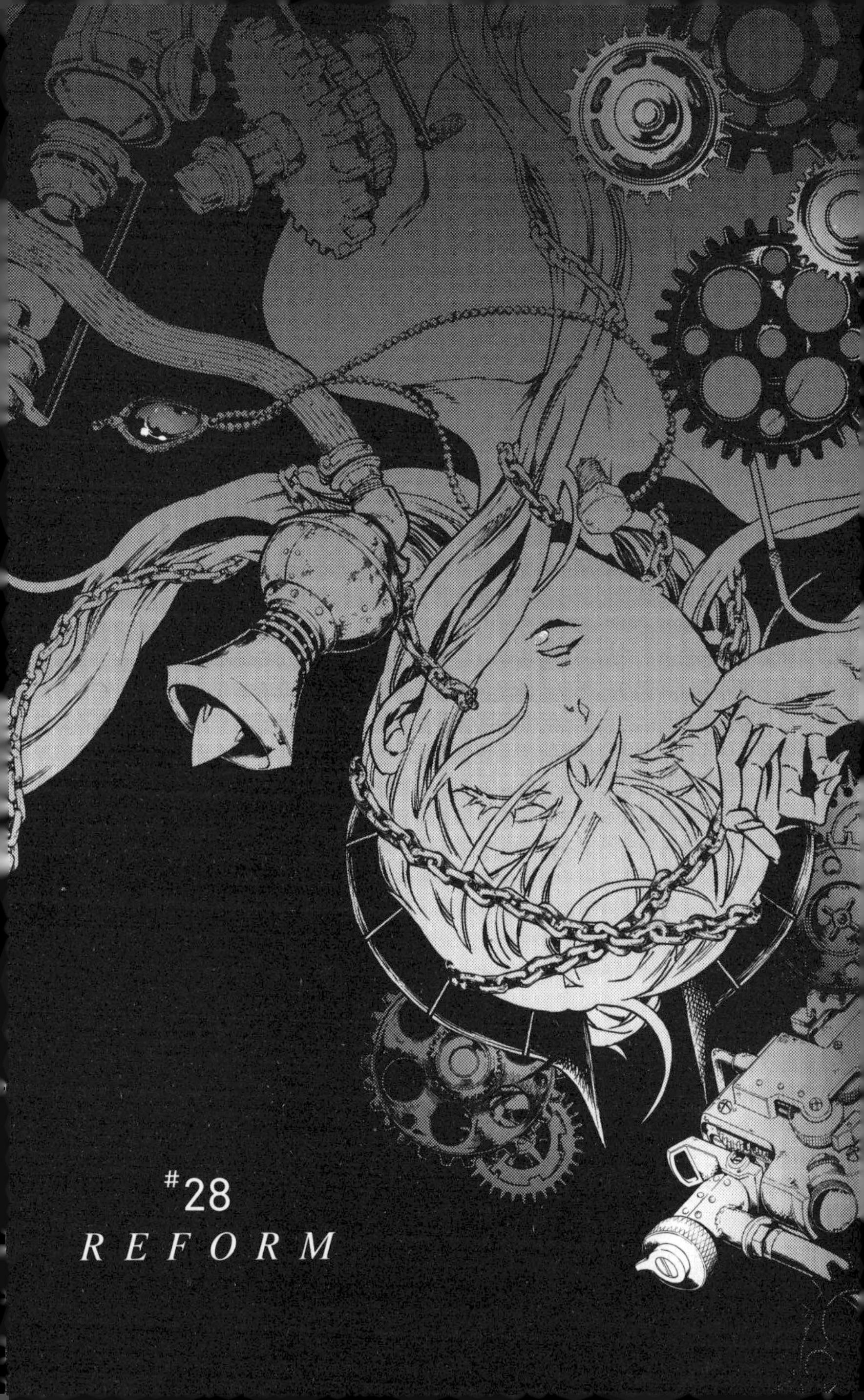

#28 REFORM

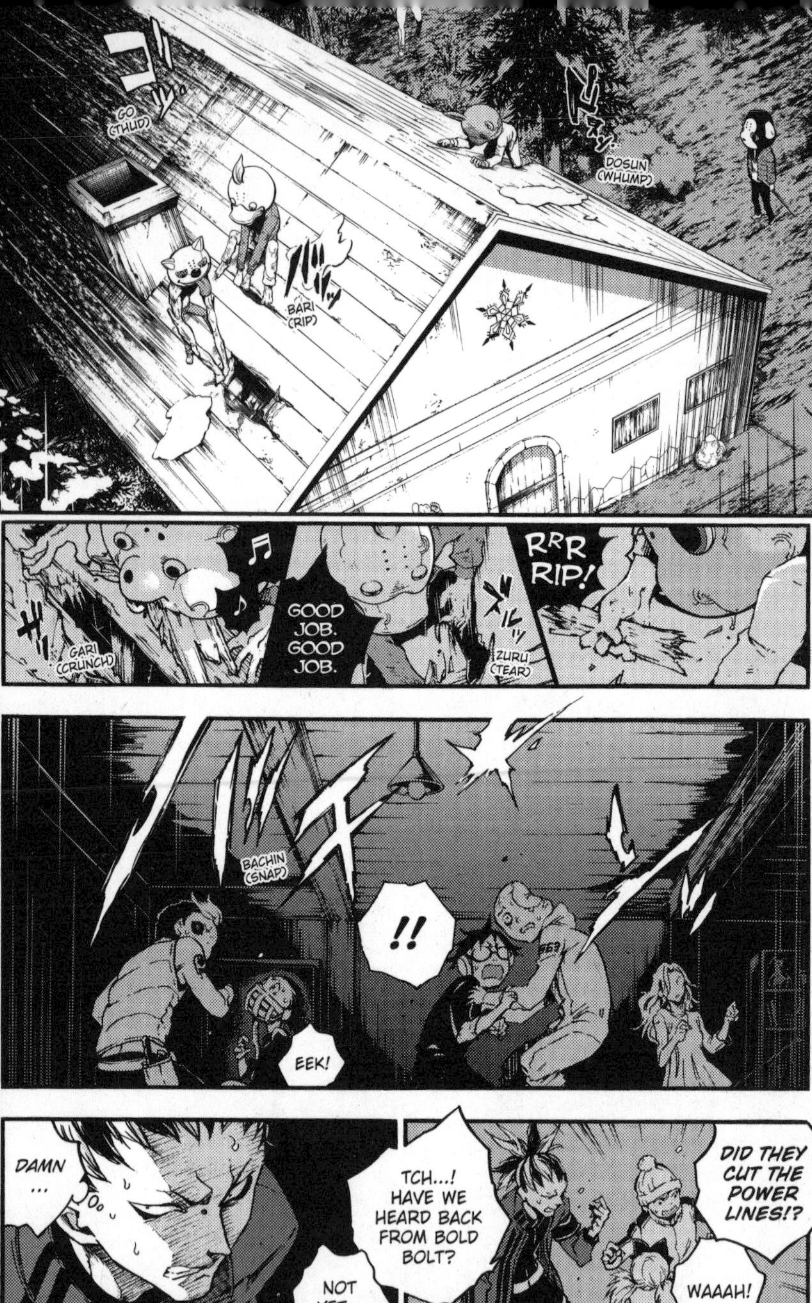
DOSUN (WHUMP)
GO (THUD)
BARI (RIP)
RRR RIP!
ZURU (TEAR)
GOOD JOB. GOOD JOB.
GARI (CRUNCH)
BACHIN (SNAP)
!!
EEK!
DID THEY CUT THE POWER LINES!?
TCH...! HAVE WE HEARD BACK FROM BOLD BOLT?
WAAAH!
NOT YET...
DAMN ...

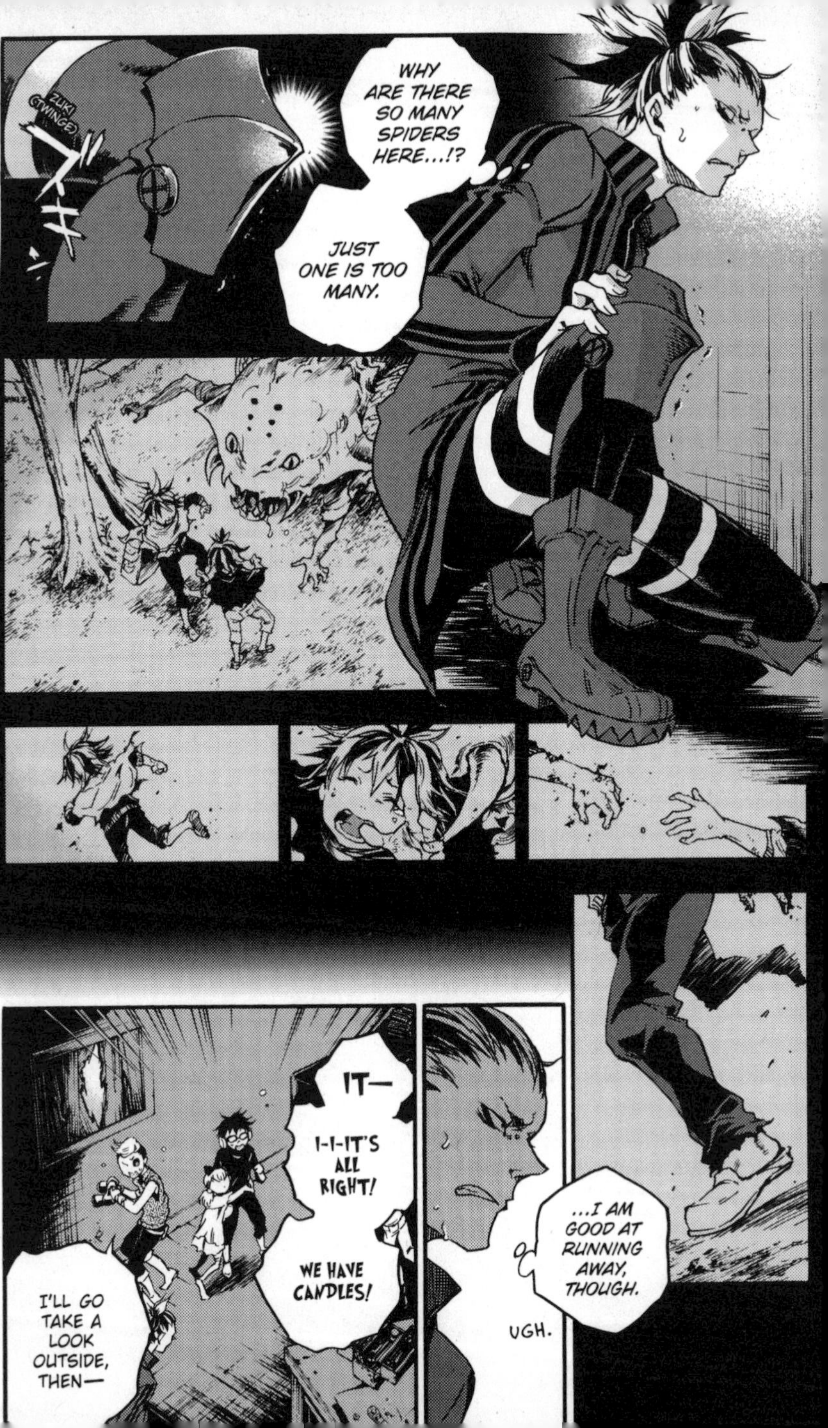
WHY ARE THERE SO MANY SPIDERS HERE...!?
JUST ONE IS TOO MANY.
ZUKI (TWINGE)
...I AM GOOD AT RUNNING AWAY, THOUGH.
UGH.
IT—
I-I-IT'S ALL RIGHT!
WE HAVE CANDLES!
I'LL GO TAKE A LOOK OUTSIDE, THEN—

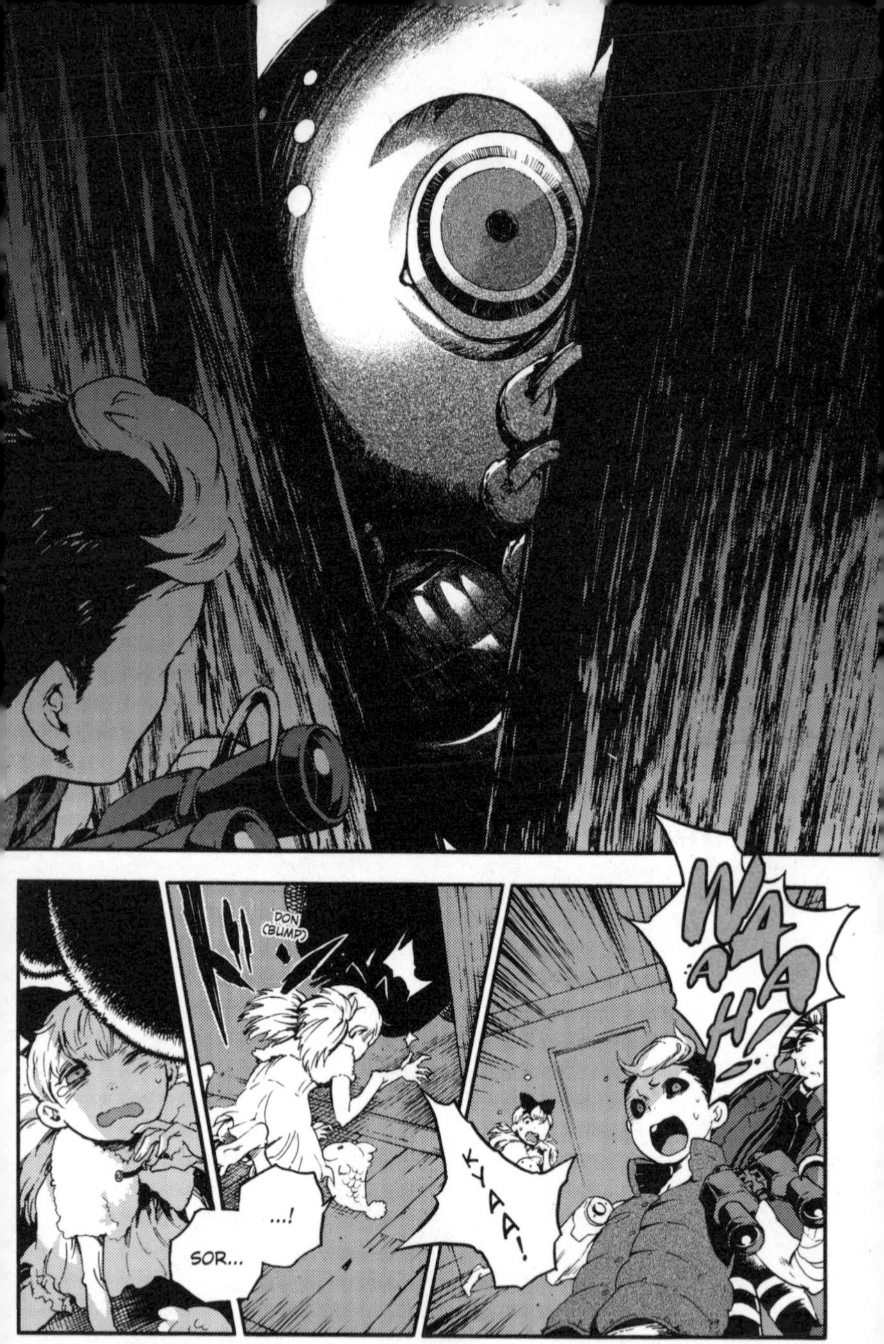
WAAAH!
KYAAA!
DON (BUMP)
...!
SOR...

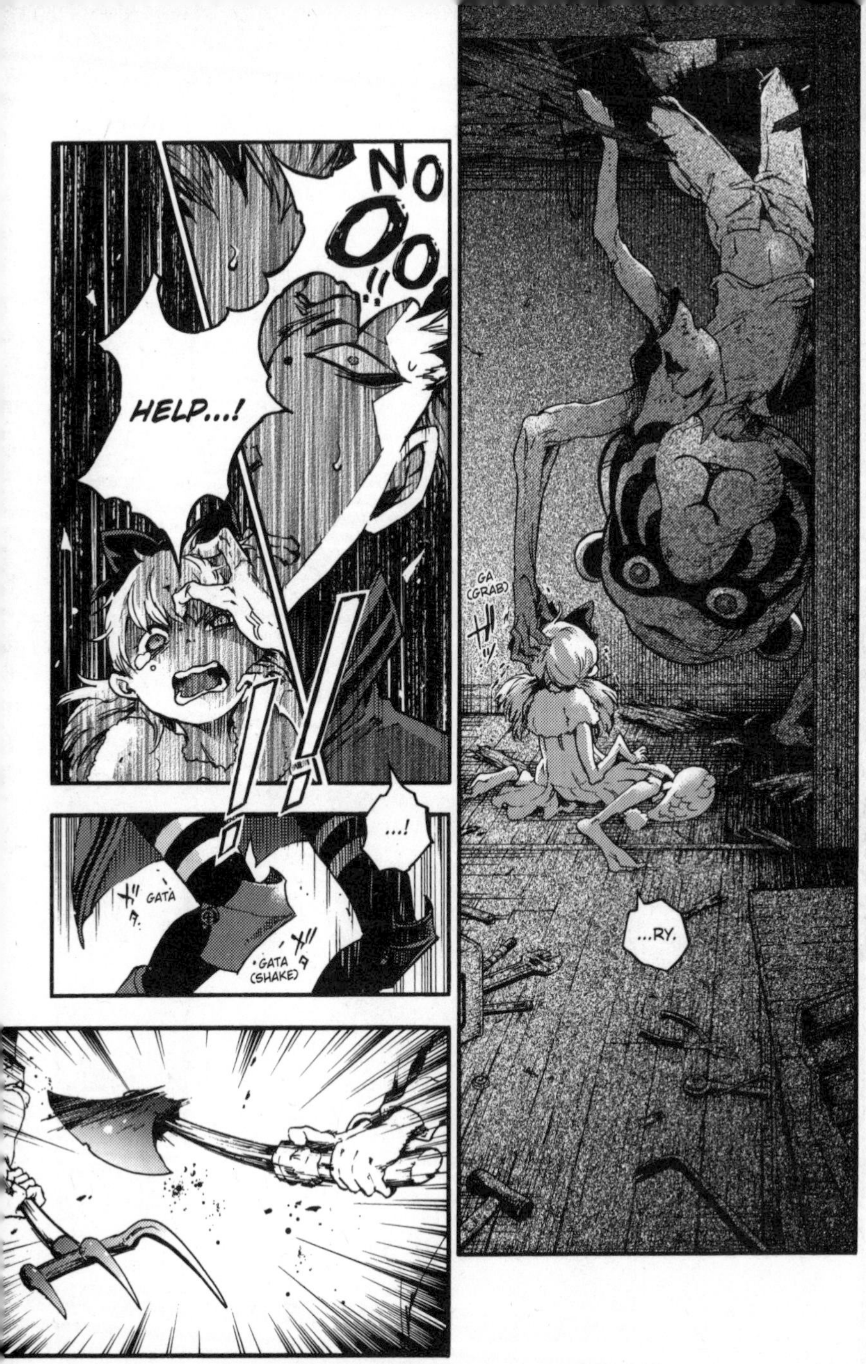
GA (GRAB)
...RY.
NOOO!!
HELP...!
...!
GATA
GATA (SHAKE)

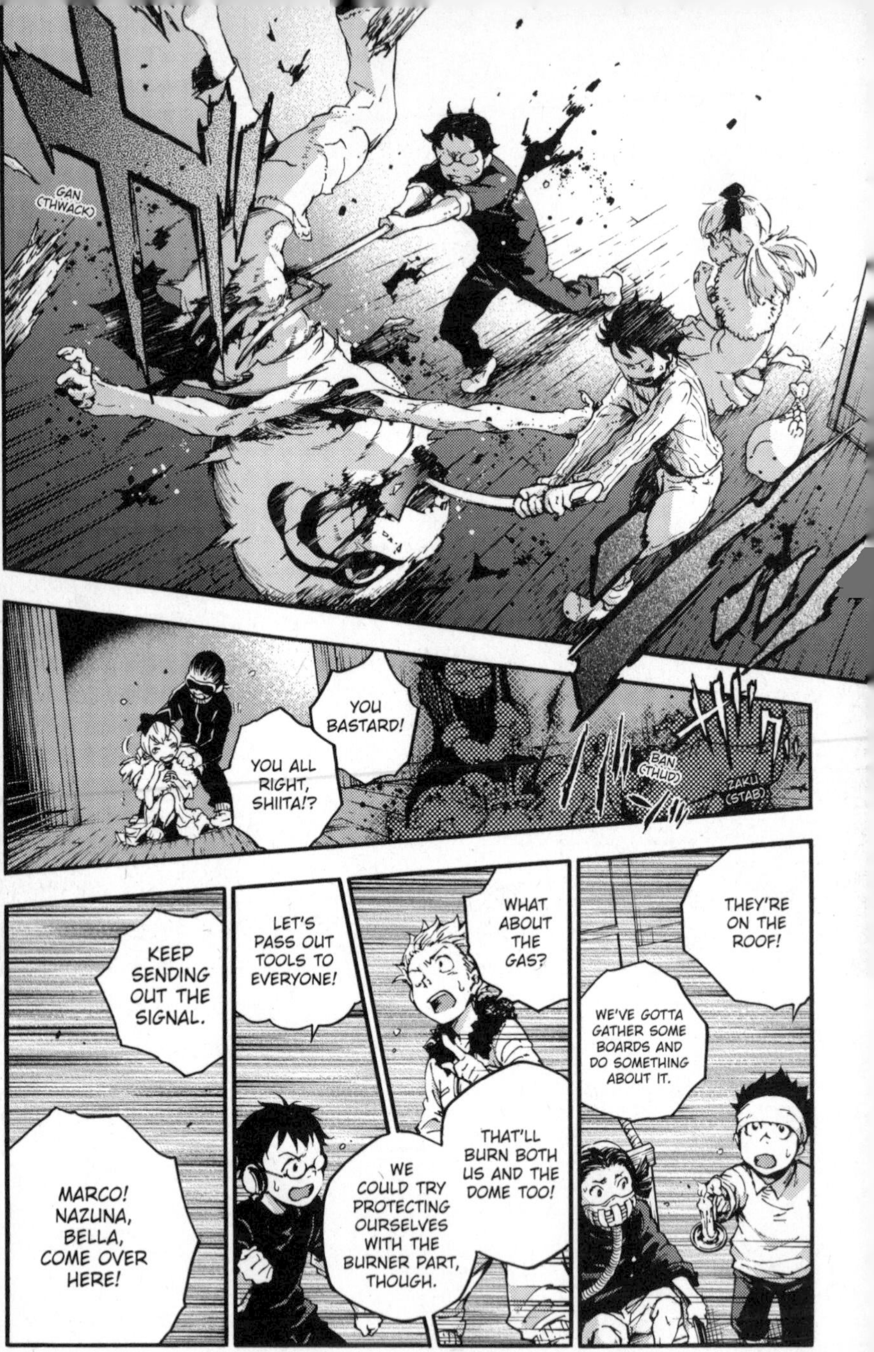
GAN (THWACK)
BAN (THUD)
ZAKU (STAB)
YOU BASTARD!
YOU ALL RIGHT, SHIITA!?
THEY'RE ON THE ROOF!
WE'VE GOTTA GATHER SOME BOARDS AND DO SOMETHING ABOUT IT.
WHAT ABOUT THE GAS?
THAT'LL BURN BOTH US AND THE DOME TOO!
WE COULD TRY PROTECTING OURSELVES WITH THE BURNER PART, THOUGH.
LET'S PASS OUT TOOLS TO EVERYONE!
KEEP SENDING OUT THE SIGNAL.
MARCO! NAZUNA, BELLA, COME OVER HERE!

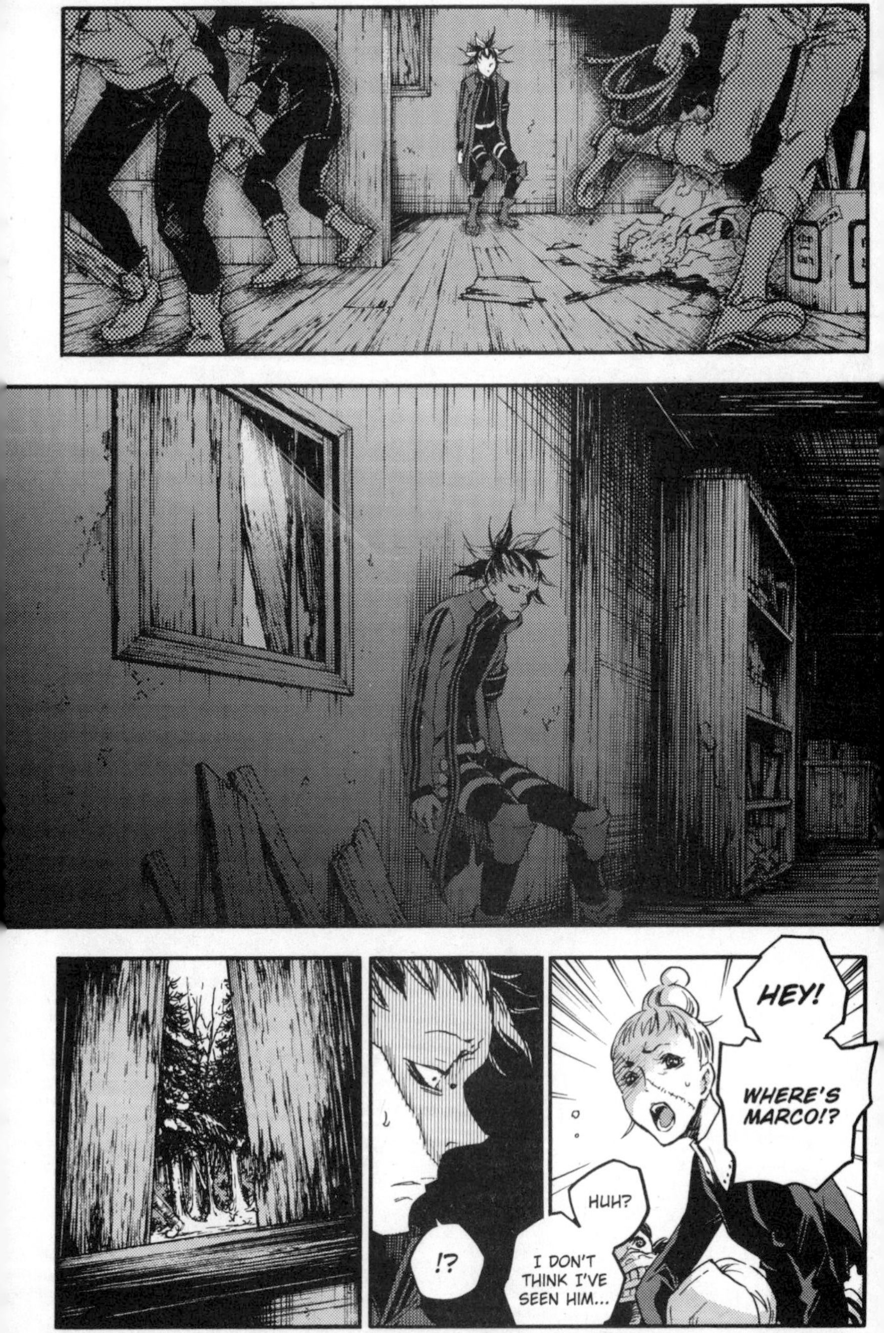
HEY!
WHERE'S MARCO!?
HUH?
I DON'T THINK I'VE SEEN HIM...
!?

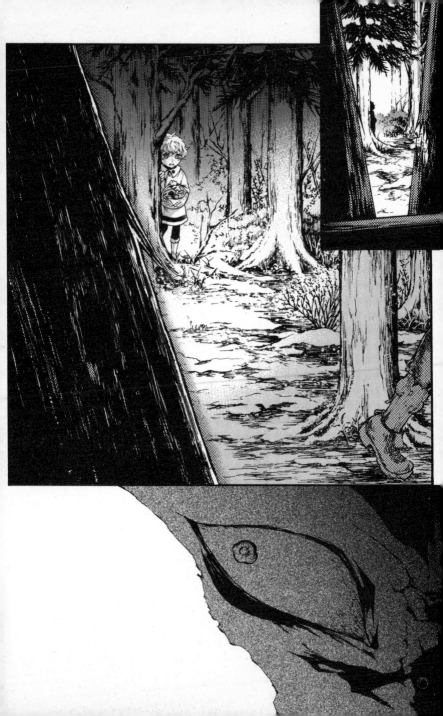

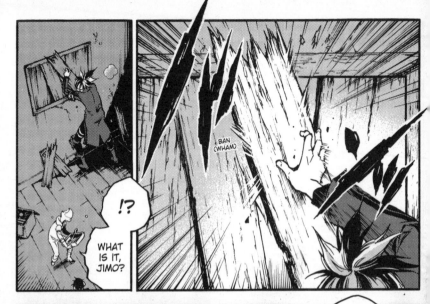

BAN
(WHAM)

!?

WHAT IS IT, JIMO?

BROTHER JIMO?

HAAH...

WHY DO I ALWAYS GET STUCK PATROLLING AROUND THE

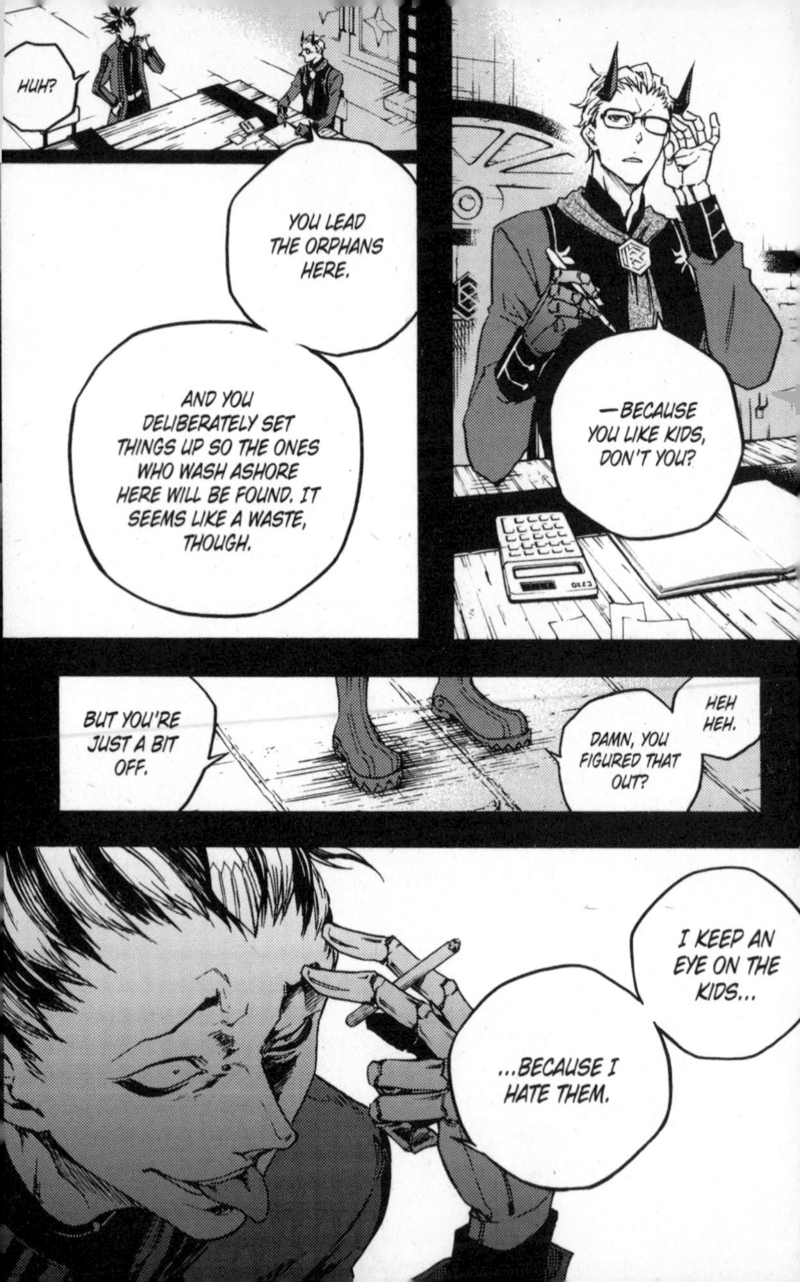
—BECAUSE YOU LIKE KIDS, DON'T YOU?
HUH?
YOU LEAD THE ORPHANS HERE.
AND YOU DELIBERATELY SET THINGS UP SO THE ONES WHO WASH ASHORE HERE WILL BE FOUND. IT SEEMS LIKE A WASTE, THOUGH.
HEH HEH.
DAMN, YOU FIGURED THAT OUT?
BUT YOU'RE JUST A BIT OFF.
I KEEP AN EYE ON THE KIDS...
...BECAUSE I HATE THEM.

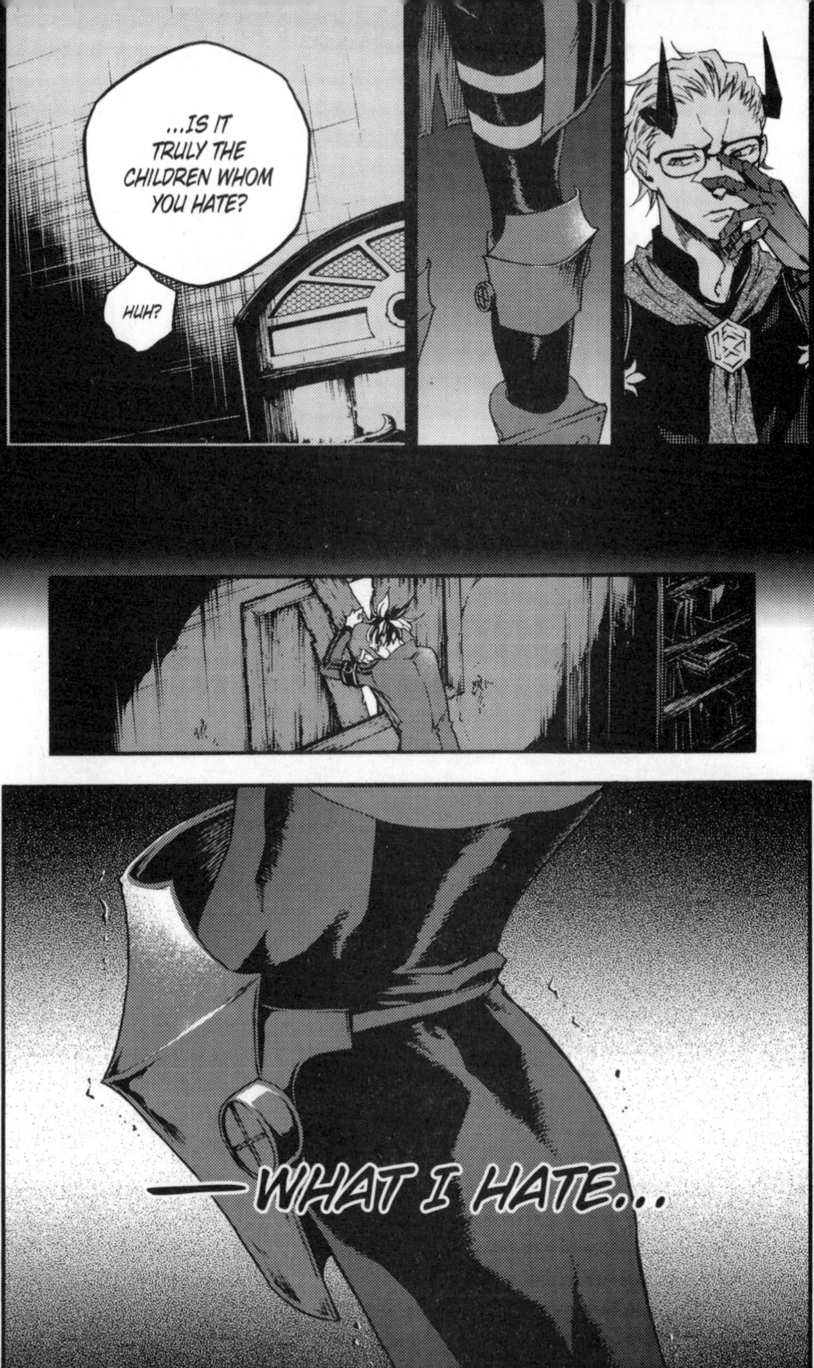
...IS IT TRULY THE CHILDREN WHOM YOU HATE?
HUH?
—WHAT I HATE...

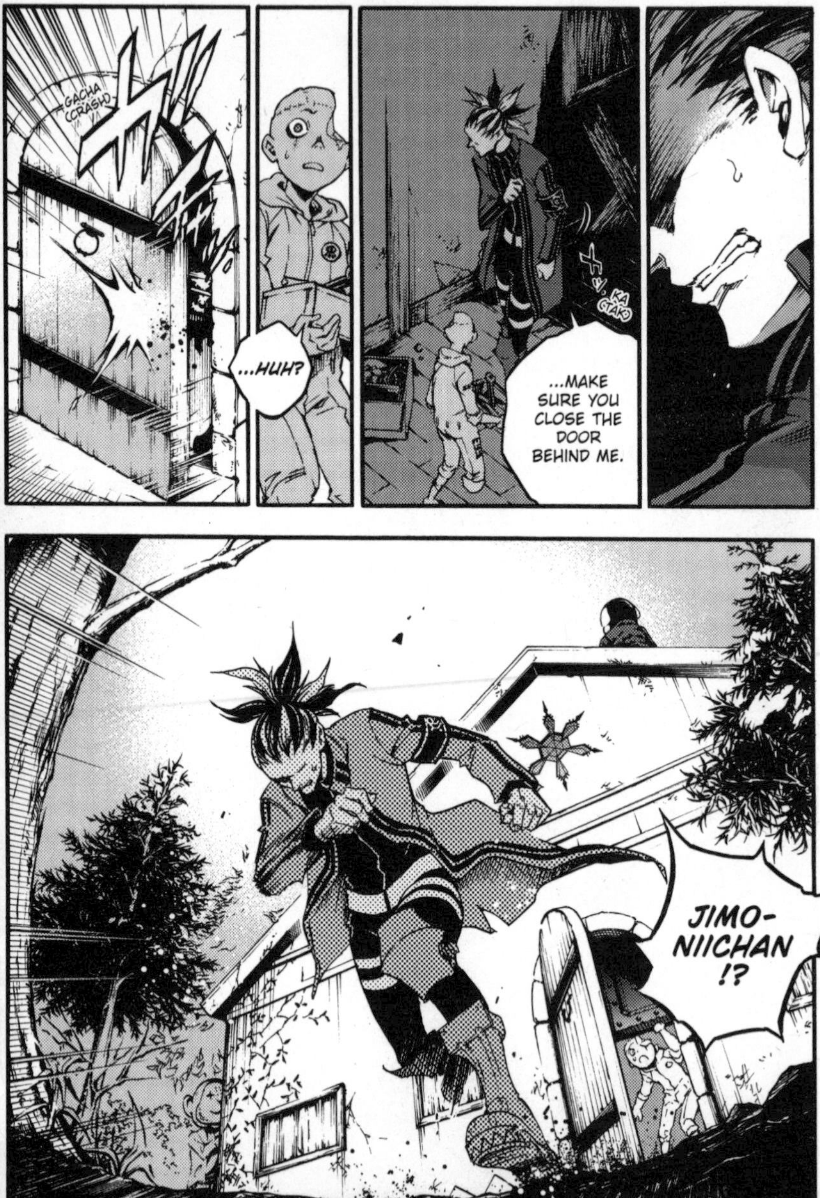
(KA-TAK)
...MAKE SURE YOU CLOSE THE DOOR BEHIND ME.
...HUH?
GACHA (CRASH)
JIMO-NIICHAN!?

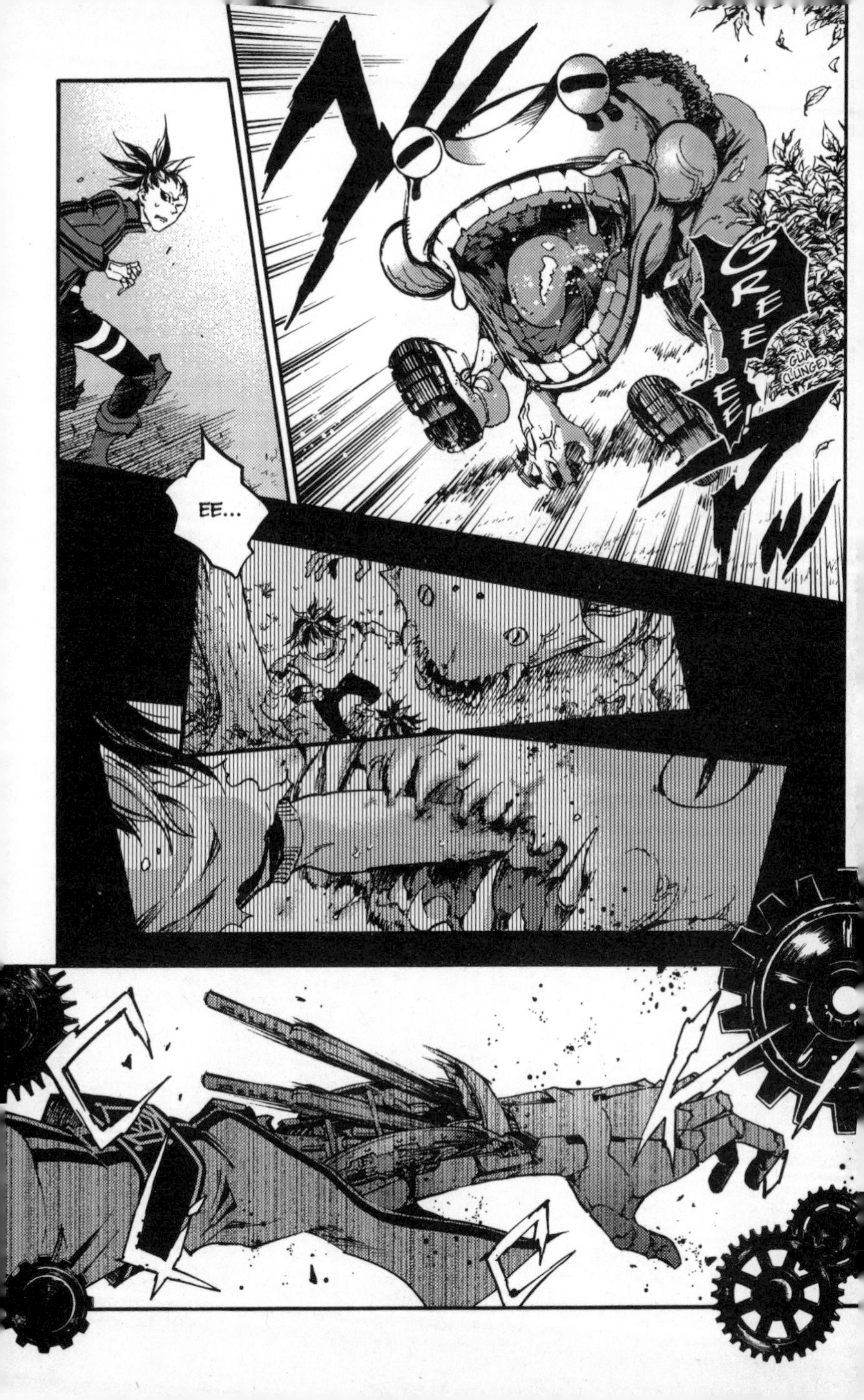
GREEEEE!
GUA (LUNGE)
EE...

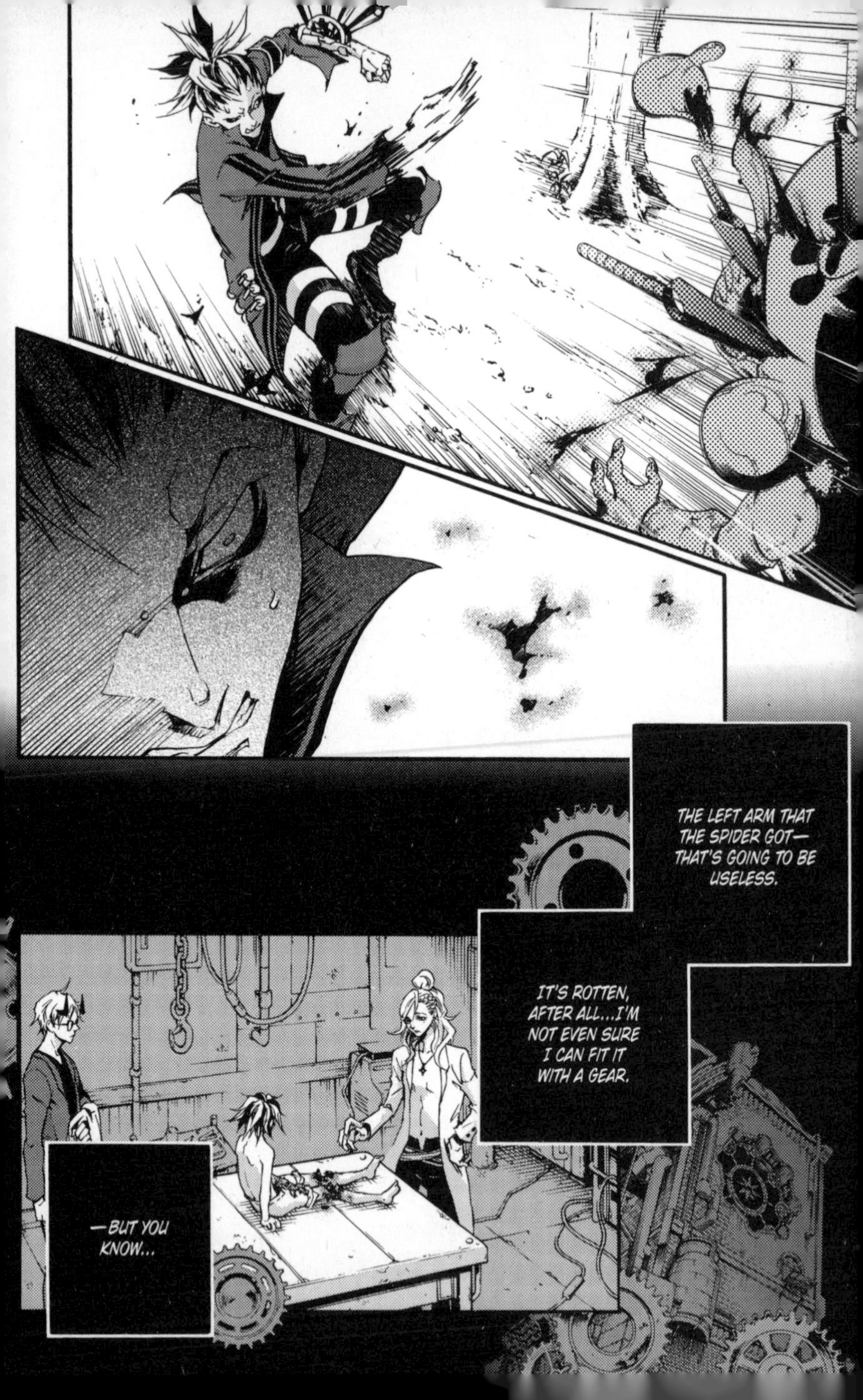
THE LEFT ARM THAT THE SPIDER GOT—THAT'S GOING TO BE USELESS.
IT'S ROTTEN, AFTER ALL...I'M NOT EVEN SURE I CAN FIT IT WITH A GEAR.
—BUT YOU KNOW...

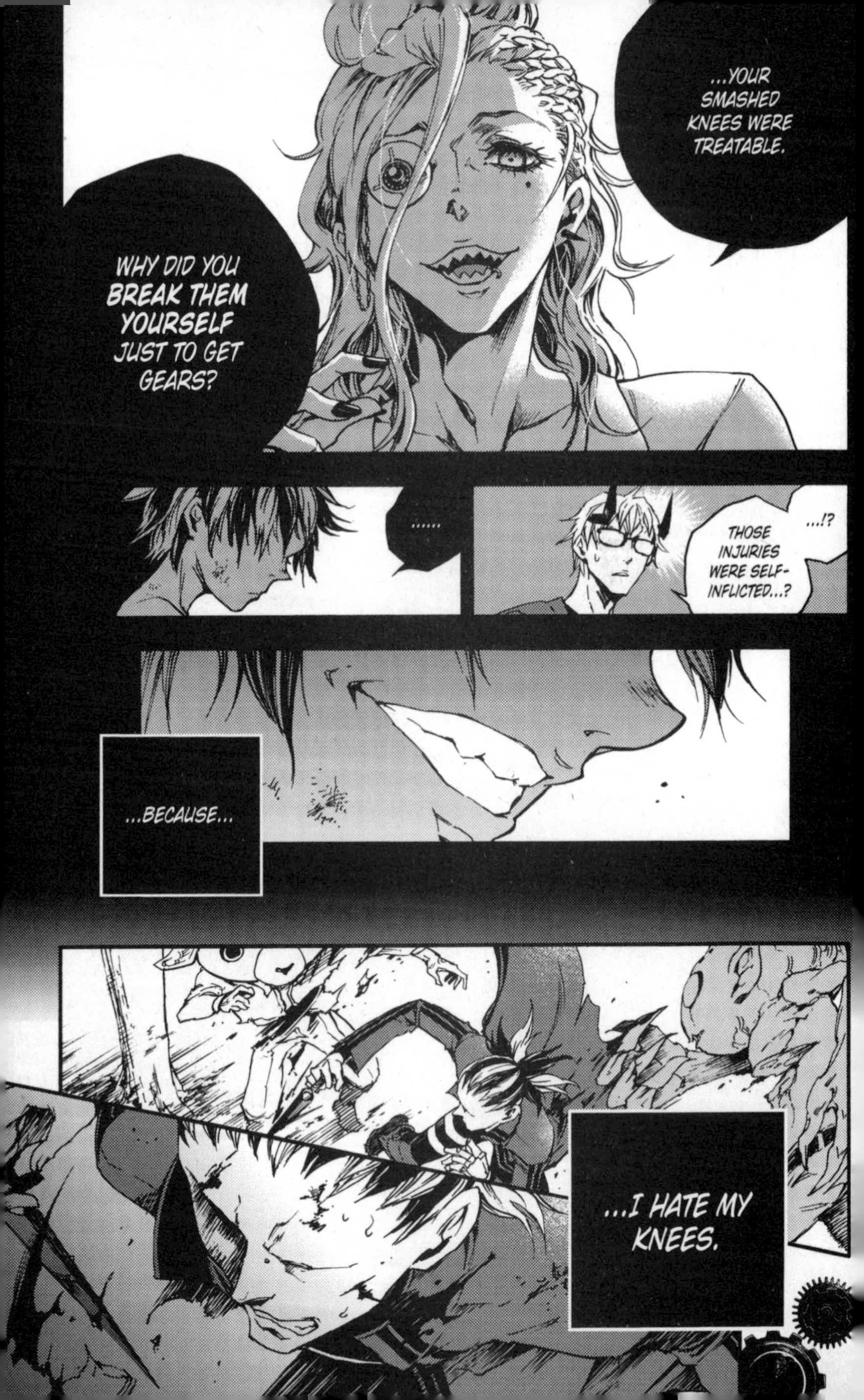
...YOUR SMASHED KNEES WERE TREATABLE.
WHY DID YOU BREAK THEM YOURSELF JUST TO GET GEARS?
...!?
THOSE INJURIES WERE SELF-INFLICTED...?
......
...BECAUSE...
...I HATE MY KNEES.

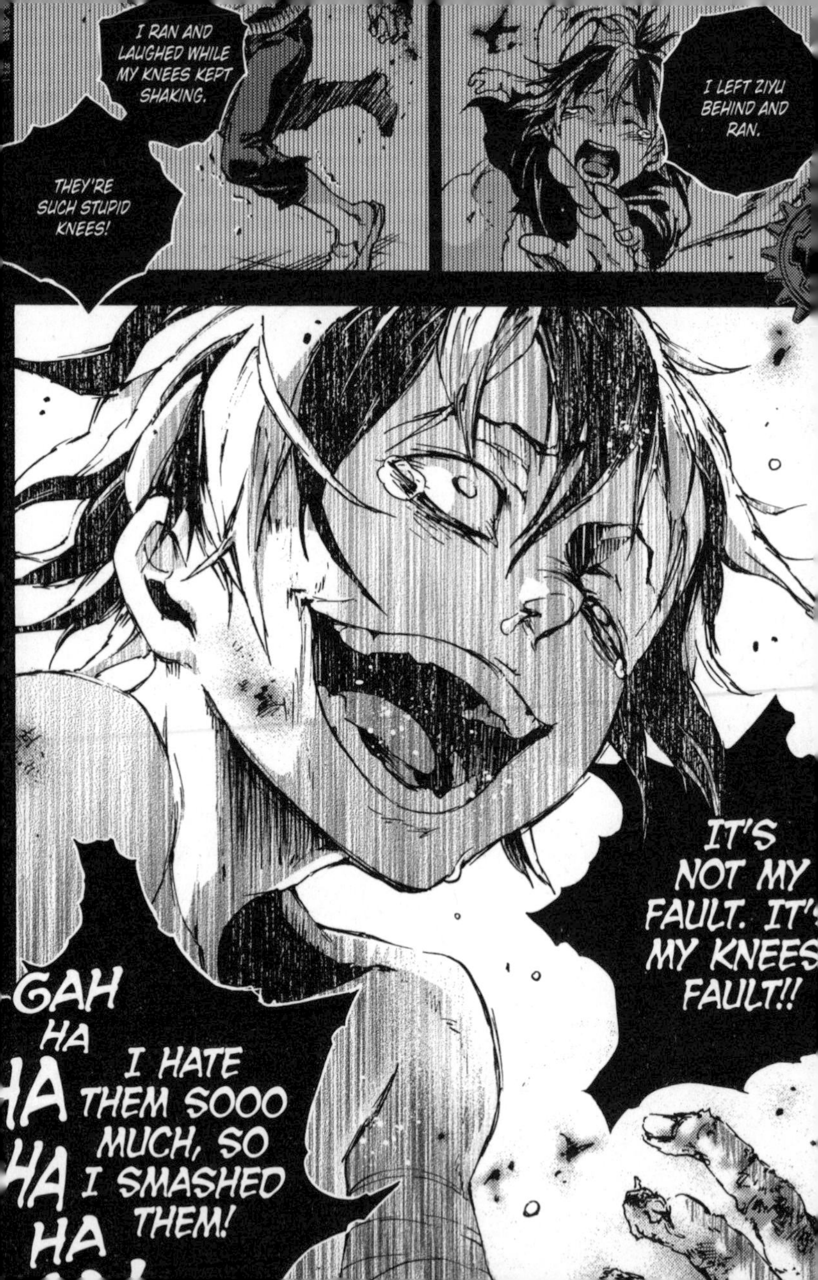
I LEFT ZIYU BEHIND AND RAN.
I RAN AND LAUGHED WHILE MY KNEES KEPT SHAKING.
THEY'RE SUCH STUPID KNEES!
IT'S NOT MY FAULT. IT'S MY KNEES FAULT!!
I HATE THEM SOOO MUCH, SO I SMASHED THEM!
GAH HA HA HA HA HA

HEH-HEH... SO HURRY UP.

HURRY UP AND JUST GIVE ME NEW ONES...

THEY'RE SHAKING AGAIN...

UGH...

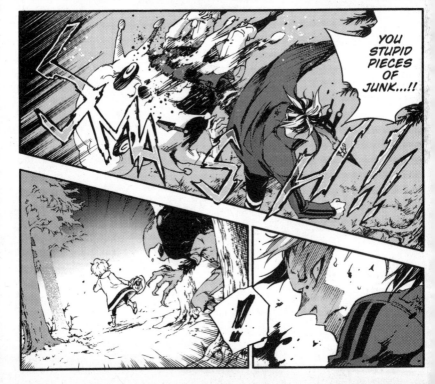

YOU STUPID PIECES OF JUNK...!!

!!

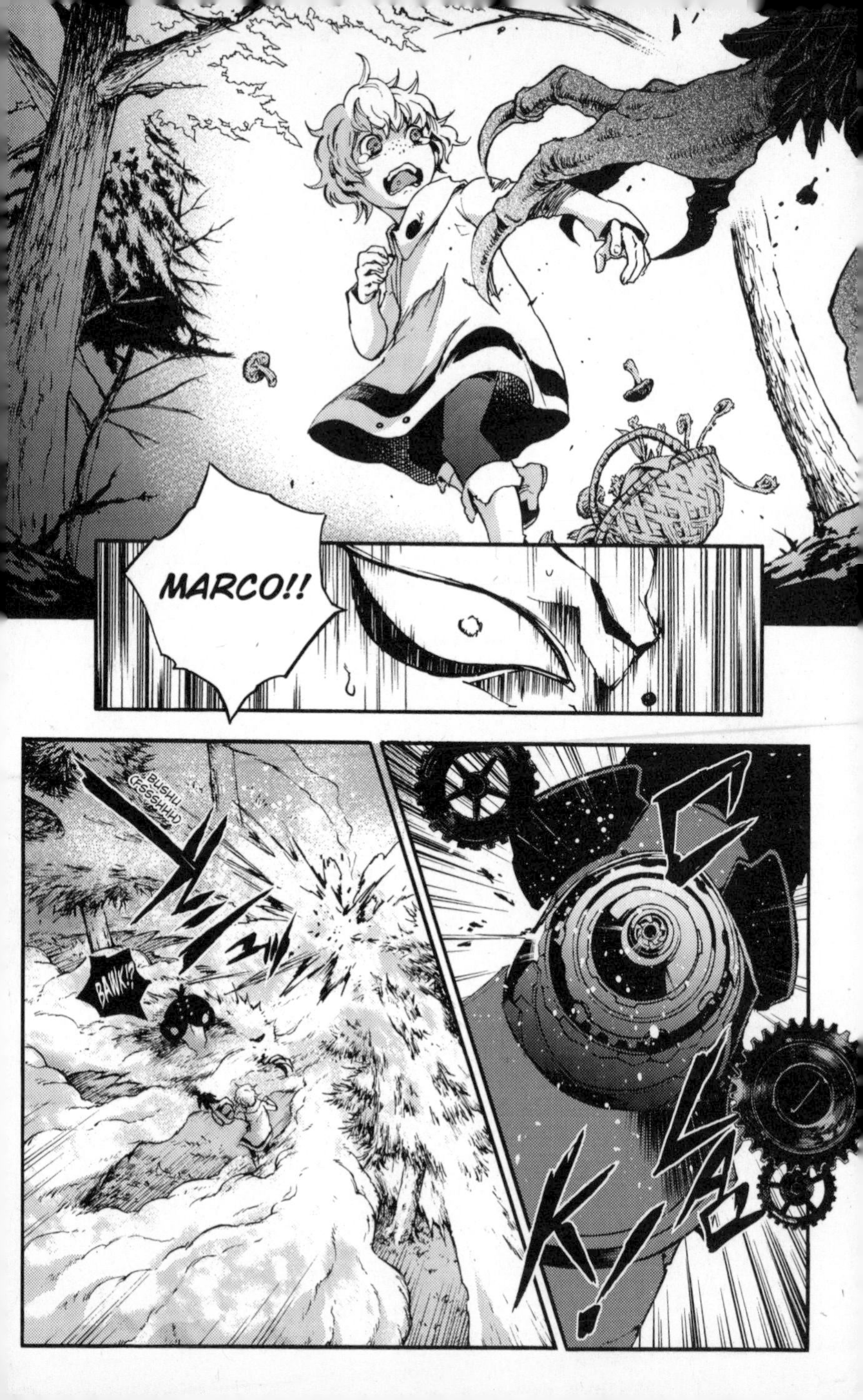
MARCO!!
BUSHU (FSSSHH)
BAWK!?

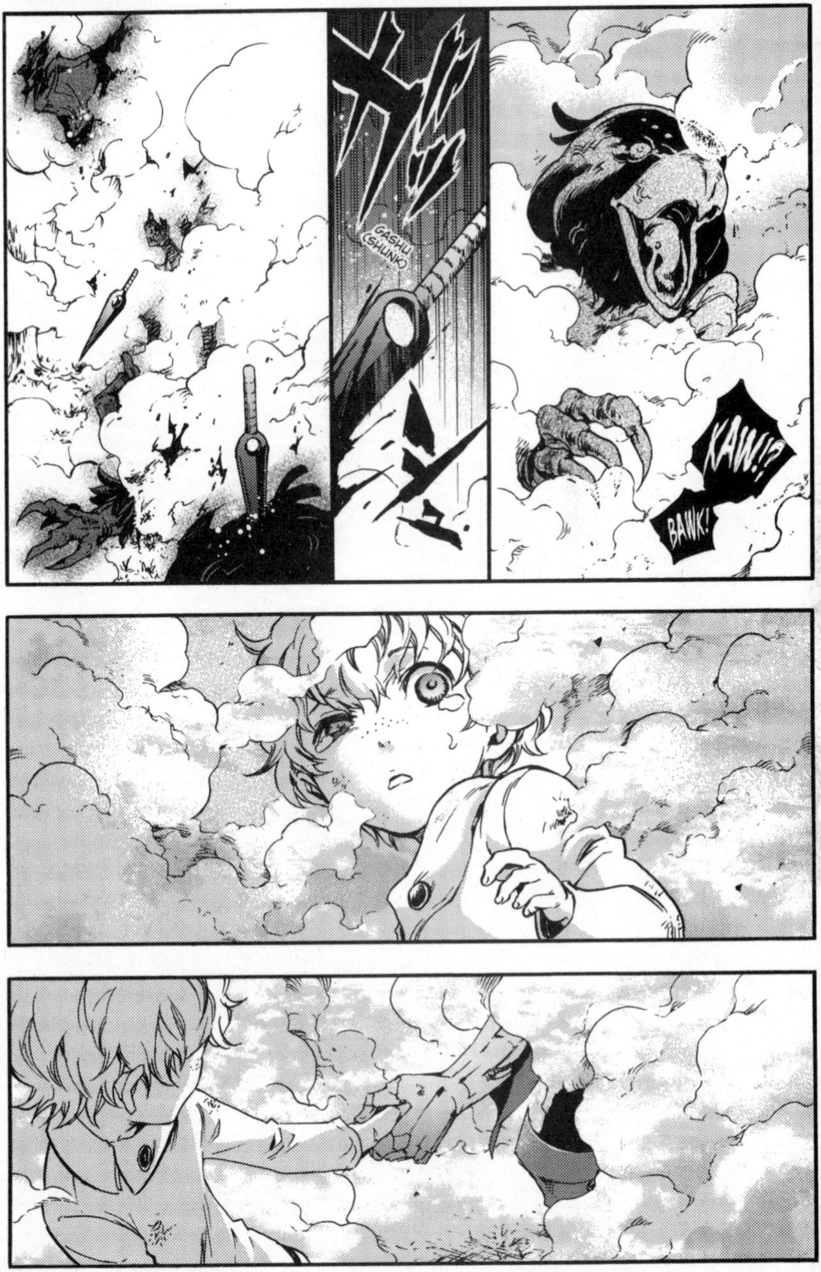
KAW!!?
BAWK!
GASHU (SHUNK)

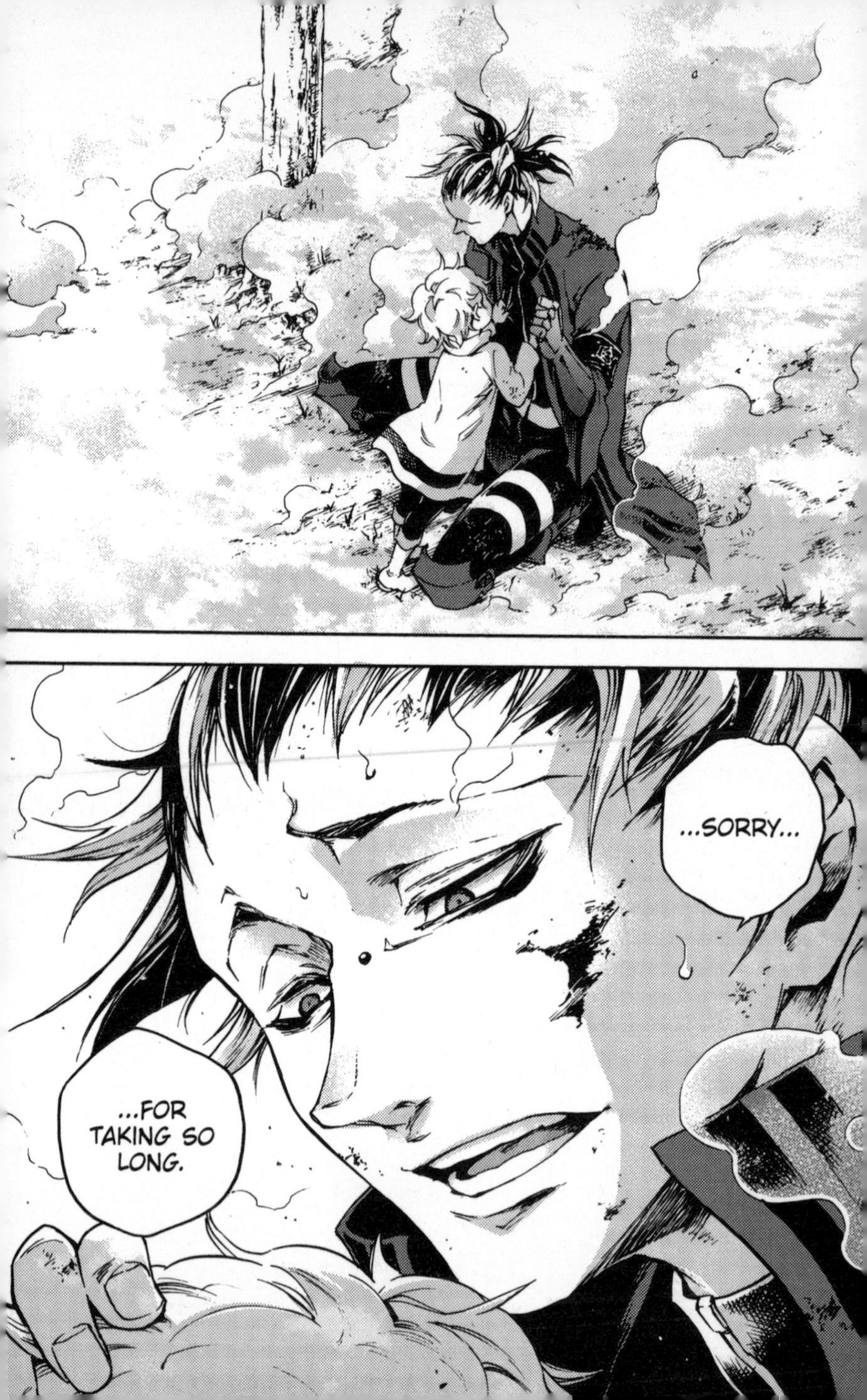
...SORRY...
...FOR TAKING SO LONG.

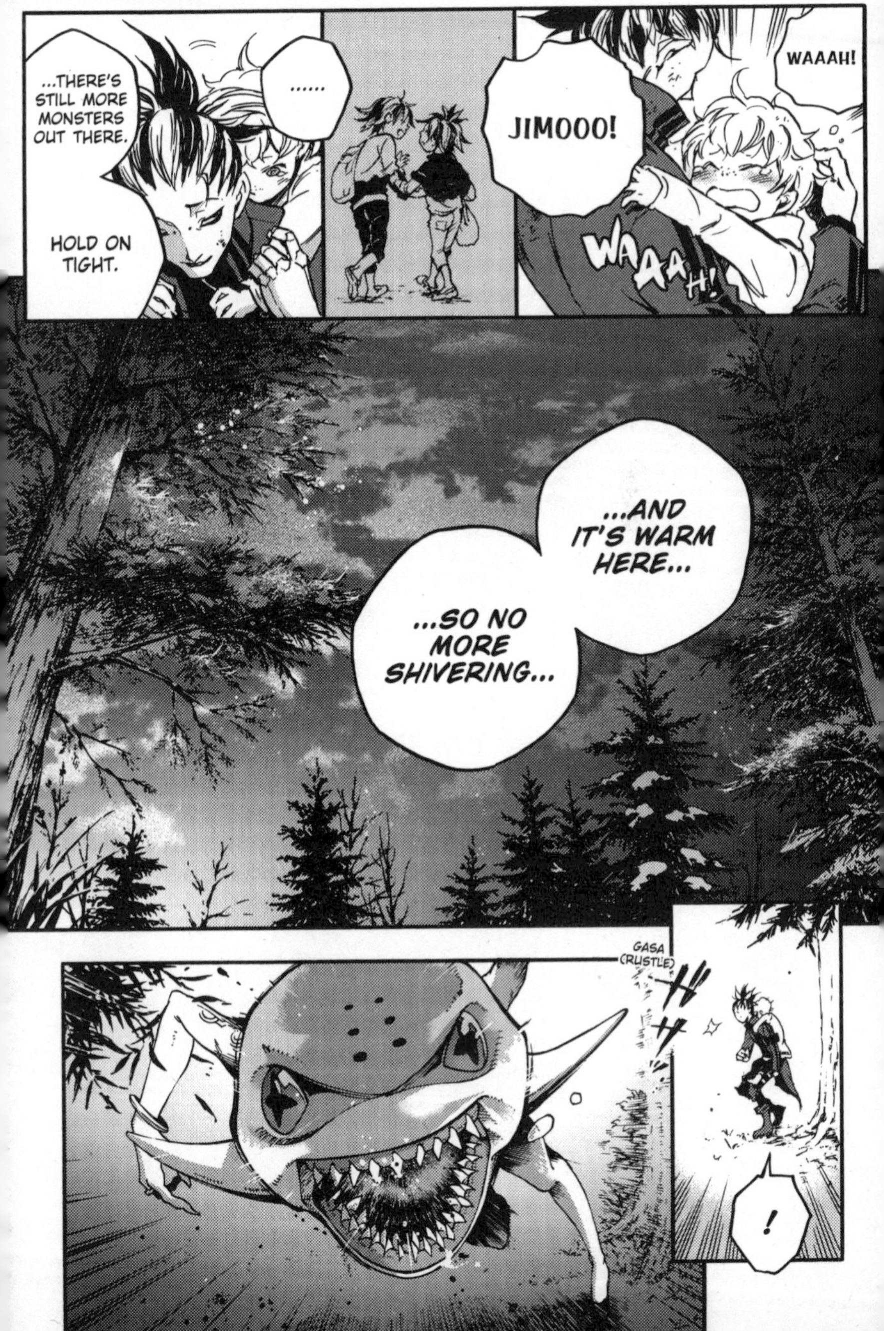
WAAAH!
JIMOOO!
WAAAH!
......
...THERE'S STILL MORE MONSTERS OUT THERE.
HOLD ON TIGHT.
...AND IT'S WARM HERE...
...SO NO MORE SHIVERING...
GASA (RUSTLE)
!

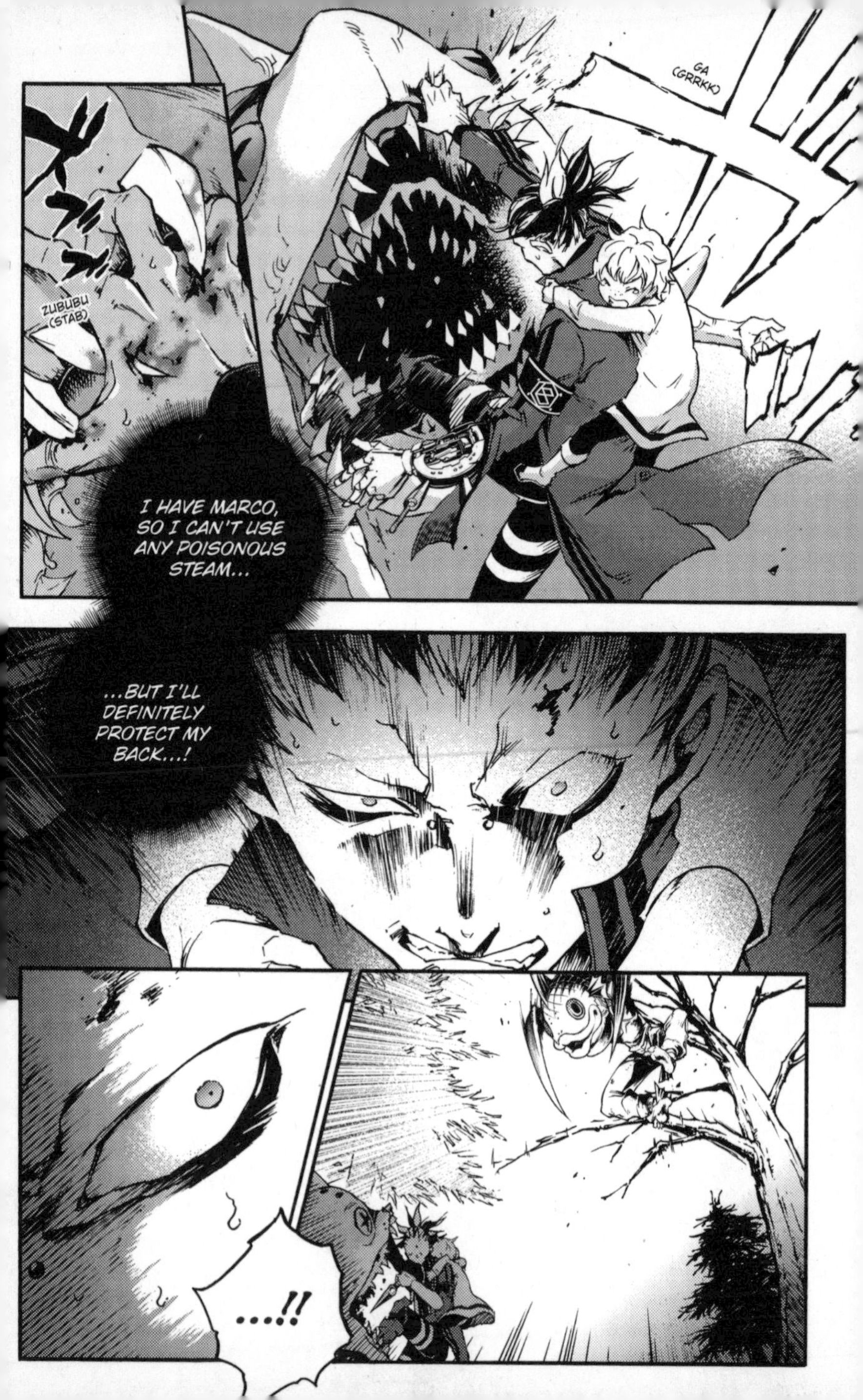
GA (GRRKK)
ZUBUBU (STAB)
I HAVE MARCO, SO I CAN'T USE ANY POISONOUS STEAM...
...BUT I'LL DEFINITELY PROTECT MY BACK...!
...!!

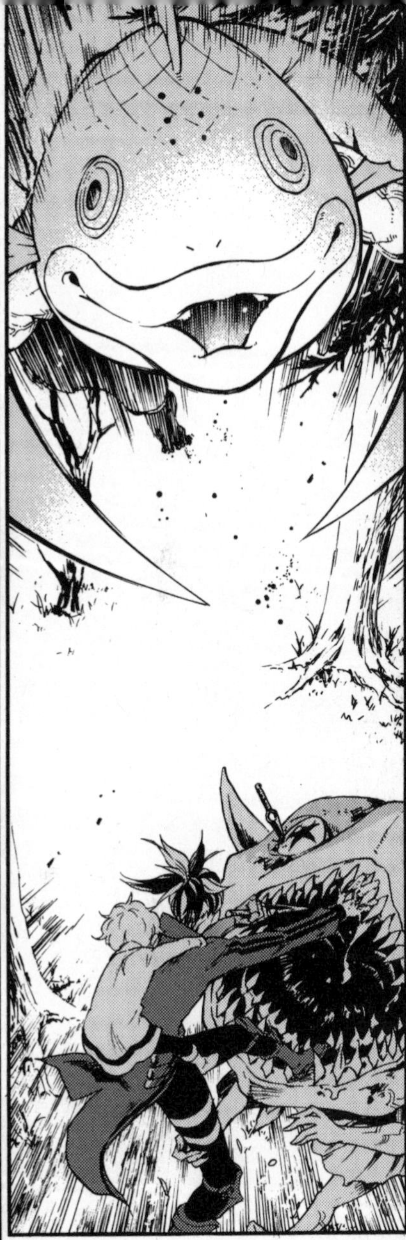
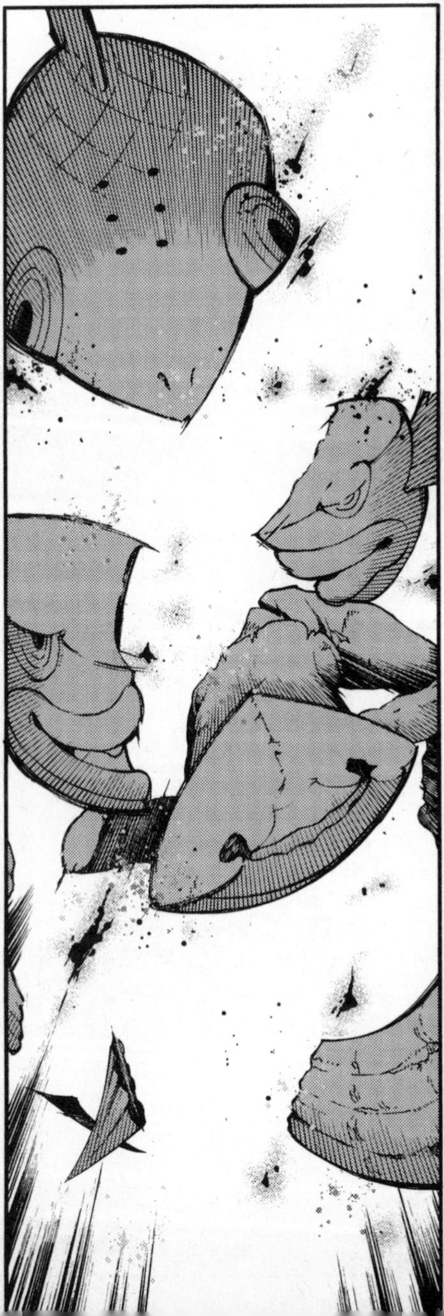

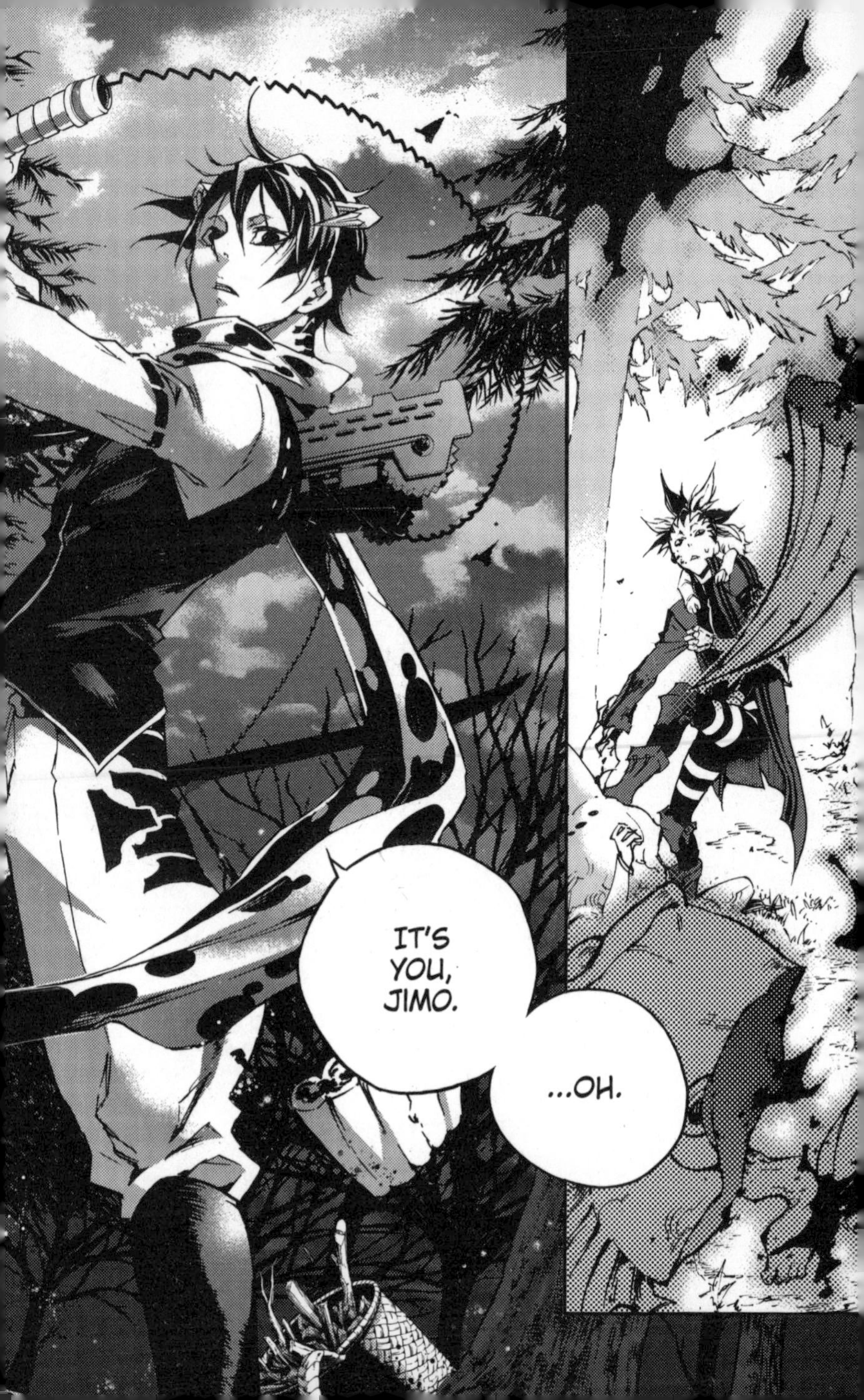
IT'S YOU, JIMO.
...OH.

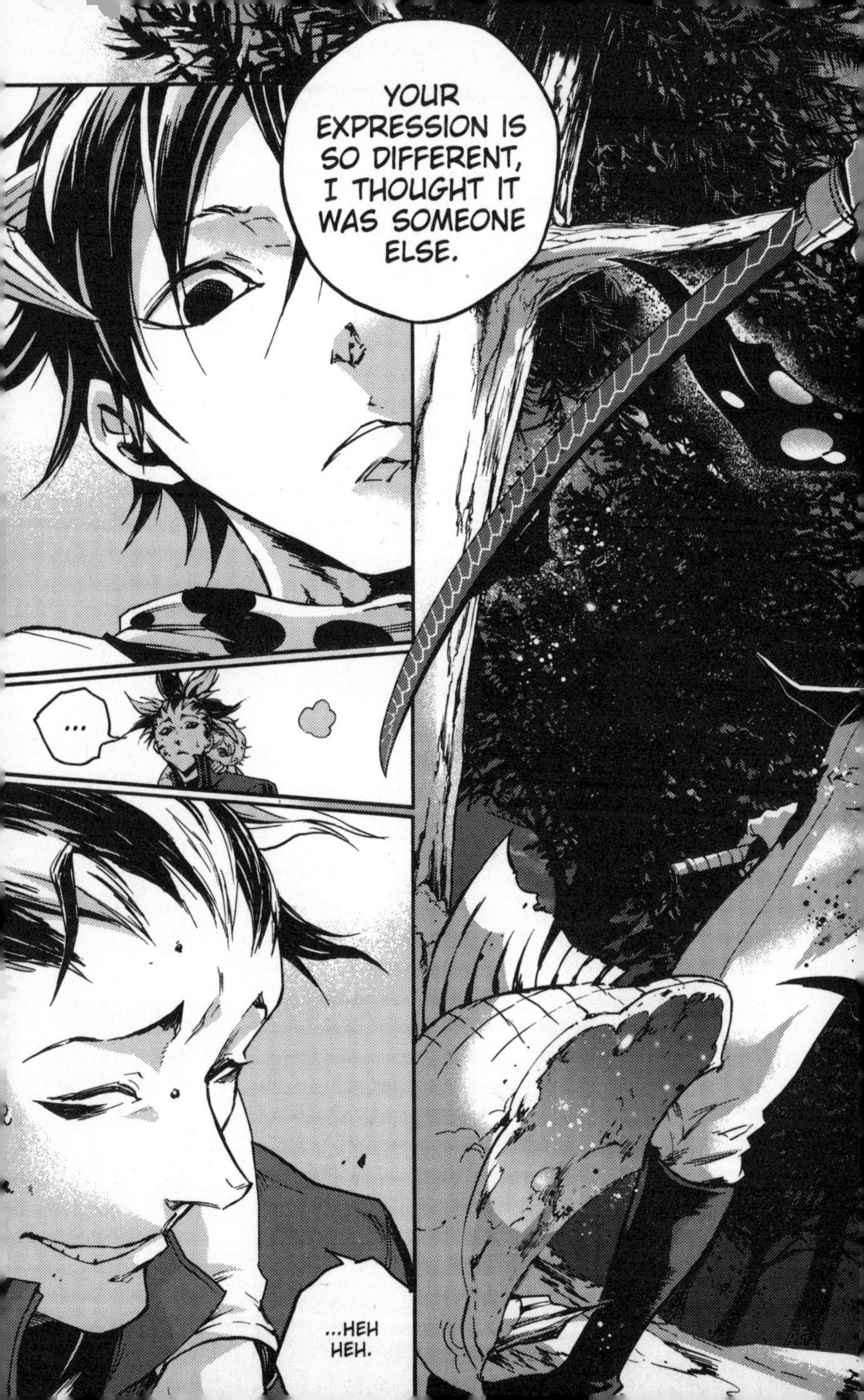
YOUR EXPRESSION IS SO DIFFERENT, I THOUGHT IT WAS SOMEONE ELSE.
...
...HEH HEH.

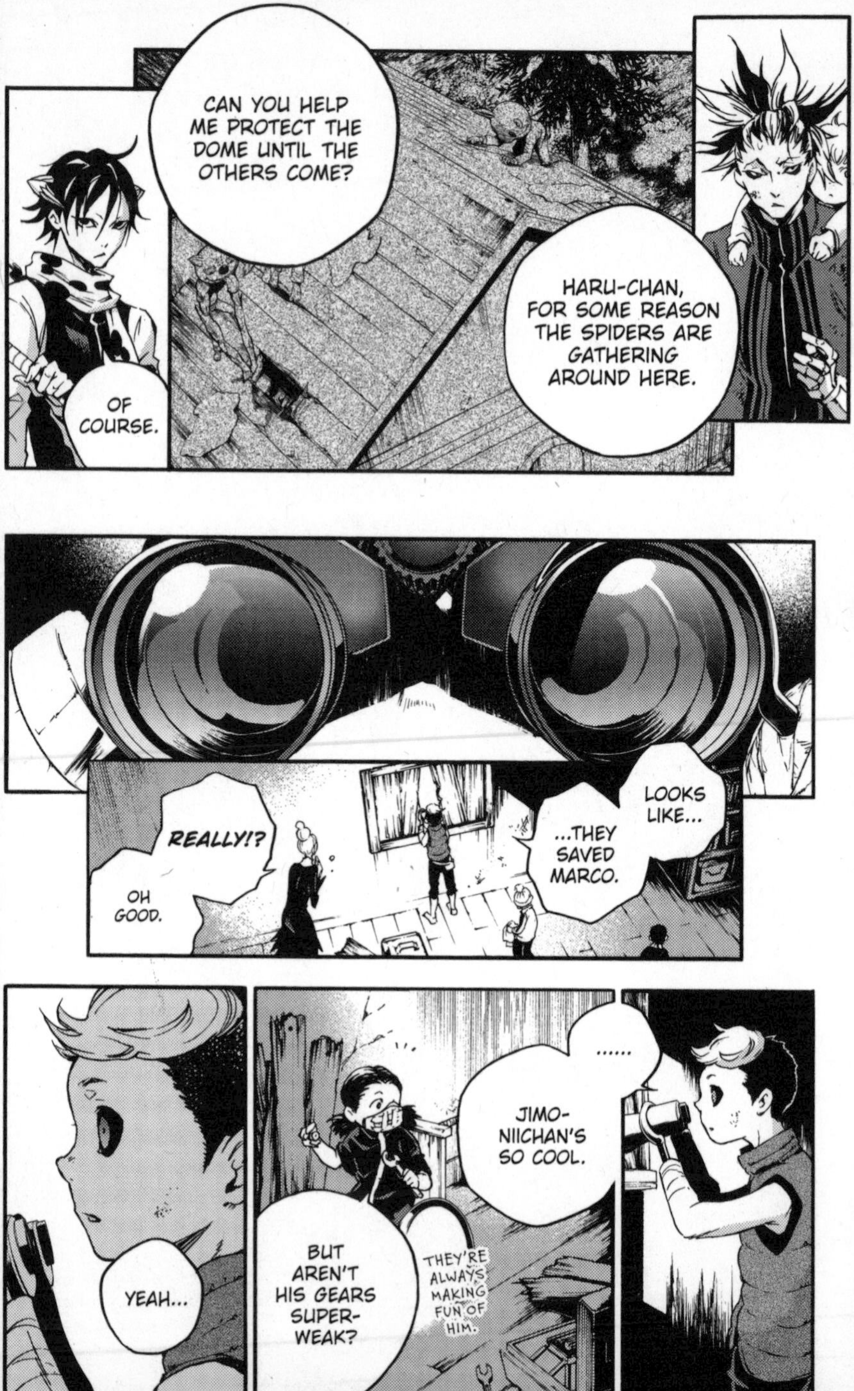
HARU-CHAN, FOR SOME REASON THE SPIDERS ARE GATHERING AROUND HERE.
CAN YOU HELP ME PROTECT THE DOME UNTIL THE OTHERS COME?
OF COURSE.
LOOKS LIKE...
...THEY SAVED MARCO.
REALLY!?
OH GOOD.
......
JIMO-NIICHAN'S SO COOL.
BUT AREN'T HIS GEARS SUPER-WEAK?
THEY'RE ALWAYS MAKING FUN OF HIM.
YEAH...

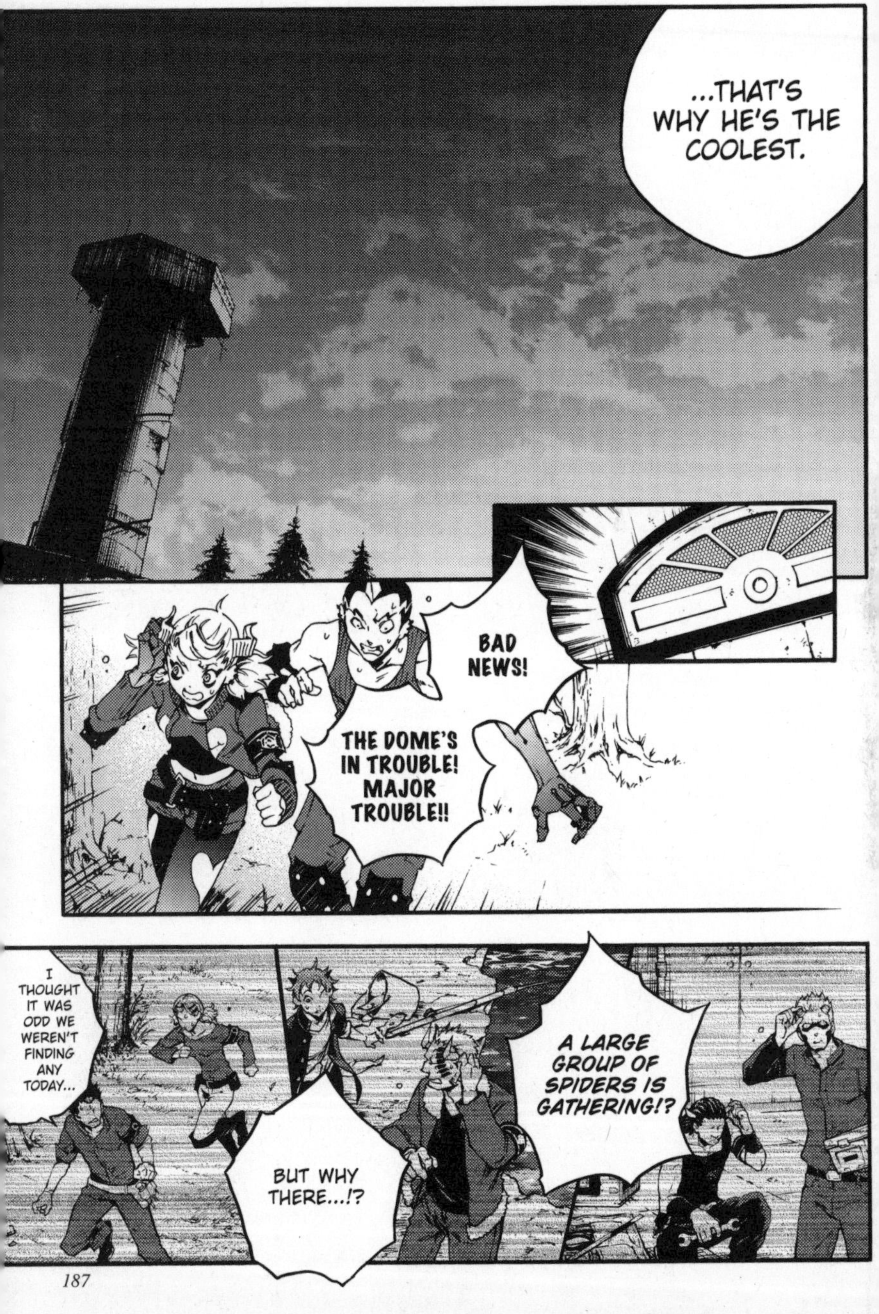
...THAT'S WHY HE'S THE COOLEST.
BAD NEWS!
THE DOME'S IN TROUBLE! MAJOR TROUBLE!!
A LARGE GROUP OF SPIDERS IS GATHERING!?
BUT WHY THERE...!?
I THOUGHT IT WAS ODD WE WEREN'T FINDING ANY TODAY...

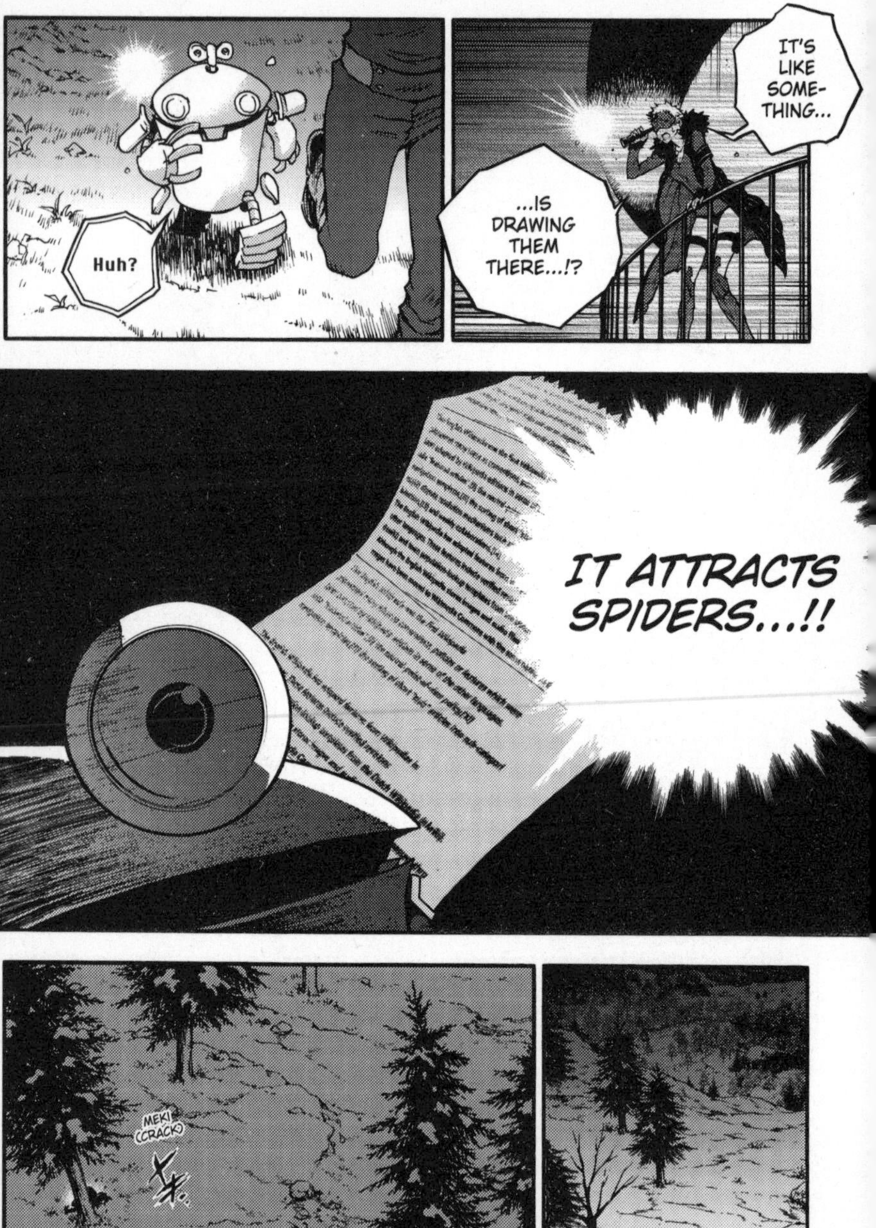
IT'S LIKE SOME-THING...
...IS DRAWING THEM THERE...!?
Huh?
IT ATTRACTS SPIDERS...!!
MEKI (CRACK)

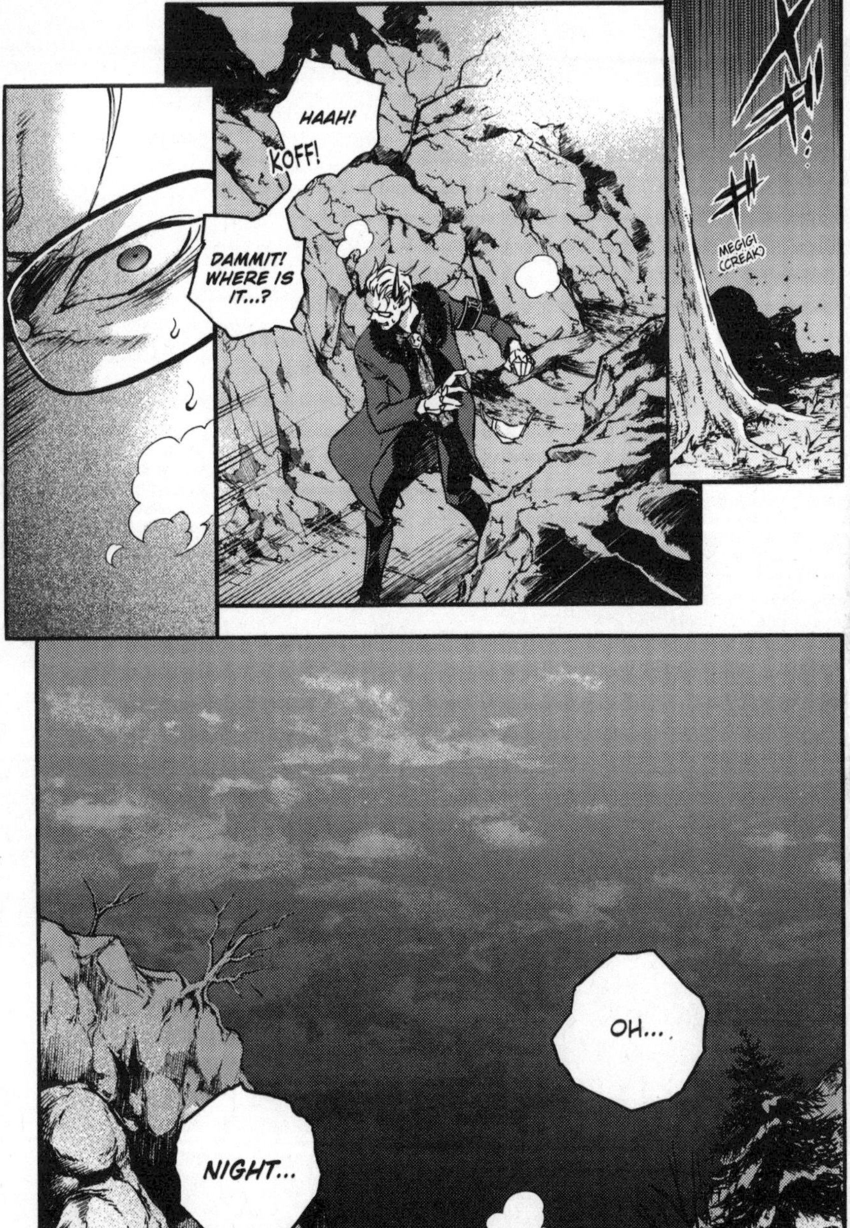
MEGIGI (CREAK)
HAAH!
KOFF!
DAMMIT! WHERE IS IT...?
OH...
NIGHT...

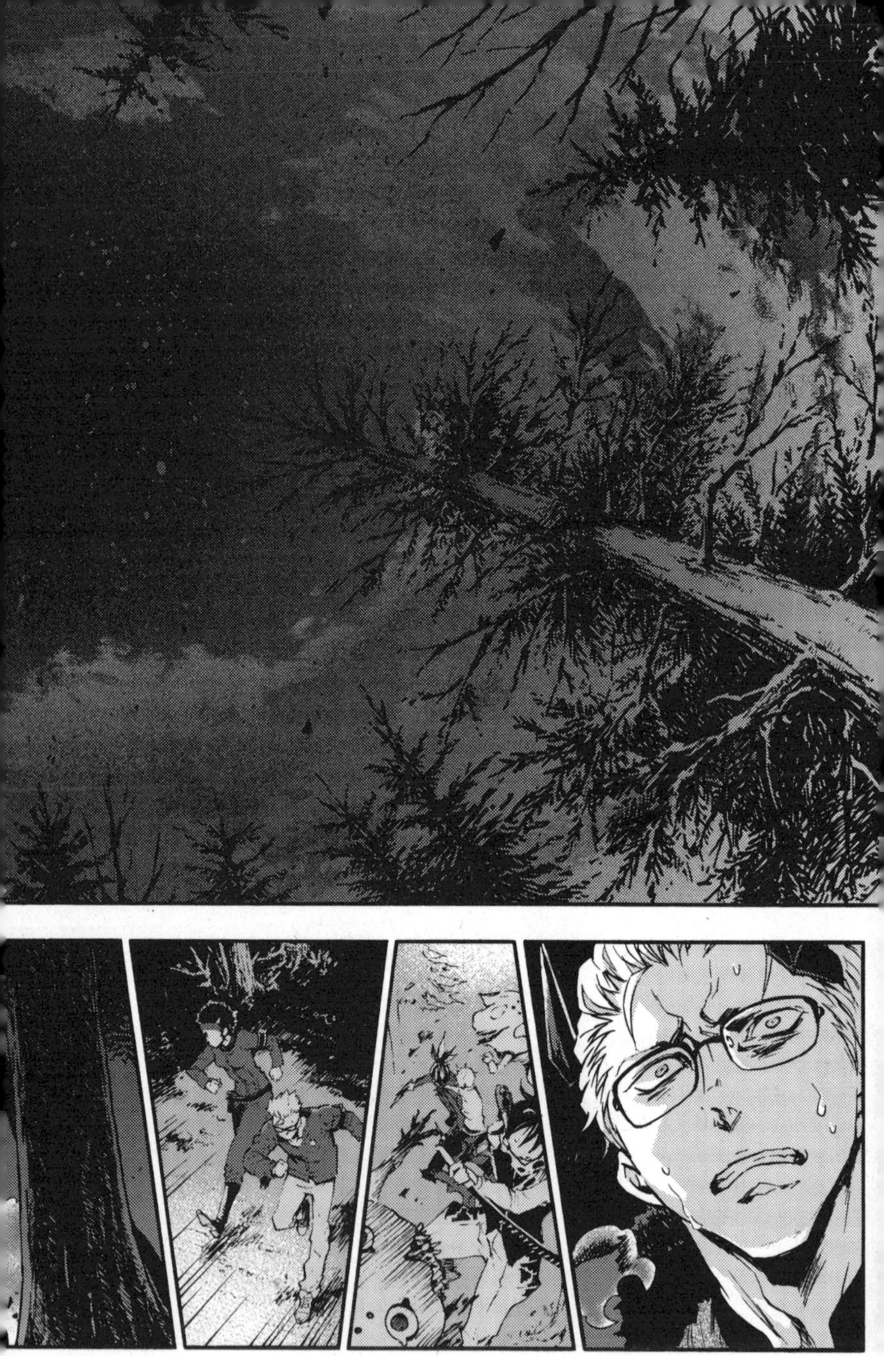

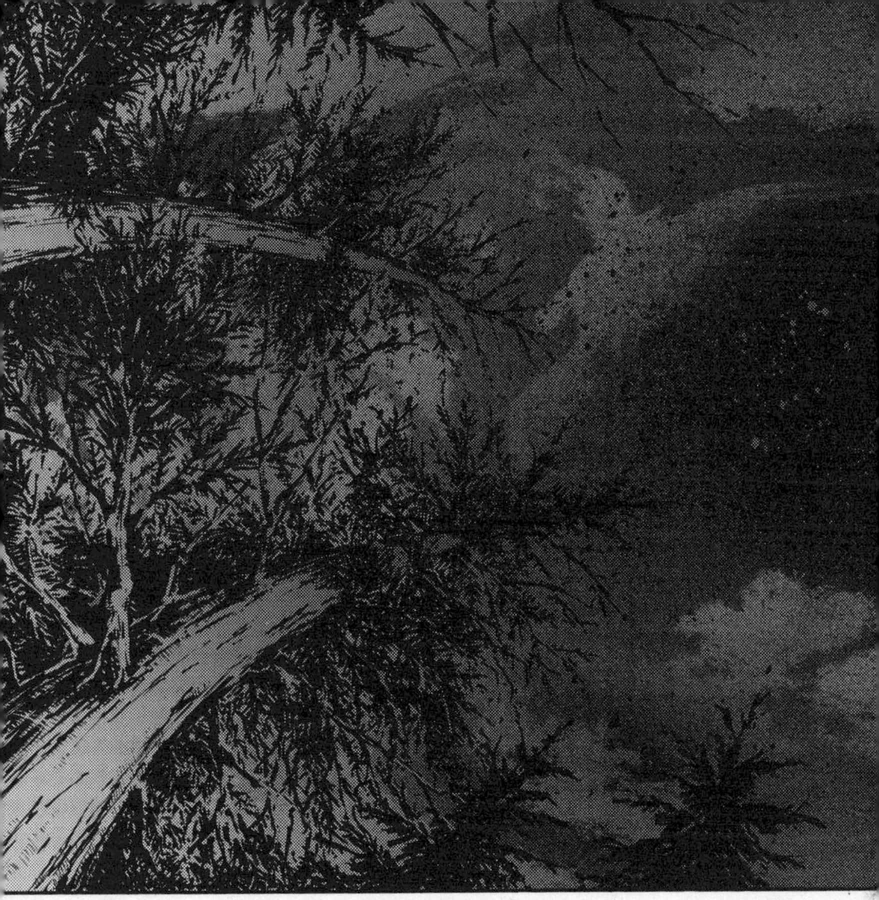

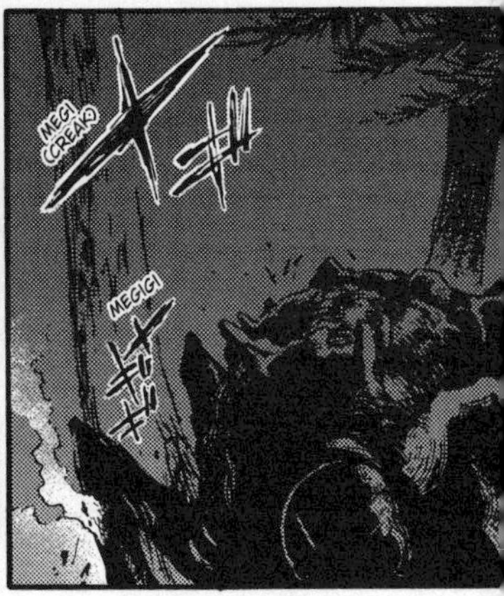
MEGI (CREAK)
MEGIGI

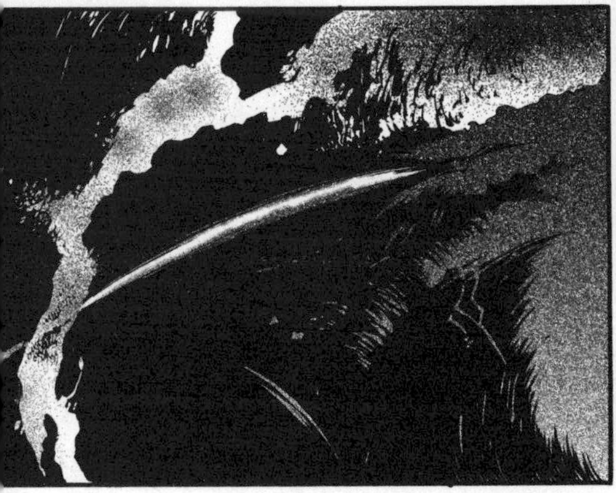

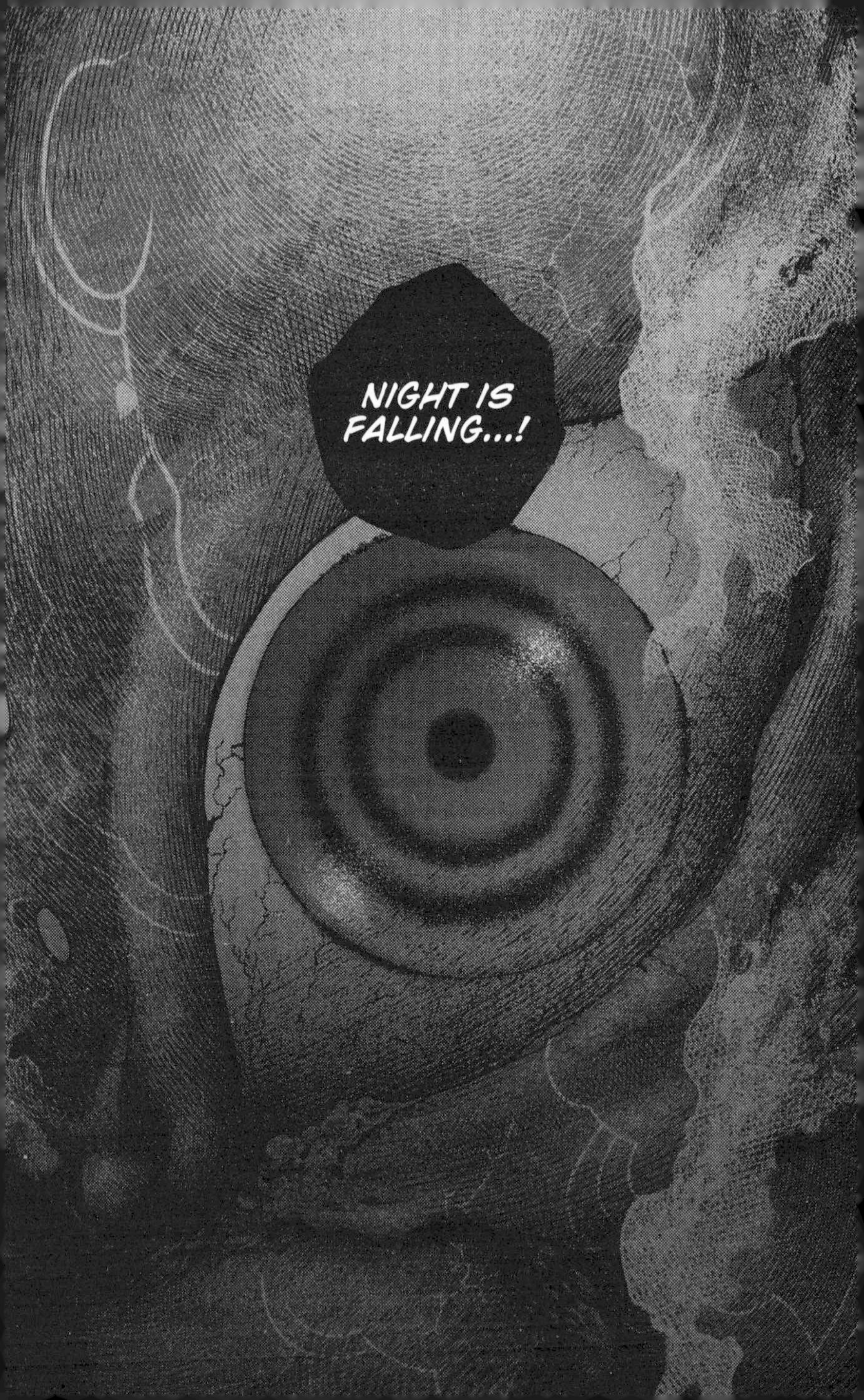
NIGHT IS FALLING...!

SMOKIN' PARADE

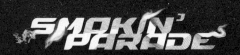

BUNGO STRAY DOGS

Volumes 1–11
available now

**If you've already seen
the anime, it's time to
read the manga!**

Having been kicked out of the
orphanage, Atsushi Nakajima rescues
a strange man from a suicide attempt—
Osamu Dazai. Turns out that Dazai is
part of a detective agency staffed by
individuals whose supernatural powers
take on a literary bent!

SMOKIN' PARADE #06

BY JINSEI KATAOKA, KAZUMA KONDOU

Translation: Leighann Harvey
Lettering: Abigail Blackman

SMOKIN' PARADE Volume 6
©Jinsei KATAOKA 2018
©Kazuma KONDOU 2018
First published in Japan in 2018 by KADOKAWA CORPORATION, Tokyo. English translation rights arranged with KADOKAWA CORPORATION, Tokyo through TUTTLE-MORI AGENCY, INC., Tokyo.

English translation © 2019 by Yen Press, LLC

Yen Press
150 West 30th Street, 19th Floor
New York, NY 10001

Visit us at yenpress.com
facebook.com/yenpress
twitter.com/yenpress
yenpress.tumblr.com
instagram.com/yenpress

First Yen Press Edition: August 2019

Yen Press is an imprint of Yen Press, LLC.
The Yen Press name and logo are trademarks of Yen Press, LLC.

The publisher is not responsible for websites (or their content) that are not owned by the publisher.

Library of Congress Control Number: 2016958477

ISBNs: 978-1-9753-0553-6 (paperback)
        978-1-9753-5919-5 (ebook)

10 9 8 7 6 5 4 3 2 1

WOR

Printed in the United States of America